D0494338

Playwrights in Rehearsal

Playwrights in Rehearsal
The Seduction of Company

Susan Letzler Cole

Routledge
New York • London

Published in 2001 by
Routledge
29 West 35th Street
New York, NY 10001

Published in Great Britain by
Routledge
11 New Fetter Lane
London EC4P 4EE

Coventry University

Copyright © 2001 by Susan Letzler Cole

Routledge is an imprint of the Taylor & Francis Group.

Printed in the United States of America on acid-free paper.

All rights reserved. No part of this book may be reprinted or reproduced or utilized in any form or by any electronic, mechanical or other means, now known or hereafter invented, including photocopying and recording or in any information storage or retrieval system, without permission in writing from the publishers.

10   9   8   7   6   5   4   3   2   1

Library of Congress Cataloging-in-Publication Data

Cole, Susan Letzler, 1940–
    Playwrights in rehearsal: the seduction of company / by Susan Letzler Cole.
    p. cm.
    Includes bibliographical references (p.) and index.
    ISBN 0-415-91969-X (acid-free paper) --ISBN 0-415-91970-3 (pbk: acid-free paper)
    1. American drama--20th century--History and criticism. 2. Dramatists, American--20th century--Biography. 3. Theater rehearsals--United States. 4. Drama--Technique. I. Title.

PS350.C65 2001
792'.0973'09045--dc21   00-059233

For David Cole—
  whose company is a blessing

Contents

Acknowledgments

This book would not have been possible without the generosity and courage of the playwrights and directors who allowed me to observe rehearsals. In addition, I want to thank the many people who offered valuable assistance of different kinds during my research and writing: Eileen Blumenthal, Peg Blumenthal, Suzanne Bradbeer, Marya Bradley, Joseph Chaikin, Linda Chapman, Olivia Corless, Irene Dash, Maria M. Delgado, Liz Diamond, Trish Finley, Deborah Frattini, Donald Fried, Elinor Fuchs, Joel Gluck, Joe Goodrich, Mandy Mishell Hackett, Kristen Harris, Karen Hartman, Harriet Holmes, Jim Houghton, Pam Jordan, Amie M. Keddy, Kevin Kittle, Benjamin Krevolin, John Lemly, Kenneth Letzler, John Leubsdorf, Jim Leverett, Kim Mancuso, Alice Mattison, Norma McLemore, Lisa McNulty, Charles Means, Julia Miles, Edward Moran, Elizabeth Moreau, Evelyn Murphy, Vickie Nolan, Kathy O'Boyle, Ruth L. Ratliff, Laura-Ann Robb, Marc Robinson, Susan Schorr, Richard Sewall, Kimberly Sewright, Catherine Sheehy, Don Shewey, Amanda W. Sloan, Annette M. Smith, Phillip Stambovsky, Tess Timidy, Dawn Williams, Patricia Yeaman.

I appreciate deeply Albertus Magnus College's granting of a sabbatical leave in 1999–2000 during which I completed the writing of this book.

I am indebted to William Germano, my editor at Routledge, for his continuing support of my work, and to Damian Treffs for his careful shepherding of this manuscript through its various stages of preparation for publication.

This book has been enriched by photographs supplied by Lia Chang, Jim Gipe, Susan Johann, Joan Marcus, Sylvia Plachy, Matt Samolis, and James Youmans.

Parts of chapter 7 appear in a different form in Maria M. Delgado and Caridad Svich, *Conducting a Life: Reflections on the Theatre of Maria Irene Fornes* (Lyme, NH: Smith and Kraus, 1999), 79–91.

My mother, Alice Parson Letzler, did not live to see the writing of this book, but she inspirits it still.

Finally, I am especially grateful to two persons. Natalie Miller read early drafts of each chapter, mailed halfway across the country, and responded with amazing alacrity and unwavering support. David Cole read successive drafts of the book with sensitivity, deep appreciation, and the wise love that has attended our life together.

Illustrations

Introduction

What is the role of the playwright in rehearsal? Having bestowed the text of the play, what else can the author bestow? The author is the original creator and first reader[1] of his or her own play: What kind of author-ity does he or she retain in the company of co-creators—directors, designers, actors—reading the text as a script for performance? What legitimacy should be granted to authorial comments in rehearsal, particularly those to do with extratextual or subtextual material? What, in fact, does the playwright in rehearsal give, and receive from, the actors and director? And what dangers may accompany a playwright's observation of the necessary exploratory work, the seeming false starts and important wrong paths, of the rehearsal process? Are the presence and the absence of the playwright, at different points in the rehearsal, equally empowering for the company?

In the following chapters I investigate and document rehearsals attended, and in some cases directed, by eight American playwrights[2] who vary in age (the youngest and oldest are separated by nearly half a century), name recognition, and dramatic technique. The plays include a script written more than two decades ago (Sam Shepard's *Curse of the Starving Class*) as well as one not yet finished as rehearsals begin—and end (Maria Irene Fornes's *The Summer in Gossensass*). The productions range from staged readings in small rooms to season-opening world premieres, with casts as small as two actors (Suzan-Lori Parks's *Topdog/Underdog*) or as large as fifteen actors playing fifty-two characters (Arthur Miller's *The American Clock*). Rehearsals occur in diverse spaces: mid- or downtown Manhattan studios, a Mount Holyoke College lecture hall, and a nineteenth-century barn. The writers' attendance runs the gamut from Jean-Claude van Itallie's two visits, separated by a year, to Maria Irene Fornes's constant presence, as director-author, from the first reading at table to opening night.

My research techniques, not very technologically advanced, were mainly those of listening—and writing down everything I heard and saw. The dozens of interviews that supplement my own observations were usually conducted during the rehearsal period. At hours anywhere from 11 A.M. to 2 A.M., actors, designers, dramaturgs, stage managers, directors, and playwrights talked with me—in rehearsal rooms or theater lobbies, on stairways and fire escapes, inside Fornes's car looking for a parking space in the East Village, on the sidewalk in front of the newly built Signature Theatre during a smoking break, at the windy corner of West Fifty-Ninth Street and Tenth Avenue, in the unisex bathroom of the Women's Project and Productions offices, on the wide front porch of a farmhouse in the hills of western Massachusetts. To the actors I interviewed the playwright appears in a variety of guises, some at odds with each other: "the source"; "a resource"; "perhaps the image of God in a symbolic sense"; "not . . . some sort of religious icon"; "the primary creator"; "a co-collaborator"; "the mouth of God"; "a griot"; "a living point of reference for clarification"; "the boss"; "a painter who keeps repainting"; "an architect"; "this treasure"; "a blessing . . . a mixed blessing"; "a large hand holding the production"; "the words themselves sitting in front of me." The most striking constant in these accounts is the paradoxical role of the playwright in rehearsal—and the ambivalence it elicits.

At times I sense a common behavior among these visiting playwrights, but there is often at least one holdout. For example, every author I observe revises the script at some point during the rehearsal period[3] (except van Itallie—who, however, says that he would have considered revisions had actors suggested them). Almost every author at some point covers his or her mouth as actors deliver lines from the play; often the writer's lips move or allow to escape a nearly inaudible sounding of the words in sync with an actor. At times I see the playwright gaze into a middle distance, as if revisiting or recovering the vanished origins of the script while it is taking on new life.

But differences abound. David Rabe never speaks to the cast after rehearsal begins; Arthur Miller speaks often and at length to the actors, as a group and one by one, sometimes giving clearly directorial notes; Tony Kushner consistently observes "the rule of filtering . . . [the writer's] opinions through the director,"[4] while Jean-Claude van Itallie gives notes almost exclusively to the full company. There are playwrights whose absence is discovered to be nourishing and playwrights whose silence is a torment; playwrights whose body language and audible responses (e.g., laughter) are openly encouraging (Arthur Miller) and others whose faces are often impassive and largely unrevealing (Elizabeth Egloff). An author may be almost preternaturally still in his attentiveness, like Shepard, or nearly always in some kind of motion, like Kushner. Some of the playwright-director pairings are based on intimacy and previous work together (e.g., Rabe and Douglas Hughes); others are newborn as rehearsal begins (e.g., Parks and David Esbjornson); at least one seems at first an odd coupling (Miller and Joseph Chaikin). Certain playwrights rewrite the script on the spot during rehearsal, their gazes alternating between the text and the actors; others either arrive without a script or else do not open it once rehearsal begins, but keep their eyes steadily focused on the actors.

Often in these rehearsals, authorial revision of the text and directorial reenvisioning of the script are in a Möbius strip–like relation. When the writer directs his or her own play, ongoing textual revision *is* a directorial reimagining of the script. (And, in the case of Irene Fornes, for whom revising the script and restaging it are intricately interactive, directing her own work is a rewriting of it.) A playwright-director knows the play in two ways: as a literary creation and as a script that energizes actors. In rehearsal the authorial director's reading of the text tends to become more fluid as actors' explorations leave their traces in the text as script-undergoing-revision.

Authors may rewrite during rehearsal in response to actors misreading lines or requesting changes—or in response to the reverberations and "music" of particular voices and bodies in motion. In addition, revisions may be suggested by directors (Hughes, Esbjornson, Garland Wright) to playwrights (Rabe, Parks, Egloff) in rehearsal—and by Irene Fornes (redirecting) to Irene Fornes (rewriting). In an age of rapid back-and-forth communication by fax, e-mail, and cell phone, when intermittent or ongoing exchange can occur semiprivately and at a distance, some of the "conversation" between directors and playwrights is necessarily veiled from even the most diligent observer. But the remarkable generosity of playwrights like Elizabeth Egloff, Suzan-Lori Parks, and Irene Fornes has made it possible for me to show, in slow motion, authorial changes *as they occur* in the rehearsal room.

Actor Joseph Wiseman says of playwrights in rehearsal: "You desperately need them, but you feel you're never ready for them." Why do they come? Elizabeth Egloff, revising her script for the first professional production of *The Devils*, says of the actors and directors: "I write in their presence and use their impulses." Suzan-Lori Parks, directing staged readings of her two new plays, says: "It's about hearing the voices you've heard in your head for years and making sure they're coming through. A writer knows." She elaborates:

> *[In rehearsal] I heard the full-color version of what I had heard in my head in black and white with stick figures.*

"What I can do," Arthur Miller says, "is to impart to the actors the original image that the character should spring out of." Then he adds: "It doesn't mean that the actors will necessarily re-create that image." Sam Shepard tells me, after listening to the table reading of *Curse of the Starving Class:* "It's a luxury to be able to do this. *It doesn't make as much sense alone* [emphasis mine]."

Actress Billie Whitelaw says of Samuel Beckett, famously attentive to the delivery of every syllable in his plays: "Once he had finished with the pen and the pencil, . . . actually, he needed me. Because all it was, was stuff on paper. I gave it life."[5] It is a fact that playwrights are invited to watch this giving of life to their plays in rehearsal. And it is clear, as Whitelaw says, that the playwright needs the company of actors. It is no less clear that, in complicated and contradictory ways, the company needs the presence of the playwright in rehearsal.

1 Sam Shepard in Rehearsal

Curse of the Starving Class

It's an animal thing.

It's 10 A.M., March 22, 1997. As I enter the fourth-floor rehearsal studio at 422 West Forty-Second Street, in New York City, I see two long tables surrounded by ten folding chairs and a few odd, upholstered chairs on wheels. A former chunky peanut butter jar filled with fresh daffodils sits in the center of one table. To either side of the daffodils are paper cups, a few coffee mugs, a box of Kleenex, several other glass jars with sharpened pencils, and a bottle of water with the name "Jim" written on it. In the corners to the right and left of the entrance are smaller tables heaped with a variety of bagels, cream cheese, green and purple grapes, bananas, coffee, tea, and more mugs.

James Houghton, the founder and artistic director of the Signature Theatre Company, greets me, introduces me to the cast rehearsing Sam Shepard's *Curse of the Starving Class,* and asks, "So you're basically looking at the playwright?" "I'm looking at you, too." He replies: "Oh? Nothing overwhelming there," and the cast laughs. But there is something overwhelming here, as in all the director-playwright interactions I observe. For the actors and the director, the reading rehearsal with the playwright present is invaluable, setting the foundation for all that follows. The script itself becomes the site of continual discovery.

Signature Theatre Company is the only not-for-profit theater in the United States that spends each theatrical season producing the work of a single living playwright. The first "playwright-in-residence" at Signature was Romulus Linney, followed by Lee Blessing, Edward Albee, Horton Foote, Adrienne Kennedy, Sam Shepard, Arthur Miller, John Guare, and Maria Irene Fornes. Houghton founded Signature Theatre in 1991 on his belief that "Playwrights are the heart of theater."[1] The company's logo, a hand holding a pen poised to write, is meant to suggest that the signature of the writer is on the work performed. But how does a playwright make his presence felt—put his signature on the work performed—if he only attends the reading at table of his play?

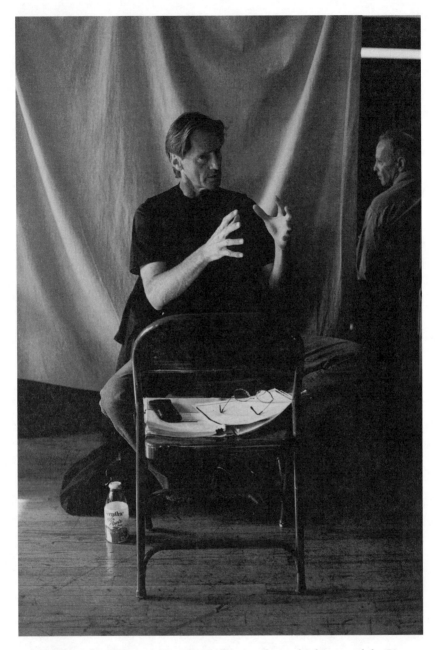

1.1 Sam Shepard and director Joseph Chaikin in rehearsal (photograph by Lia Chang/© Lia Chang Gallery)

The rehearsal of *Curse of the Starving Class*, the last production in the 1996–1997 Sam Shepard season at Signature, tells that story.

Sam Shepard's plays have been produced in this country and abroad for almost four decades. Eleven of his plays, including *Curse of the Starving Class*, have won Obie Awards; one, *Buried Child*, received a Pulitzer Prize. Shepard has toured with Bob Dylan's Rolling Thunder Revue and has written, directed, and acted extensively in films. He has directed his own plays, including *Fool for Love*, which was awarded an Obie for his direction. Shepard also wrote *War in Heaven: Angel's Monologue* in collaboration with Joseph Chaikin, who starred in it.

Curse of the Starving Class, presented at the Joseph Papp Public Theater in New York City, April 27–May 25, 1997, is a play about a family dispossessed of its homestead by the greed of land developers and its own gullibility. Not literally starving, the Tate family is "cursed," poisoned from within and without. The echoing names of father and son (Weston and Wesley), mother and daughter (Ella and Emma), suggest inescapable inheritance.

I arrive on the fourth day of reading the play aloud at table.[2] The playwright is expected on the following day. Stage manager Donald Fried hands out a two-page "time line," the sequence of events specified in or implied by the script, worked out by the director and cast. Jim Houghton explains the significance of the time line: "We need to be grounded; otherwise it will be shallow. There are certain things we need to know, for example, the time scheme, so we're all working in the same context. . . . We got information from Sam [Shepard] that the fair [mentioned by Emma in act 1] is in July or August. So we decided it's August."[3]

The time line begins on Wednesday, August 3, 1976, at 2 A.M., when Weston breaks down the front door to his house. At 2:30 A.M. Weston leaves as the police arrive; at 5 A.M. Weston's wife, Ella, falls asleep. At 10 A.M. act 1 begins. On Thursday, August 4, Wesley and Emma get up at 8 A.M. At 10 A.M. act 2 begins as Wesley builds a new front door and Emma makes charts on the correct way to cut up a frying chicken. On Friday, August 5, at 6:30 A.M. Weston "walks around property and has epiphany. Does laundry, puts on coffee." At 10 A.M. act 3 begins. Weston leaves for Mexico at 10:30 A.M. At 10:45 A.M. Emma leaves and the family car is blown up. (It is not clear whether she is inside it.) In the time line, each act begins at 10 A.M. and ends by noon. There are no indications in Shepard's script of the times at which any of these events occur.

The time line is referred to explicitly in rehearsal. After the read-through of act 1, the director says, "Good. Now it's 10 A.M., act 2"; after act 2, he says, "Good. Let's go on to act 3. It's 10 o'clock in the morning." During a break, Jude Ciccolella says the time line helps him as an actor: "The director and the actors inferentially arrived at it from the events in the script. It's good to know what they're coming from and what they're going to."

Houghton establishes with the actors a time line that they will adhere to (just as each actor creates his or her own subtext that exists independently of the script),[4] but, at the same time, he acknowledges in rehearsal the playwright's point of view. During the reading of act 2, an actress asks what time of day it is. The director responds: "We can ask Sam, but Sam hates this kind of question!"

During the reading at table the director frequently interrupts with questions. For example, he asks: "Why do you [Ella] take action when you do in the play?" "What do you [Emma] *do* [at home]?" "Do you [Wesley] go to school?" "Do you [all the actors] have a television?" Deborah Hedwall, playing Ella, responds, "Black and white . . . the kind with the tinfoil on top that doesn't work." The reading aloud of act 2 continues. After Gretchen Cleevely delivers Emma's first monologue, a fantasy vision of her future as the only mechanic in a little town in Mexico, Houghton says: "That's great. So you're fourteen years old. Where is this coming from? You don't watch TV; it's broken. . . . You know a lot. . . . Are you in a place where anything's possible?"

The director's characteristic style is to ask actors questions and invite them to consider the actable implications of their answers. He is interested in how what he calls "information" affects acting choices. His directorial notes typically begin with phrases like, "How do you know . . . ?" or "Just consider that . . . ," and often end, "Just make that specific for yourself."

Exploration and discovery are privileged activities not just at the table but throughout rehearsal. "You hear different things in the text at different times," Hedwall says, and this is also true of the playwright in rehearsal. Two days earlier, Sam Shepard listened to the actors reading and made revisions in the rehearsal script.[5] "You think it's Mr. and Mrs. America who're gonna buy this place" is now "You think it's Ozzie and Harriet. . . ." The playwright, I am told, dictated changes in a neutral tone, without indicating any particular emphasis or inflection. For example, he added a sentence, "It's always been confidential," to one of Weston's speeches in act 2. As Ciccolella reads the line aloud today, he emphasizes *confidential*. The actor has received new text directly from the playwright's mouth, but the inflection is his choice, and he may experiment with it, he says.

Shepard's rehearsal revisions of the script are themselves never revised, unlike those of Elizabeth Egloff and Maria Irene Fornes. New lines and phrasing are absorbed effortlessly by the actors and accepted by the director. Ciccolella (Weston), whose speeches receive the most frequent alteration, says: "None of the revisions or additions change the fundamental spine as I feel it. These additions are, in Sam's words, in some cases, to add humor, and, in some cases, for specificity and clarity." When I ask if he had felt a lack of specificity or clarity in the speeches that Shepard revised or added to, he answers: "No. That's from his perspective. Perhaps in listening to us read at the table, he may have heard something new, learned something."

Asked why he never disagrees with the playwright's rehearsal revisions, the director says:

> *The playwright's revisions come out of a natural evolution and process. . . . Most of the playwrights I've worked with at Signature Theatre make discoveries in the*

rehearsal process. Things are revealed to you in rehearsal as individuals come to-gether. That's why Sam has the impulse to change the script. He is not locked in. If I were to make arbitrary cuts in the text, he probably wouldn't like that. I don't do that. I have a deep respect for the writer's impulse.

Then he adds:

If there's something there that gives trouble, I think it's my job to reveal it, either through the rehearsal work itself or through a question to the writer. It's a process of discovery. The actors are constantly discovering. And so are the writer, the director, the designers. The discovery tells you where to go. . . . If I came to the table assuming that I know everything—assuming that I know where every piece should be—that would be ridiculous. My job is to point the discoveries in a certain direction. . . . I raise questions.

A critical question raised early in rehearsal has to do with the delivery of the play's aria-like monologues. Discussing Ella's act 2 monologue on the "curse" referred to in the title, the director tells Deborah Hedwall: "I'm not committed to what Sam says is 'out' [delivered directly to the audience]." The actress says, "I need to deliver this speech *within* the play,"[6] and the director replies, "Yes. I can provide the 'out'—with light, for example." There is no stage direction indicating how the problematic monologue should be played. The director is prepared to experiment with various possibilities, raising questions about each. Here, his response to Hedwall's "need" is to ask her to explore its implications: "The question is *why* are you saying this to *Wesley*?"

In act 1, Weston, alone on stage, discovers a live lamb in his kitchen and asks, "Is this inside or outside? This is inside, right? This is the inside of the house. Even with the door out it's still the inside. (*to lamb*) Right?" (156). Weston's lines comically allude not only to the difficulty of determining what is "inside" and what is "outside" but also to the difficulty of finding an appropriate or stable audience in the play. Weston's first monologue is addressed to the lamb, to himself, to the lamb, to himself, to the house in general, and to himself, in that order. Even after Wesley enters, Weston delivers one more speech to the house.

As the afternoon wears on, the rehearsal room becomes warmer. A window is opened, four stories above West Forty-Second Street. Wesley talks about the "zombie invasion" of "land development" (162–63). Outside the window a dirty steel overpass looms above the occasional honks and repeated swishing of cars and buses. The sounds of the city drift through the humid air of the brick-lined rehearsal room, bringing back Weston's act 1 question: "Is this inside or outside?"

Suddenly I am jolted by the actor's electric reading of Weston's monologue in act 3. I see other members of the cast visibly moved by Ciccolella's evocative, understated delivery:

I kept looking for it out there somewhere. I kept trying to piece it together. The jumps. I couldn't figure out the jumps. From being born, to growing up, to droppin' bombs, to having kids, to hittin' bars, to this. It all turned on me some-

how. It all turned around on me. I kept looking for it out there somewhere. And all the time it was right inside this house [194].

The "volatile discontinuity"[7] of "the jumps" marks the cast's experience in rehearsal as well as the audience's experience in the theater.

At the end of rehearsal, the director's wife, Joyce, brings him his young son, Henry, who remains sleeping in his arms as he gives notes to the actors. Houghton's final note, to Emma on the child's perspective in this family, seems to arise from his double role as director and parent: "You've always been included, and suddenly you're not. That's something that kept you here. Without that, there's no reason for you to stay."

Rehearsal on the following day is filled with quiet anticipation of the playwright's arrival. This will be Shepard's second, and, as it turns out, last appearance. The entire cast assembles at 1 P.M. on Sunday, March 23, 1997. The daffodils are somewhat wilted but there are more coffee cups and bottled water. A kitchen sink filled with large pots has been brought into the rehearsal studio and placed off in a corner. On his earlier visit, Ciccolella tells me, Shepard gave no interpretive comments to the actors on lines or line readings. He will talk about ideas, if asked, or provide information, when needed. For example, Ciccolella asked why lambs were gelded, and Shepard told him that one ungelded lamb was kept for breeding and the gelded lambs were fattened up and sold. Gelded lambs apparently are fatter than ungelded. The actor adds, "I don't know anything about lambs." He says that the playwright also told the cast how to pronounce "coyote": *kai´-oat.*

The director announces that Shepard will arrive in a few hours. Until then, he says, "what we'll do is read." As Hedwall reads the part of Ella, it is easy to forget that the actors are simply sitting at a table, reading. Her voice and the entire upper half of her body are performing the play, its particular rhythms, its sudden shifts from the comic to the grim, from the bizarre to the ordinary, from the expressionistic to the literal.

Houghton has a small, black digital clock in front of him, giving the exact time in large black letters. It is 1:35 P.M. We are still in act 1, waiting for the playwright. It is a cold spring Sunday in the city, very different from yesterday. Wind chill is 18 degrees and there are high, fierce gusts of wind, then sudden bright sunlight. There is one empty space at the table, to the right of the director, reserved for the missing playwright. The vacant chair seems a dramatic image of the "absent" father figures in the play.

The actors begin reading act 2. I listen again to the lines describing Weston's father: "He lived apart. Right in the midst of things, and he lived apart. Nobody saw that" (168). Today in rehearsal these lines have an added resonance: they seem to characterize the playwright who is "in the midst of things" even in his apartness, undeniably present and yet unmistakably absent. When will the playwright join the company, I wonder; what speech will call up his presence? It is 2:14 P.M. by the director's digital clock. We are now in the middle of act 2.

There is a ten-minute break after the end of act 2, followed by discussion. The director asks open-ended questions and gently points out how the actors' responses will affect line readings and acting choices. The director does not intrude on the actors' private creation of subtextual or extratextual material. He simply insists, through continual questions, that each actor make specific choices in every moment of the play.[8] Just before the reading of act 3 begins, Jim Houghton mentions that after talking with Shepard the cast established that the Tate family lives about thirty miles out of town on a run-down ten-acre farm.

The reading of act 3 begins at 3:07 P.M. At 3:17, as Ella asks: "What's that lamb doing back in here?" (187), the playwright arrives. Sam Shepard wears dark blue jeans, a black T-shirt and black overshirt, a dark brown vest, brown work shoes with brown laces, white socks, and serious glasses. He sits behind the director, not at the table in the chair reserved for him. He has arrived with a male friend who listens appreciatively to the rest of act 3 and leaves.

The rehearsal has continued without a pause. The playwright, sniffing a bit from the cold, follows the read-through, looking mainly at the script, not at the actors. He holds the script on his right thigh, his right leg crossed over his left knee. He has surprisingly delicate hands. He gazes intently at the text, listening to the actors' voices at the table. Occasionally, he looks up and glances at an actor reading. He sits two feet behind my chair, three feet from the director seated at table. Shepard's brown hair is brushed back from his forehead, up over the top and the sides of his head. His lean, intense face is nearly expressionless. His lips are close together. I see an ink stain on his left hand as he rubs his cheek. Brow furrowed, he follows the script closely as Weston and Wesley talk in act 3. The actors' voices, at first quieter after the playwright's arrival, pick up energy.

Shepard seems almost totally occupied with the text, his facial muscles taut, concentrated. He is very still. Occasionally, his left hand reaches up to his face or neck for a moment. Otherwise his head and body are motionless, the head tilted slightly to the right toward the pages of the script, which he holds in his right hand. His left hand rubs and then remains on the back of his neck briefly until it is lowered to turn a page. His body is now utterly still except for that moving left hand that goes to his mouth to cover a cough. There is a strong smell of cigarette smoke coming from his general direction. His companion, without a script, gazes at the actors, laughing often.

Toward the end of act 3, the playwright sits with both feet wide apart on the floor, holding the script in his left hand, stroking his chin with the right. Suddenly he laughs audibly at Clark Middleton's deft comic delivery of Emerson's lines, "Oh that! [the blowing up of Weston's car]. That was just a little reminder. A kind of post-hypnotic suggestion" (198), and continues to laugh during the dialogue between Emerson and Slater (Joe Caruso).

At the end of the reading of act 3, the director asks the playwright if he has anything to say. Shepard responds in a relaxed, friendly voice: "Just a few little things. Sorry I missed the front of it. I wanted to add something for

Ella. Add 'How long have I been sleeping?' to Ella's speech [after her line, "I must've slept right through it" (199)]. And then add the same line again at the very end of the play: 'How long have I been sleeping?' [to Deborah Hedwall]. Just try that." The "little thing" the playwright has just added in rehearsal is a new final line. The reception of this revision is uneventful. Hedwall's response is, "Yeah. That's cool," although she will say to me later, on March 25, "I think it's amazingly incredible that Sam Shepard would change the last line and say, 'Try this.'"

Shepard's attention is now concentrated on the actors. He is giving line revisions and additions directly to the cast, not to a director or dramaturg. Without losing a beat, he continues talking to the actors: "I missed the front part of that. How did it read? Any hitches?" This is, of course, exactly what the actors would wish to ask the playwright.

Shepard begins to talk about the implications of the new question—"How long have I been sleeping?"—that he has just added to the play: "In a truly alcoholic situation, people grow to not know each other *radically* and then there are these moments when things start to come back. So all those questions you're asking are the truth." The playwright, who is also an actor and a director, says to Hedwall, "I'm not trying to give you an attitude." He adds: "In the play there are periods of drastic alienation so that people are strangers; then things come back."[9] In response to an actor's question, he says: "Yeah, this is an old couple. They obviously know things about each other—but because of this schism, this information comes back almost like in a dreamlike situation. You know what I mean? So it's good if it has this resonance, that it's not just one thing." Speaking to Gretchen Cleevely, the actress playing Emma, Shepard says: "You've gone through a little realization yourself. She [Ella] ain't stopping you. It's not like you're tiptoeing around her." The director listens, without commenting. The playwright continues to talk directly to the actors: "I think the whole third act is about the fact that they're going through momentous changes, *radical* changes, *everybody*. Whether or not they're permanent, they are huge changes in fundamental personalities."

The director now asks the cast to reread the last seven pages of act 2 "so Sam can hear it." Shepard rises and moves to the table where he sits in the chair reserved for him immediately to the right of the director. As the actors begin to read, the playwright's gaze is again focused on his script, now placed on the table in front of him. His left hand touches his left cheek, his right rests between his knees. He looks up only rarely. He is now much more visible to the actors at table.

Shepard turns a page of script carefully and then clasps his hands together in front of his knees. He makes a note directly on his script as Ellis (Jack R. Marks) reads. The blue pen in his right hand remains pointed toward his script as he continues to listen. He puts his pen down on the table and continues to gaze at his script. Next to him, the director suddenly leans forward in his seat, smiling, as he glances at the actors reading at the far left and the far right ends of the table. Shepard smiles faintly, his eyes still fixed on the text. Previously a study in contrasts, the director and the playwright now both gaze at their scripts, turning the pages simultaneously. The director writes notes on a white pad to his right; the playwright writes directly on his script. At the table Shepard's right hand is rarely still. His fingers slowly rub his forehead, then make another note during the dialogue between Sergeant Malcolm (Kevin Carrigan) and Ella.

At the end of act 2 the director stops the read-through and says, "Sam, you want to give us what you got there?" Shepard says, "Yeah. On page 42, Ellis, put in 'I hate artichokes.'" The cast laughs. "On page 44, Ellis, change 'steakhouse' to 'steak joint.' On page 48, Ella, add 'We're going away,' and add 'I'm by myself' after 'I'll be all right.'"[10] Shepard reads aloud the line preceding each addition or revision, then reads the new phrase or line in an uninflected voice. He is clearly not giving line readings, just dictating words.

The actors begin to read act 3 again. The playwright sits listening, his right hand under his chin, the fingers of his left hand delicately raised above the page of script. He turns the page. Jude Ciccolella is reading the long opening monologue about an eagle stealing lamb testes, "Those fresh little remnants of manlihood" (183). Shepard is eerily still, his left hand resting on his left thigh. The director, to his left, sits quietly for a moment, characteristically looking now at the actor and now at the script. The playwright continues to sit nearly motionless in relaxed attentiveness, staring at the text of his play, the blue pen now in his right hand.

Houghton leans back in his seat, and I see Shepard make a note as Weston delivers another of his act 3 monologues. Shepard makes another note. I watch more closely. The blue pen starts to mark the text, just grazes the page, hovers, grazes it again. The playwright, all concentration, writes briefly on his script. I see him again begin to make a note, pause, then carefully and deliberately set down a few words on his script. He whispers to the director, who stops the read-through. I am watching a playwright writing as actors read his play aloud. The two processes occur almost simultaneously: actors read, writer writes. The playwright is continuing the process of writing, and rewriting, as he listens in a way that only the presence of actors in rehearsal makes possible. Later Shepard will tell me: "It's a luxury to be able to do this. It doesn't make as much sense alone."

Shepard now reads aloud to the cast the changes he has made during the read-through: "Change 'And that gave me a great feeling' to '. . . a great sensation'. . . . 'Some of your crusty socks' [he adds the word "crusty"]. Change 'Chicanos' either to 'wets' or '*Mojados*.' Which do you prefer, Weston?" Ciccolella replies, "'*Mojados.*' How do you spell it?" In a very casual way, the playwright enlists the actor as a co-creator of text: "Which do you prefer, Weston?" He addresses the actor as the character, as if it is the character who knows best which word he would prefer. "*Mojados*" replaces "Chicanos" in rehearsal and performance. The playwright tells Ella to change "I'm very grateful" to "That's big of you," and then says, "That's it." There will be no more revisions of the text.[11]

Shepard asks if the cast has any questions, prefacing his invitation with a disclaimer: "I may not be able to answer your questions, but if you have any. . . . " An actor asks why the lamb in the play is killed. The question is not answered directly, but the playwright's response is more revealing than any literal answer:

> *I think there are two levels to look at the play on. One is the rational: cause and effect. The other is the spiritual where the transformations are overwhelming occurrences, beyond reason. . . . Your character [Wesley] is the most raw of all. Everybody has a little bit of armor. You don't. Wesley is totally vulnerable. It leads him into a transformation of self, so to speak. It's more like a spiritual awakening, beyond rationality. . . . That's all okay, acting [what you can figure out rationally]. . . . But the power of it is in this emotional thing that starts to move like an earthquake. [To Wesley] I don't know if that helps.*
>
> *It's not an ordinary drama of psychological realism. That's the external part. This other thing is the meat and potatoes. It's intended to be radical, primitive, almost biblical—the sacrifice of the lamb.*

Shepard inverts the usual connotation of "meat and potatoes," as if to imply that what is most substantial in the play, what he wants the actors to feed on, ought to feel as nourishing as psychological realism.[12] He continues:

> *It's coming from the heart. Why did those ancient people sacrifice? What is this about? Something is being sacrificed for something else—it's not just brutality. They're in the grips of something. Everybody is in the grips of something. It's not any more a psychological drama about the psychological problems of people in the twentieth century. It's ancient . . . symbolic. There's something powerful moving you.*
>
> *I don't know exactly why you slaughtered the lamb. If the audience can be taken into this territory that they don't understand, that's when something happens.*
>
> *The play starts with a violent act, tearing the front door down. The whole question of violence, it's not just a social problem. It's more than that. . . . It's an animal thing.*

As actors in rehearsal so often do, the playwright talks about the play in the play's own language: "[It was] an animal thing" (186).

Paul Dawson asks why his character, Wesley, is depriving himself of food. Shepard says: "Fasting is another mysterious thing that Wes is caught up in. Wes doesn't know he is on a spiritual quest. It's just happening to him. This is true of people on spiritual quests. They know *something's* happening to them, but they can't get hold of it. Fasting causes certain processes to start, causes vulnerability. Something has taken over, and it's happening to him [Wesley] in a very domestic, dysfunctional—I hate that word—family situation. . . . I hate this newly invented word. We didn't have it in the '50s."

Dawson responds: "Your speaking of the play in these terms is very helpful because we've been talking about the play very rationally, but the places I have trouble with don't work that way." The playwright confirms the actor's sense of the play without undermining the rehearsal work: "You need the rational for the surface level but that's not the foreground of what's happening; that's not the underbelly of the play."

Cleevely, the actress playing Emma, asks, "Why did you write the play?" When Shepard replies, "Nothin' better to do," she persists: "Can you say?" and he says, "I don't want to get into it. It's irrelevant. It's there." In a 1971 program note, in fact, Shepard wrote, "I got into writing plays because I had nothing else to do."[13] But this answer to what is probably the question a playwright most dreads, understandably, is the one unhelpful moment in the author's conversation with the actors. The actress tells me later that perhaps she should have rephrased her question but "it was a little hard to hear that it was irrelevant. I felt stupid. My interest in asking that was a personal interest, because I read and like his plays. I like to know 'Why am I doing this?' 'Why am I in this play?' 'What would you like people to know about me?'" Then she adds: "I got . . . ideas from his comments that fed me. He talked about things being very ancient and about a spiritual force taking hold of people without their knowing. That was answering my question, 'Why did you write the play?'"

The director, entering the conversation at the table, asks about the dialect in the play: "Anybody getting it?" Shepard's laconic reply, "Deborah is," is followed by an intense, detailed discussion of accent. The voicing of his text clearly matters to this writer, who is as interested in music as he is in words:

> A lot of southerners founded the gringo culture in the Southwest, mainly from Tennessee and Kentucky. . . . The accent is distinct from the traditional southern accent. R, for example, is harder-sounding in the Southwest than it is in the traditional South. The accent in the play is basically a Tennessee accent.

When Ciccolella asks, "Is my accent too far south?"[14] Shepard replies, "Yep. Harden it up a bit. Make a's 'A,' never 'ah.' Hit r's harder."

The director asks the playwright to read aloud a speech, not from the play in rehearsal but from *Buried Child*, to demonstrate the accent in *Curse of the Starving Class*. Shepard reads aloud for a few minutes—an actor's assured, understated reading. He pronounces the word, "roof" *roove*, and tells the actors to "say *muh*, not 'my,'" adding: "It's not a pretty accent but it does something to the air."

Shepard is fine-tuning a generic "south–of–New York" accent common among actors in the Northeast. He suggests that in parts of southern New Mexico and rural southern California you can hear the accent he wants in the play: "Just sting it a bit. It shouldn't jump out at us."

The playwright then begins to talk about the "social . . . [and] psychological problems of people in the twentieth century" that he had earlier deemphasized:

> This part of the country [southeastern California] was more or less established by World War II veterans—midwesterners and southwesterners. This part of the

country was being sold as the promised land. There were even fliers distributed by land developers that had pictures of cactus plants with oranges *on them. They had just gone out and put Valencia oranges on a cactus and photographed it. After World War II, everybody was up for renewal. Particularly the men who came out of that war were attracted to such promises. My old man was a pilot.[15] These men turned to booze when the promise collapsed. Their families suffered terribly. This era—the Eisenhower era—was a very repressed era. These men and their families suffered terribly. Take this as the immediate background for this play.*

It was like a migration that utterly failed in its profound destiny. These men felt: "We won the war"—you know, the '50s—"we're going to grab America by the balls." The men were crushed in this trauma and the women suffered horribly behind this thing of alcohol. There was a psychological damage to these men and families that is still a mystery to me.[16]

Shepard brings back the mystery but in a psychological, familial context. On the one hand, his description of the "background" for the play strongly suggests a sense of cause and effect; on the other hand, his final emphasis, as in his earlier comments to the cast, is on an "overwhelming occurrence, beyond reason," territory not fully understood.

Shepard has said to the company: "If the audience can be taken into this territory that they don't exactly understand, that's when something happens." And that's when something happens for the playwright as well:

I feel like there are territories within us that are totally unknown. Huge, mysterious, and dangerous territories. We think we know ourselves, when we really know only this little bitty part. We have this social person that we present to each other. We have all these galaxies inside of us. And if we don't enter those in art of one kind or another, whether it's playwriting, or painting, or music, or whatever, then I don't understand the point in doing anything. It's the reason I write. I try to go into parts of myself that are unknown. . . . I'm not doing this in order to vent demons. I want to shake hands with them.[17]

Sam Shepard lights a Camel. No one else ever smokes in the rehearsal room. There are signs in the stairwell—the only way into this fourth-floor studio—stating, "This is a smoke-free building." Shepard continues to talk as he smokes, his face lighting up as he describes the scams by means of which people were sold land in the desert. He mentions the arrival of Brecht, his "favorite playwright,"[18] in California in the 1950s and Brecht's diaries in which he comments on Americans watering their lawns.

Shepard is relaxed, smiling, conversational, not pontificating. The actors are listening, responding, questioning. The director remains an appreciative, unobtrusive presence. Comments that seem to come from and go nowhere in particular are telling. Shepard says, suddenly and simply: "The desert is very powerful. Hot winds always there—coming off the desert."[19] The room grows silent as Shepard talks about the effects of land "development":

> It takes one hundred and fifty years for an olive tree to grow only as tall as this room. There were olive trees planted by immigrants out there that were bull-dozed. [Cast sighs.] And vineyards. I remember groves of olive trees out there. Gone. I can't think of a place in this country where there are more dramatic changes in the culture in a short time.

The director asks if there are any more questions for the playwright: "I know we'll think of hundreds after he's left." Deborah Hedwall asks, "Do you usually add stuff?" Shepard replies, laughing: "No, I usually take away." To the entire company, he says, "The play sounds great. I thought I would have to do more doctoring." He smiles.

After rehearsal I express amazement at the playwright's addition of a new final line to the play and ask Shepard why and how he makes revisions during rehearsal. He explains that he does not intend to change the published text: "These changes are just for this production." Then he smiles and says:

> It's like listening to music. You hear a note that can be elaborated on or elimi-nated. Sometimes it's in order to clarify an idea. . . . It's in response to live actors, not just to their voices but their intentions, too—the whole thing. . . . It's a luxury to be able to do this. It doesn't make as much sense alone.

Harold Bloom has remarked of Huckleberry Finn that he, "like any American, does not feel free unless he is alone, and yet solitude makes him fear he is no part of the creation, however the world happened or came about."[20] Shepard, like the figures in his plays, is elusive. He will not appear again in rehearsal and he does not attend the performance of his play at the Public Theater. That the playwright in rehearsal is a kind of disappearing act makes perfect sense. "Theater is a place to bring stuff from . . . your life experience," Shepard has said. "You bring it and you" (pause) "you send this telegram and then you get out. There's no use hanging around in it."[21] But in the rehearsals that follow his presence is still felt.

Two days later the long tables are gone. The wood floor is marked with strips of bright green masking tape indicating the length and width of the Shiva stage at the Public Theater. Exits and entrances are indicated upstage right and center. A square wooden table occupies the center of the newly marked playing area. A smaller table, representing the stove, has been placed stage left. The sink is gone.

Jim Houghton sits in the playing area with three of the actors. After discussion with the playwright and consultation with the set designer, E. David Cosier, the director wants to make the set "more abstract": "Sam likes this, too." Shepard, who had talked movingly about the vanished olive groves in the last rehearsal, has suggested having olives in the refrigerator, the direc-tor says, "so the set will be past and present simultaneously." (I saw no olives in performance.) The director continues to present the new concept for the set: "I want to heighten the sense of the lie these people were handed [the "background" provided by Shepard in rehearsal]. The appliances will be from the '50s—very simple design. . . . All the design choices will reflect the '50s."

In performance on the raked stage of the Shiva Theater the audience sees a bright yellow linoleum kitchen floor, a vintage 1950s red Formica kitchen table with three color-coordinated chairs, a Super Chef stove, and, upstage center, a Frigidaire facing out, and miked so as to amplify the groans, moans, and bellows it emits every time it is opened or shut.[22] There is no kitchen sink. Surrounding the set on three sides, raised about six feet above the stage floor in front of thirteen-foot black curtains ("teasers"), there is a narrow panoramic mural of open land, a few strands of trees, and a big blue sky. Brightly lit as one enters the theater, the dazzling blue sky seems to change colors during the course of the performance. A painted landscape changes its appearance under different stage lighting to suggest a sky seen in different weathers and at different times of day.

"We're losing the tree, losing any sense of the outside," the director tells the actors in rehearsal. "What I like about [the new set design] is that it really reflects the lie Sam was talking about on Sunday. . . . It basically comes down to 'less is more.' I don't know whether there will be a sink. I'm going back and forth. . . . I was going to have Wes washing his hands." Discussion continues—an actress says, "I want a sink," and the director replies, "Maybe we'll keep the sink with the plumbing exposed"—but the sink's fate is sealed.[23]

The director reports to the actors that the playwright, praising them, told someone after the last rehearsal, "They're reading the hell out of it." He adds: "I feel Sam really helped us out. He doesn't always get involved in the production of his work. When he's here, he's so helpful. . . . I think we've really tapped into where the play is rooted through the work we did last week, and then Sam put a cap on it."

Stage manager Donald Fried tells me how the set design evolved:

> *The idea to revise the set came from Sam. Sam came to rehearsal Thursday [March 20, 1997], on the spur of the moment, without having seen any of the drawings of the set design.[24] The first thing he saw was a model of the set. He and Jim had a brief discussion about the set design during a break. Sam's immediate reaction was that the set was too "cozy." It bothered Sam that the refrigerator was center right, facing stage left, so when you opened it you couldn't see into it. Jim liked it because when you opened it you were center stage and there would be a spot flooding you with light from inside the refrigerator. Sam thought the refrigerator had to take on more prominence.*
>
> *The floor had several different rakes built into it to control the flow of the artichokes and the [simulated] pee.[25] Sam didn't like that. Though he understood the practical reasons, he thought it didn't serve the play. After discussion among Sam, Jim, and David [Cosier], Jim hit on the idea to heavily abstract the set, i.e., to make the refrigerator, table, chairs, and stove icons, . . . quintessential icons of*

the '50s, with the idea that when Ella and Weston were married in the '50s, there was a sense of hope and great promise. The floor is a brand new yellow; the appliances are all very new. This was Jim's idea, and Sam liked it. The set is very clean and new, and the family is not, especially Weston. [The play is set in the late '70s. The characters are wearing '70s clothes in a '50s set.]

The original set design was the result of collaboration between the director and the set designer. The final set design is the result of collaboration among playwright, director, and set designer.[26] The implications of the change in scenic design, from heavily realistic to what Houghton calls "more abstract," become a kind of invisible compass in rehearsal.

At the outset, the director characteristically encourages the actors to find their own blocking, then comments, questions, and suggests adjustments. During the play's first rehearsal on its feet, an actor asks: "Should we go with the stage direction or just with instinct?" The director replies: "Just go with your instinct." In act 1, Ella says to her daughter: "Why can't you just cooperate?" and Emma replies: "Because it's deadly. It leads to dying" (148). Rehearsal work that began with slavish conformity to the stage directions in the text would be similarly "deadly."

At one point, the actress playing Ella sits at the opposite end of the table from Wesley who is removing pieces of the front door from the floor. She suddenly says, "I wonder if I should be sitting closer to Wes," and the director responds: "Sure. Try anything you want. . . . We are not tied to anything. This is all about trying, and finding, stuff." Immediately after this, the actress asks if they can replay the scene "so I can try to follow Sam's stage directions about cooking this bacon sandwich." The rehearsal trajectory is a creative back-and-forth between a freedom to depart from and an instinctive drawing nearer to the authority of the playwright.

"When Sam and I were talking about the play a long time ago," the director says, the playwright spoke about "not just the sight but the *sound* of the bacon cooking, just a hint of that." (In performance the audience hears the sizzle of the bacon cooking on top of the stove.) Even with a trash can representing the refrigerator, a small wooden table standing in for the stove, and nonexistent bacon fried and eaten by Ella, the text is beginning to breathe, its sounds and smells sensuously articulated by the director and actors. When Paul Dawson says a few minutes later, "It helps me to watch her eat the bacon. I'm hungry, and she's eating," it is startling to realize that the bacon exists only in the actors' imagination.

Certain props are a source of curiosity and hilarity. This is especially true of the prosthesis and IV bag of water with a rubber tube strapped around the actor's body that will allow Wesley to simulate urinating on his sister's 4-H charts in act 1.[27] Since the same actor will enter completely naked in act 3, there are a series of rehearsal jokes, culminating when Dawson uses the prosthesis for the first time in the playing area, "peeing" very carefully into a large aluminum pot. All three actors in the scene deliver their lines through their own irrepressible laughter, echoed and magnified by the director's laughter. This laughter continues to interrupt the scene, bursting out intermittently on both sides of the downstage edge of the playing area. There is a particularly loud explosion of hilarity when Ella tells Wesley that he is circumcised just like his grandfather, "almost identical in fact" (144). The laughter continues for three pages of the script, but the actors stop giggling long before the rest of us do.

During the lunch break, I ask Deborah Hedwall and Gretchen Cleevely how they were affected by the presence of the playwright in rehearsal. Cleevely says: "It made me nervous. You have your own reactions to the play and the director's feelings and the other actors' feelings. When the playwright responds, it's as if it's coming from the mouth of God." Hedwall's reaction is equally direct: "He wasn't in on the casting. . . . 'Will he approve of me?' 'Will he like me?'" and she continues:

> Because so much of this is his stories and the places he comes from, he has information that is forever interesting. But because he offers it as information that you may or may not find interesting, he doesn't seem to offer it to form your own responses, to make you see this family in a certain way.

I ask about her response to Shepard's comments on the spiritual "level" in the play. Hedwall begins with a definition of acting that recalls Marianne Moore's definition of poetry ("'imaginary gardens with real toads in them'"):[28]

> "Living truthfully in the imaginary circumstance of the material"—Sanford Meisner—means that I have no understanding of the symbolism or the spiritual level in the play. Acting is completely about the reality of what you're doing, not about what you're thinking. It's always propelled forward by need, even in Waiting for Godot.[29] [What Shepard said about spiritual awakening in the play] is very freeing because he's written it. You don't have to act it and you can't. [The characters in this play] blame everything on the externals. There's no rich inner life. If there is, it's accidental. He's already written it. You just have to live it.
>
> If you don't [know] what Sam told us, you start imposing a hideous burden on yourself to be deep and interesting. What's interesting is the simple truth of what he's written. If any actor or character were aware of the deep material in this play and felt obligated to the metaphors, the fun would be over, for the actors and the audience. If you go ahead and do all the work, it doesn't work.
>
> There are intellectual plays, like Pinter, that require a greater awareness of what you're saying. In Sam Shepard's play there's no heavenly connection to the earthly action. Not as my job. My job is to be clear about and make clear my own [Ella's] needs and what I'm going to do about them.[30]

In refusing to feel "obligated to the metaphors" and denying "heavenly connections to the earthly action," the actress seems to be opposing or rejecting what the playwright has said in rehearsal: "It's more like a spiritual awakening, beyond rationality. . . . It's ancient, symbolic." But she is making a point about acting, not literary criticism, or rather she is making a point about a literary work from *inside* the literary work.

"Who knows in the moment when they're living a metaphor?" Hedwall asks. "Nobody does. . . . Basically, Sam Shepard gives you the permission to not know about it. In that way it's liberating. It's hard enough to make sense of it, no matter how off the ground. And this play is off the ground."

More than a week later, in rehearsal on April 2, I listen to Ella's "curse" monologue in act 2. She begins by talking to Wesley, then delivers the rest of the monologue out to the audience in a semirealistic, meditative style. Hedwall has found the realm where the speech exists. She is there, utterly there, as always, in the scene, on the ground, rooted, as an "earthly" person. At the same time she is a figure searching a mystery, something unseen but felt: she is investigating the meaning of the title of the play she's in. Without willing it or considering it her "job," the actress lifts her character a little bit off the ground for a moment—but it is the right moment.

During a break on March 28, I ask the actress: "Where does all your obvious understanding of the spiritual dimension and the symbolism that Sam Shepard talked about in rehearsal *go* when you perform the role of Ella?" She responds:

> *Great question. I hadn't thought about that [pause]. I have an answer. For myself. I put it in my heart and it goes into my soul and I leave it alone and see where it comes out. It's on its own. I have nothing to do with it after that. Then it becomes impulse, pure god-impulse, not on the intellectual plane at all. It's bigger than us, like Sam's plays.*

And without losing a beat she quotes from Ella's "curse" monologue: "It goes back and back to tiny little cells and genes. To atoms. To tiny little swimming things making up their minds without us. Plotting in the womb. Before that even" (174). The script is the site of discovery, including the discovery of what cannot be known. To adapt Yeats, in one of his last letters, the theater can embody what it cannot know.[31]

Paul Dawson clearly has been affected by what the playwright said in rehearsal. Today I see a Wesley more in tune with Shepard's comment: "Your character is the most raw of all. Everybody has a little bit of armor. You don't. Wesley is totally vulnerable." It's in his eyes: alternately bewildered, angry, coldly empty, uncomprehending, pleading, sullen, meditative, suddenly tender with painful openness to the gradual revelations of what is happening to this family. During the lunch break on March 26, Dawson tells me: "I think when Sam wrote this play he probably identified most with my character. It was valuable having him here, especially valuable to me, because he introduced a new way of talking about the play, which was talking about the less rational, the less practical, aspects." The actor offers an alternative view to that of Hedwall:

> *Previously, we as actors and the director had been talking about the factual givens of the play. And as an actor I think it's valuable to sit outside the play and*

metaphors
+ symbolism

try to objectively view the work as a piece of literature. And I don't think it's all
that common a perspective among actors. So I was glad with Sam to be given
the opportunity to talk about the metaphors and the symbolism because I think
there are as many clues there as there are in the factual givens, the practicalities,
if you will.

I just think it's fatuous or foolish to ignore these things. With Wes, in particular, I think, as Sam said, there is something spiritual and unconscious that is
going on that you can't get to just by adding up the givens. It wasn't even so
much that Sam gave me any new information. He just confirmed what my instincts, my feelings, already were and validated them.

It is not surprising that the actor playing a character who is perhaps a surro-
gate for the playwright seems to feel most fully the necessity of finding clues in
the author's notes in rehearsal. Whether it is a difference in the characters they
portray or in acting technique or in the willingness to share what feeds them in
their work, Hedwall and Dawson express different degrees of wariness about
the writer's comments on symbolism and spirituality in the play.

Jude Ciccolella takes a modified position, somewhere between Hedwall's
not knowing more than the character knows and Dawson's interest in viewing
the literary work "objectively." During rehearsal on March 26, he says to the
director: "I think Wes has had an epiphany, *as Sam said, but I also think* he's
conscious of some of it. . . . There's truth to it, but in the end the curse finally
wins out" (emphasis mine). During a break in rehearsal, Ciccolella tells me his
responses to the presence of the playwright at the table reading:

You want a sense that he digs what you're doing, that you're in the right zone.
All actors want that. Apparently, Sam generally thinks we're in the right zone so
that is positive. My feeling is that he's impressed with the general tone. . . . The
thing with Sam Shepard in particular is that he has an encyclopedic mind, so that
he knows a lot about a lot of things, and he's acutely perceptive and intelligent
without being ostentatious about it. He has that laconic style. Also, though I
think he has clear ideas about the tone or style of his play, there's not a rigidity
for the actors. . . .

Kris Kristofferson and Morgan Freeman are very rooted, honest, at-ease
people when you speak with them. Sam has that quality. There's no dissembling
at all. There's a strong presence. So in speaking with him, his comments about
the play are not frivolous. They're well thought out. I thought that was
impressive.

Clarity without rigidity is what the actor values in the playwright's comments
to the company; it is also exactly what seems most useful in rehearsal work on
his play.

In rehearsal on March 27, the director comments to actor Clark
Middleton: "What's wonderful about having the writer [present] . . . is that
there is such authority there. You don't question it." Of course, one does, at
times. But Jim Houghton clearly demonstrates his sympathetic relation to the

"author-ity" of the playwright by his frequent reminders of authorial presence in rehearsal.

Sam Shepard has said that all his plays are "musical." "There are many possible rhythmic structures that an actor can hit, but there's only one true one. There's one moment that he has to meet." He defines rhythm as "the delineation of time in space, but it only makes sense with silences on either side of it. You can't have a rhythm that doesn't have a silence in it."[32] In rehearsal the director tells the cast: "I think the pauses indicated by Sam Shepard are very important—the silences. We may add or take some away later, but let's try to be sensitive to them now." He asks the actors to observe closely the pauses, particularly the stage direction following one of Weston's speeches in act 2: "*(long silence)*" (166). "Try to think in terms of *not* taking pauses except where Sam has indicated." The directorial note on silence stands in for the playwright, reinscribing the writer's "delineation of time in space" in rehearsal.

During the playing of act 2, Ciccolella stops midscene and asks, "Is this one of those pauses?" Off book already,[33] the actor has had no opportunity to reread the stage directions. Once again during the scene the actor asks if there is a marked pause that he has missed. Both times the stage manager answers no. A few speeches later, stage manager Donald Fried, anticipating the question, says quickly, "long silence." Weston takes the long pause and continues his speech. The playwright's silences are observed in rehearsal.

Directing Emma's fantasy monologue about a future life as a mechanic in "a little place called Los Cerritos" (161), Houghton uses the playwright's personal storytelling style in rehearsal as a model for storytelling in the play: "There aren't any pauses. . . . Even Sam, when he speaks about the whole history of the trees, he's pouring this information out, and it's right there, and it's so interesting." The delivery Houghton elicits becomes more and more interesting, and effective, in rehearsal and in performance.

During an act 3 work-through (a stop-and-start rehearsal), the director tells Weston and Ella: "I'd like to do the scene again without the two of you looking at each other. I think a lot is not being said here. There is a lot between the lines that's not being said." As if in imitation of the playwright's style, the director's rehearsal note asks for less (elimination of visual focus on the other) to produce more. When Houghton asks later how the new blocking worked, Ciccolella replies, "I think it's right. It's also what Sam wants, what he's indicated in the script." The stage direction in the text reads: "*WESTON, who keeps cooking the eggs . . . knows she's there but doesn't look at her*" (187). Hedwall responds:

> *The whole thing seems forced. There are times when I want to look at Weston. I wanted to do the exercise [not looking at each other]. I peeked at his back a few times. I liked that, listening to his voice. . . . There's a strange forgiveness in this scene that's never spoken. We've both been so hideously deceptive with each other. But now there's something that has allowed me to fall*

asleep with him in the room. I don't want to play *all this . . . but it's very interesting.*

The playwright's stage direction prohibiting looking refers only to Weston. The actor for whom the stage direction is intended feels comfortable with the directorial note. The actress who is given no indication in the text of where to look peeks at Weston's back but also feels "something" that allows her to close her eyes altogether and sleep while he cooks.

The actor's sense that directorial and authorial choices coincide supports his reading of the scene. The actress finds the gap, the breathing space, between the playwright's textual "note" and the director's rehearsal note. As she reads "between the lines," she considers what implication to play and not to play: "I don't want to *play* all this . . . but it's very interesting."

Rehearsing a scene in which Ella cooks while Wesley sweeps the floor[34] as he delivers one of the play's extended monologues, Hedwall says: "I'm confused about the broom pushing. I don't know if that's supposed to be my reality." The director replies, "You're just cooking," and the actress responds: "Great. I'm here, in my space. I have my [imaginary] window. I can look out." During the next run-through Wesley delivers his monologue almost motionless. Ella stares out her "window," mouthing soundless words for a long time before she begins to "cook," then she stops, fork in midair, gazing at the frying pan, as if she is both in her own space and also silently responding to the boy who is speaking about her in the third person, as if his reality touches hers, his stillness becomes hers.

In tension with the company-created time line, the monologues stop time.[35] Ella's realistic motions of cooking are checked by Wesley's stillness on stage; the time line is overtaken by the timeless moment of Wesley's reverie: "Mom crying soft. Soft crying. Then no sound" (138).

The delivery of the monologues out to the audience is at first resisted, consciously or involuntarily, by the actors. Directing Emma's act 2 monologue, Houghton tells Cleevely: "Think of it too as a kind of pitch you're making to someone. . . . You have a kind of ownership of it. This time, pitch it to *me*; talk to *me*." His specific realistic directions ("pitch it to me") are calculated to achieve the illusion-breaking effect of a speech delivered directly to the audience. He does not ask the actress to deliver her monologue out; he simply gives her a new personalized audience, replacing Wesley with himself. Eventually, the theater audience will replace the director.

After the monologue is run again, Houghton says: "You're obviously not going to direct it to me in performance. . . . I'm not going to be sitting out there every night." "You're not?" the actress asks, in mock surprise. They both laugh. In the first preview performance on April 15, 1997, Emma plays her fantasy monologue out. The speech is quiet, paced as directed. I glance over my shoulder. Jim Houghton is seated at the back of the house. The actress is again delivering her monologue to the director, but he is now literally the audience.

The evolution of the playing of the monologues in rehearsal clearly seems keyed to Shepard's comments to the cast: "In the play there are periods of drastic alienation so that people are strangers; then things come back. . . . So it's good if it has this resonance, that it's not just one thing."[36] In rehearsal on March 26, Houghton identifies what he calls "major shifts" in act 2: pauses, either indicated or implied in the stage directions, just before a monologue. The director tells the actors that he will "be doing light shifts here." (In performance, when monologues are played out, the lights slowly dim.) During rehearsal two days later, the director says: "I'm going to try something. I'm going to hit the floor with a hammer just at the point where there is a major shift in the scene. Just as an exercise." He hits the floor just before and just after Wesley's first long monologue in act 1 and Ella's "curse" monologue in act 2. The sound of the hammer signals a light change but it also signals the boundary between different temporal and spatial realms in the play. The playwright's "two levels" are, in a sense, present in rehearsal work on the monologues.

Just as Houghton at times "stands in" for the playwright's choices—"I think the pauses indicated by Sam Shepard are very important"—he, like other directors I observe, also at times blurs the boundary between what is directorial and what is authorial. "Was that Sam's decision?" Ciccolella asks, referring to the raked stage. The director replies: "It was an evolution. . . . It will be a raised platform with a rise." There is a protection for the cast in this seemingly united front, as actors in subsequent chapters will attest. At Signature Theatre Company the gap between directorial and authorial preferences may be narrower than in other productions,[37] but there is always a gap, even when the author and the director are the same person.

Today I glance over at the director's notes on the white pad to the side of his script. They are almost illegible. I see a W circled, then "Emma!—Go to door"; a WE circled and then "Head on table"; a W circled, followed by "X Further D." After he gives his notes, the director crosses them out and begins a new set. Unlike my own, his notes are ephemeral; once shared, they are gone like yesterday's rain.

In directing certain monologues out, Houghton is effecting a preference of the playwright not stated in the script. With scripted stage directions, he is more eclectic. Houghton says: "Some of the stage directions may work beautifully and others may not. It depends on the individual actors. . . . It's been my experience that the writers aren't so overly precious about everything. It's more often the interpreters, the people who write about the play, who are."

In rehearsal on March 28, Hedwall remarks: "What he's saying as a playwright about my relationship with this family is hard to understand and yet fascinating."[38] The director replies: "We have to understand what Sam intends from the indications he gives us in the script." Some indications are easier to follow than others. Rehearsing act 2 on April 2, the director gives the actress this note: "Ella, when you say, 'I have a car,' there's a written pause. Why don't you try sitting down after that line?" The playwright wants a pause; the director suggests blocking that reinforces a scripted stillness.

Not so easily understood or choreographed is an exit near the end of act 2. The stage manager points out that "the text strangely has Taylor exit stage left" (180), when all the other characters exit through the (missing) front door, stage right. During the break the director sits beside me, studying the script and drawing diagrams for a blocking of five separate exits. Then he works the scene for thirty to forty minutes, creating an intricate new blocking that incorporates the seemingly odd exit stage left.

Blocking a single mysterious stage direction opens up the space dramatically. What was tight and congested in the previous staging is open and clean and fluid. The new blocking of a very busy scene is the result both of the director's openness to experimentation and of his adhering more strictly to the playwright's stage direction. In rehearsal, an inexplicable exit—Taylor needs to leave the house but there is no indication that anyone can leave the house by exiting stage left—becomes one more stageable mystery, an act "beyond rationality" that eerily opens up the stage.[39]

Shepard's scripted positioning of the lamb in the play is consistent throughout: center stage.[40] In performance on the raked stage of the Shiva Theater, the lamb is foregrounded downstage left. Ciccolella says of his long monologue to the lamb in act 3: "This speech should be stark different from [Weston's] . . . previous drunken rages. This is like a man talking to his child." Houghton replies: "I agree with you totally. It's a whole different thing."

A member of the company with the potential to upstage everybody, the lamb is a subject of increasing interest and not a little concern in rehearsal. Ciccolella, who has previously performed in *Curse of the Starving Class,* predicts that the lamb may jump out of its little fenced-in enclosure on stage once it begins to grow. The director asks the actor if the lamb will make noise when Wesley picks it up and carries it offstage in act 3. "The lamb will make noise," Ciccolella says. "The audience will have to ignore it." Clark Middleton asks, "Will I have to share my dressing room with the lamb?" and stage manager Donald Fried replies: "No. And he won't have to share his with you."

"He" turns out to be Peg, who gets a bit chunky sitting in her outdoor pen in between performances and is replaced midrun by a littler lamb named April. Right before her debut I visit Peg and her companion, Hector, just outside the Shiva Theater. Peg and Hector are both a few months old, not siblings but former stallmates on a farm in Connecticut. After the end of the show, the cast has been assured, they will be taken to a petting zoo. Hector turned out to be too big for the role but he is here to keep Peg company.

Peg has a leg problem. Though she is weaned, she is being given a bottle with formula to help the muscles in her left front leg develop properly and a splint, removed when she is onstage, has been applied to strengthen it. Hector becomes very upset when she leaves for the theater.

On April 10, 1997, the lamb makes her first onstage appearance during technical rehearsals at the Public Theater. Animal handler Todd Serenbetz places some hay in a corner of her fenced-in enclosure downstage left. Peg bleats loudly and frequently on arrival. Serenbetz, sitting in the front row about four feet from the lamb, says to her: "Don't worry. I'm here." The bleating continues. The director says to the lamb: "It's all right, sweetie." He receives a much louder bleat.

In the first technical run-through of act 3, Peg steals the show. During the long opening monologue addressed to her, she bleats very loudly, wanders and slides about on the yellow floor, faces out appealingly, licks her lips, and investigates the tiny pile of hay. There is much laughter from the cast and crew. The lamb abruptly lies down and focuses her gaze on Weston as he says, "It was an animal thing" (186). Utterly silent, she continues to look at the actor whose lines now take on new resonance.

Peg bleats once as Ella enters, covering her opening line, "What's that lamb doing back in here?" (187), the line on which Sam Shepard had last entered rehearsal. Ella repeats her question, and the scene continues. The lamb is silent, lying inside her little pen, her back to the audience, focused steadily on the human actors, upstaging no one. It is so quiet we can hear the sizzle of the ham and eggs Weston cooks.

Wesley enters center upstage, wet and fully naked, in bright light.[41] He walks downstage left, picks up the lamb carefully, and carries her off stage right. Peg does not make a sound.

Weston worries about the lamb: "That lamb needs to be kept warm" (190). He eats the ham and scrambled eggs he has just cooked.[42] Then Wesley reappears, dressed in his father's old dirty clothes, his hands and lower arms bloodied. He announces that he has butchered the lamb because "We need some food." Weston replies:

THE ICE BOX IS CRAMMED FULL A'FOOD! (191)

The moment remains as mysterious on the stage as in the rehearsal reading at table attended by the playwright.

The "story" of the lamb is an inner conundrum in the play. The first question addressed to the playwright by an actor concerned the slaughter of the lamb and is never answered. The longest speech in *Curse of the Starving Class* is addressed to the lamb: an animal story with a delayed conclusion that is narrated at the very end of the play. In his act 3 monologue Weston tells about an eagle who steals the testes of lambs he has been castrating. When Wesley enters and asks, "What happens next?" Weston replies, "I was telling it to the lamb!" and refuses to repeat or develop the story for his son: "I ain't tellin' it again!" (184). Later Wesley inexplicably butchers the lamb he had brought into the house to heal. Near the end of act 3 a character who has just blown up Weston's car enters with a skinned lamb carcass and drops it in the downstage pen. Ella "wakes up" from an ambiguous sleep, stares at the lamb carcass, and says, "Something just went through me. Just from looking at the lamb" (199).

What "went through" her is a story Weston used to tell about an eagle and a tomcat, a continuation of the monologue addressed to the lamb. Only now do we realize that Wesley knows the rest of the story, that he asked his father to tell it again the way a child asks a parent to reread, or retell, a familiar bedtime story. The mother replaces the father as narrator and with her son completes the monologue, changing it to a dialogue:

ELLA: You remember the whole thing?

WESLEY: Yeah.

ELLA: I don't. I remember something about it. But it just went right through me.

WESLEY: Oh.

ELLA: (*after pause*) I remember he keeps coming back and swooping down on the shed roof and then flying off . . . . What happens next?

And Wesley remembers:

WESLEY: A cat comes.

ELLA: That's right. A big tomcat comes. Right out in the fields. And he jumps on top of that roof to sniff around in all the entrails or whatever it was.

WESLEY: (*still with his back to her*) And that eagle comes down and picks up the cat in his talons and carries him screaming off into the sky.

ELLA: (*staring at lamb*) That's right. And they fight. They fight like crazy in the middle of the sky. The cat's tearing his chest out, and the eagle's trying to drop him, but the cat won't let go because he knows if he falls he'll die.

WESLEY: And the eagle's being torn apart in midair. The eagle's trying to free himself from the cat, and the cat won't let go.

ELLA: And they come crashing down to the earth. Both of them come crashing down. Like one whole thing. How long have I been sleeping? (199–200)

A story has been reconstructed, shared, once again addressed to a lamb, now slaughtered. It is the story that both Weston and the playwright have been telling about dying animals locked in mortal combat.[43] "An animal thing" evokes the completion of the narrative and is its subject and audience.

Deborah Hedwall offers her own perspective on the scene and its effect on the audience:

The text gives actors the opportunity to explore a kind of thinking and not necessarily to be responsible for the wallop that it lands. Clearly at the end the woman has come out of a deep sleep which has involved her house and her children. Identities are all mixed up. She witnesses a slaughtered lamb and never once mentions it, and then goes off on a story that is told by her husband earlier in the play. Each person in the audience will walk away with their own feelings about that. Each actress playing the part will have to find her own truth and clarity in that story.

> But ultimately Sam Shepard has completely shaped the end of the play him-self because of what he's chosen to have happen. He has not drawn spiritually conscious people. He has drawn earthly people without a great facility of rich inner life. So the audience really has to do with it what they will.

Sam Shepard has said that he has "always had a problem with endings":

> I never know when to end a play. I'd just as soon not end anything. But you have to stop at some point, just to let people out of the theater. I don't like endings and I have a hard time with them. . . . A resolution isn't an ending; it's a strangu-lation.[44]

In this production, Shepard has and has not, in Hedwall's words, "completely shaped the end of the play himself." He has added a new last line (Ella's "How long have I been sleeping?"[45]) "in response," he says, "to live actors, not just their voices but their intentions too—the whole thing," with the ironic result that "one whole thing" no longer ends the play.

But the "end" of the play is not the line Ella speaks. The final tableau—*"They stay like that with WESLEY looking off upstage, his back to ELLA, and ELLA downstage, looking at the* [slaughtered] *lamb. Lights fade very slowly to black"* (200)—is a fractured, ironic version of the original last line. The play closes with a complex stage image of "one whole thing": alive, dying, dead; absent and present; asleep and awake; not comprehended fully by any onstage perspective or gaze—light fading slowly on an unanswered question.

2 David Rabe in Rehearsal

A Question of Mercy

If the writer doesn't know, who's going to know?

David Rabe is best known for his Vietnam trilogy, beginning with *The Basic Training of Pavlo Hummel*, which opened off-Broadway to rave reviews in 1971. The next year the Broadway production of *Sticks and Bones* received a Tony Award for best play of the year. The final play in the trilogy, *Streamers*, had its world premiere at Long Wharf Theatre in New Haven, Connecticut, in 1976. Like Sam Shepard, David Rabe has written screenplays and directed theater productions of his own work. The film version of his 1984 play, *Hurlyburly*, finished shooting during the New Haven rehearsals of *A Question of Mercy*, performed at Long Wharf Theatre, February 18–March 15, 1998.

Rabe's *A Question of Mercy* had its 1997 world premiere in a New York Theatre Workshop production directed by Douglas Hughes. When I mentioned that I planned to write about a restaging of the New York production of *A Question of Mercy* during Hughes's inaugural season as the new artistic director at Long Wharf Theatre, a friend asked quietly, "What can there be to write about?" It's a good question, and one this chapter intends to answer. How can the restaging of a play whose author, director, and set designer remain unchanged be a site of exploration, discovery, revision? In what sense can the playwright take an interest, or a role, in such a project?

A Question of Mercy "boldly address[es] the subject of assisted suicide . . . while offering no sentimental heroes or moral conclusions. And the work's conscious stiffness reflect[s] a culture that has never found a vocabulary for dealing with death."[1] In Rabe's play, Thomas, a gay man whose partner, Anthony, is dying of AIDS, asks Dr. Chapman to help Anthony commit suicide. Reluctantly, the physician becomes involved, as does Susanah, a friend of the gay couple's. Ultimately, the intricate suicide plan breaks down.

A Question of Mercy had its genesis in Rabe's reading of a 1991 article by Dr. Richard Selzer[2] who, like the playwright, is present at rehearsals in New York and New Haven. Selzer, who has himself adapted Thomas Mann's

2.1 David Rabe and director Douglas Hughes (standing) in rehearsal of *A Question of Mercy* (photograph by Joan Marcus)

novella *The Black Swan* for the stage, is no innocent about matters of authorship: "Although the adaptation is very close to the [article] . . . and many lines of dialogue are those I recorded, I wasn't a collaborator. He did it."[3] Still, there is the ambiguity of two authorial figures in rehearsal, further complicated by the fact that, as Selzer acknowledges, the dialogue he has written, some of which Rabe follows quite closely, contains "the words . . . as they were spoken" by people who still reside in New Haven at the time of the Long Wharf production.[4] Who is the "primary source" of the play is one of the questions the play poses.[5]

Douglas Hughes distinguishes between a documentary about "life" and the play David Rabe has written: "*A Question of Mercy* comes from 'real life testimony.' But we don't look upon it as a true life event. The incident occurred but it is theatrically distilled. It is not a documentary."[6] In 1997, following the resignation of Arvin Brown, Hughes became Long Wharf Theatre's first new artistic director in thirty years. Introducing himself in an open letter to Long Wharf subscribers, Hughes writes: "Theatre is, after all, the most human of art forms, the place where we practice being alive."[7] The director presents eloquently the compelling questions raised by Rabe's play:

> What happens when the renegade act of self-slaughter, existentially a tradition with a lone perpetrator in isolation from society, suddenly wants society to give it the civilized nod? When rational standards have been applied to something that is beyond reason in the end?
>
> We are determined to banish mystery, to have everything explicable. But what happens when reason fails, when we come to an ultimate moment?[8]

The first read-through at table takes place on January 13, 1998, in Rehearsal Hall A at Long Wharf Theatre. By 1 P.M. more than forty people are milling about in a clean, spacious room. Two long rectangular tables sit side by side in one corner. Windows fill the upper half of an entire wall. Outside, seagulls fly by almost continuously. Cake, cookies, fruit, coffee, and tea are placed on a table in a small anteroom. An Equity meeting preceded the rehearsal; small paper bags containing juice and bananas have been left behind.

Douglas Hughes enters, followed by David Rabe. The playwright wears dark green corduroy pants and a long-sleeved collared black jersey beneath a brownish plaid shirt. He is cleanshaven with a full head of white hair and piercing blue eyes. His glasses, not worn during the reading, hang from a cord around his neck. In front of him at the table, where he sits to the left of the director, is a script of the play. Directly across the table from David Rabe sits Richard Selzer. The two writers are cordial, speak briefly, and later appear together in the rehearsal room for a photo session. During the "Meet and Greet" that inaugurates rehearsal, Hughes asks everyone to introduce himself or herself. The playwright introduces himself simply as "David Rabe, writer." "It's taken twenty years [since] *Streamers*," the director announces, "and we're [finally] doing another David Rabe play, almost exactly one year since I came here. I'm thrilled."

After the members of the Long Wharf staff have left, Hughes addresses the actors:

This is about an utter mess, right? The interest is in the human [experience] of dancing away from the issue. Suddenly all the texture of the experience, the sustenance of ambiguity and behavior that seems so apt and true [pause]. . . . The play is about triangular *relationships. . . . A loving conspiracy is engineered. . . . It's about mundane fear which gives the play its overvoice beyond matters that would interest the Hemlock Society. It's that ambivalence that interests me the most. It's the fact that it's called "A Question". . . .*

He continues to weave directorial notes into his opening comments to the company:

The play came with very realistic set descriptions. Finally, I suggested that it be done in a different way, with a minimum of scenery. David said, "Oh, yes. That's the way I'd like it to be done."

I think of the stage as a microscope. [He mentions that he was a biology major in college.] It is a powerful internal metaphor for me, and I hope for you, though it will be lost, I think, on the audience.

The actors' faces are intensely focused on the director, who, having removed his brown wool cardigan, says, "I just realized I forgot to put a belt on today." The cast laughs. "Very Dr. Chapmanlike." (Dr. Chapman, the physician in the play, doesn't appear to notice the tie he wears.)

Everyone has lived through the way we keep mortality at bay. . . . [There is in the play] a loving, well-intentioned conspiracy that proceeds by inference, gains confidence and loses confidence. . . . There is only that issue alive in the play. There is history, of course, but the scheme is to create a breathlessly sealed world.

Who is going to be leader? Who is going to be Dad?

So I asked for the stage of a microscope in a way, and that's what we'll have at Long Wharf. . . . A smear of red, almost as if one is looking at a smear of blood—blood which is so human—will be the backdrop, projected as slides.

The director points to a small model of the set on the table directly in front of him as he talks to a rapt cast. The playwright sits motionless, right arm and hand resting on his thigh, chin cupped in his left hand, meditative, listening, his gaze straight out across the table.

Hughes alludes to Justice David Souter's separate opinion in the Supreme Court's recent decision of June 26, 1997, not to recognize "a limited constitutional right of terminally ill and competent patients to the help of a doctor in ending their lives, in order to avoid further pointless suffering and anguish."[9] "It's come back to the states," Hughes says. "We're left with a status quo that we know is being violated all the time, sometimes with zero consequence and sometimes [not]."

In the midst of these concerns, Hughes introduces further staging choices that depart from the rehearsal script:

> *Anthony [dying of AIDS] will take the pills in a very orderly way as Dr. Chapman has prescribed, and Dr. Chapman will check his vitals and give him morphine if it is needed. [To the actor playing Anthony:] What is of interest in this scene is not slides of your past. [Anthony wants to commit suicide listening to Bach and watching "the slides of my life, . . . of my friends and loved ones."]*
>
> *I've checked with David [Rabe]. My idea is that . . . we see you seeing what you choose to see. The only realistic props in the play are hospital equipment brought in to resuscitate Anthony. Then the world crashes in on what has been a very sealed-in world. There's an invasion. Onto the stage come the apparatus of life sustenance. Floating down from the grid come, very realistically, breathing tubes, monitors, the sounds of heroically trying to save his life. Anthony is taken over by the experts, as Dr. Chapman says. And thereby hangs a tale, as you know.*[10]

The rehearsal script indicates the use of actual projected images: *"a picture of Anthony as a child. . . . The slides will progress, moving through Anthony's life—a new slide every twenty seconds or so"* (92–93). The director announces, in the presence of the playwright and with his tacit approval, that he is overriding the stage directions in the rehearsal script, exchanging naturalistic depiction for a doubling of acts of imagination: actor and audience will "see" what they choose to see.

In the Grove Press edition of *A Question of Mercy*, published just before the play opens at Long Wharf, appear the following revised stage directions: *"ANTHONY moves forward and sits down facing out. He turns on the projector, which flashes forward on automatic. Blink after blink."*[11] In performance at Long Wharf, the slide projector faces the audience. Beams of light flash at regular intervals: we, the audience, are the slides Anthony sees.

In Signature Theatre's production of *Curse of the Starving Class*, Sam Shepard sought a less cozy, more abstract set. In the New York and New Haven productions of Rabe's *A Question of Mercy*, the director argues for a nonrealistic set; its abstract backdrop, designed by Neil Patel, will appear on the front cover of the published edition of the play. In the presence of the playwright, the director speaks for the silent author.

"The play is really about . . . the human politics, about trying to keep a band together," Hughes says to the company. "As Susanah [a friend of Anthony and Thomas's] says, 'There are limits to love.' This play forces us to examine the limits of our love. As with Didi and Gogo we see the loops of human behavior." The director relies on dramatic texts (both Rabe and Beckett) to explicate the dramatic text.

Like James Houghton, Hughes privileges the reading at table: "We'll spend a good bit of time at the table as a group. We'll read it once today. Next time it's a free-for-all. *Anyone who wants to pull the plug* and take us back *can.* And I may do that" (emphasis mine). Hughes's metaphor for stopping rehearsal is startling in the way it conjures up the very questions raised by the play. But connections between rehearsal work and the action of the play are not fortuitous: the company in rehearsal is also a kind of "well-intentioned conspiracy that proceeds by inference, gains confidence and loses confidence" and, for a time, creates "a breathlessly sealed world."

Dr. Richard Selzer is the first of the two writers to speak to the actors:

> *This play is based on a true experience I had in New Haven. This play is true. Watching it in New York, I had the feeling I was watching myself. It was frightening.*
>
> *A Yale acquaintance I knew phoned me up one night. He wanted me to meet with a gay couple, one of whom was suffering from AIDS. I said I was retired but I would come. As I entered their apartment building, the doorman, who had been a patient of mine, recognized me. When I first met with them, we were all very tense. It was claustrophobic. There was no air coming in. I was trapped, drawn in over and over. I went to visit them over twenty times. I went back because, well, I had gotten to know them. I was ill at ease because I had been so long away from medicine. I knew well what they wanted from me and I kept refusing and refusing. But I asked the inevitable question: Would I want someone to help me die? And the answer was: yes. And from that moment the die was cast. From that moment we were a kind of secret cell. We were domestic. Cookies were served. It went on inexorably. Then there was the introduction of the fourth person [Susanah]. I was shocked because we were sworn to secrecy. The doorman always greeted me. I was so dumb. I didn't think about it.*
>
> *The woman who was their friend was like a sister I had always wanted. She was very strong, almost cruel. We men were weak, vacillating. It was with an enormous sense of relief and guilt and anguish that I accepted her [last-minute argument that Selzer not assist at the time of the attempted suicide]. . . .*
>
> *There will be people in the audience in New Haven who will know the story and the people [in it]. It had become a* cause célèbre. *This [production] will in fact awaken this sleeping event.*

The director's concept of "a breathlessly sealed world" corresponds to Selzer's representation of the scene as claustrophobic ("There was no air coming in"), just as his view of the characters as a "well-intentioned conspiracy" is confirmed by Selzer's presentation of the participants as "a kind of secret cell."

David Rabe has remained silent. Now he addresses the actors:

> *I read [Selzer's] piece in the* New York Times. *The focus for me was on the scene in the hospital [after Anthony's suicide attempt] when Anthony says he wants to live. Originally it was written for television, which accounts for the original stage directions. Then I decided to write for the theater.[12] I hadn't solved the problem of the central metaphor. I don't like multiset plays.*
>
> *It's a collision of the enormously painful with the ridiculous. . . . The plan is an attempt to turn reason into prophecy, but it breaks down constantly.[13] The emotional life is the core. You want to be friendly and nice and not to be in this mess, but you are.*

> *I didn't choose to leave out the professions [of the characters], but I just did it instinctively.*

Rabe's phrase, "in this mess," echoes the director's opening statement ("This is about an utter mess, right?"), but his "instinctive" omission of the occupations of his characters distances him from the other author in the room, who specifies that the AIDS victim is a doctor and his partner is a poet and minister.[14] "The essay is very spare. I didn't discuss it with Richard. I asked suddenly: how did she [Susanah] get there? I had to figure it out. That's the issue you have to work out." The indeterminate "you" includes the director, the actors, and possibly the audience.

Rabe was not present when Selzer spoke to the New York cast. The read-through at Long Wharf is the first time the two writers have appeared together in rehearsal. In an interview, Rabe says: "In the beginning I only spoke to Dr. Selzer on the phone—and we didn't discuss the events at all—although I've met him since. I haven't met any of the others. I wanted to work off the essay as it existed, and my response to it. I didn't want anyone to veto it."[15] The playwright says of Selzer's comments to the New Haven cast: "He was really helpful in that he had a sense of his own absurdity in some parts."[16] What Rabe most wants no one to "veto" is that sense of absurdity: "I do think that deep down, a lot of my work is about people trying to make reasonable accommodations of situations that are insane or absurd."[17]

Rabe's comments to the cast before the first read-through end with a Yogi Berra-like statement, wiser than it first appears. "Most of us live a civilized life," he says, then pauses. "*After* I wrote it, I thought about this: for people who can kill people, it's easy. For people who can't, it's impossible. These are people who *can't*." Selzer, addressing the company, adds: "There is a feeling that death is being usurped from Thomas by the doctor. It is apparent to me, from watching the New York production, that Thomas has been replaced." Each writer comments on what is learned after writing. In particular, Selzer's account of watching the staging of a play based on his own life shifts the "source" of knowledge from experience to art.

At 2:30 P.M. the table reading begins. I sit directly behind the director, on a diagonal to the playwright. Hughes laughs easily and audibly at the comic lines. His script is open on the table in front of him, and to its right are a pencil and small white unlined pad; I see him look at the script and make a note on the pad. Rabe sits, staring at the actors, his left arm across his upper abdomen, his right hand touching his face near his mouth. The thumb and forefinger of the right hand press against his lips as the actors read. In front of him on the table his script is closed, a pencil to its right. The fingers of his right (writing) hand are often in motion. The fingers of his left hand are bent, unmoving. When Thomas makes clear Anthony's desire to die, the playwright's lower jaw clenches. During the first encounter between Dr. Chapman (David Chandler) and the Doorman (Michael Kell), Rabe looks at Kell, the only member of the cast to have been in the New York production, and makes a note on the title page of his unopened script. Now the playwright appears more re-laxed. He gazes, smiling, at the actors during the scene in which Dr. Chapman has tea and homemade chocolate chip cookies in his first meeting with Anthony (Seth Gilliam) and Thomas (Richard Bekins). As the scene continues, Rabe leans forward, elbows on the table, the fingers of his right hand extended vertically until they join the fingertips of the left hand, together covering both mouth and nose. Only his eyes are visible. He opens, then closes, a blue folder containing the rehearsal schedule and contact sheet for the production, and places it beneath his still unopened script. Sipping coffee, he gazes across the table at the actors reading the lines of Thomas and Anthony, and then makes a second note on the title page of the script. He picks up his pencil while Anthony and Dr. Chapman talk, writes again, looks down at his writing with the pencil held lightly in his right hand, and returns his gaze to the actors.

Meanwhile, Hughes sits back in his chair, the director's script in its red three-ringed binder open to the page from which the actors are now reading. Production stage manager Charles Means is turning the pages of his own copy of the script in its larger, black, three-ringed binder: a diagram of the staging is on the right, the corresponding page of script on the left. The actors read in low, emotionally resonant voices, occasionally making eye contact. Once or twice they touch each other, or gesture with head or hand, in quietly restrained movements. The entire company—director, actors, and stage manager—are all reading the text, either silently or aloud; only the playwright has not yet opened his script. Rabe's gaze is almost always on the actors, unlike Shepard's nearly continuous focus on his text during the table reading of *Curse of the Starving Class*.

The voices of the actors are at times so low that with the slight whirring noise of the heater in the rehearsal studio anyone not sitting at the table must strain to hear. Rabe makes a note, this time on the back of the final page of his script. He writes at great length. When he seems to be finished, he twirls his pencil in his right hand, looks at the actor playing Anthony, then writes more. Now he resumes his characteristic posture (left arm across upper abdomen, thumb and forefinger of right hand pressed against mouth), gazing across the table at the actors. They are an unexpected contrast, director and playwright: one continually following the text along with the actors, the other not once looking at the words in his own play.

Rabe sits back in his seat for a moment, and picks up his pencil. As he leans forward, he turns the pencil upside down, then rights it, repeating this maneuver several times. He holds the pencil poised to write, writes, erases, writes again. The actors read aloud the shockingly casual negotiation of a mu-tually convenient date for Anthony's suicide:

ANTHONY: (*studying the calendar*) Are you free on February tenth? . . . .
DR. CHAPMAN: The tenth. Yes. I'm free. I have one thing, but I'm sure I
              can switch it. . . .
ANTHONY: So we have a date? [38–39]

On Anthony's line, "So we have a date?" Rabe sits with his arms at his sides, staring at the actor, then makes a note.

Susanah's entrance and opening lines elicit the first audible response from the playwright, who laughs openly along with the director. As the scene continues, Rabe reassumes his characteristic position. I see his lips move, hidden from the actors. He bends forward and makes a note on the next to last page of his script, about fifty pages ahead of where the actors are reading.

Rabe is not writing "on the script" in the same sense as other playwrights I observe in rehearsal.[18] The page he chooses has no particular relevance to what he writes except as available space. His notes are private, conveyed only to the director; they will not appear as textual revisions in the next day's rehearsal. The "sealed-in world" of the play has its counterpart in the very private world of this playwright in rehearsal. Even his own text on the table in front of him remains largely sealed off.

The reading continues. Rabe leans forward, his hands loosely clasped on the table, as Susanah says: "The certainty is so difficult. I don't know how anyone can know what is right absolutely in this kind of situation" (51). The dialogue that follows, an increasingly detailed discussion of where Thomas and Susanah should be while Anthony commits suicide (in the next room? at the movies? out of town?), recalls the playwright's comment to the cast: "It's a collision of the enormously painful with the ridiculous."

DR. CHAPMAN:	You could wait in the living room with Susanah. . . .
THOMAS:	What are you saying? That we would be somewhere in the apartment waiting the whole time until he dies?
SUSANAH:	We wouldn't have to. . . . We could go out . . . and return to find him dead.
THOMAS:	Where would we go? . . . .
SUSANAH:	We could go out. . . . For a walk.
THOMAS:	I couldn't just walk around.
SUSANAH:	Or to the movies. We could go to the movies.
ANTHONY:	What movie? (54–55)

I hear the playwright laugh.

During the break between act 1 and act 2, Rabe talks to the director after the actors have left the table:

> *The play wants you to embrace the whole thing. If it's funny, so be it. Then that moment can jump out in fullness. Otherwise everything is leveled. . . . More theatricality. It's like a revealing. . . . So much of the writing is so mental. They're continually coming up with a plan which is destroyed. Then they have to scramble around and reconstruct it. . . . The more pleasant it is—Anthony is ready to manipulate that niceness into a concession.*

These "authorial notes" on behalf of the text ("The play wants . . .") are not addressed directly to the actors. Clearly, the playwright trusts the director to sift through, distill, and translate in rehearsal what he has communicated privately.

Rabe talks with me for a few minutes at the end of the break. He speaks slowly and elliptically, not always finishing his sentences, as if his thought is steadily unfolding beneath a silence that is occasionally broken. Our conversation is interrupted by the stage manager's call to resume the reading.

The read-through of act 2 begins at 4 P.M. At times, actors ask how to pronounce certain words (e.g., Metuchen, Levo-Dromoran), and invariably the director, not the playwright, replies.[19] For the first time, I see Rabe open his script and study a certain page. He closes the script and makes a note inside his blue rehearsal folder.

It is late afternoon. The actors take longer pauses between phrases and sentences than in their reading of the first act, perhaps feeling the enormity of the play's climactic event or perhaps simply feeling tired. As the stage manager reads the horrifyingly graphic description of Anthony's solitary, botched attempt to commit suicide, Rabe sits with his arms crossed over his chest, head bowed, eyes closed. Suddenly I hear and see him heave a sigh.

The playwright has told the actors that his initial "focus" was on the moment in the hospital when Anthony says he wants to live. Elsewhere Rabe has referred to Anthony's "reversal in the hospital after the suicide attempt" as "this shocking and moving and intolerable thing."[20] As he listens to the reading of that scene, the playwright's jaw clenches, and clenches again. His lips move visibly against his fingers. Once more I hear his sigh. Again his jaw clenches.

It is 5 P.M. The reading is over. The director says simply: "I think we'll leave it alone there. Tomorrow we'll start again at 11. Thank you, ladies and gentlemen." David Rabe says to me afterward, "I'll definitely be back. I'm intrigued."

Rabe's opening comments to the actors as well as his ongoing private discussions with the director will find their way into rehearsal in the weeks that follow. He will return to watch two later rehearsals, but more and more the director will offer himself as a liaison between the playwright and the actors, at times initiating inquiry about the text.[21] For example, he says to David Chandler early in rehearsal: "One line I need to talk to David about is [Dr. Chapman's comment], 'I have to get back to my office.'" Later the actor says privately: "I'm very glad Doug brought that up. It's a very strange line."

In rehearsal on January 15, Hughes says: "The whole introduction of Susanah is without plan. There's no formality. It's just *lobbed* at the doctor." Chandler asks: "Why does *she* need to be there? For a smart guy, I say 'I don't understand' a lot." The director responds at first with statements, and then with questions: "There's a personal disorientation. . . . Is she there to bolster Thomas? Is she pushing some button of your own?" The playwright is not there to answer the actor's or the director's questions, though it is unlikely that he would do so if he were. "[Selzer's] piece is very fragmented and impressionistic," Rabe tells me. "There is no attempt to explain. When I read it, I said to myself, for example: 'How did she *get* there? Dr. Chapman wants her *out*, but how did she get *in*?'" He laughs.

In his talks with the cast, the director does not immediately try to answer this question but acknowledges, and shares responsibility for, the difficulties the play presents for the actors: "I and the play are asking you to leap over some water hazards." One of the "hazards" of the play is the tone. Rabe tells me:

> *There are pitfalls, so many options in doing a play. It's been my experience in most of my plays that the actors have been conditioned by their training and experience in other plays to act in a certain way that isn't necessarily the best way to treat my material. I find what I can offer is to try to talk to them about my play. They've got to be in the right zone of experience of theatricality—.*[22]
>
> *The [actors] perform in many plays. If they bring themselves to bear in the way they do in other plays, it may not be right for my play. What they give is always flesh and blood. But it's got to be in the right zone.*

Hughes says to Babo Harrison, the actress playing Susanah: "What is true, what is genuine, in this play is that it is absolutely possible to sit in the midst of death and talk about trivia. It's not about desperate backpaddling. Remove the friction so [the discussion about a movie Susanah and Thomas saw together] is delightful, is really about the subject." Later he adds: "David did have some very specific movie in mind. . . . I've forgotten what it was. . . . The truth is so terrifying. We want you sealed up from [that terror]." The "we" seems clearly directorial and authorial. Perhaps if the actors knew which movie Rabe had in mind or simply agreed on one of their own choosing, the conversation would become more convincingly "sealed up." In this early rehearsal it sounds forced. The subtext of death is unsealed, almost palpable.

The scene being rehearsed is a perfect example of why getting "in the right zone" is tricky in this play. Susanah and Thomas are debating the merits of a movie Anthony has not seen. After the discussion has gone on for some time, Anthony says to Dr. Chapman: "Tell me about death." He is inquiring about the physical details of his bodily death, and after some hesitation the doctor answers. In the midst of Dr. Chapman's response, Anthony says: "The body is a single-minded bore. Live, live, live. That's all it wants" (48–49). As the scene is read, some actors' eyes are wet with tears; the faces and bodies of all those sitting at the table are taut with suppressed feeling. In the rehearsal room, listening deepens.

One of the "hazards" to be avoided by the actors is becoming, like the body, "a single-minded bore." The director interrupts the rehearsal, talks to the actors for a few minutes, and asks them to reread the scene. This time during the dialogue Hughes laughs intermittently, providing an aural counterimpulse to the textual shifts in content and tone. The director is "embodying" a private authorial note, as he will do again in rehearsal.

Hughes's laughter is appropriate, yet the scene ends with scripted weeping as Thomas says of his lover, Anthony: "Even as he is, with all his suffering, he's here. He's here. But if we do this he'll be gone and there's not a thing I can do about it" (50). The shift from laughter to tears as appropriate responses within a single brief scene is part of what the director calls "the jangling music of the play."

On January 31, Rabe tells me:

> *There's something about the first act through to the monologues [of Susanah and Thomas]—maybe the second Beacon [a scene in an all-night diner where Susanah and Thomas meet with Dr. Chapman and convince him not to assist in Anthony's suicide]—where what the actors are required to do is different from what the actors are required to do after that. I'm still trying to find out how to say what it is. I can see it, but I can't say it yet. . . . You can't just tell the actors to leave something out. I have to talk to Doug about this. The characters are trying to condition themselves to be clinical, to be objective. But it's like . . . I feel like as things get out of control, humanity returns. I have to talk to Doug about this. I think if we can find the right way to say it, they'll do it.*

Alongside Rabe's sense of the difficulty of finding "the right way to say it" is the writer's confidence in language: if "we" can say it, "they" can do it. The playwright's "we" embraces the director who joins in the search for language appropriate to its task.

Hughes will enlist the actors in the project of discovering a special rehearsal vocabulary for *A Question of Mercy*. On February 7, I am startled by his phrase, "a Thomas vortex," which the actors, laughing, seem to understand as a directorial note. During the lunch break, Hughes tells me:

> *David and I had a meeting that went on for a long time after that first run [on January 31, 1998]. David was very excited because he was seeing in lightning flashes the jangling music of the play that I saw when I read it and he felt when he composed it. But it wasn't being sustained in the playing of the play.*

This is a remarkable instance of interactive states of consciousness: in rehearsal, the playwright "sees" the music of his play being "seen" by a director whose staging rekindles what the author "felt" as he composed it. Just as important as this mutually confirmatory seeing of what is there is noticing what is missing. "When I came in the next day," Hughes continues, "I said to the actors: we have to commit to the supremacy, the sovereignty, of the plan [to assist in Anthony's suicide], the search for the solution, the perfect plan. We conceive of the state the actors are in as an Orwellian state where emotion and human mess and moral fuss are not allowed. . . . The state will not accommodate my humanity, so my humanity must be ignored." The director is finding "the right way to say it [so] they'll do it" in the right zone.

A rehearsal vocabulary is emerging, particular to this play, and "a Thomas vortex" is part of it:

> *So we get more contrast into the play. So emotion blisters up like a bad burn and has to be covered up. The way to do it is to commit to our emotional doubt and then, sometimes in the next breath, to commit willingly to stifle our emotion.*

Then we formulated a kind of vocabulary. We added to it today—for example,
"a Thomas vortex." That's when Thomas [whose emotions vacillate more wildly
than those of any other character] lets his doubts rupture up, bleed up, and they
begin dragging the others to a chaos of emotion. The situation insists that that
kind of emotion leads nowhere if your goal is to kill a man and make it civilized
and not get caught.

Hughes had asked the cast at the first table rehearsal, "Who is going to be
leader?" Three weeks later the company in rehearsal arrive at an unsurprising
answer, and make another discovery about the structure of the play as they
continue to add to their "vocabulary":

Paradoxically, or perhaps not so paradoxically, the dying man is the most power-
ful man. And that gave us a kind of hierarchy that we could use in playing the
play. And so we realized that in this play emotional shifts work the way plot
turns work. So you have to commit to them as forcefully as you would to turns
in the plot. Since then [the actors] have gotten even braver, even riskier. . . . These
are people who are trying to be heroes for the dying man and a lot of what they
do is not so heroic. And you've got to commit doubly to the effort "to be a good
soldier"—another phrase in our vocabulary—to separate yourself from your
humanity to wage war effectively.[23]

The complex relation between emotional shifts and plot turns is illustrated in
a moment of exploratory blocking on January 22. Hughes muses aloud, "I
wonder if the move here is . . . ," and suggests a staging in which Thomas
"gives his back to Anthony." After watching this several times, Hughes says,
"I was mistaken," and reverses the blocking, asking Thomas to cross downstage *toward* Anthony. The two antithetical blocking choices suggest a basic
paradox in the play: turning toward Anthony, Thomas turns his back on his
lover's desire to die.

Raising questions and being patient about when answers arrive, creating a
company language through rehearsal work that exposes hierarchical patterns
and emotional shifts—these require collaborative explorations and reenvisionings for director and actors alike. And the playwright who returns "intrigued"
may, like Dr. Selzer, be coming to know more intimately what he has written as
it seeks "the right zone of . . . theatricality."

Hughes says of his staging of *A Question of Mercy* at Long Wharf: "This
is, of course, a second production. In many ways for me it took a second production to finally get my hands on what initially drew me to the play." In rehearsal on January 15, I watch the director make textual revisions in Rabe's
script. At the end of act 1 there is a "coda," Susanah's monologue, written by
the playwright during the New York previews. In the Long Wharf rehearsal
Hughes dictates two small revisions in this monologue: "Add 'three' before
'comrades' so it reads 'like three comrades.' Substitute 'Frisbee' for 'beach
ball.' I think that will be better."[24] These changes do not appear in the 1998
published edition of the play.

What seems a directorial intrusion of the kind James Houghton would eschew in rehearsal of *Curse of the Starving Class* is an option granted by the playwright. Hughes says during a break:

> *I have a confidence about . . . [the play's] power and structure, having done it once. . . . I can explore what drew me to the play in the first place: the disorienting phenomenon of people puttering around the subject of suicide and making plans as if they were for a vacation or a dinner date. So I'm more interested in the mundane. And "beach ball" seems less mundane than "Frisbee." I remember David saying to me after he wrote "beach ball": "Maybe it should be 'Frisbee'?" I said, "No. Keep 'beach ball.'" So now I feel free to go back to "Frisbee," an option David gave me, left over from the New York rehearsals.*

This change, retained in performance, is a small but telling example of director as "author-ized" collaborator in revising the script during a restaging of the play. A more significant revision[25] is the creation of a tiny new scene, when a change in blocking produces a new exit, with additional dialogue, for Thomas and Anthony.

On January 22, the director opens the morning rehearsal by telling the cast of a conversation with Rabe earlier in the day:

> *He's very interested in attempting—and I am, too—a slight rewrite for the scene with Susanah. It won't change anything significantly but it will influence the traffic on stage. Rather than tucking it up right, we can work out an entrance and exit so we can play this [private conversation between two characters] up center if we can figure out a way that the conference can really have its weight at center. Something I was unhappy with in the previous production so I've asked him [Rabe] about that. We won't have that revision today.*

As Hughes works the scene, he says at one point, "This may be a vestigial proscenium idea."[26] An almost entirely new cast, a different theatrical environment,[27] and the task of reblocking a play originally produced on a proscenium stage for a three-quarters thrust stage—all these seem to underlie the director's diary entry on January 27, 1998: "Tomorrow I will walk into the rehearsal room and learn for the thousandth time how malleable, how thrillingly and frighteningly alive great writing for the stage really is."[28] While they wait for the playwright's faxed revisions, the actors improvise new lines in a playful parody of reauthoring the text. Seth Gilliam (Anthony) asks, "Where are my sandals from India?" In a replaying of the scene, the actor says: "Where are my boots? The wooden ones. From Norway." Several members of the cast comment that they find the latter improvisation "more David Rabe"—"especially in three sentences," one actor adds.

The actors are rehearsing an anticipated change in the script. The faxed revision that arrives on January 24 reads, in part:

ANTHONY: Thomas, can you help me? [. . . shoes . . .]

In a January 27 revision, the speech becomes:

ANTHONY: Thomas, I can't find my shoe. I only have one shoe.

In the last revision (February 5), this new exit has precipitated a scene that appears in the New Haven performances but not in the published text:

ANTHONY: Thomas, I can't find my other shoe. It's the pair from Siena.
THOMAS: (*as THOMAS joins ANTHONY*) They were right by the bed.
ANTHONY: I don't want to have lost it.
THOMAS: No, no, no.
  (*They go off. SUSANAH looks up at DR. CHAPMAN.*)[29]

Rehearsing on January 22, before any of the three revisions arrives, Hughes asks an assistant to "check the front office to see if there is a fax from David." When none appears, the director makes provisional alterations himself, reassigning one speech, "I've put some water on for tea," from Thomas to Susanah, and changing "I've" to "I'll" (43).

Richard Bekins interrupts the reading: "God, I'm really having trouble with the transition [in one of Thomas's speeches]." Hughes responds: "This may sound ludicrously technical, but it's almost like dropping something as a way of triggering it." The actor experiments with holding a tea tray as he speaks. Hughes says: "Let's just try 'writing in' an exit. Let's just try that." He asks the actor to move far right, and drop the tea tray on a table just before the speech that begins, "And I'm losing Anthony. That's what I can't bear" (50). The exit the director "writes in" does not appear in the rehearsal script, but in the published text there are stage directions that somewhat correspond to the rehearsal blocking: Thomas moves upstage right, carrying a loaded tea tray, and then at the end of the speech on losing Anthony, Thomas "*turns and walks off.*"[30] The restaging of the play continues a process of mutually supportive reenvisionings of the text by director and playwright.[31]

Later Rabe comments on the newly created exit:

> *I had always wanted to do this in the New York rehearsals. But I had a reluctance to revise it as we were about to open. In the television version [where the camera directs the viewer's gaze], Susanah and Dr. Chapman went into the kitchen to talk. But I didn't want them thrust upstage. I wanted Susanah and Dr. Chapman center stage and I thought it would be stronger to get Anthony and Thomas off stage.*
>
> *I talked about the problem with Doug. He worked on a version in rehearsal before he got my faxed revision. His revision was simpler than mine. What we ended up with was a compromise.*

The playwright and director are in a complicated dance, not synchronizing steps but ending together.

In the New Haven rehearsal, Hughes responds to the particular tones, rhythms, and pacing of a largely new cast; he is watching closely their instinctive gestures and movements, their sense of boundaries, of when and whether to touch each other. As he collaborates with and redirects the actors' impulses, I feel the energy that gathers, rises, subsides, and continues to fluctuate in the rehearsal room. The director allows the actors' sense of trouble, confusion, awkwardness, and questioning a respected place in a rehearsal process in which problems are engaged, and mainly worked through, with candor, laughter, and patience, the director's patience at times exceeding that of the cast.[32]

Altogether Rabe is present at three rehearsals: the first read-through at the table and two run-throughs. After his initial visit, Rabe never again speaks directly to the actors, whose responses to his presence and his silence range from appreciation to paranoia. Michael Kell, the actor playing the doorman, says:

> I actually live for these situations: rehearsals. I almost wish they could go on endlessly. In this room is a kind of family. Doug is a sort of father. I know David personally. He's usually very quiet and thoughtful and speaks very rarely. He's the origin of why we're here, and he holds a very high opinion even when he's quiet. I don't have a lot of education so it's a sense of being with a scholar. I learn about life through his view of the world.
>
> I was in the New York production. David Rabe first let Doug answer questions. Then he'd give his feelings and always try to complement what Doug was saying. They were basically in agreement but with different ways of expressing it.[33]

"The director is always the father figure to the actor," Richard Bekins tells me. When asked who the playwright would be in this configuration, he replies, "That's an interesting question." He pauses. "I was going to say 'grandfather,'" he continues, laughing. "Perhaps the image of God in a symbolic sense, not a religious sense. . . . [Rabe] didn't say much, did he, when he was here. But it was nice, just having the image of him here." The actor's language of appreciation is suggestive: somewhere in the vicinity of rehearsal is the "image" of the creator of the world his character inhabits.

The following week, Bekins revises his metaphor:

> I thought about my image of the director as the father later. It's more the mother, allowing it to unfold instead of imposing. Doug is so good at both. [Directing] is also the maternal nourishing. Sometimes the actor is in the state of "I don't know" and looking for guidance, . . . approval. In that sense, the director is the father. Supporting, nurturing, allowing, unfolding—these are very feminine aspects, I think, of the director.[34]

Seth Gilliam points to the positive aspects of an absent playwright: "On the one hand, it's kind of freeing to be working on a play when the playwright is dead: if you have a specific idea, you can fight for it, because there's no one from the source to contradict it." The actor's view is reminiscent of the playwright's keeping his distance from the source of his material because he "didn't want anyone to veto" his response to it. Gilliam appreciates "access to the playwright if there's something that's muddled or unclear," but, he says, "I always go with the director first."

> The director has the number one power position in the rehearsal process. The writer is pretty much there as a resource. If things break down in the exchange

with the director, then I'd go to the writer. I'm okay with David Rabe's not being here a lot because I trust Doug, especially since they've done this show before, that Doug really understands what David wants. Doug's ego is not such that he's averse to going to David with a question the actor has.

David Chandler[35] is the actor who most desires communication with the playwright during rehearsal. "David's the boss," Chandler says, "because it's David's words and it's David's story and it's David's metaphors. Richard [Selzer] is source material, but ultimately it's David's vehicle. And of course he's not here," the actor adds, laughing. Gilliam's "source" is the playwright, from whom he would wrest authority. Chandler reduces the physician-writer on whom his character is based to "source material" and, bypassing parental metaphors, presents the playwright as the absent "boss." But he is ambivalent toward the actual presence and role of the author in rehearsal:

I think when a playwright's around—especially when he's a well-known play-wright—sometimes it can be a little . . . claustrophobic. Some [playwrights] are very supportive, and others are wrapped up tight, and that affects the actors a lit-tle bit. When a playwright is around, you want to be really exact with the words. You don't want to mess up the words. When the playwright's around a lot, he becomes part of the scenery. When he drops in just a bit, you feel it more as an event, and you have to fight the impulse to make it an event, to perform it.

He elaborates on the actor-playwright relationship in rehearsal:

I think . . . with a living playwright and a new work . . . the actors have to give him the benefit of the doubt for as long as possible, by which I mean two days into it you can't say: "I don't get this. This doesn't work for me. I need this." You gotta assume that he's lived with it for a long time and at least for a few weeks you have to assume that he knows best. And then there may be a point when the actor and the director know better and the playwright may recognize that and say, "I need to fix that," or "There's a gap here." I hate when actors start play-writing. It's a collaboration in terms of playwriting but with extreme humility on the part of the actor and with boldness in terms of the actor's commitment to what he does, which is to act. Do you know what I mean?

Chandler has begun to wrestle with a problematic passage in one of Dr. Chap-man's monologues that "doesn't work" for him. His frustration continues as he attempts unsuccessfully to get a direct response from the playwright to the questions that he insistently raises in rehearsal.

On January 15, Hughes interrupts the reading of Dr. Chapman's act 2 monologue: "There's a destructive stage direction here: 'Chapman faces out.' I think it should be different from the speeches where you're dramatizing your doubts for us. This speech is born fully grown. It's more interior. . . . My point is simply that it's quite different from the other ones." The director's use of the word *destructive* for the stage direction highlights its departure from a realis-tic mode of presentation. Like James Houghton rehearsing the monologues delivered "out" in *Curse of the Starving Class,* but with greater explicitness and speed, Hughes is both calling attention to the "difference" of such a speech and encouraging the actor to enter into it. But the monologue is not easily entered.

The speech has to do with the doctrine of the resurrection of the individual embodied self:

> Our gravesites are dark holes, dark cells in which we are deposited and contained, walled off from nature and from one another, encased in caskets which, like our egos, isolate us as we wait to be recalled through the doctrine of the Resurrection whose stipulations condemn us to live forever as our desperate singular selves. (80)[36]

Chandler objects: "As a Christian, I don't think that's what the resurrection is about. I don't know what David's getting at in this speech." Hughes responds: "David was raised Catholic with the notion of resurrection and damnation. I think David's spent a lot of time paddling away from Catholicism. There's no way I can argue that this is exact . . . but that's of no help to you. I think it's the idea that for a Christian there's some other place." The actor replies: "But it's not a place which insists on 'desperate singular selves.' It makes my hair stand on end. It seems a very singular distortion." The director says: "Obviously, I've been around the block with this play before, and this question was not raised." He laughs. "Obviously, I was doing it with a bunch of pagans." He and the cast laugh. "It's well worth looking at what is meant by the doctrine of the resurrection."[37]

Hughes and Chandler continue to discuss the contested passage for a few minutes during which the director speaks for the playwright: "I'm still myself, packaged in a body. I know that's what David wants to get at. I also know that it's somewhat narrowed as it reads." Hughes confidently voices the writer's position but at the same time supports the actor's sense of difficulty ("it's somewhat narrowed as it reads").

The playwright's absence may allow the actor a more open, uncensored questioning of the lines, but it also leaves the actor with a lingering problem. During a break, Hughes tells me that he will ask Rabe about the disputed passage: "My answer will do for me. But will it do for David Chandler, the actor? Like Holden Caulfield in *Catcher in the Rye,* my definition of a great author is someone I want to call up. And David is someone I can call up."[38]

Hughes does call Rabe, but, as he anticipates, what will do for the director will not necessarily do for the actor. Meanwhile, problems develop in the reading of Thomas's long monologue in act 2. In rehearsal, the director speaks for the other absent writer in his note to the actor: "I remember something Selzer said to me. When Anthony indicated that he didn't want to die, Selzer used the word *hollowed.* I feel there is something about that word that is applicable to Thomas." Bekins's problem, however, is not with the monologue's words but with its intended audience. The actor asks: "Who is he speaking to?" And the director responds simply: "I believe he is speaking to the audience. . . . I think you *should* address the audience." (In the rehearsal script, only Dr. Chapman's speeches are designated "out," with the exception of Susanah's "coda" in act 1.) In the published text, Thomas's monologue is delivered "facing out"[39]: Hughes's directorial note in rehearsal is in the right zone, though he does not invoke the authority of the absent playwright.

In the late afternoon the director reads aloud to the company an authorial statement that will appear in the Long Wharf program for *A Question of Mercy*: "I do think that deep down my plays are about people trying to make reasonable accommodations of situations that are insane or absurd."[40] After the cast leaves, Hughes says:

> *It falls to me to worry about what goes on between the actors. I don't need to endow the event itself with significance. I'm not here to duplicate David's job. I'm here to bring something else forward that is in the writing but is harder to get to: the effort to cope rationally with something that's insane or absurd, as David says.*

What Michael Kell observed of Hughes and Rabe—that they are "basically in agreement but with different ways of expressing it"—seems true. They are perhaps as close as a director and playwright in rehearsal can be without inhabiting the same body.

In rehearsal on January 22, Chandler asks if the playwright has responded to his question about the speech on the doctrine of the resurrection. Hughes says: "Frankly, David's in California right now working on a film [*Hurlyburly*], so I just spoke to him for the first time today." He adds that Jeanette Plourde, assistant to the director, has "very carefully delineated a list" of questions for the playwright and he will talk to Rabe about them. During a break, Chandler tells me: "I don't think [Hughes] did satisfy me on the issue of the doctrine of the resurrection. It would be interesting to see what David's response would be. I don't know if I'm muddying it with my own" (pause) "religious feelings." Then he adds:

> *I think I need the playwright. Doug didn't write the play. Doug doesn't have all the answers. Or the one he gave me may be the answer. That may be all I can get. If the writer doesn't know, who's going to know? It would be exceedingly hubristic of me to say now I've got all my ducks in a row.*

Two days later, the director speaks to Chandler just before rehearsal begins:

> *[Rabe] said that it's about belief in the resurrection of the body. The Nicene Creed says, "I believe in the resurrection of the body." [Rabe] says it's about the Christian concept of the resurrection of the body in the creed. So he said he was interested even to talk it through with you. The soul is always encased in this envelope.*

The actor says: "I'm just confused about it. He talks about death ripping us away from the only thing we know." When Hughes replies, "Maybe you and

David and I can talk about it on the phone," Chandler says: "Well, I think we're *at* it."

When the actor next delivers the monologue in rehearsal, he stumbles verbally several times and seems more uncomfortable than in his earlier readings. The director walks toward the actor and initiates what will be a thirty- to forty-minute private conversation. Director and actor sit facing each other on wooden chairs in the playing area. There are long reflective pauses in their dialogue. The other actors wander to the peripheries of the room.

Hughes says: "In a broad stroke he seems to be saying—even for a Christian—you're going to be this flailing unintegrated soul forever." The "he" is indeterminate; the director may be speaking for the playwright or for the character. The actor says, with some anguish: "I'm not clear in my heart and head. What is he saying? What is he saying?" The director responds: "The world of the play is so cruelly lonely. . . . Their connectedness to others was their way of understanding themselves." Hughes reads the lines of Dr. Chapman's monologue aloud himself as he talks. Then he sits quietly, meditating. Finally, he says to the actor: "I think it's a mourning, this speech, for a way of being alive. . . . I think it's spoken very much alone." Hughes's responses have modulated deftly, as so often, into directorial notes. The actor writes on his script. There is a long pause.

Director and actor, alone with a text that is no longer accompanied by its author, each become simply readers of the same speech. The director says to the actor: "Even as you read it, you make sense of it." And the actor responds: "I can make sense of it, but that's faking it. I want to be sure it's really laid in. I can keep the balls in the air."

After a break, Chandler, sitting in the same chair in which he had discussed his monologue with the director, reads the speech. He delivers it with more meditative pauses, as if thinking while he reads. It is not so much a performance as a new meeting with the text. Afterward, the director says, "That's much more aware," and again enters the playing area where he continues to talk privately with the actor.

In the afternoon rehearsal on January 24, Hughes says: "I'd like to try something as an exercise now. I'll check with David about it. I'd like to pass the ball to Susanah here, as an experiment." The director playwrites "as an experiment" in rehearsal: he takes a sentence from the middle of Dr. Chapman's speech and assigns it to Susanah, changing one proper noun to the first-person pronoun.[41] This change is retained in the following rehearsals and in performance. Babo Harrison, the actress whose character receives the newly assigned line, asks in an interested, slightly hopeful tone: "Will [the playwright] be here today?" The director responds: "No, he's squirreled away in that house. I'll call him."

Later, during a break, Babo Harrison says:

> What I particularly love about working with a living author is the opportunity to get in synch with their vision, with their linguistic world, in a way that is very, very profound, very personal. It's like a marriage. If he's there and a part of the

rehearsal process, then you really are catching the wave together. Perhaps I'll do something in rehearsal that stimulates the playwright to rewrite, and that's very exciting. And similarly the actors can avail themselves of the playwright and get an answer "from the source." I can't think of any other way to say it.

Like Chandler, Babo Harrison would like "an answer 'from the source,'" but her deeper desire, as she says, describing rehearsals of Joan Ackerman's *The Battling Cage*, is to be "an active part of the author's process."

In an interview, Rabe explains:

At the first reading I tried to pick up on certain themes Doug had laid down and help [the actors] understand the tone and themes I was most interested in. I wanted them to understand that a lot of the writing is about losing track of what the central issue is. I think they did that well in the reading.

There is also this other part that is giddy and has an absurd quality that's about getting the plan straight. And how hard that is [laughing], whether it's a vacation or suicide.

At the table reading, Rabe had told the cast that his focus was initially on the scene in the hospital when, after his suicide attempt, Anthony indicates that he wants to live.[42] But when I ask about this, he says:

In the actual writing of the play the focus moved. The shock and power of that scene take care of themselves. The writing is about the tracing of how to get to that moment. The characters all present their own problems and then continually put aside their problems and yet in the end they abandon him. And that's what I wanted to write about. In Selzer's piece the moment in the hospital is diamond-clear and powerful. But in the movement toward it I tried to fill in all the gaps.

Rabe now clarifies what he had earlier called "the problem of the central metaphor" in his comments to the actors:

In the past I had written plays with multiple settings. I always had the physical metaphor—a go-go bar or a physical training ground—so that many settings could be worked out from it as a core metaphor. In this play, which was originally written for television, I had been literal. I went to the different places. There was no need for a central metaphor in the staging of it. I don't like plays with turn-tables so I said, "We'll solve this later."

"Later" is ongoing:

Doug first tried to make it work with the various settings in the original script. Then he approached me with his idea. We evolved together. He wanted it to be a little more abstract than I wanted—for example, without the [four prop] tele-phones. I felt we needed those objects to ground it. We're still talking. I still wish there was a way to make . . . [Thomas and Anthony's] home cozier, not so ab-stract. You need something that's a little protective and friendly so the actual physical location will be warmer. An abstract set inhibits that sort of coziness . . . and perhaps the absurdity that it's cozy and yet you're trying to kill this guy.

The cookies do it in a way. In New York the backdrop was so towering that it dwarfed the people. Here the audience looks down [onto the stage]. It will be less daunting.

The set in New York and to some extent here has a statement to it that resists something I want. But it's Shakespearean [smiling]. Shakespeare says it's a park, and it is—right? No scenery. It's Shakespearean to have that fluidity. It's just that I think I want something *to make it cozy. But we'll see. Maybe not. We're still talking.*[43]

Rabe is called away by Kimberly Sewright, media relations manager at Long Wharf, for a photo shoot with Dr. Selzer in the rehearsal hall.

Richard Selzer and David Rabe enter the playing area together. Mara Lavitt, staff photographer for the *New Haven Register,*[44] positions the two writers behind a hospital bed, upstage far left, Rabe sitting with his chin in his left hand, upstretched fingers covering the edge of his mouth, and Selzer standing to his side, bending slightly toward the camera. Rabe wears olive corduroy pants, a brownish-black plaid long-sleeved, open-collared shirt, and black laced shoes. Selzer wears a bright pink long-sleeved, buttoned-down shirt, open at the collar, under a black sweater-vest, dark pants, and black shoes. Lavitt engages the two writers in light conversation and encourages them with laughter, as she turns that tiny corner of the rehearsal room into a well-lit studio in which the men almost seem characters in their own writing. The photographer says several times: "Nice window light. But one of you may be out of focus."

After the photo session, Rabe leaves the rehearsal room briefly to find coffee. An actor asks, "If Mr. Rabe walks out, should we keep going?" There is tension-relieving laughter from the cast. The run-through begins at 2:30 P.M. Director and playwright are seated side by side between the director's table and the stage manager's table. Rabe sits, legs spread wide apart, feet planted squarely on the floor, slightly slumped in his chair. His right elbow rests on the arm of the chair, the fingers of his right hand pressed against his lips. Hughes sits, left leg crossed over right knee, his hands clasped over his stomach, wringing his fingers at times, gazing at the actors. I hear him laugh appreciatively.

Today Rabe is without glasses and script. A small yellow pad and pencil sit atop a large container of whole-milk yogurt near his feet. His right hand moves in front of his mouth; he smiles and laughs soundlessly behind his hand. When the Doorman enters, the muscles of the playwright's throat move as if he is speaking lines. During Dr. Chapman's first meeting with Thomas and Anthony, Rabe makes notes on his small yellow pad. The run-through is entirely off book; there are no scripts anywhere in the playing area. Actors occasionally call for lines from production assistant Sarah Foote. Rabe removes a small thermos and mug from a well-worn "WNET Thirteen" cloth bag and begins to eat his yogurt as he continues to watch and listen.

In the ten-minute break between the two acts, the director and playwright remain seated, looking at the playing area as they talk. I hear only fragments: the word *intimacy* is repeated several times by Rabe. Hughes consults his script; Rabe does not look at the text. Just before the actors return, I hear Rabe say: "I think they're a team."

The run-through continues. Gilliam asks for lines. The production assistant reads aloud: "The two of us first, Thomas and myself alone, and then the three of us" (73). Gilliam returns to his earlier position in the playing area, and then asks again for his line. The line is repeated. Without a pause, the actor says: "Jesus. Who *wrote* this?" I hear the playwright's first audible laughter in today's rehearsal, along with the director's.

Rabe's note to Hughes after the first table reading—"If it's funny, so be it. . . . Otherwise everything is leveled"—found its way into rehearsal two days ago. Hughes said: "The first time I went through the play, we were all terribly careful about to whom that responsibility belonged." Babo Harrison responded, "So it became too weighted," and the cast began to experiment with hilarity as they rehearsed the scene in which they plan in minute detail the assisted suicide. During today's run, as the actors discuss the details of the suicide plan, they break up in laughter several times. I cannot tell whether this is a misfired directorial note or actors' jitters.

Chandler delivers his "doctrine of the Resurrection" monologue while putting on a tie. The actor loses one line but reads the disputed passage with a jarring painfulness that reverberates in the room—a performance that cannot have been merely "keeping the balls in the air." The playwright watches, the fingers of his right hand characteristically covering his mouth.

The stage manager plays a recording of Bach's "Goldberg" Variations. Anthony sits alone in a bathrobe, with a slide projector, a large glass of water, a pitcher, and many white pills (Tic-Tacs) on a table in front of him. The production assistant says, "slide," at regular intervals. Ever more slowly Anthony attempts to swallow the pills. He falls, gets up, stands with the pills in his hand, tries to drink. Pills and pitcher fall from his hands. He attempts to gather the pills from the floor, finally collapsing amid the spilled water and strewn pills. The face of Babo Harrison, watching Gilliam from outside the playing area, is pained. I see tears in her eyes.

It is 5 P.M. As Thomas and Susanah enter to discover that Anthony is still alive, the director rises from his seat: "Sorry. We have to end here. It's end of rehearsal." The playwright sits silently. What is it like for him, I wonder, to watch his play "end" before the final scene? The actors leave by one door; he by another. On my way out, I ask if it is hard to have the play stopped at this point. "No," he says, very firmly.

The following day, just as rehearsal begins, two actors exclaim: "The playwright never said anything," and Hughes responds, "He never talks." An actor asks, "Is he happy?" and without pausing adds: "You wouldn't tell us the truth. We're just paranoid actors." "Yes, he's happy," Hughes replies, and then in a closed session, during which I am asked to leave, he talks for three-quarters of an hour with a nervous cast. There are hazards in the presence of a silent playwright in rehearsal.

On February 6, David Rabe comes to a run-through I do not attend. I am told that, again, he says nothing to the actors. This time the run-through includes the hospital scene and Anthony's death three days after he is resuscitated, but rehearsal ends before the playing of the very last scene.

During a break in rehearsal, I visit the main stage. Large squares of sheet metal are placed over two-thirds of the surface of a square platform five inches above the stage floor. The upstage backdrop is a series of Rothko-like bands in shades of red and orange-gold. I walk across the stage of the empty theater. Above me, from an intricate black grid, hangs a small sky of lights that, in performance, will create silvery swirls on the stage floor below. Unexpectedly I find myself stage center, gazing at the seats where the not-yet-present audience will crowd in so closely and intimately on three sides of the performance space. To one who all her life has had serious stage fright, it feels shockingly exhilarating.

I sit in the front row, center. It is so still that I hear the sound of my pencil writing. I feel the mysterious waiting energy of the stage. I can see why the actors want to be there. There is life in the theater, even before they arrive.

At the beginning of rehearsal on February 7, Hughes tells the actors: "David's not coming back. He says he thinks it's great, so why come back. He'll be here for the show." The director voices the playwright's responses to rehearsal work:

> David said, "I just feel so happy." He said the play got into the zone he wanted. . . . He talked about the fact that he'd come across a phrase in his reading the night before—"the disembodied voice of logic whispering in your ear like a muse"— and this is the zone we entered.
>
> Another thing he said last night, that I was very moved by, was that the thing that really moved him to write was his experience in Vietnam. When he came back, he read everything he could about Vietnam, including books about My Lai, the carnage that swept through that village and that American platoon. At the height of it people would come out of their huts and begin watering their gardens and tilling their little plots of vegetables. They just tried to do anything that was normal, even though they knew perfectly well what the situation was, and, of course, they were slaughtered instantly. He said that was the stone in his shoes that made him write everything he writes, especially Sticks and Bones—that quest for normalcy and the belief that logic can cure everything. And he said he realized now how this play is connected to what he's written before. It was very exciting. He was delighted with what he saw us doing here.

Autobiographical material that fed the writing of the play, transmitted directly to the actors in rehearsal by Sam Shepard and Arthur Miller, is here communicated to them by the director.

Now Hughes speaks in his own voice: "There are a lot of things in David's play that have to do with characters who are streaming in and out of each other, with souls that are colliding. I just think we're a beat late. I just want to track that middle section. But I liked . . . [the run-through] hugely yesterday." Hughes had begun rehearsal by speaking for the author; he intended to give the cast his own notes after they rehearsed the ending of the play. But first one and then all of the actors ask that notes be given before they begin the work-through.

It is less than a week before the first preview. The actors bring their chairs into the playing area and sit facing the director, who remains seated in his usual location midway between the director's and stage manager's tables. I notice that two actors move apart from those who are seated, Chandler pacing and gesturing as he responds to Hughes's comments, and Gilliam, who had been the first to ask for notes, doing a few physical warm-up exercises as he listens. The director says: "You're so in the tissue of the language of the play that we're now able to talk about things—pauses, for example—that we couldn't before." Speaking of a particular scene, Hughes says: "Like so many things, it just fell into place and then we began to indulge it a little. . . . I think we just need to *chasten* ourselves." The elegance of the directorial phrasing suggests that Rabe's confidence in the finding of "the right way to say it" is not misplaced.

The director's understanding of the work that language alone can do is evidenced in his comment to Thomas: "I'm not sure there's a laugh there. It helps float you up. But . . . what I wrote was: 'Are we doing the audience's work for them?' . . . The sharpness of it is so much clearer potentially . . . if it hasn't been *trumped* by the laugh. Do we let the *language* take care of it?" Hughes voices what might sound like an authorial perspective, but it is also his own.

The director says to Michael Kell: "This is from David, an extra line that came into the published version. If you would add, just ahead of 'It's a torture': 'What are they doing! What are they doing?' just so you can get . . . [Dr. Chapman's] attention."[45] Hughes dictates the authorial revision, immediately adding his own directorial note ("just so . . . "). The roles of playwright and director are distinct yet interdependent, like two-voice counterpoint.

Hughes's notes continue to enfold those of the author: "He so *loved* that [new] scene—the introduction of Susanah—and how we finally figured out how to get her in the play, because that was vestigial from the New York production. It's *tiny* but it *is* a scene so it becomes something that isn't just stage management, getting you guys off the stage." Like the actress playing Susanah, the director seems to relish active participation in "the author's process," collaborating with the playwright in the creation of what he calls "[not] just stage management" but a "tiny . . . scene." In his comment, "We finally figured out how to get . . . [Susanah] in the play," he credits the company in rehearsal with a solution to what may remain a problem in the text.

Chandler says to the director: "The whole resurrection thing is moot, then?" "Well," Hughes replies, "[Rabe] *loves* the way you do it. . . . Just do it badly [if you want it to be an issue with the playwright]" (laughing). Later I ask Chandler if the playwright has ever talked to him directly about the monologue on the doctrine of the resurrection. He says "no" with a rueful smile. "I guess I'll just have to live with it."

For the last time in rehearsal I watch the actor perform the problematic lines:

> *Our gravesites are dark holes, dark cells in which we are deposited and contained, walled off from nature and from one another, encased in caskets which like our egos isolate us as we wait to be recalled through the doctrine of the Resurrection whose stipulations condemn us to live forever as our desperate singular selves.*

It is a curiously depressive passage. As he will in performance, Chandler sits stage center, facing out; his hands, clasped against his chin, move toward his mouth. It is, for me, his finest moment in rehearsal, unseen by the playwright. The coughing and chair squeaking and shoe scraping that have peppered rehearsal vanish. You could hear a pin drop. And then I notice that the physical position the actor with an unfulfilled desire to hear directly from the author has adopted, consciously or not, resembles that of the playwright in rehearsal.

3 Elizabeth Egloff in Rehearsal

The Devils

Let me think about this. It may require a little rewriting.

Elizabeth Egloff's *The Devils*, inspired by Dostoevsky's novel *The Possessed*, dramatizes the plotting of a group of provincial revolutionaries, led first by Nicholas Stavrogin and later by Peter Verkhovensky, who is responsible for the group's murder of Ivan Shatov, one of its own members, and also for the assassination of the governor's wife, Mrs. Lembke. Stavrogin, described by one critic as "the book's Hamlet,"[1] returns to his hometown with a guilty secret: he once raped a child, Matryosha, who then hanged herself, as he himself will do at the end of the play. Stavrogin has an inconclusive affair with his mother's protégée, Dasha Shatov, whose brother, Ivan, is later murdered by the revolutionary cell (Shigalyov, Virginsky, and Liputin).[2]

The rape of Matryosha appears in a chapter suppressed by Dostoevsky's nineteenth-century publisher and presented as a supplement at the end of later editions of the novel. Egloff opens *The Devils* with the scene of rape and repeats it as an "instant replay" in scene 3.[3] Throughout the play the apparition of the dead child haunts Stavrogin, who later rapes Dasha. "I think the play ultimately is about the fact that politics *are* personal, and that is why change doesn't happen unless personal change happens—and personal change almost never happens," Egloff says. "I call what I've created radical adaptation. It's telling my version of somebody's story."

Radical adaptation is not new to "the much praised young playwright,"[4] whose works include *Phaedra*, an adaptation of the Greek tragedy; *The Sin of Akaki Akakiyevich* and *The Nose*, very free versions of two of Gogol's short stories, "The Overcoat" and "The Nose"; *Wolf-Man*, loosely based on the life story of Freud's famous patient; and *Peter Pan and Wendy*, adapted from J. M. Barrie's classic, which opened at American Repertory Theatre in December 1997. Her comedy *The Swan*, produced throughout this country and in Europe, was awarded the 1990 Kesselring Prize for best play. *The Devils*, presented in a

3.1 Elizabeth Egloff (photograph by James Youmans)

workshop at New York University's Tisch School of the Arts under the direction of Robert Woodruff in the spring of 1994, received its first professional production, directed by Garland Wright, at New York Theatre Workshop, May 20–June 8, 1997. *The Devils* was advertised as "the largest production in New York Theatre Workshop history."[5]

Egloff says: "Being able to write in rehearsal is very particular to working with Garland." Wright, former co-director of the directing program at the Juilliard School in New York, was for ten years the artistic director of the Tyrone Guthrie Theater in Minneapolis. An actor who once played Orsino in Shakespeare's *Twelfth Night* and a co-founder of the off-Broadway Lion Theater Company, he staged his own adaptation, the Obie Award–winning *K: Impressions of Kakfa's The Trial*, and received a second Obie Award for his directing of *On the Verge*. During rehearsals of Egloff's *The Devils*, Wright undergoes chemotherapy for the disease that will take his life the following year, on July 22, 1998.[6]

Despite the success of its most well-known production—Jonathan Larson's *Rent*—New York Theatre Workshop, an off-Broadway theater company founded in 1979, is "almost defiantly noncommercial."[7] Artistic director James C. Nicola says, just before *The Devils* opens: "Two years ago, I'd come to work and wonder whether we'd be here tomorrow. Now I wonder whether we'll be here two or three years from now."[8]

Rehearsals of Egloff's *The Devils* take place next door to the theater in a third-floor studio at 83 East Fourth Street in New York City. On a cold, windy morning, April 1, 1997, I edge past four men carrying long wooden planks. David Rabe's *A Question of Mercy* ended its extended New York run at the theater two days before, and the building of the set for *The Devils* began the following day.

In a small anteroom to the studio on the third floor are a child's mattress and several toys that belong to the playwright's four-month-old son, William, who sometimes accompanies his mother to rehearsal. On the walls of the brightly lit studio are two large sketches of the set and photographs with captions describing critical events in nineteenth-century Russia (e.g., "1861—Alexander II announces the emancipation of the serfs"; "November 21, 1869—the Nachaev affair. Sergei Nachaev, known as the most nihilistic nihilist, murders a fellow revolutionary and dumps the body in a frozen pond in the park. Dostoevsky based . . . [*The Possessed*] on this incident"). On the wall behind the stage manager's desk is a map of the world with boundaries marked for Russia, France, Austria, Prussia, and the Ottoman Empire in 1865.[9]

Garland Wright begins rehearsal with the words, "Let's just stumble our way into this." He is blocking, for the first time, a scene (act 3, scene 6) between Dasha (Kali Rocha) and Stepan Verkhovensky (Frank Raiter), father of the revolutionary leader, Peter, and lover of Nicholas Stavrogin's mother. The director stops the scene almost immediately: "Question?" In response to Kali Rocha's questioning of one of Dasha's lines, Wright says, "She doesn't want sympathy." Rehearsal is interrupted by the director's note that Dasha rise from her knees. The actress responds:

> *I need to take this very slowly. I don't know who I am in this scene and I don't know who he [Stepan] is to me and what I need from him. It seems clear that I need to know if Stavrogin did poison the governor's wife. Is Nicholas Stavrogin not who I think he is anymore? Maybe that is who she is if she doesn't know who she is in this scene.*

The director replies: "Yes. That sounds like a director's comment. I'm delighted you said it instead of me." The actors laugh. "If Nicholas is not the person you think, no one is. In some ways you've been tossed out on the alleyway. The world you knew six days ago basically no longer exists." Discussion continues, the scene is replayed, and Wright again asks the two actors to find the action inscribed, like many of Shakespeare's stage directions, in the dialogue: "Get off your knees" (Stepan's line).[10] Though I do not know it at the time, this tiny moment in rehearsal is paradigmatic: in the next version of the scene, the line will be cut. The script will remain fluid through previews. For the director seeking to respect authorial intent, rehearsal can be vertiginous.

The text behind the playwright's text is present in the rehearsal room. On the director's table is his copy of *The Possessed*, heavily underlined, with red tabs marking particular pages.[11] Stepan's last speech in act 3, scene 6 ends:

> *"Love is the crown of human existence."*
> *Who said THAT? (163)*

These lines are "a kind of Pirandello moment, as if Stepan knows that he is a character in the novel," Wright tells assistant director Kathleen Dimmick. During a break, he reads aloud from Stepan's speech in the novel as he is dying:

> *And what is more precious than love? Love is higher than existence, love is the crown of existence; and how is it possible that existence should not be under its dominance? [emphasis mine]. If I have once loved . . . [God] and rejoiced in my love, is it possible that He should extinguish me and my joy and bring me to nothingness again? If there is a God, then I am immortal.* Voilà ma profession de foi.[12]

"It's that conversion moment," Wright says to Dimmick, "that he writes over and over as if to convince himself."

Egloff, who will attend rehearsal in a few days, tells me later: "Adaptation was a way for me to work on my story skills and also a way to get back to poetry, where I had always been so comfortable." For the playwright, one of the attractions of Russian literature is that "meaning is hidden under layers and layers of metaphor and [it] therefore approaches sublime poetry. I think that women tend to speak indirectly and as a woman that's one of the reasons I identify with Russian literature."

Many readers of Dostoevsky's novel find Nicholas Stavrogin irresistibly fascinating, and some reviewers of Egloff's *The Devils* seemed to expect her Stavrogin to play a more central role.[13] But Egloff resists finding Stavrogin irresistible: "I tend to come down on Peter Verkhovensky's side. . . . I think Peter loses his idealism in the play—and, believe it or not, Peter is an idealist— and at the end of the play he is such an idealist that he is Stalin, i.e., there's something Stalinesque about his idealism at the end of the play." Parts of Peter's final speech "are strongly influenced by a Neruda poem which ends, 'Come and see the blood in the streets.' I think Neruda repeats it three times. Both the poem and Peter's final speech are elegies to something that is lost."[14]

"It's clear that Dostoevksy was responding to a real event," Egloff says.

> *The story that to me was so magnetic was the story of a group of friends who turn on one of them and murder him [Shatov]. My murder scene is virtually exactly as Dostoevksy wrote it. The only thing that's different is that some pieces of evidence from the actual trial are included in my play but not in the novel. I wanted to get back to the historical events themselves.*

The playwright's relation to "the historical events themselves" is not slavish:

> *I think my job as a writer is to tell everybody's story. . . . I take complete license with historical events and do not feel guilty about it. . . . When I do an adaptation, I look for a central character or a central event that seems to have a life of its own. I use that to spin off the whole story. In this case, it was an event, not a character, from which the whole rest of the story comes [emphasis mine].*

Like Rabe's *A Question of Mercy*, Egloff's play is inspired not simply by an earlier narrative but by an actual event that calls out to her as if, in what Wright called a "Pirandello moment," it wants to become theater in order to "have a life of its own."

"This play is written for people who may or may not have read the novel," Egloff explains. "I don't care if they have or not. I have quite aggressively staked out my own territory."[15] When asked if he recommends that the actors read the novel, Wright says:

> *I told them it was up to them. I told them my experience: I read the novel after I read the play. At the time it didn't help me at all because the novel and the play are so different. It's good research. Ordinarily, it would have been a requirement. Reading the play, you have a feeling that you have to read the novel. I felt that I had to be authoritative on the novel if I was going to be working on an adaptation. When I read the novel I realized that she hadn't adapted it. She has responded to it and created her own work of art.*
>
> *Liz said the thing she responded to first was the trial, that such a thing had actually happened. That's why I've . . . [been emphasizing] that ideology and political actions are a result of individual relationships rather than individual relationships being a playing out of ideology.*[16]

The fifteen actors in the cast have varied opinions about the usefulness of reading the text behind the text. Frank Raiter [Stepan] says he has not read the novel. "We were told [by the director] not to read it, if we hadn't already." Patrice Johnson (Marie Shatov) bought the novel, "perused it, and decided to take the director's advice not to read it," she says, because "Liz [Egloff] is the source." Lynn Cohen (Mrs. Stavrogin) reads *The Possessed* early in rehearsal: "My having read the novel goes into my body in some way; however, I'm doing *this* play. That's where my decisions are made: this script, this play."

During lunch break on April 3, Bill Camp (Nicholas Stavrogin) sits on the steps of the fire escape, bent over a copy of *The Possessed*. Saying that the novel opens up Stavrogin's "search for danger, sensation," the actor reads aloud to the director Dostoevksy's portrayal of the character he plays.[17]

For the director, the text's relation to the play is problematic. During rehearsal on April 3, Wright says: "Can we talk awhile? We're going to do this scene [act 3, scene 15] in complete darkness." The actors sit in a semicircle in front of the director's chair. "It's a scene where a guy has to be shot." This is the scene in which the revolutionaries murder Ivan Shatov, one of their own members. Wright says to the actors: "In the novel—I don't know whether it matters, but it has resonance for me—this park is on the estate of Mrs. Stavrogin. It's like a synthetic forest. It's private property. And lastly there's something weird, even creepy, about where the murder happens." Then he adds: "But in the play this is never mentioned at all."[18]

For Nathalie Paulding, the twelve-year-old actress who plays the raped child, Matryosha, there is another kind of problematic relation to the novel. Asked if she would like to question the playwright about the character she plays, the actress responds:

> I would ask her about a character if a book wasn't done on it already. I haven't read the whole book but I have read about the part that happens to my character. Learning background and relations makes me feel comfortable acting on stage. I also thought about the relations between characters from reading the book. . . . My mom is reading the novel and then she points out the parts about me and then we read it together, because a book like this has words I don't understand.

Paulding says she decided to read *The Possessed* because "I thought I heard the director tell other actors to read it."[19]

Rehearsing act 3, scene 7,[20] on April 1, Denis O'Hare (Peter Verkhovensky), after questioning the tone of one of his lines, says: "It's an out-loud thought." "The very thing we're looking for," Wright replies. Then he adds: "I think I have to ask the writer about a line I do not understand on any level." The actor who delivers this line asks, "Could it be a joke?" and the director replies: "I don't think so. I think it may be coming out of several drafts; it may refer to two different characters."[21] Five days later, Egloff, watching a run of act 3, writes "cut?" next to this line in her script but does not cut it. The maelstrom of rehearsal revision is tricky; sometimes it pulls in everyone but the playwright.

The afternoon rehearsal is at first dominated by a discussion of doors.[22] Several actors study the model of the set which sits atop a black stool next to the director's chair. The director must imagine the timing and location of entrances and exits on a multilevel set filled with doors. Wright mentions to the assistant director that he is raising "the dramaturgical question whether in this culture a locked door is inviolable." The question hangs in the air.

During a break in rehearsal, the director walks out onto the fire escape by himself and remarks to no one in particular, "God, this is a good play." Returning to the director's table to resume rehearsal, he says to the assistant director and stage manager: "Do you think we will ever *do* this *whole* play?" and laughter erupts. But he doesn't rush the actors when the play demands a pause. Like James Houghton rehearsing *Curse of the Starving Class*, Wright honors scripted silences. Directing act 3, scene 13, Wright asks that "everyone *play* the silence" after Marie Shatov's scream of pain in childbirth: "NOOOOOO *(Suddenly, silence)*" (183).

It is 6 P.M. The director says: "Very nice work. Thank you. So go home." As the actors are leaving, faxes from the playwright are arriving. Production assistant John Giampetro gathers them and says: "It's twenty-five pages!"

Egloff is expected at rehearsal on April 3 but does not appear. She will attend many rehearsals in the weeks that follow; when not present in person, she is nevertheless present in the form of frequent faxed revisions. Wright, dressed entirely in black, including a black baseball cap that never leaves his head, spends forty-five minutes blocking the murder of Shatov. As with Houghton's rehearsal of multiple exits in *Curse of the Starving Class*, a slow process of trial and error eventually becomes a few minutes of playing time. As the actors rehearse, Wright reads aloud the stage directions in the script, giving voice to the voice of the missing playwright.

Wright tells the actors: "Don't get thrown by all the capital letters in the script. Find whatever values you can in the speeches. Obviously, she [Egloff] is indicating high intensity. There's a lot of repetition in the script. Don't take that as a merely formal device." "Poetry," Egloff tells me, is "where I started as a writer. Poetry was all I did until I was thirty."[23] On the page the speeches have the look of free verse, with their short unpunctuated lines and distinct stanza breaks, as in Dasha's monologue at the end of the play:

And in the summer house
the roses were

so fragile
always and forever fragile (213).[24]

For some actors, the language is self-directing. Patrick Kerr (Liputin) says of the playwright:

We're friends, and she's a poet, and her language is the most important element
of the production for me as an actor. I have a strong sense and understanding of

her humor and her rhythms. All you need to do is add water. She really has spelled out how to do it—where to take little breaths, the thoughts. The intentions of the lines are evident in the way in which she's written the lines, with capital letters and lack of punctuation. The lines seem to show how they should be delivered.

In contrast, James Colby (Kirilov) feels a freedom in the way the lines are written: "One of the things that really attracted me to the play was the writing, especially the rhythm of the language. There's not a lot of periods, question marks, or stage directions. That gives the actor more possibilities." Colby likes the options offered by a script in which a given line "doesn't have to be either a statement or a question. . . . There are a lot of ways to interpret the line—a lot more possibilities—which is quite nice."

Christopher McCann (Shatov) takes a position midway between Kerr and Colby:

I trust the words on the page. If I have a question about, for example, why is this line written in capitals, was there a specific thing that she imagined—because a lot of the lines are written in capitals and the intent is not the same for all of them—I have asked her. And the answer is not necessarily definitive. . . . I asked her about the lines in bold letters, and she replied that it indicated some kind of change, not necessarily louder.

But the actor's sensitivity to language can also imperil him in a rehearsal where the script is in flux. "It's very exciting to create a role and to have it be molded as you're rehearsing it," Daniel Oreskes (Blum) tells me.

It's also scary. You get to a point where you understand the scene and get confident in its rhythm and then even the littlest rewrite can change it dramatically, and that's scary because a word or phrase is extremely powerful. A different word is or can be a different character. A different rhythm can be a different character. . . . *A word in a way is like a tree because the roots of it go much deeper: the changing of a word can create many changes in implication for what the character does or feels. [emphasis mine]*

Nathalie Paulding (Matryosha) arrives in the late afternoon on April 3, accompanied by her mother. I overhear the director answer her inaudible question: "Not quite dead, but not the way you were playing it earlier." Later he tells an actor, "I asked Nathalie to go only halfway toward the dead voice of the earlier scenes." The problem for the actress playing the raped child who hangs herself is not the language but its context. Egloff has said:

The first scene [the rape of Matryosha] and the instant replay of it in the third scene were there in the very first draft. The game that leads to violence in that scene is sort of what the whole play is about. That episode was in an appendix in my edition of the novel. I think that translated into that episode standing outside the reality of the play.

It is that "standing outside the reality of the play" which Paulding must locate in rehearsal—a difficult task for an actor several times her age.

The director rehearses act 3, scene 20, in which the confession and replaying of Stavrogin's rape of Matryosha merge with his rape of Dasha. At the climactic moment, both Matryosha and Dasha cry out in unison:

> *Nicholas don't*
> *Nicholas don't*
> *Nicholas don't (207)*

These are the lines uttered by Matryosha in the opening scene of the play. At first the actors read the script seated in chairs. Wright reads aloud the fairly explicit stage directions.[25] There is a stillness in the room as the director voices what the audience will see, not hear. Dasha's face is anguished; Matryosha's face has a deathly immobility.

As the actors begin to rehearse the scene on its feet, the director interrupts it and enters the playing area to demonstrate how he wants Nicholas to pull Dasha toward him. Suddenly the child actress asks a startling question: "Are my 'Nicholas don'ts' for her or for my own little scene?" At first, the director does not understand the question. After the assistant director paraphrases it, he says: "No, you're not telling him not to do it to her. You're telling him not to do it to you. I'm not sure, Nathalie, that you ever look at him in this scene until the very end."

Nathalie Paulding's question recalls Deborah Hedwall's quandary in rehearsal of *Curse of the Starving Class*: "I don't know if that's supposed to be my reality." Like Hedwall's Ella, Paulding's Matryosha shares stage space with a character who speaks but not to her, a character she does not look at yet responds to.

The rape of the child stands "outside the reality of the play." The sexual violence the playwright imagines and the actors simulate is performed not on the twelve-year-old body of the actress playing Matryosha but on the body of the adult actress playing Dasha. As the actors continue to rehearse, ironically laboring to achieve mutual agreement on every detail of an act that is in every way the opposite of mutual agreement, Paulding's Matryosha looks a little bored, then turns on her stomach and lies still.[26] The scene progresses. Stage manager Charles Means whispers to the director and then asks the child actress to sit with her mother in the kitchen/green room "while the adult actors rehearse."[27]

When the scene is run, a slightly comic effect is created by the heavy white knee pads worn as protection for the actors during the rape scene. The unnervingly self-possessed Paulding keeps herself apart in a delicate stillness. She lies on the floor, facing away, as directed. After the run-through, I see her quietly begin to make a lasso out of the black rope with which she is represented as hanging herself—and dance through its noose while the director gives notes.

The director is staging the rape of a child replayed as the rape of an adult: what is presented is Dasha's and Matryosha's rape. Even though they are, in a sense, as the director indicates, in separate scenes, they share one language. We hear the same words for the same events but see different choreographies: the child collapsed on the floor, looking away; the adult in fierce, active, futile resistance.

Egloff both illustrates and subverts the act of suppressing Stavrogin's rape of a child. She too suppresses the event by refusing to dramatize it literally and yet she begins her play with it, repeats it, and then presents an implicit double version of it near the end of the play. She deconstructs the nineteenth-century editor's suppression of the rape of a child by boldly highlighting it and at the same time never showing it.

On April 4 the playwright is again expected at rehearsal and again does not come. Wright directs Dasha's final speech in the play:

> *My love for that man*
> *was the high point of my life*
> *J'aimais cet homme toute ma vie*
>
> *but then I remember that day*
> *Remember that day we were all on the roof*
> *and the sun was shining. . . .*
>
> *And in the summer house*
> *the roses were*
>
> *so fragile*
> *always and forever fragile.*[28]

Kali Rocha says: "There's something I don't understand. Why am I saying 'but' here?" The director responds: "There was an even better day than that one." Once again there is a problem with a line that, along with several others in this speech, will be cut. The actress continues to question: "The roses were 'fragile.' Is that good?" "Yes," Wright responds, without a pause. "She doesn't say one negative thing. She doesn't have one negative thought."[29]

When asked in an interview if she would have preferred to question the playwright directly in rehearsal, Kali Rocha says: "Great question. No. I think ultimately most voices in the room should defer to the director. It's a very tricky balance. . . . The fact that Liz wasn't in the room that day didn't mean that I had to resort to asking the director, because I would have anyway. It is his vision of the scene that I would ultimately serve." Unlike actor David Chandler painfully questioning lines in his "resurrection" monologue during rehearsal of *A Question of Mercy*, Rocha is "satisfied with the director's answer." The director and the playwright, she says, "seem to be speaking the same voice."[30]

Egloff later tells me:

> *My principle is that usually when somebody in rehearsal has a comment or question that requires revision, I say, "Let me think about it," and go home. I trust*

Garland implicitly. That's because of his attitude toward writers. He has a very hands-off approach to the writing itself, and he's very respectful of writers.

I generally am not embarrassed about changing a text over and over again, and I seem to have a reputation for writing a lot of drafts. I think you have to lower the stakes. If you went into rehearsal wanting this to end up a perfect script, you'd drive yourself mad.[31]

On April 4, the director says: "I have some changes, but they require talking to Liz first." Expecting Egloff to be at rehearsal today, Wright intended to direct a new version of the opening of act 1, scene 10 (the governor's disastrous tea party), a scene that will undergo many revisions during rehearsal. In the March 15 script, Dasha enters *"trilling an aria from Offenbach's operetta, 'La Vie Parisienne,' a capella. . . . She is not very good"* (39). In a faxed revision, dated April 5, Dasha *"is playing a spirited folk song on a spinet"* (40). In a rejected version, dated April 8, Dasha's musical endeavors are eliminated entirely.[32] In the earlier script, Dasha's singing of the aria overlapped with a great number of loud speeches, all in capital letters. Egloff wishes to cut the aria. Wright wants the song there to establish the atmosphere of the salon, but suggests that Dasha sing only the end of the aria.[33]

The director's proposed revision would preserve the singing but shorten its duration and would also eliminate the overlap with shouted speeches by moving forward several speeches complimenting Dasha's singing. But Wright will not rehearse his version of the scene without the playwright's agreement. After a telephone conversation with Egloff, Wright tells the cast that he and the playwright have decided that Dasha will sing only the end of the aria. He explains that in an earlier workshop production Egloff could not hear clearly the shouted speeches at the opening of the scene and sensed that the audience was mainly listening to the singing. Eventually, Dasha's singing is replaced by violin playing.[34] Later there is one further revision of the opening stage direction. Egloff explains:

Dasha is giving a dramatic recitation of the last stanza of Shelley's "Hellas" in my version, but she's playing the violin in Garland's version. I put this in the text a week before tech but Garland wanted me to keep watching the rehearsal version.

There are three texts. There's the text in my head, there's the text in Garland's head, and there's the text in production. Various parts of these three texts are rather fluid. If something works for Garland and if I think it works for the production, I don't fight it—but I may change the text in my computer.

In rehearsal on April 4, an actor proposes a solution for a problem he is discussing with the director and then quickly adds, "But that's cheating because Liz wouldn't have written it that way." "Right," says the director. When the same actor asks, "Why am I always apologizing [to Stavrogin]?" Wright replies sympathetically: "I know, I know. From Liz's point of view, your whole life is an apology"; he prefaces this by saying that he and Egloff had been in conflict for months about that apologetic stance. The director makes his reservations, even his disagreements, known when actors question particular aspects of the play, but he privileges the playwright's point of view. When Wright does not know how Egloff would respond to a question that arises in rehearsal, it is added to "the Liz list," to be discussed with her. Some questions, however, dematerialize on their own. After running a scene in act 2, the director asks Dasha if she has a question. She says, "I was just breathing." "Good," Wright replies, "the very thing we want." An actor standing nearby says: "Continue down that path."

"The great thing about having the playwright in the room," the director tells me, "is that they're someone to talk to."

> *It's great to turn around in the room and say, "What did you mean by that?" and if she doesn't know, maybe there's work to be done, and if she does know, you're able to create a more authentic version of the play with the author there. I actually like the playwright in the room. Some directors just hate it. I don't—unless they're pigs. There are lots of pigs—by that I mean control freaks. Most playwrights are not pigs.[35]*

On April 6 the playwright is present in rehearsal for the first read-through of a recently faxed revision of the longest scene in the play (act 2, scene 20; later, act 2, scene 10), a ballroom scene during which the governor's wife is poisoned. Before Egloff arrives, I overhear the stage manager ask Wright, smoking on the fire escape during a break, what the three chairs in the playing area represent. "Chairs," the director says, wearily.

The assembled cast sits in the playing area. Elizabeth Egloff sits beside me at the director's table. She is wearing olive jeans, a black sweater, a jersey with horizontal green and white stripes, white socks, white running shoes, and no makeup. Her dark hair falls below her shoulders. Immediately approachable, warm and gracious,[36] the playwright tells me her son, William, whom she is breast-feeding, has been awakening every two to three hours all night, ravenous.[37] Before the reading begins, Wright briefly discusses one of Liputin's lines with Egloff. The playwright says: "Let's wait until we hear it and see if we should cut it."

The actors begin to read aloud. Egloff leans far forward in her seat, a blue pen in her right hand. She clasps her hands together in front of her mouth, covering it from view, as she gazes with great concentration at each actor as he or she reads. Occasionally, she makes a note on her script; otherwise she looks away from the actors only briefly to turn a page. Assistant director Kathleen Dimmick sits between the playwright and the director, as if in symbolic representation of her additional role as production dramaturg.[38] Wright leans over and asks Egloff an inaudible question; she pauses and whispers back; her gaze returns to the actors. The actors, who have been rehearsing for about ten days, read with great expression, very much in role. Again the director, not the stage manager, reads the stage directions.

Egloff exchanges her blue pen for a pencil. Her right hand touches the right side of her face for a moment. She writes on her script more frequently as the scene progresses. When the read-through ends, Wright says, "Now we have to *do* this." The cast laughs. The playwright asks if she can first make some changes in the already revised scene. She cuts the line she and the director had discussed.[39] After consulting audibly with Wright, she also cuts Stepan's line "SIC TRANSIT GLORIA," explaining that she doesn't think it will be understood.[40] An actor says, "I thank you for this rewrite," and Egloff expresses her appreciation. "No," he replies, "I thank you selfishly, for me."

The director tells Egloff that he blocked as much of the scene as he could last night until he couldn't keep all the characters in his head any longer. As he begins the work-through, Egloff and Dimmick quietly discuss additional changes in the script. When Wright stops rehearsal to make a blocking adjustment, Egloff dictates further revisions, cutting three lines and adding one. The actors rehearse these changes.[41] Egloff suggests another cut in the script, then quickly asks: "Would you rather have me shut up and wait until you've finished blocking?" "Yes," Wright replies, and, more playfully: "Yes, shut up. [To the cast] Liz has agreed to be quiet during the rest of the scene" (laughter). Randy Danson (Mrs. Lembke, the governor's wife) suddenly looks at the actors playing the revolutionaries and says: "I've never seen you before. I feel like I'm in a movie!" In the presence of the playwright, the government and the revolutionaries meet for the first time in rehearsal.

As the work-through continues, Egloff and Dimmick discuss textual revisions. I do not hear their whispered conversations but see the results. Even as the actors read the following lines, I watch the playwright cross through them on her script:

> MRS. STAVROGIN: TWO HUNDRED PEOPLE FROM MOSCOW
> WHAT'S THAT ST. PETERSBURG DON'T MAKE
> ME LAUGH. . . .
> BLUM: . . . AND TURGENEV.[42]

Daniel Oreskes (Blum) asks the playwright if she might restore a line of his that she has cut. Egloff says: "Let's try it and watch it and decide. I did cut it intentionally." Oreskes later tells me: "I felt that in the rewrite [of the ballroom scene] my character had lost the quality that made him who he was. . . . I mentioned that to Liz and she was extremely sympathetic. I felt that what I said to her was a factor in the next rewrite. And that rewrite really helped a lot."[43]

As Wright continues to block the scene, Egloff writes "cut?" next to one of Mrs. Lembke's speeches. A little later she cancels her query. The director stops rehearsal to reblock. Egloff writes "cut?" next to one of Mrs. Lembke's lines later in the scene. After a few minutes this line is crossed through in heavy pencil. Now Egloff looks back at the passage she had earlier considered cutting and in definitive dark pencil crosses through the first line of one of Mrs. Lembke's speeches that she will later cut in its entirety.

As rehearsal continues, Egloff crosses through Mrs. Lembke's line, "CALM DOWN BLUM," and writes above the crossed-out words, "SHUT

UP"; to the right of the revised line she writes, "or 'HAVE A CHAM-PAGNE.'" Noticing my steady transcribing of her revisions, Egloff laughs. When I explain, "I'm interested in your process," she laughs again, and says: "My process is to make continual changes." And this is almost true. Mrs. Lembke's "CALM DOWN," altered to "SHUT UP," is later changed to "STOP IT," and then revised back to "SHUT UP," the final form of the line echoing the earlier playful dialogue between director and playwright.[44]

Taking a ten-minute break, the director says, to laughter, "I want a drink." Then, "I'm sorry. I'm very cranky today. This scene in this space!" The playwright replies: "It doesn't help you but I feel the same way textually." The playwright cannot get a fix on the scene on the page; the director cannot get a fix on it in the playing area. When rehearsal resumes, I watch Egloff writing "cut?" next to particular speeches; crossing out stage directions; rewriting, reassigning, or inserting lines of dialogue. She adds words which as I copy she erases, replacing the previous revision with a new phrase or a question mark.

The scene is played again and again. Egloff, looking at her script, listens over and over to actors speaking words she is deciding to cut. It is as if I am watching lines audition, already knowing which ones, despite their best efforts, must face rejection.

The playwright makes an increasing number of small revisions. After discussing some of these with Dimmick, who records them in her script, Egloff passes me the newly revised pages and I enter the changes in my script. Rehearsal suddenly pauses at one of Mrs. Stavrogin's lines. The director asks the playwright, "To whom is this line addressed?" Egloff, who is making a note on her script, says: "I'm sorry. I was writing something." Wright repeats his question and Egloff whispers, "To Blum." "To Blum?" the director asks. Egloff whispers again: "To Blum, *if* it's going to work. But Ray doesn't know that yet." The actor, hearing his name, asks the playwright what he doesn't know. She smiles, says nothing. Lynn Cohen (Mrs. Stavrogin) asks: "When I say, 'STEPAN VERKHOVENSKY YOU'D BETTER NOT'—'better not' what?"[45] The director responds quickly, "Make it up." It is striking that the director consults the playwright about a missing stage direction but not about a missing thought.

As the work-through draws to a close, the playwright's revisions seem to accelerate. I can barely copy one before the next appears. Egloff writes a new stage direction—"*Dasha pounds on the closet door*"[46]—which Wright immediately accepts. In fact, the playwright and director never disagree in the presence of the actors. When Egloff speaks directly to the actors in rehearsal, she receives, and perhaps anticipates, the support of the director. When she whispers an answer to a question Wright asks or silently makes notes during rehearsal, she is staking out territory to be negotiated privately.

Just before the lunch break, Wright says: "Okay, everybody, there will probably be some snips and cuts, but this script is the one we'll be using. So get rid of the earlier one." Feeling the sheer weight in my hands of the subsequent versions of this nearly 20-page scene, I feel certain that the director was whistling in the dark.

While Wright is at lunch, Egloff and Dimmick remain at the director's table, discussing further revisions. Dimmick says: "I wonder, dramaturgically, about the fire [the town is burning during the ballroom scene]. . . . I wonder if there would be an opportunity for a mention of smelling something to do with fire?" The playwright adds a new line: "Do you smell something burning?" (138). This addition necessitates further changes. Dimmick says: "The problem is that you're taking this character out of the argument by having him obsessed with the smell. It's a trade-off." Egloff has been experimenting with the placement of the new line in the scene as blocked. Dimmick now raises the question whether the audience "will think something's burning in the kitchen." The playwright says that she is becoming "a little bleary." Eventually, she will add a second, more explicit reference to the smell of fire "outside" (139-A). She and Dimmick discuss further cuts as I leave. I walk past Lynn Cohen and Frank Raiter running lines in the green room even as the playwright is changing them at the director's table. In the rehearsal of a script undergoing "continual changes," an ordinary event—actors learning their lines during a break—is suddenly jarring.

"Garland has such a good dramaturgical eye—and so does Kathleen [Dimmick]—that I really need their help," Egloff says just before rehearsal resumes. "I've worked with Kathleen as a dramaturg on this play for a short time two years ago. And at home I reach a stopping point where I can't go any further, in this case, with this play, because there are so many characters." She explains:

> Stage time is moving so fast [in the ballroom scene] that I can't picture it when I work on the computer. There is a point when it has to stop becoming literature or it will lose life. As a writer I like the literary aspects of playwriting more than anything but there does come a point when I hit a dead end with the literature and I need to turn the reins over to the director and this scene is one of those cases.
>
> I generally hate improvising as a way of writing but this particular director and these particular actors are very literary-minded and so in this case I feel I can trust them to guide me. Therefore, I write in their presence and use their impulses.

For Egloff, giving over the reins is not surrendering complete control.

> Each of these actors is tracking his or her character better than I am. I need to keep enough control so the actors don't feel it is out of control even though I'm giving over the reins to the actors. I try to use their impulses but not to give all control to them because the actors need to know that the writer and the director are in control. It's a delicate balancing act at those moments.

Egloff's final words recall Kali Rocha's description of the relation between the actor and the playwright and director in rehearsal: "It's a very tricky balance."

Nathalie Paulding has arrived for the first run-through of act 3. The director says to the cast: "It's hard to rehearse on one level a play that will be performed on six levels. Just be where you are, not where you think you *should* be. This is a stumble through." Egloff looks at Patrice Johnson, highly padded over both the buttocks and the belly, in preparation for her role as the pregnant Marie Shatov, and says to the director: "I'd like to know where she got that idea. Certainly not from *me*." "Hmmmm," Wright murmurs to great laughter. At 3:30 P.M., the run-through begins. The director whispers to Egloff who writes "discuss" on a page of her script. As the actors perform that page, there is a brief whispered discussion between Wright and Egloff. The playwright crosses through a stage direction in act 3, scene 1, and writes "fix" in the right margin, along with an alternative stage direction. In the May 9 script a new speech is inserted exactly at the point where the playwright has written "fix."[47] As rehearsal continues, Egloff makes heavy cuts, crossing through lines that will remain crossed through in the May 9 script.

During the run of the twenty-two scenes in act 3, not until today performed in sequence, actors' scripts are scattered throughout the playing area (on a bed or table, in the lap of a seated actor), although almost every actor is off book. The director and playwright are in identical postures, both gazing at the actors; then Egloff bends her head, makes a brief note on her script. A moment later, director and playwright are simultaneously writing on their scripts; then only the playwright's eyes lift and focus steadily, intently, on the actors. She turns the pages of her massive script without breaking her gaze.

Hearing the actors make slight inadvertent alterations in the text during the run-through, as is to be expected and as they may do in performance, I marvel at this or any playwright's ongoing effort to get the language right. The author's "improvising" of her writing[48] is part of an intricate exchange of impulses that actors, director, and designers take from a script and from each other, and that a playwright in rehearsal takes from all of them and gives back in her rewrites; then the whole process begins again. I cannot possibly witness or record all that is happening in this small room. No one can. As Shatov says of the birth of Marie's baby in the scene I am now watching: "The mystery . . . /is an incomprehensible/mystery" (184).

During the playing of the "double rape" of Dasha and Matryosha (act 3, scene 20), Egloff's gaze is focused on Nathalie Paulding as she performs her "own little scene" of "Nicholas don'ts" and then falls to the floor, facing away from the simulated rape ten feet to her left. The playwright's right hand reaches underneath her glasses to wipe her eyes.[49] The run ends. No one moves. The director says, "Okay. Good."

After rehearsal, the playwright says to the director: "You've done a huge amount of work. I think it really holds." Egloff, Wright, and Dimmick now talk for an hour and a half. Wright says: "I think Dasha's speech at the end is too long." Egloff asks how much of the speech he wants cut, and Wright says, "About half." Dasha's last speech is in the form of a letter to Mrs. Stavrogin. In particular, Wright questions whether Dasha would say to her lover's mother: "My love for that man/was the high point of my life." While the director speaks to one of the actors, the playwright, still sitting at the table, makes revisions in her script. "Fabulous," Wright says when Egloff shows him the new version of Dasha's final speech. "We hassled that for months and months," Egloff tells me. In the rehearsal room a resolution of this hassle is achieved.[50]

Egloff and Wright discuss the opening of the governor's tea party scene (act 1, scene 10). The cast has now been given a revised script with the new stage direction, "*Dasha playing a spirited folk song on a spinet*," followed by Stepan's response, "Brava/Brava."[51] The director and the playwright study this version together. Egloff says: "Have we reached a dead end with the shouting over the music?" and Wright replies: "We'll see."[52]

During more detailed discussion of act 3, the director says that he misses some lines now cut; Egloff and Wright agree to look these over again. Wright suggests a certain cut. Egloff makes it, proposes other cuts in act 3 and suggests adding a line to clarify one scene (act 3, scene 17). Wright immediately agrees, and Egloff dictates the new line to the stage manager.[53]

Together Egloff and Wright study act 3, scene 16. The director says: "I don't think this requires rewriting"; almost simultaneously, the playwright says: "Maybe the scene needs to be rewritten. Dasha shouldn't necessarily just be sitting there. . . . Let me think about this. It may require a little rewriting." The scene opens with the stage direction: "*Dasha sitting at Mrs. Stavrogin's window, in the dark. A candle wanders in*," and ends with the stage direction: "*The candle wanders out*."[54] Egloff says: "*Dasha* leaves and the candle *stays*." "Possibly" is Wright's laconic reply. The director walks to the fire escape where he smokes; the playwright rewrites. Then I hear the playwright read aloud to the director an entire rewritten scene, the text in rehearsal voiced by its author.

Wright asks Egloff how Marie Shatov, having just given birth, would negotiate stairs. The playwright gives an explicit answer: "Her legs would be like noodles, like broken legs. Her back would be killing her. And her vagina would be sore, so she'd be stiff there." Wright asks her about the timing of Marie's contractions, and the volume and intensity of her screaming during labor. Responding in her dual roles as playwright and new mother, Egloff says: "She would just be panting during the last part of her pregnancy scene. I think the screaming *has* to come down." Behind the text is the voice of "the playwright in the room . . . someone to talk to." In rehearsal on April 12, Wright tells the actress playing Marie Shatov, "Remember my note. Play the pain as written and not at other times so we don't get to birth too soon." In his phrasing, directorial authority ("my note") is aligned with that of the text ("as written").

A more complicated matter is the location of the intermission, a decision that has both structural and practical implications.[55] Egloff says: "If we don't give two intermissions, the audience may become exhausted and start laughing." Wright, Egloff, and Dimmick consider placing one intermission between scene 12 and scene 13 of act 2, and another after the ballroom scene (act 2, scene 20). Egloff, however, thinks that opening the second act with scene 13 (a scene between the Governor and Blum) may be "a feeble beginning." In three days, she will come back to rehearsal to see a run of the restructured first act.

Wright asks questions about act 3, scene 6, the scene between Dasha and Stepan that had given trouble in rehearsal. Egloff says she will "look over" that scene,[56] and then adds: "So I'm going to generate a new ballroom scene." A look of horror passes over the director's face: "I can't tell you the rate change in my heart." There is laughter. Dimmick comments: "There are some other little changes that Liz and I have discussed that we haven't talked about with you yet." Wright says, "My heart is going there again." To restore normal heartbeat, Egloff reads aloud a few examples of small stylistic changes in the script, adding: "So that's what I mean by 'generating a new scene.'" "I have too many notes in this version of the scene," Wright says. "I need to have the changes recorded in my present script. I can't put in a new script for the ballroom scene at this point." Egloff responds sympathetically: "Maybe the actors will feel that way, too." Stage manager Charles Means, who has rarely spoken during the past hour and a half, says quietly: "We can generate a master revised ballroom scene."[57]

There is one last discussion of a speech in which Shatov tells Marie that he won't leave her alone while she is in pain. Wright says: "But he does leave her alone. Why not cut that line?" "I like the contradiction," Egloff says.

It is 7 P.M. Dimmick shows Egloff the set in progress on the stage of the theater next door to the rehearsal hall. The playwright silently observes the beginnings of the massive wooden scaffolding. We walk outside into a drizzling rain, and she waves goodbye.

Two days later, on April 8, Charles Means and assistant stage manager Antonia Gianino hand out revisions of act 1, scene 4: pages 14, 14 (pre-A), and 14-A. "New pages: authors!" an actor says, half playfully. Sitting at a table in the green room, an actor explains: "I'm studying my script." "You are?" another actor asks. "You will be, too, when you get the new pages."

Actors who have rehearsed this scene on its feet now sit in the playing area and read aloud the revised text. Before me as I write are four versions of page 14: the March 15 script, with handwritten revisions by the playwright; a faxed version dated April 1; a Xerox of the director's handwritten revisions of the faxed revision, approved by Egloff and handed out to the actors on April 8; and the May 9 script. The tendency is generally in the direction of more cuts and occasional reassignment of speeches. The version of page 14 read by the actors in rehearsal today is a collaborative revision by the director and playwright. To distinguish precisely what is directorial from what is authorial would be, as Horatio tells Hamlet, to consider too curiously.[58]

In the afternoon the playwright arrives. The director immediately asks her a question: "Who is Peter [Verkhovensky] having breakfast with?" and then announces to the company: "We're *considering* making *this* [all the scenes through act 2, scene 12] act 1. So this run is for us to see if this is possible. This is not a decision. We just want to see if this is a possibility."

Egloff, wearing a purple wool sweater and gray jeans, sits at the director's table. The run begins. She holds her pen in her right hand; three fingers press lightly against her forehead as she leans forward, her script on the table in

PETER VERKHOVENSKY

```
I'm talking about every job in this town
whether Mr. Somebody wants you to repair his porch
or Mrs. So-and-so wants you to carry her groceries
and your wife Virginsky
She's going to have to stop baking bread for other people

Nobody works for anybody Anywhere Period
until we have a system in this country
that makes everybody equal
We're talking about founding a nation based on Community
not Hierarchy
```
Equality ⟶

```
where nobody can kick you out of your apartment
because the Community owns the apartment
where nobody can deny you food
because the Community owns the land and the farms and the
grocery stores and the bakeries
```
we all *we all*

```
We're talking about starting a Community
where banks give money to people who need money
not people who have money and want to make more
Now does anybody have any more questions
```
founding a nation and the banks

(Pause.)

where people who need money are every bit as good as people who have

SHIGALYOV

```
Fuck it
```
Now does...

3.2 Elizabeth Egloff's rehearsal revisions of script: "people who need money are every bit as good as people who have money"

front of her, her eyes focused on the actors. She laughs quite freely during the rehearsal, making brief notes on her script. During scene changes she lists the page numbers of her revisions on a separate sheet, along with other notations, such as "Track Mrs. Lembke using 'comrade.'" Act 1, scene 10 begins without the aria. When I ask if Dasha's singing has been completely cut, Egloff whispers: "I don't know. There are about four different versions floating around."

In the morning and early afternoon rehearsals, Wright directed voicing, tone, pace, gesture, and movement with meticulous attention to detail. Now, in this late afternoon run, much of what was achieved earlier seems to be lost, and this is the "version" the playwright is watching.

Egloff writes on her pad: "Shall we reorganize scenes in early act 2?" She marks a possible revision of phrasing and a significant cut in scene 4. In rehearsal the playwright is reimagining her play, structurally and stylistically. Like the director, she is checking the fit of language and action; the fluidity and juxtaposition of scenes until now rehearsed nonsequentially; the clarity of reference and consistency of motivation. "*Trim* Lembke's world," she writes on her white pad. "Trim widow's speech by half." "Cut Shig's kerosene scene?" Then she writes: "pp. 95–97 cuts" (act 2, scene 2). The run ends. The director says, "Thanks," and the playwright says, "Yeah." It is 5:30 P.M. The actors leave for the day.

Egloff and Wright talk. "As I was watching it," Egloff says, "I think it *does* need to be reshaped, and trimmed. . . . The play *lives*, I think, in the [revolutionaries'] world and in Nicholas's world. As a principle of cutting, I think it needs to focus there. I think the focus is almost too equal now. . . . I'm interested in sitting down and actually going through and doing cuts." Wright and Egloff try to find a time when they can meet. The playwright says to the director: "I feel like the text work in this chunk we've just seen is a *primary* thing to be addressed. I'm thinking of cutting and shaping. It would be like a waste of your time to work on some of these scenes." Wright asks: "Do you know which ones?" Egloff mentions Shigalyov's kerosene scene and several others: "I need to go through and weigh them out." The director tries to ascertain which scenes will not be changed and which will. Egloff says again that she needs to "weigh out" what cuts to make, adding: "It's so hard to hold the whole thing in your head."

Wright leaves the room for twenty minutes to attend a previously scheduled meeting. Egloff tells assistant director and production dramaturg Kathleen Dimmick: "When I watch the actors running the 'stumble through,' and they lose their way, that's a great key."[59] In her discussion with Dimmick, the playwright "rehearses" cuts and alterations she later presents to the director. On Wright's return, Egloff proposes either trimming several scenes heavily or cutting them entirely. The reshaping and cutting of the scene (act 2, scene 2; later, act 2, scene 1) in which the pregnant Marie returns to Shatov is what Egloff calls "my most radical suggestion."[60] The director listens without comment. Then he asks: "These would be cuts to make this act structure work?" I miss the playwright's reply, but her proposed rewrites suggest more complex ambitions. She asks the director if a particular cut ("losing the Kirilov tea scene") would "disturb" him, and he responds: "I think it's the scene that shows what those characters' relationship really is." The director continues to talk quietly about why he wishes to keep some of the parts of the play the playwright is considering cutting.

Together they determine those cuts Wright needs immediately: Egloff will fax revisions in three scenes from act 2 that evening.[61] The playwright then suggests that another scene be cut. The director responds, "Don't cut anything [just] because it's dragging now or not working yet." Afterward Wright says to me: "It's quicksand."

Four days earlier, the director, smoking on the fire escape, told me:

A new play is an embryo forming, and working on it is midwifery in some sense, which is quite different from working with a play that is already an adult. There are dangers in feeling superior because we're grown up and wise and the play's just getting started.

What was most frightening for me just before I left New York was that people rewrote plays and rewrote plays and rewrote plays because they thought that's what they were supposed to do. And they didn't actually make it better. The issue of panic, particularly in New York, is so high on a new play that we sometimes overwrite a new play. That's why I'm not a big fan of playwriting workshops. Somehow I think playwrights should not be influenced by so many opinions.

The thing I loved about Liz's play when I read it on the page was that it was strong and assertive and, I thought, quite finished, not that there's nothing left to do, of course. It was well-formed and ready to be born.[62]

On April 12 the director informs the actors that he and Egloff have made cuts. I overhear an actor tell Wright that the playwright has changed one of his lines and he explains why he feels the earlier version is better. During a work-through of revised scenes, Wright says: "The minute we go slowly, Liz starts cutting scenes, so we've got to cover our flanks." The cast laughs, and the same actor responds: "So we have to chip in and send her to Mexico," which prompts more laughter.

Asked how she responds to the playwright's revision of her scene with Ivan Shatov, Patrice Johnson (Marie Shatov) says:

It helps if . . . changes are happening as an ongoing process and not after you have made and rehearsed decisions and are about to perform them. Otherwise you get a train wreck with a bunch of confused actors. . . .

In this production it helps immensely to have Elizabeth around from time to time. . . . [If] the writer is constantly changing the text, cutting, rewriting, that can throw you off in the process if you've already absorbed and rehearsed the original script. I've had some cuts that have thrown me, but it's happening early enough in the rehearsal that you have time to work with it and discover it.

There were lines that the writer told me in advance she was going to change—lines about Marie's travel—so I was prepared for that. What I didn't expect was the revision of the first bed scene which condensed the whole scene, but it's coming as we're rehearsing so it's great. Actors are always married to lines that they've already memorized. Actors are always against less lines.[63]

Lynn Cohen (Mrs. Stavrogin) offers another view of rehearsal revision:

I used to say, "I must and I shall," in the earlier version. . . . The new line is, "I shall go, I shall see, I shall conquer." This revision shows a woman who is fit for battle in every sense of the word and knows she's going to win. This revision was also in response to Garland's request for a specific kind of heightening, . . . to see this woman in full battle dress. I feel this revision works very well . . . [but] it could be changed again at this point.[64]

I am sitting on the bottom step of a stairway outside the rehearsal hall. The actress, seated in a chair near me, continues:

Let me explain. You're walking up the staircase and you have a series of lines, all having to do with not wanting to leave a person at the bottom of the stairs. In the rehearsal process you may find that you don't need all those lines and that you end up stopping halfway up the stairs, turn around, and say, "John." In other words, you ask if I'll miss a line if it's cut. Sometimes you do but you've already lived through that line so it's there *and sometimes you don't need it any more.* [emphasis mine]

Randy Danson (Mrs. Lembke) tells me:

I like working with plays-in-progress and playwrights who are present in rehearsal because I like feeling that I have an effect on the process. I think that there are things you can know as an actor being inside something that someone has written.

It's like [the difference between] someone who builds a house and someone who lives inside it. You might find that the placement of the doorway into the closet or the width of the hallway when you live there actually just doesn't work for you in that kind of day-to-day usage. It might be better one foot over. Even though the playwright invented it and is perfectly right about it, there's something about living in a house that brings a whole new dimension.

When you're living in this house, you've got to assume that the architect is brilliant and knows what she's doing, not that the architect is a fool. It's not because I feel that you have to automatically respect all writers—though I think all artists should be respected—but because it is exactly by giving in to the structure you've been handed that you will find the more interesting original creativity out of yourself. Because it pushes you beyond your first thought.

Kali Rocha (Dasha) says:

As an actor, my receptivity to the playwright's revisions during rehearsal comes down to a matter of trust. When you're working on a new play, you gotta trust the playwright, so that when they come at you with revisions during the rehearsal process—rather than resist them because it's not what you had in your head from the beginning—you can incorporate them as another rich layer from the playwright's head. Why would you refuse such a gift?

I watch Kali Rocha and Frank Raiter read aloud two new revised pages of act 3, scene 6, faxed by the playwright. Raiter (Stepan) says he has trouble making a transition to his line, "Say why don't we run away together?" (163). The director replies: "But that's not a change!" "Yes. I'm *still* having trouble with it" (laughter). "I'll see what I can do to help you," Wright says. He spends more than an hour closely analyzing and redirecting the revised scene; there is a thirty-minute discussion of a single line, "I'LL NEVER FORGIVE HER" (162). At one point Wright comments, "I'm just not sure what that 'DON'T' is." In the May 9 script, Dasha's "DON'T" is crossed through (162).

Rehearsing act 3, scene 17, James Colby (Kirilov) tells the director that he needs something, perhaps a word, to help him when he picks up a gun and aims it at Peter Verkhovensky, who is pointing a gun at him. Wright says, "I could ask Liz," and then immediately, and brilliantly, redirects the scene as written. He slows down the action so that the urgency of Kirilov's shaking hand as he lifts his gun enables the actor to play the moment without adding a single word to the text. Later Colby says he likes some lines now cut from one of his monologues, "but it's not important."

On April 15 the company again rehearses the ballroom scene, located at the end of the restructured second act. "It's the scene in the play that is most like the way the play *used* to be," Wright says to an actor. "The play used to be a lot more farcical. She wisely decided to revise. This scene is right on the line, on the razor's edge, stylistically." In the ballroom scene, lines overlap during vigorous physical activity—pushing, hitting, falling down, jumping about, biting people. Wright has been rehearsing this long and much-revised scene over and over for days, trying to pace the scripted frenzy inside the governor's salon while outside the town is burning. There are nine actors in the scene, all—after a certain point—in constant motion.

In preparation for a run of the first act that afternoon, Wright rehearses the fourth version of scene 10, which now begins with Dasha playing a violin. Egloff has cut two and a half pages and has placed Stavrogin's nose- and ear-biting, actions originally separated by three pages, in close proximity to each other. Movement consultant Christopher Burns rechoreographs Stavrogin's biting as the director watches. While the scene is rehearsed, Wright dictates a new line to clarify the action: "He's biting him on the nose." This line, never added to the script, is what I would call directorial reauthoring in the service of rehearsal: a "textual" revision extinguished when its function is served. In the same way, Wright later introduces experimentally a line cut in an earlier version (Stavrogin's "but I have to whisper").[65]

The playwright arrives for the 4:30 P.M. run of the revised first act. The assistant director tells Egloff that the director has added a few lines in act 1, scene 10. The stage manager announces changes in act 2: scene 5 has been cut, scene 10 has become scene 17, and scene 9 will be followed by scene 11. The director tells Nathalie Paulding that a scene in which she appears (act 2, scene 4) has been cut by about two-thirds. The director tells Egloff that he has moved one of Shatov's lines to a slightly earlier position in act 1, scene 10.[66]

During the run Egloff writes frequently in the margins of her script and in a notebook in her lap. Selected examples: "pp. 14–15B, trim dialogue"; "p. 30, another word for 'see'?"; "p. 43, put back Mrs. L's line"; "fix biting lines (Does NS have to stay on his feet?)." More urgent notes appear: "The salon scenes have no reality. . . . Is it because they aren't listening to each other? Or is it text?" "This is just an endless series of gags—I can't follow a story," she writes after watching a scene early in act 2.

Mandy Mishell Hackett, the NYTW literary adviser who has observed the run, remains for a discussion with Wright, Egloff, and Dimmick after rehearsal ends. Although neither Dimmick nor Hackett has the official designation of dramaturg, they both function in that role. Egloff says that she is thinking of cutting one of the "gang [of revolutionaries]" scenes. Hackett describes the scene as "an important brush stroke"; Wright asks Egloff not to cut it.[67] Egloff says to the director: "What about putting Dasha into Mrs. Stavrogin's first scene [act 1, scene 6]?" Wright replies, "I could do that." "I like that," says the literary adviser.[68]

Egloff and Dimmick have remained seated at the director's table; Hackett stands midway between them and Wright, ten feet away by the open door to the fire escape. Visually, the playwright is flanked by "dramaturgs" while the director is liminally placed, neither quite inside the rehearsal space nor quite escaping from it. Wright says: "The train scene [act 2, scene 3; later, act 1, scene 13] needs to be one-half shorter." "Do you want me to make cuts?" Egloff asks. Wright replies: "But that's the beginning of tracking the pogrom, so we have to cut *and* underline." ("Pogrom" is the rehearsal designation for act 1, scene 19, a scene in which the governor's men brutally assault Stepan, Mrs. Stavrogin, and Dasha in their futile search for Peter Verkhovensky.) The director asks: "Couldn't we mention Peter's name directly? Because it's not clear whether they're looking for Nicholas or for Peter." Egloff says: "Actually, I can write that a lot more clearly." Wright elaborates: "I just think the audience is disoriented. I didn't know whom they're looking for, and so I didn't know why they're beating up people. They're in Mrs. Stavrogin's house, but they're looking for Peter." Hackett adds: "We get two new big information scenes in the [restructured] first act. Marie really seems to me to be *second act* information." Egloff asks: "Are you suggesting moving Marie to act 2?" Wright says: "You *could* transfer her to act 2."

The literary adviser's idea excites great interest. After a brief discussion, the playwright and director decide to move Marie Shatov's first appearance to the second act. Then Wright suggests that this scene should open act 2, following the intermission.[69] What Egloff had earlier characterized as "a feeble beginning" of the second act has been replaced with a scene that seemed to be seeking a new location in the play.

Egloff now says: "I think there are too many jokes." Wright suggests that what the playwright perceives as a problem in the text may be a problem in the acting that he can remedy in rehearsal. Hackett says to Egloff: "I think you should wait until you see a full run and feel the rhythm before you make too many cuts in the jokes."[70] The playwright has not seen a run-through of the whole play. No one has.[71]

On April 17 Wright rehearses a new version of act 2, scene 18, in which Peter Verkhovensky offers to travel to China with Nicholas Stavrogin and is rebuffed. Before he works the revised scene, line by line, the director tells Denis O'Hare (Verkhovensky): "The minute a scene is reordered, that changes what the scene is about. That's part of what makes Liz a good writer." O'Hare later says: "Because we have parts of the earlier version in the rewrite, I may have trouble getting this down." "Of course," Wright responds.

Bill Camp (Stavrogin) remarks that the playwright's "adjustments in scenes . . . enhance the structure of the piece as a whole so there's more of a payoff for the things we've already done. . . . What China now means to me is a new color in our conversation in the course of the scene." Camp talks about the relocation of a single line:

"Please don't" used to be my response to Peter's humiliating himself in this scene. Now it refers to his talking to me about China. He doesn't realize that China means death to me now. . . . It's like a painting that the playwright has provided and the director and the actors bring their own palette, their own colors, to the painting. . . . Liz keeps repainting, and making it better, and then we take that and we apply our own textures. . . . It may throw me for an afternoon or an evening, having to learn a new scene or the values of a new scene for a character I'm playing. But I wouldn't expect a playwright to give me a rewrite of values that are 180 degrees different from the ones I've already absorbed. I think Liz is simply enhancing the values already there. It's trust.

When I ask, "Trust of what?" he replies: "The playwright. Your own instincts. The director. All of it."

On April 17 there is an afternoon run-through of the restructured second act. Michael Arkin (Governor Lembke) says: "And at least for today this is act 2." The playwright, wearing a green and blue plaid shirt, gray pants and white running shoes, arrives a little late, with her son, William, sleeping in her arms. She stands in the far right upstage corner of the rehearsal studio, near the door through which actors must pass to reach the green room. Unable to take notes, Egloff is watching the run from "backstage." I can see the playwright's face; the actors performing cannot. Members of the company not in a given scene react to the run with visible appreciation and audible laughter. Egloff's gaze, serious and steady, is interrupted by smiles only when actors greet her quietly as they pass through the open door where she stands holding her baby strapped in front of her. William is now awake and is also staring intently at the men speaking in loud voices very close to him and his mother. The playwright continues to stand in the open doorway, liminally placed, like the director after the previous run. She sways slightly as she rocks her son in her arms, the hand that would have been making notes clasping him. William makes a few baby noises; his mother disappears into the anteroom and is back one minute later. The playwright seems to have to choose between not seeing parts of her play or seeing it disrupted by the sounds of her infant. In addition, she is seeing her play from a perspective that no member of the audience will share.

I watch simultaneously the faces, gestures, and movements of actors in a high-energy run-through of a revised script and the face of the playwright on whom this is registering. As the actors perform the new version of act 2, scene 18, rehearsed by O'Hare and Camp earlier today, the baby again makes tiny noises, but Egloff does not leave the room. On her face I see a look of total concentration, neither critical nor admiring: the still, focused intensity of the playwright's gaze. At that very moment William makes more insistent audible demands to be the sole object of her concentration, and Egloff retreats further into the anteroom where she can hear but not see her rewritten scene. During the ballroom scene that ends the new second act, I see Egloff once again watching, as she stands upstage breast-feeding William.

After the run Egloff talks with Wright, Dimmick, and Hackett about trimming parts of the play. Hackett says she thinks it makes "perfect sense as it is." Wright asks Egloff for an adjustment that will mesh with the blocking in one scene, and she agrees. The playwright asks Christopher McCann (Ivan Shatov) if the revisions in his scene make sense. Yes, the actor says, then moves into the playing area where he inaudibly discusses and then demonstrates something as she watches. Together they look at the script; she makes a note.

That afternoon while William is having a late lunch, I ask Egloff to characterize the playwright-director relationship in rehearsals of *The Devils*. She describes Wright as "a wonderful dramaturg who at the same time is a very talented director," and explains:

> What I needed with this play was a dramaturg because it is so huge I can't keep a perspective on it. This is the largest play I've written by a long shot. To me, a dramaturg is an in-house critic. You need particular qualities. I think it's ironic that the director of this piece has been the best dramaturg I've ever had.[72]
>
> I needed—and every playwright deserves—a first production that as closely as possible emulates the production in your head. And after that a director can do whatever production he or she wants. Garland and I are on the same wavelength aesthetically.[73]

Still breast-feeding William at the end of our interview, the playwright adds, "When I'm writing I'm on a very solitary path of discovery. So I come to rehearsal because it's not so lonely."

On April 19 Egloff arrives without William to watch a run of the revised act 1. Wearing a brown leather jacket, a black-and-white checked shirt, a black sweater, and black pants, she sits at the director's table with a pad of lined yellow paper on which she makes infrequent, brief notes. The new sequence of scenes, announced by the stage manager, is pasted on the walls of the rehearsal room. During the run actors consult these lists; sometimes they are called into a scene by the stage manager.

Nathalie Paulding sits in the rehearsal room holding her large purple and pink three-ringed binder with small pasted-on unicorns decorating the cover. She follows her script whenever she is not in a scene, is word-perfect, and never requires a cue for an entrance, exit, or cross. Today when Matryosha says, "I/ Killed/ God" (70), at the end of act 1, scene 14, she makes the sign of the Russian orthodox blessing. This unscripted gesture is her own idea, she tells me, and she received permission of the director to "try it" in the run. Later it is cut, but the director's willingness to incorporate the suggestions of this utterly serious child actress in a rehearsal observed by the playwright is unsurprising.

After the April 19 run-through of the new act 1, the playwright and the director speak in private, provisionally agreeing to make heavy cuts in the production but not in the text, including the elimination of an entire scene "because of budgetary and space problems."[74] These cuts, however, are not made in the run-through the following day.

On April 20, three days before technical rehearsals begin, the entire play is run for the first time. In attendance, together with the playwright, director, assistant director, literary adviser, stage manager, assistant stage manager, and production assistant, are James C. Nicola, artistic director of New York Theatre Workshop; Susan Hilferty, costume designer; James F. Ingalls, lighting designer; Zhanna Gurvich, props mistress, representing set designer Douglas Stein; Christopher Burns, movement consultant; Jill DuBoff, sound engineer; and Rhonda Celestain, wardrobe supervisor. The downstage side of the rehearsal room is filled with the chairs of the fifteen observers, exactly as many as the number of actors in the cast.

Nicola and Hackett sit between Egloff and me. The playwright's script is at first not on the table before her, but during act 1 I see her looking at it. Actors silently consult lists of the order of scenes pasted on the walls of the rehearsal room. Every run is a new run. Dasha appears for the first time in the revised version of act 1, scene 6. As the actors perform this scene, everyone within range is writing: Egloff, Nicola, Hackett, Wright. In the upstage wall mirror, behind the actors, I see the faces of six other observers, all holding pencils and pads, in various postures of attentiveness. But none of us has the stillness and intensity of the playwright's gaze, not even the director, whose focus on the scene before his eyes is both more mobile and somehow more relaxed.

I watch Egloff watching the newly rewritten scene between Peter and Nicholas that she had only heard, not viewed, during the run-through she attended with William. Her expression is veiled, as it so often is, by the stillness of her head and body. Her right hand is under her chin, all five fingers covering the lower half of her face. I see only her eyes, open wide, unsmiling—her characteristic demeanor during runs.[75]

During the break following the run-through, Nicola, Hackett, Egloff, and Dimmick sit at the director's table, discussing plot and structural issues, and possible revisions. Wright stands apart, smoking on the fire escape. Costume designer Susan Hilferty glances at the group discussing the nearly four-hour-long run and says: "You look glazed. Are you?" There is a general affirmative response.

Nicola tells the playwright he thinks there are too many story plots and there is a need to simplify. He suggests some cuts and redistribution of emphases, including more explicit mention of the strike incited by the revolutionaries.[76]

After Nicola leaves, Wright gives notes to the actors while Egloff and Hackett continue to talk quietly. As in the play, voices in the same room overlap. Some of Nicola's suggestions, Egloff says, "would require massive rewrites." "Whenever you can make a choice that takes us forward four or five seconds," Wright says to the actors, "do." "My mind is so tired," Egloff whispers to the literary adviser. A moment later an actor asks her a question about one of his lines. The playwright responds: "In my head he's a moment short of saying it coherently." Wright tells his cast: "I should warn you—I really *do* tech. . . . I need you to learn the places where you have contact with the stage."

The actors leave. At the director's table, Egloff, Dimmick, and Hackett discuss cuts in scene 8 of act 3. The playwright, flanked on either side by a dramaturg, reads aloud Shatov's lines. At times one or the other encourages her to cut less or more. I hear Egloff say: "This whole thing I could lose," and a voice at her side says: "You don't want to lose that. It's great."

Further cuts in the much-revised ballroom scene are discussed. Dimmick says: "We have to cut for clarity, not for time." Egloff suggests cutting one speech and reassigning another in act 2, and then says: "Act 2 is the one I'm having trouble following. Jim [Nicola] briefly suggested that we get rid of the assassination [of the governor's wife at the end of act 2]."[77] Wright, still standing near the door to the fire escape, remains silent. Hackett says, "The question I have is: how does the assassination get us forward?" Egloff responds: "It's a big enough question that I think we should have a longer conversation about it." The conference has moved to the door of the fire escape. "I think I have to throw down a red flag," Wright says. "I don't think we have time for leisurely conversation now. I don't have much time left for tech. . . . There's a point at which this becomes dangerous. We'll shoot ourselves in the foot. The cast hasn't really rehearsed yet." Egloff says: "Act 1 works. Act 2 and the top of act 3 need work." The director asks that any "trims" in the play be faxed as quickly as possible.

On April 23 the cast assembles in the theater for the first tech rehearsal. I arrive at 12:30 P.M. The crew is still working on the set. The noise of machines obliterates human voices. Sound cues are being tested nonstop as figures move in a kind of surreal dance on all levels of the intricate, multilevel set, opening and closing doors, climbing stairs, removing odd nails, vacuuming sawdust. Actors peer out from the edges of the set, half-costumed. I see Marie on the uppermost level, stage left, without her pregnancy padding, slowly walking through the door to Shatov's room, sitting on the bed, rubbing her back. Kirilov stands directly below her on the stage floor, investigating the shelves in his room. A minute later Kirilov is replaced by the costume designer, who stares out into the auditorium. The props mistress walks across the stage holding out plates, bowls, and glasses for Shatov and Kirilov, now in the auditorium, to approve. Actors, designers, artistic and technical staff, and the running crew mingle and mix, flowing through the performance space; boundaries dissolve and then reconfigure.

The stage manager addresses the company, seated on the stage in makeup and full costume. After alerting the actors to particularly splinter-rich areas, he begins to conduct a formal group tour of the set, room by room. But the actors escape, exploring the spaces where their scenes will be played.[78] Dasha shuts the door to her room on the upper stage, far right, then laughs as Nicholas opens the door and walks in. Matryosha carefully takes the measure of the parts of the stage where she will appear as an apparition haunting Stavrogin.

I am startled to see actors entering rooms they will never visit in performance. The actors' tour has become a kind of carnival, a necessary prelude to the rigor of the technical rehearsal about to begin.

The director invites me to explore the unit set. Spatially smaller than it appears from the auditorium, it is a complex wooden structure with many playing areas; some belong to a single character (e.g., Shatov's room, Kirilov's room), while others are multifunctional (e.g., center stage, the apron). I count thirteen doors, four windows, and six different levels of playing area on a stage forty-eight feet wide and twenty-two feet high. The wood is salvaged lumber, chosen to decrease costs but also "because nobody could make lumber look that old that well."[79]

The playwright arrives at 1:20 P.M. She looks at the set with the costumed actors moving about it. For several seconds her face is radiant. Egloff sits in the auditorium next to Nicola, a cup of coffee in her right hand: no script, no pencil, no pad. She is, for the moment, no longer the writer writing in the presence of the actors.

The lights are dimming. The windows and the doors of the set are backlit. There is the sound of heavy machinery. Then the director stops the rehearsal. Light and sound cues are rechecked several times. The lights dim again. The set is waiting, and so are the actors; I feel a shiver of anticipation. The first scene begins and is immediately stopped by the director. This is repeated four more times. Slowly my sense of excitement is scaled back to a patient waiting and watching, a reluctant admiration for the director's willingness to consider the technical possibilities of sound and lighting as meticulously as he had explored the actors' vocal and physical choices in the rehearsal room next door.

After the first break, the stage manager mentions that there will be a sound of water dripping. The director says: "I don't recall water dripping, but let's hear it." Means replies: "It's in the script."[80] A woman's laughter is heard somewhere in the darkened auditorium. The stage manager smiles, asks quietly: "Liz? Is Liz here?" She is not, but the question hangs a moment in the theater.

In addition to other revisions, there are now more pointed references to the strike.[81] When I arrive at tech rehearsal on April 27, the stage manager hands me twelve new faxed pages of the beginning of the ballroom scene. The lights go down for act 2. I hear a tiny baby noise; in the dark it is difficult to know its location. As I glance back at the sound booth, I see Egloff sitting in the rear of the auditorium nursing William, her gaze visible even in the semi-darkened theater.

During a break, the playwright tells me that she is "very happy with all of the design." An actor interrupts our conversation: "I have a word question. In scene 4, can I change 'Well' to 'Now'?" Egloff responds: "The 'Well' doesn't work? It seems like equivocating? And you're saying that 'Now' gives more of a jump start?" "Yes. Yes," the actor replies. "Go ahead and do it," Egloff says. "That's cool. Please tell Chuck [Means]."[82] The actor adds: "I love the changes in the ballroom scene. Even on first reading yesterday."

The playwright's revisions have been arriving almost daily so far during tech rehearsal.[83] On April 29, Dimmick tells the stage manager that "more cuts have come in," that some actors have been informed and others have not, and that one actor will have to carry newly revised pages of the script with him for several days.[84] She tells me that I "cannot imagine how complicated this is."

Revisions of the text continue during previews. On May 7, the actors rehearse rewrites they receive that morning in preparation for a 7 P.M. performance. The ballroom scene has been revised again, one change in the text inviting playful, at times exuberant, experimentation with new gestures and blocking.[85] The director, who has left his copy of the script at home by accident, says he is lost without his "charts," but this is not apparent during the hour and a half he spends meticulously redirecting nine revised pages of act 2, scene 10. In less than five hours the actors will perform the ballroom scene, rewritten and reblocked.

In rehearsal of *Curse of the Starving Class*, the final line is changed at the table reading, and is performed as revised, but is not altered in the text. The final stage direction in *The Devils*, reinvented again and again during technical rehearsals and preview performances, also remains unaltered in every version of the text:

(A pistol-shot.

A trap-door in the ceiling opens up, and a body falls through. It kicks. A second trap-door in the ceiling opens up, and a second body falls through. A third trap-door opens, and a third body falls through.

The bodies are all hooded. They kick a few times, then stop. After a moment, they begin to turn slowly in the air, revolving.) (214)

On April 30, production manager Joe Levy reviews the history of rejected final stage images: "In this show we were supposed to have three bodies drop with nooses around their necks at the end. Then they became silhouettes, or dummies. Then the nooses were cut completely. Now the final three hangings are reduced to a sound effect: the sound of a taut hemp rope being stretched. From my point of view, it works better because it's less expensive and easier to do. . . . You still know what's going on."

On May 7, after four nights of previews, house manager Jonathan Pascoe tells me that he and others in the audience "couldn't tell what was going on" at the end of the play. That afternoon the director laboriously rehearses a new staging in which the revolutionaries (Shigalyov, Virginsky, and Liputin) are led across the darkened upper stage, hands bound behind their backs. We hear a low drum roll, then Blum's voice: "READY" (213), followed by the unscripted words "Aim" and "Fire." Three bodies simultaneously register death wounds. In the performance I attend on May 9, the three actors, eyes blindfolded and hands bound, neither dummies nor in silhouette, no longer "reduced to a sound effect," are executed by being shot, not hanged.

Responding to this restaging of the end of her play, Egloff says: "I think Garland came up with that final image, and he did ask for my permission. . . . When I watched what Garland had done, I was convinced that the shooting worked, in a different way from the hanging, and I haven't decided which one I prefer."

The play is "frozen" during previews, but the playwright is still writing:

There are cuts I've already made in my text that are not being used in perfor-mance because the actors couldn't deal with further cuts. This was about ten days into previews. The play was frozen two days later. Perhaps it's simpler to say that the play got frozen earlier for some actors than for others.

Asked how it feels to watch a performance of *The Devils* that does not incor-porate her ongoing revisions, Egloff replies: "Sometimes it's agony. Sometimes I detach and take a longer view." Then she says:

The text is retreating from its produced manifestation and it's becoming an ab-straction again for me, which is the way it was before rehearsal, and I am begin-ning to imagine it in other manifestations as I'm watching.

On opening night I began imagining how the ballroom scene should be and I fixed it in my head—it's in an entirely different room. It was agony to continue to watch it in this particular version.

Garland Wright, rehearsing a revised speech during previews, emphasizes that Kirilov is "furiously" writing in his notebook what he says in his mono-logue.[86] Kirilov's "voice," as he writes "*frantically in his journal*," "*as fast as he can*" (142-C, 48), ends the first two acts of the play. When, just before he kills himself in act 3, he writes for the last time, falsely confessing to the mur-ders committed by Peter Verkhovensky, his recorded voice speaks the words he writes, and "*As Kirilov writes, his voice goes on without him*" (197).

"I firmly believe," says Elizabeth Egloff, rewriting lines even as her actors speak them in rehearsal, continually "revoicing" the text she hears, "that any given production of a play is just one more step in its writing." In the end, Kirilov, setting down words that go on without him, that are voiced elsewhere, is a figure of the playwright in rehearsal, always writing for a voice that is and is not her own.

4 Suzan-Lori Parks in Rehearsal

In the Blood and *Topdog/Underdog*

My first thing is I gotta get the script right. If I can just hear the words, I can make cuts.

Just give in to the rhythm of the words.

"**I**n my opinion," Tony Kushner says in a 1994 interview, "the best playwright in the country today, and she's quite young, is a young black woman named Suzan-Lori Parks. . . . She's completely extraordinary. I'm insanely jealous of her, and I think people should see her work."[1] Suzan-Lori Parks is a two-time Obie Award–winning playwright whose plays include *The Death of the Last Black Man in the Whole Entire World, Imperceptible Mutabilities in the Third Kingdom, The America Play,* and *Venus.* Her film, *Girl 6,* was directed by Spike Lee; she has completed a second screenplay for Jodie Foster. Parks established the Harlemkids Internet Playwriting Workshop in 1996 and teaches playwriting at the Yale School of Drama. A reading of her play *Topdog/Underdog,* directed by the author, was presented at the Public Theater's New Work Now! Festival on April 24, 1999. After a series of author-directed readings, the world premiere of *In the Blood,* directed by David Esbjornson, opened the 1999–2000 season at the Public Theater in New York City, playing November 2–December 5, 1999 (extended through December 19, 1999).

"Theater," Suzan-Lori Parks writes, "is the place which best allows me to figure out how the world works. What's going on here." And she adds: "As a playwright I try to do many things: explore the form, ask questions, make a good show, tell a good story, ask more questions, take nothing for granted."[2] In the summer and fall of 1998, and the winter and spring of 1999, I watch Parks direct rehearsals for sit-down readings of *In the Blood* and *Topdog/ Underdog* in three different settings with four different casts.[3] "In principle there is no reason why a first-rate dramatist, with rich experience in theater, should not also be a first-rate director," French director Jacques Copeau has

4.1 Suzan-Lori Parks in rehearsal of *In the Blood* (photograph by Jim Gipe)

written. "For there is a stage economy that corresponds to dramatic economy, *a performing style engendered by a literary style* [emphasis mine]."[4] George C. Wolfe, the producer of the Joseph Papp Public Theater/New York Shakespeare Festival, puts it succinctly: "The rehearsal process has to do with understanding the rules of the rhythms of the language."[5]

"A reading is a first hearing," says director Liz Diamond, who has staged several of Parks's plays.

> *It lets you have a preliminary outing with the playwright during which you explore formal considerations of language, tempo, and rhythm as well as character. It's also crucial in getting a theater involved.*
>
> *I think that the presence of Suzan-Lori Parks in rehearsal results in a meticulous attention on the part of the actor to the concrete facts of the text as they appear on the page: punctuation, spelling, apparent rhythmic structure, typography—white space versus black space, that is, negative space versus filled space. She insists on a meticulous attention to the physical facts of the text, which are in fact stage directions.*[6]

"Words are spells in our mouths," Parks writes. "[F]or me, Language is a physical act. It's something which involves your entire body—not just your head. Words are spells which an actor consumes and digests—and through digesting creates a performance on stage. Each word is configured to give the actor a clue to their physical life."[7]

I arrive at the Public Theater's first-floor rehearsal room at 9:50 A.M. on June 29, 1998, for the first read-through of *In the Blood*. Jonathan Earl Peck enters a few minutes later and is handed an "updated script" by intern Joe Salvatore, who will read aloud the stage directions. The actor laughs and says: "That's what I get for doing my homework. It's about ten pages thicker." Kathleen Chalfant enters with a dog-eared script. A minute later the playwright arrives, wearing a blue-and-white patterned skirt with a slit on one side, a black tank top, and black platform sandals. "So how many more pages is it?" Peck asks her.[8]

Parks calls *In the Blood* "'the alien baby play.' It leapt out of another play and said, 'Here I am.'"[9] What leapt out is a play about a black welfare mother with five fiercely loved, fatherless children, one of whom she kills brutally, in a frenzy, at the end of the play. A month before the reading Parks tells me:

> *Right now it's like a little chamber play, showing Hester and her five children, any one of whom can double as the people in her life who are giving her hell. So it's nice for the actors to play children and adults. The oldest [female] child doubles as the Welfare Lady. The youngest child is the minister. Her second son is named Trouble who is also the doctor. . . . It's funny, but it's very sad. It's very like* Woyzeck. *. . . This play is like a series of woodcuts—nine scenes. Everybody has a Confession.*[10]

In the rehearsal room the playwright and six actors sit at a long black table piled with revised scripts, white pads, yellow Post-its, pens and pencils in a plastic cup, a water jug, paper cups, and a variety of bags filled with yogurt, bottled water, and sandwiches. After introductions, Parks says: "Any questions before we start? Anything weird?" Peck says: "You want to tell us anything?" "All I want to talk about are the 'spells,'" Parks replies. "All the characters breathe together." These spells, which appear frequently in her plays, are a typographical arrangement in which several speech tags follow each other without dialogue, for example:

ALL:
HESTER:
ALL:[11]

An actor asks: "And the 'rests' are real rests?" and the playwright replies: "Yes. And you don't say 'rest.'" The word, "(*rest*)," appears sometimes in combination with a spell and sometimes by itself, for example:

HESTER:
JABBER/BULLY/TROUBLE/BEAUTY/BABY:
(*rest*)

and then:

HESTER:
(*rest*)
All right.
(*rest*) [15].[12]

Parks's spells present a difficulty for the actors. "It's hard to do in a reading," she tells me. "No thoughts usually. It's a suspension of all thought, all stage business. Maybe an inhale and exhale. A moment of high focus and high concentration. It's not a rest."[13]

The opening line of the prologue is "wissa," repeated eight times. The authorial director does not explain the repeated word; she simply asks that it be spoken in unison by all the actors. The subsequent lines, which appear without speech tags, are delivered individually by the actors in the order in which they are seated at the table. Parks pronounces the opening word: *wis*-ah. The actors repeat it, and then continue reading at a fast clip with high energy. The playwright herself takes the double roles (Jabber and Chilli) of an absent actor.

Speech tags appear in scene 1, the pace slows down, and an actor misses his cue. Parks reassumes her directorial voice: "Let's go back to 'The letter A'." (Except for the letter A, Hester can neither read nor write.) As the actors continue, Parks becomes more visibly the playwright revising in rehearsal. While Karen Kandel reads one of Hester's long monologues, Parks studies preceding pages of her script, then looks again at the monologue. The fingers of her right (writing) hand tighten. Now she reads aloud the lines of the missing actor. She picks up her pen, holds it poised above her script, pauses, puts it down. A minute later, during another of Hester's monologues, she writes on her notepad, then again turns back to earlier pages in the script while laughing at Peck's comic timing as he reads Reverand[14] D.'s lines: "That is what they call living, friends. L-I-V-I-N, friends" (18). As he continues, Parks laughs so hard she cries. Speechless, she waves at him with her left hand after he has finished his monologue.

During the reading of scene 2, the author picks up her pen, crosses out lines on a page of the script, makes a note on her pad, crosses out more lines, and makes another note.[15] The first page of her white pad is now filled with her writing. "Authorial" and "directorial" notes appear side by side: "Doc— more expansive. Kindness will cut against the cruelty of the scene. p. 31 2 cut[s]." "Kindness" is doubly underlined, with an arrow pointing toward the word "cut."[16] As Michael Potts reads the Doctor's Confession, Parks holds her pen like a baton, point down, her fingers wrapped around it. At other times the pen seems to function as Greek worry beads, or as an object of contemplation, before again becoming an instrument of writing.

Unlike Egloff, who wrote *The Devils* entirely as free verse, Parks alternates prose and poetry in her play. The speeches marked as Confessions are written as verse, and her revisions reflect this. For example, she adds the word "once" to a four-word line in the Doctor's Confession, and then moves the previous end word to the beginning of the next line, giving each line the same strong two-beat rhythm: "We did it in/That alley there" becomes

We did it once
in that alley there (38).[17]

As Peck reads Reverand D.'s opening monologue in scene 3, Parks, utterly still except for a gradually emerging smile, stares at the text. She laughs with the rest of the cast as Peck says, "I stand atop a cornerstone!" (40). A minute later her right hand clenches; she picks up her pen and makes a note. For an instant I see her gaze into a middle distance, a space no one else enters. The actors turn the pages in their scripts; the playwright doesn't. The fingers of her right hand caress her gray pen. Suddenly the missing actor appears. Parks speaks in a mock-directorial voice: "Let's take a break. Here is James [Urbaniak]. James, here is all the people."

When rehearsal resumes, Parks gives notes as author and as director: "You're reading great. I hear things that I don't hear when I read it at home."[18] She tells the Doctor: "It's a brutal scene. But he's approaching her as if he wants to help. I think he's an expansive, friendly guy. I think you'll get more mileage out of it—I think you'll take us further—if you're kind. It's complicated." The words "kind" and "expansive" are lifted from her notes written during the read-through, but her presentation is more detailed, both actor-friendly ("you'll get more mileage out of it") and audience-sensitive ("you'll take us further"). To the other actors she says: "The impulse is good. . . . You don't have to *play* evil. You are evil."[19] To Kandel (Hester), she says: "You're tightly wound. She's just *talking* to herself." Parks makes a rapid, swishing

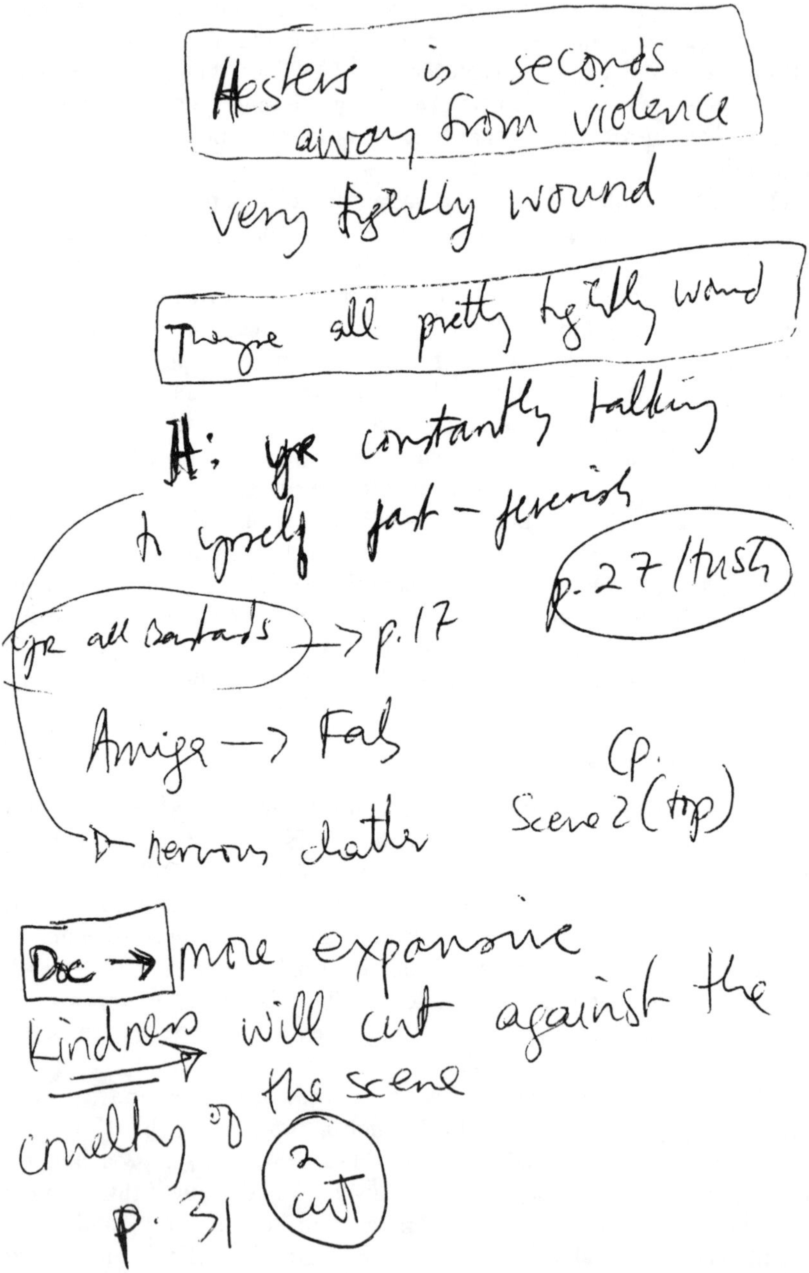

Hesters is seconds
away from violence

very tightly wound

They're all pretty tightly wound

A: yr constantly talking
h yrself fast — feverish

yr all bastards → p.17

p.27 /tush

Amiga → Fab

D nervous chatter

(p.
Scene 2 (top)

Doc → more expansive
Kindness will cut against the
the scene
cruelty of
p. 31
a
cut

4.2 Suzan-Lori Parks's rehearsal notes for *In the Blood*: "Kindness will cut against the cruelty of the scene"

sound. "It's hard to do, I know, because you're just reading." Without transition she dictates changes in the text, explaining the two cuts noted on her pad: "I gilded the lily. I tend to do that when I'm writing by myself." In rehearsal the playwright is never writing by herself.

The actors begin the play again. In the middle of the prologue, unaccountably, a dog barks somewhere in the Public Theater. The playwright looks up, slightly surprised, amused. No longer reading a part in her play, Parks sits with arms crossed over her chest, the fingers of her right hand splayed; her left hand tangles and untangles her hair. As the actors collectively page through parts of scene 1, the playwright turns pages in the opposite direction. Chalfant's Amiga Gringa begins to play directly to Kandel's Hester. The two actresses, seated next to each other, respond spontaneously to each other's rhythms and pacing as they gesture and wait for the other's gesture. At the table Hester now plays *to* Shona Tucker's Bully and her brother, Trouble; Bully plays to Hester and Trouble. Quickly, paths of energy are inscribed, and then reinscribed more confidently, as the reading continues. Parks continues to revise the script as the actors read, again lagging behind them. For example, as the actors read page 33, the playwright writes on page 31, rereads what she has written, studies previous pages, finally rejoins the actors on page 35, then turns back to an earlier page, stares at the script, and makes further revisions.[20]

After a break, Parks again gives notes. In her responses to the actors, Parks moves easily between the authorial and directorial modes. To Chalfant, she says: "Play the high status just as you're doing." The actress replies: "Good. That's a good note." To the Doctor, she says: "I cut some of your lines. The writing was over the top." She says to the cast: "The Confessions are really strange." "Shall we do them to the audience?" asks Chalfant. "Yes," Parks replies.

Rehearsal resumes. One spell in scene 7 is accompanied by two bars of music. Parks laughs and says, "Just go on." In scene 8, the following line appears: "————nnnnnnnn————"(97). Kandel asks: "What is that?" Parks makes a sound; the actress makes a sound. Their sounds mingle, become almost indistinguishable. "That's right," Parks says. "The sound is the sound of something I shouldn't have done." Hester has just killed her oldest child, Jabber. The last line in the play is: "Aaaaaaaaaaaeeeieieiehhhh!" (104); Kandel is not asked to rehearse the scream at the table.

The read-through ends at 1:45 P.M. Peck tells of a story on television about a mother whose children didn't appear at school. Finally, the two older children were found in the house, scalded to death. Chalfant jumps, shivers, utters, "Aiiii!" The six-month-old baby, says Peck, was unharmed: "Gives you a perspective on that." Parks compliments the cast: "Great job. We have the reading at 3 P.M. I know you have to take some time for yourselves. I have a few things. . . . The high-status is going fabulously. . . . It's read as an attitude but it's not an attitude for the person doing it." Interweaving directorial and authorial notes, she continues: "Needs to be as fast as you can go. . . . There's a big cut on page 46." Peck interrupts: "You're cutting.

Playwrights don't like to do that." Parks replies: "As my mother says, we're not everybody." The cast laughs. She dictates cuts and then replaces the word "squalor" with the phrase, "difficult circumstances," explaining: "I think that will give you more openness. 'Squalor' is a stingy word."[21] Tucker asks a question about Welfare Lady's reaction to Hester. Parks replies: "It's like you send your dog to obedience school and he comes back untrained. You kick your dog. You're angry." "Don't worry," she adds. "I don't have dogs." To Peck she says: "There's a way to find in the [Reverand's] Confession a lack of bullshit you have in the scene [with Hester]. It's real." She presses her hands to her chest. "It's not cartoonish. It's not about *feelings*. It's about what you're interested in. But it's very real. Imagine the real situation. Here you are, a good guy. Not a woman-hater. And that's the difficulty. . . . That's the trick. They're very real. But they're very. . . ." She makes a sharp, shrill, weird sound: "beeeeei." (Reggie Montgomery, the actor playing this role a year and a half later, is still asking troubled questions about the Confession on the last day of rehearsal.) The authorial director tells one actor, "I want more volume," and then gives a general note that she has circled on her pad:

> *Everybody, take two steps down from the Southern accent. We started in*
> *Delaware. Then we went to Virginia. At the end we were in Mississippi. [Laughter]*
> *If we're sliding down the continent, let's slide down* west, *so we end in Texas.*

Peck says: "I don't know what a Northern preacher sounds like." "If you're in Atlanta," Parks replies, "just don't go to Mississippi." Like Sam Shepard, Parks has a musical sense of language. The distinctions she makes, and hears, are precise. Every syllable, every consonant, every sound in her play counts. A few minutes later, she says to an actor, "Let me hear the 't' in 'slut,'" and then jokes, "Do they say the 't' in Atlanta?"[22]

"After he drops the club and goes inside," Parks says to an actress, "take a breath." Asked to repeat her comment, she rephrases: "You're at the end of your rope." But breath is, for Parks, an essential note. Now Kandel tries out two different versions of Hester's "nnnnnnnn," saying: "I was listening to you and got a different sense of it." "I try all this out beforehand," Parks says. "That's a suggestion at this point. Basically, you're cracked. You're open. That's what these Confessions are, for everyone. It's like as much as you want." Parks voices the 'n's' again. She dictates further cuts, some of which are retained in the revised script, and then says: "I don't know what to do about the song. I have the song in my head." The playwright has composed the lyrics and music of a song Hester's first lover sings in scene 7. Now she sings the tune for the cast and then assigns each of the song's five stanzas to a different actor.

During the break, Kathleen Chalfant tells me:

> *It's a great resource to have the playwright present because you can actually ask*
> *them what is meant instead of going through an endless process of thought trans-*
> *fer, usually inexact transfer. In the early part of the rehearsal it's wholly positive.*
> *There's a period in the middle of rehearsal when the play becomes unrecognizable*

4.3 Suzan-Lori Parks's rehearsal notes for *In the Blood*: "everybody back away from the Southern accents" *to anyone. It's deconstructed for everybody's purposes. It isn't conscious, but it happens. The actors need to do it. The director needs to take it apart and try things in different ways. For the writer it must be agony. As an actor there's a point where you're not sure you'll be able to put it back together. If the playwright is a person to whom this causes pain, it's distracting to have the playwright there because you try to fix it for them. You want to remove the anguish from their faces. You do that terrible sin of going for results. That is the only down side. And even when it doesn't cause anguish to the playwright, you have to be a little bit careful of playing to the playwright, satisfying the writer.*

Then she adds:

It's lunatic not to have the writer there when you're doing a new play because they're the only person who knows what it's about. I think the primary creator in the theater is the writer and actors are somewhere between the cello and the cello player or the horn and the horn player—because we are to make life of the text, but without the text we have nothing to do.

The playwright, who overhears Chalfant's last sentence, says to the actress: "It's the breath. You're the breath. You breathe it."

Parks continues: "I was raised as a Catholic. The pope as mediator. Now I'm going to be a little bit of a Protestant. There I am. I can talk to you directly. . . . Before it was on the page I tried it with my voice and body. Hester spends so much time crouching down emotionally, so when she opens her arms to the Reverand or her son," she says, stretching her arms out to either side, "it's completely opening up. I gotta try it all out to see where the emotions are." More than a year later, in the first read-through on September 28, 1999, as she delivers Hester's lines, "Cmmeer. Cmmeer. Mama loves you" (17), Charlayne Woodard instinctively stretches her arms out toward the actors on either side of her at the table.

In preparation for the afternoon reading on June 29, 1998, the actors' chairs are arranged in a semicircle and the table is removed. The playwright decides, with the cast's enthusiastic backing, that she will sing the song in the play. An audience of about twenty-five people gathers. Producer George C. Wolfe enters; the room grows silent. Parks says simply: "Thank you for coming. Thank you for having me here." She sits in the front row, far left, pen in hand. During the reading her attention is divided between the text and the actors; she turns pages when they do. Wolfe, wearing black slacks, an orange-red shirt, bright orange socks, and white running shoes, sits in the center of the third row, a yellow pad on his lap, watching the actors intently.

There has been only one complete rehearsal read-through of the play. The reading begins at a low level of energy. At first, there is not much audible response from the audience. Appreciative laughter greets Bully's speech in scene 1. I see Wolfe shake with silent laughter at Reverand D.'s line, "I stand atop a cornerstone!" (cut later in Esbjornson's rehearsals when the cornerstone in scene 3 becomes a soapbox). Peck also gets a big laugh from the audience as he reads Reverand D.'s monologue on "L-I-V-I-N" (cut in the first preview, November 2, 1999). The playwright's right hand presses against the right side of her face, concealing it from the audience.[23] Suddenly her left hand becomes a fist pressed against her mouth.

The reading resumes after an intermission during which Wolfe and his staff check phone and e-mail messages in their offices. Parks's right hand is clenched in her lap. The fingers of her left hand are folded gracefully over the right, as if comforting, restraining, embracing it: each hand has a life of its own. In scene 7, the playwright sings the song she composed (a country-western tune) from her seat in the front row. The actors begin to pat their thighs in rhythm, smile, and laugh. She says, "One more stanza" (unscripted line), and an actor responds, "Bring it home, Suzan-Lori." At the conclusion of her musical performance, the actors applaud loudly, and the reading continues. Peck enunciates the final consonant in "slut." Southern accents have been adjusted "two steps down." Urbaniak's Chilli is louder, as directed, and more riveting. Kandel's "nnnnnnnn" is her own—negotiated with, but not in the least imitative of, the playwright. Without having rehearsed it at the table, Kandel emits a harrowing scream at the end of the play. The audience claps loudly as do the actors, who look at the playwright. Parks says: "Thanks again for coming," and hugs each actor.

Jonathan Earl Peck (Reverand D.) was in Parks's first production, *Betting on the Dust Commander*, in the East Village:

> This is just a reading. If it were a rehearsal for a full production, it would be difficult if she were there, even as a playwright. In the first production, whatever came to me came filtered through the director, Lori Carlos. Suzan-Lori's role was just to be there and make changes, if she felt they were needed. At that point she was younger, and we were all younger. And she didn't have the kind of confidence she has now.

Like some of the actors in Egloff's *The Devils*, Peck finds revisions, especially cuts, problematic:

> In my experience it's much easier to work with dead playwrights. There will be no rewrites. . . . It's so much easier to learn something than to unlearn something, especially if it gets into your muscles. Muscle-memory, I like to call it. . . . With this [reading], you're just trying to create a picture with words.

For Kandel, however, the playwright's presence in rehearsal "made all the difference in the world."

> She was telling us what her intent was, what she heard in her head. . . . I had read the script twice before I walked in. In the reading of it, there was no way to anticipate what the spells were or what "rest" or "rest/rest" meant. . . . The words that come after the "rest" are not necessarily what you feel, but what you feel is revealed anyway. It was interesting to go back after her comments and read the script again. It feels like it's orchestrated—with all the dashes, the rests, the spells—for all of us, like music. . . . The dashes are not quite rests; they're something else.

The actress is clearly paying, in Liz Diamond's words, "meticulous attention . . . to the physical facts of the text, which are in fact stage directions." As for the playwright's voicing of Hester's "nnnnnnnn," Kandel says:

> *I don't mind line readings. I ask for them sometimes. I don't feel bound by them. I don't feel I have to reproduce what Suzan-Lori did when she made the sound, but I want to experience what she experienced. Sometimes I've got to see it or hear it and then I understand it in my body. It will come out differently because I'm a different person. She said it's the sound you make when you do something wrong, but the sound she made wasn't the sound I would make. But when she made that sound I understood it.*
>
> *Usually you get a character description and clues from what the other characters say about your character. But you don't have those same clues in her plays. It's like learning how to read another kind of play. It's like learning how to read Beckett. She's fabulous. And she's getting better. And she's scaring me.*

During a long interview on June 30, 1998, I asked Parks what she likes about directing her own work. "There's no mediator to my understanding of the play," she says.

> *I think the director can be a magnifying glass or a microscope. Or they can be the Hubble telescope. Sometimes maybe you want a microscope when you're doing* Hamlet. *Sometimes you need a magnifying glass. Or the Hubble telescope.*
>
> *I haven't directed nearly as much as I've written. My fear is that my shortcomings as a director will get in the way of the writing. But that can happen whether I direct it or not. What I want now—for this new play—is to find a director who really gets it and who isn't afraid. If I don't find that, I'll direct it myself.*

Usually, attending rehearsal of one of her plays is "not interesting" to Parks.

> *I have nothing to do. I watch, go away for a week, I come back. I may cut, revise a little. Usually just sitting there and watching them try to figure out the characters and the director's doing all the talking is not interesting. I'm not really even seeing the actors' process. The actors' process is going on inside. It's boring to me. I'd rather go home and write something else.*

But the author-directed rehearsal of *In the Blood* was "great," Parks says:

> *I got to do everything. I got to communicate the play to people. I found that I do it very well. I'm not squeamish; I'm not afraid of any of the issues; I don't have issues with the issues. I don't have any agenda except to do it.*

In the reading rehearsal of *In the Blood*, Parks directs, rewrites—and acts. "That's what I do when I write," she tells me. "I'm the actor, the writer, the director."

The playwright elaborates on her writing of *In the Blood*:

> *I used to write in longhand, then type it out, print it out, and then scribble in the margins. . . . With this it was from my head to the computer. . . . After I*

printed out the first draft, I was already writing the second draft in my head. This is the first time I've ever done this. I usually put the first draft away in a drawer for several months. . . .

I wanted two things: I wanted nine scenes, and I wanted the actors to double only once. It's like The America Play. *It was a wilderness experience. But it came out whole. But dealing with that was difficult.*

I feel as if every play I do is a different manifestation of the same experience. The experience is this: writing along, minding my own business, working hard at it, then something happens resembling a psychological crisis—a breakdown of something. Then you're at a crossroads, and you feel I will either lose my mind or write the play. It's a physical thing. It happens with every play.

She makes a sound. I ask how she would write that sound. She says, "Try 12 r's, 3 i's, 4 p's. How does that look?" I write it and say: it looks like "rip." "The horror that mitosis must feel like, if you're just a cell," she explains. "It's frightening. Everything's changing. You never know. You write the play. But you might go down the other path." "There I am," Parks says at the end of the interview, "out in the wilderness, having alien babies and looking for father and finding Lincoln" (laughing).

In the fall of 1998, Mount Holyoke College, Parks's alma mater, sponsors a "Theatre in the World" symposium that features a public reading of *In the Blood*. As if characterizing the reading rehearsals I observe, Tina Packer says in her keynote address: "You have to let the word tell you what it is."[24] At 9 A.M. on Saturday morning, October 24, 1998, Professor John Lemly, head of Mount Holyoke's Theater Arts Department, conducts Parks and several actors to the "New York Room," a rather formal academic hall with even lines of chairs, a blackboard, a podium, and a microphone. Parks asks for a rectangular wooden table and eight chairs to be placed in the center aisle, and begins rehearsal. Handing out more than a dozen revised pages, she says to the actors: "You get a new improved script." As at the Public Theater read-through, actors have studied one version of the play and receive another as they begin to rehearse.

Parks is relaxed, warm, casual, impressively organized, and articulate, despite the fact that she has the flu and is running a fever. She dictates minute revisions of punctuation—cutting a dash, for example, or replacing a comma with a period—saying to the cast: "This is like those quilts where you turn it around and there are all these little stitches." She pauses. "But it's important." As before, she comments briefly on the first line: "The 'wissa-wissa-wissa' is everybody talking together." The actors read the prologue with great vitality and expressiveness, at a rapid pace, each actor assigned a separate line by the order of the seating at table.

Wearing blue jeans, a light purple shirt, black hooded sweatshirt, and running shoes, Parks sits at the head of the table, script in lap, her left hand holding her right wrist. Occasionally she picks up her gray pen and makes a note on her script or notebook. As in the Public Theater read-through, at times she falls behind the actors' reading and turns pages rapidly to catch up. Her long, lean legs are stretched out under the table as she sits, impassive, looking down at her script, writing intermittently. The actors hit a snag, stop. Parks's calm, directorial voice restarts the reading: "Let's do that again."

Rehearsal resumes. The playwright's gaze is focused on her own writing; she makes further notes and pages ahead. Then she stops the read-through: "You all are great. There's a lot of humor in the oddity of it. There are sad moments, but there's a lot of humor." An actor asks where the play is set, and Parks replies: "Let's start in Indiana. Think of Midwest. If we start in Alabama, we'll all slide into a Southern dialect. . . . It could be anywhere." In the fall of 1999, when I ask Charlayne Woodard what accent she's going for in Hester's speeches, she says: "I'm just following the text. It changes." She quotes from memory two very different lines in a single speech: "Picture, it *comed out* pretty good. . . . and dont he look like he got everything *one could want* in life? [emphasis mine]" (30).

The actors continue to ask questions in the Mount Holyoke rehearsal. When Robbie McCauley asks, "Any thoughts on Hester?" Parks responds with a directorial note on pace, one that she will repeat: "Technically, she's quick time. . . . Like those street women in New York who are operating on no food, she's [snaps her fingers rapidly]. . . . Then later she spins out of control." Predictably, the actors request an explanation of the speech tags without dialogue. "They're called 'spells,'" Parks replies. "It's tricky in a reading. . . . It's a moment when the characters will take a breath together." An actor responds: "When you see several names together, it's not separate moments?" and Parks says: "It's more so I can keep in mind what I'm going for. It's really for performance." Lyle Denit (Doctor) asks about his character: "Is this stuff on his back a kind of street clinic or is he a loser?" "He's a street clinic loser," Parks replies. "He's a man with problems. He really needs to show some results here. He's a little more rounded out. *Well, we'll see. You're gonna read it.*" (emphasis mine). Parks refrains from detailed explanation or interpretation of character. Listening to voices, she responds to textual problems by revising the script and to acting problems by giving clear directorial notes. In a sense, she trusts the precision of her writing to direct the actors in rehearsal.[25] Robbie McCauley (Hester) says: "It's as if the writing speaks, and you give voice to it. That is the kind of writing that attracts an actor. And that's what this particular play is."

After lunch break, Parks gives notes. "Hester, quick time. You know *Jaws*? If the shark doesn't keep moving, it will die." John Hellweg asks: "With Jabber, should I energize the slowness or . . . ?" "Energize the slowness," Parks answers, without a pause. The playwright tells McCauley to keep the word "money" that the actress had spontaneously added in the morning read-through (the word appears in the September 1999 script, 21).

The read-through resumes. The playwright sits, looking at her script, writing alternately on the pages of her play and notebook. Now she places her notebook on top of the script; for a moment her rehearsal writing supplants the playtext the actors are reading. Her right hand nestles in her left hand, its fingers moving slowly as Hester reads a long monologue. As the afternoon wears on, the "quick time" slows. Parks presses the fingers holding her pen against her lips. At the table, McCauley, like Kandel, begins to deliver her speeches *to* various actors, taking her eyes off the script. The expressive movements of her hands, shoulders, and head accompany her reading. But Parks's gaze is not often on the actors. "I can hear them better when I don't look at them," she tells me. "My first thing is I gotta get the script right. If I can just hear the words, I can make cuts. I like to cut."

After a break, Parks dictates further cuts and repeats her earlier note on quick time. When an actress asks, "What am I up to?" Parks responds, as director James Houghton often did, with a question: "What do *you* think you're up to?" She makes substantial cuts in the Doctor's Confession, explaining: "Not because you didn't do it well but because it's overwritten." Giving a note to Reverand D., she says: "Breathe into every word." To the whole cast, she says: "None of these people are cardboard characters. They're all trying to figure out this world or how to make it work for them or figure out their past, like Chilli [Hester's first lover]."

The actors sit in a semicircle. The director stands in front of them, listening for the first time without her script, as they reread the prologue and epilogue. Rehearsal ends. McCauley says: "I missed the answer to the question about what to wear. Nothing?" The cast laughs. An actor says: "That's another play."

During the dinner break, Parks tells me:

> Every time I hear it, I hear something I want to cut instead of hearing something I don't understand. . . . I told the actress playing Amiga [Julie Nelson] that she's reading it like I hear it in my head. And that's happening with other actors too. So it's written so that I don't have to be around for them to figure out what I want. . . . I'm saying that there's a rhythm there—with Amiga and Chilli and Bully—that they get it on their own, for example, "Troubles doing girls work." Every time without fail the actor gets the rhythm right. And that's exciting. And they're conveying it the way I mean it, like a musician who knows how many beats there are and where the rests are.
>
> It's not [a question of being] an over-controlling playwright. If you just give in to the rhythm of the words, it's exciting; it's not boring. And the creativity of the actor comes from other things. They fill it out, they connect with it emotionally—if they're not fighting the language, if they give in to it. Because the language isn't fighting them. It's not there to trip them up. It's a wonderful ride.

I ask Parks if *In the Blood* is different from her other plays. "Yes," she says, "I'm a different playwright. I knew I was a different playwright after I wrote *Venus*."

> I feel as if I've combined a kind of poetic rhythmic swirl with really solid characters and story. It's unflinching. That happens in the Confessions, the language in them. I think this play is better. All the things I've been doing are in this play: the

character-doubling, the joy in the theatrical event. It's not just an issue play. The joy in the theatricality of the thing. The joy in the language. And the compassion-ate, caring characters who are trying to understand something. They're trying to figure out their relationship to Hester and to themselves. . . . It's difficult. The characters do bad things but they're not completely bad people.

At 8:30 P.M., Parks stands on the stage of Rooke Theatre introducing *In the Blood.* "We'll take questions afterwards. We don't promise answers." Without script, notebook, or pen, she sits next to me in the last row. At times she listens with eyes closed. After a while volume and energy levels drop; the pace drags. What was hauntingly moving as a chamber piece in a small room is losing life in the theater. During the intermission Parks gives a note on pace. When the reading resumes, "quick time" returns and energy levels rise. The actors seem more rooted in their roles; Hester's final scream, rehearsed at the table, is deeper, even more piercing.

During the "talkback" with playwright and cast, Parks says: "This is the first [reading] . . . in a theater. There were a lot of laughs. . . . It's a comedy! But it's difficult, because people laugh a lot and then they get mad at *me.*" The audience laughs. Rochelle Calhoun (Welfare Lady/Bully) says: "For me the rhythm is so strong in your language. You really have to get into the rhythm of the language," and Parks replies: "You all weren't resisting the rhythm. You were playing with the rhythm rather than against it."

"When I opened the script I realized I was home," Robbie McCauley, an Obie Award–winning visiting artist at Mount Holyoke College, says. "It speaks to me as an actor." She alludes to her work with director Joseph Chaikin on Adrienne Kennedy's plays: "You do it and you're there."

The best note that I got from Suzan-Lori seems simple, and she was so right about it, was pacing, and that had to do with my character. And that was my intermission note: make sure you keep that "quick time." . . . A reading is a strange animal to me. . . . Finally, what you're doing is using what you know as an actor to transmit the play while holding the script.

"The one thing I must have," McCauley adds, "is that the content of the work . . . transmits some possibility for transformation."[26]

"She listened and we listened," John Hellweg (Chilli/Jabber)[27] says of the authorial director.

She didn't seem to be waiting for a correct reading. . . . Her responses helped us to catch the spirit of a line or a scene, to gauge the style of the play.

But it wasn't that her responses were leading us. In fact, they gave a kind of latitude, encouraging us to experiment and to open up to the unexpected, to unanticipated possibilities in a scene. . . . As we continued to work, we began to hear and feel the poetry in the play, how words and images would resonate as they were sounded at different points in the play. We would dampen those reso-nances, lose the rhythm, every time we weren't really listening. Or if we were pushing for emotional weight. So we had to listen for nuances, sense the transi-

tions and be ready to catch the shifts of direction in the play. Scenes could swerve from being very funny to brutal . . . within the space of a few lines. . . . The inflections, the rhythms, the pacing are precisely calibrated to communicate the spirit, the sensation of what is haunting, what is driving these characters [emphasis mine].

The following winter and spring Parks directed two readings of *Topdog/ Underdog*, a new two-character play[28] about brothers: Booth, the underdog, a shoplifter who changes his name to 3-Card Monty, and his older brother, Lincoln, the topdog, an ex-cardshark who, like the Foundling Father in *The America Play*,[29] has a job impersonating Abraham Lincoln.

As with *In the Blood*, a little play is leaping out of a big play, but Parks's metaphor has changed: "It was underneath that play for years. *The America Play* was working on, writing, *Topdog/Underdog*."[30] *Topdog* is "about personal history, and family history, and about this overriding history that they can't escape," Parks tells me. "Their history catches up with them. Lincoln quits playing 3-Card Monty. Booth changes his name. And the cards are their death."[31]

On March 4, 1999, Parks directed a reading of *Topdog* with Chad L. Coleman (Lincoln) and Michael Potts (Booth) in the Public Theater's rehearsal room. Later, on April 24, 1999, the play was presented in a reading at the Public's Anspacher Theater with Ruben Santiago-Hudson (Lincoln) and Jeffrey Wright (Booth). Parks's notes to the actors in her rehearsals of *Topdog/Underdog* recall those she gave during rehearsals for readings of *In the Blood* in their attention to pace, punctuation, line delivery, spells, and rests.

Parks's suggestive comment in rehearsal on March 4, 1999, "Lincoln is a Great Dane; Booth is a terrier," produces a change of pace, like her repeated note on "quick time" in rehearsal of *In the Blood*. Booth's delivery of his lines is rapid, rhythmic, like jazz riffs; Lincoln's is slower, more deliberate, with more pauses. A later comment to Coleman, "You're doing the 'high-status' thing—that's what I call the Great Dane—beautifully," recalls Parks's note on "high status" to Kathleen Chalfant.

Wearing elegant black pants, a black long-sleeved sweater, and a black jacket, Parks sits at the table in the rehearsal room at the Public Theater, revising the script of *Topdog* as the actors read, cutting and making minute alterations in punctuation—adding a period, inserting an exclamation mark. The playwright's idiosyncratic punctuation again functions as a director of voice and pace. For example, one speech in *Topdog* is enclosed by three parentheses, another by six.[32] Parks explains to the actor: "These triple parens are like . . . whispering." She reads the lines aloud in a fast-paced, chugging rhythm:

(((Watch me close watch me close now: Who see thuh red card who see thuh red card? . . . Cop C, Stick, Cop C! Go on—))). (9)

Later in rehearsal Potts reads these lines in a jagged, rapid whisper, as directed; Parks smiles. She continues to give specific notes on voicing. For example, she tells Coleman: "That's a change of tone," and asks Potts to emphasize the verb in his line, "Who are they mostly?" (35). She asks an actor to deliver a line enclosed within double parentheses more softly, adding: "Don't rush that word." To intern Keira Fromm, she says: "Just don't rush the stage directions. Just be friendly to them."

On April 24, Parks gives this note to Jeffrey Wright: "It's rhythmic but it's klunky. It's *not* arhythmic." She stands near him on the stage of the Anspacher Theater and makes fists, plunging her arms upward and forward, and then back in toward her body. Parks also "performs" her reading of her text in a note to Coleman's Lincoln: "You're struggling. You don't want to hustle your brother, you don't want to take his money, you don't want to take his inheritance. . . . So there's a rope pulling you from the back of your pants and you're digging your heels in against that." She stands up and presses her heels into the floor as if to resist being pulled backward by an invisible rope.

As she did with Kandel's Hester, Parks anticipates the familiar question of whom a character addresses. "You're talking to yourself," she says softly to Coleman's Lincoln. "This is a horrible place you're in," she says to Potts's Booth. "It's a chasm. . . . I don't know if the stage direction [*"in a state of extreme agitation mixed with a strange calm*," later cut][33] helps you." In rehearsal Parks replaces a straightforward authorial stage direction with a directorial metaphor ("a chasm"). She also talks about subtext metaphorically: "There's an undercurrent that turns into an undertow." Later, in an elegantly phrased note, she refers to "the unaddressed reality underneath."[34] In response, Potts (Booth) makes a physical gesture, as if twisting a knife pointed at Lincoln across the table. "Yes, Michael," Parks responds. "That's what's happening in the scene."

In contrast with *In the Blood* rehearsals, here at times Parks's notes are gently or firmly resisted. For example, after a lengthy discussion with the playwright, Coleman (Lincoln) says: "It seems like something more is at stake. . . ." "It's 2 A.M.," Parks says. "You lost your job at 10 in the morning. You've been walking around since 10 A.M. You just want to come home and sit down. I think that's a lot to play. If you play more, it's going to get obscured." She adds: "You're so incredibly depressed because you just lost your job." Her directorial note echoes the stage direction in the script: "*LINCOLN comes in. . . . He is very depressed. He sits in his recliner chair not noticing anything*" (43). In rehearsal for the later (April 24) staged reading, Ruben Santiago-Hudson also resists one of Parks's notes on Lincoln: "But it's more than that. It's deeper than that. It's more complex." Again the actor wants to play more; the authorial director asks him to play less.

Jeffrey Wright asks a familiar question with precision: "I have a question about this piece and your writing. You leave space for 'rests,' for 'spells.' And the implication is that there's a musicality to it and that there's no rest where it's not written as a rest or spell." "Right," says Parks. "It's like that [she snaps her fingers quickly]." As before, Parks pays meticulous attention to spells and rests, cutting and revising them. For example, in the March 4 rehearsal she cuts a spell, saying: "You can write in a 'rest' there. There's almost no moment. There's a very brief moment." "A spell is a bigger moment than a rest," Parks tells me the next day. "It's like a major chord with left hand and right hand, like a chord played on an organ." The playwright's sense of the nature and necessity of rests and spells is unerring, yet others question it.

"This is a sensitive area," Santiago-Hudson says:

> [Your] being the writer and also the director is a little difficult. Another director might see where we're coming from. Certain places where you have a "rest" I don't feel a "rest." I'm in a box. You wrote a "rest" which is actually correct because you wrote it. But I don't hear it. It's like I'm hearing another symphony. So I'm in a box. But I don't want to miss your level because your level is important.[35]

Parks responds: "I do this a lot—directing my own plays. It's a good point. Maybe there's not a rest there. . . . But we're rushing along here. You guys are so good that you're bringing a lot of complexity to it." "After rehearsal yesterday," the actor says, "I looked over one speech and read it aloud differently, without looking at your notes. Then I looked at your notes and they were the same as what I had done. Maybe we're on the same psychic rhythm . . . or maybe I remembered what you said in rehearsal."

The playwright-director knows the text both ways: as a complicated, subtle creation of her own dramatic imagination and as a theatrical script that energizes actors accustomed to taking their impulses off a text mediated by a director. When the mediation is conducted by the author-acting-as-director, what I call "authorizing energy" is complicated for the actor. And the more "directorial" the writer becomes as she takes impulses off the text-as-script-under-revision-in-rehearsal, the more her "reading" of her own play risks becoming as fluid as the actors' explorations that are confirmed, overridden, or abandoned on the way to performance.

What happens to the author-director relationship when a new director enters the rehearsal process?

In late September of 1999, rehearsals of *In the Blood*, directed by David Esbjornson,[36] begin at the Public Theater with the playwright in attendance. The play is publicized, and described in the theater program, as a "modern-day riff" on *The Scarlet Letter*. Unlike the nineteenth-century novel that inspired Egloff's *The Devils*, Nathaniel Hawthorne's *The Scarlet Letter* is neither present nor alluded to in rehearsals of *In the Blood*. Parks tells me that the novel "was just a springboard: a woman and an A." "People are going to be looking for connections," Parks says, on September 18, 1999, "and aren't going to see them. There's nothing there." She observes that Reverand D. keeps making speeches (like Hawthorne's Dimmesdale), and Chilli comes back (like Chillingsworth) and her Hester sews, or tries to (like Hester Prynne), and her last scene even bears the title of Hawthorne's first chapter ("The Prison-Door")—but *In the Blood*, she says, "is more like *Mother Courage* or *Woyzeck* than *The Scarlet Letter*."

David Esbjornson, who headed Classic Stage Company in New York from 1992 to 1998, is an Obie Award–winning director. He staged the American premiere of Tony Kushner's *Angels in America* and, more recently, Maria Irene Fornes's *Mud* and *Drowning* at Signature Theatre.

In the Public Theater's rehearsal hall on September 28, 1999, sixty people gather. The room seems to expand. Tables heaped with bagels, fruit, cheese, coffee, and juice are pushed against the walls. George C. Wolfe enters and asks all those present to form a circle and introduce themselves. Esbjornson says: "Director of *In the Blood*, this week." Before the laughter subsides, Wolfe says, "And you'd better watch it." Wolfe welcomes "Ms. Parks" and her "brilliant play."

That afternoon at the table, before the first read-through, Parks announces a textual revision. Like Sam Shepard at the reading rehearsal of *Curse of the Starving Class*, Parks changes the last line of the play. Hester's scream is cut. In its place Parks dictates, without explanation, a new final line: "Big hand coming down on me," uttered three times.[37] "How do we do this?" an actor asks of the opening "wissa's." "It's all whispering," Parks replies. The director's voice enters the rehearsal: "Let's just explore it together." The playwright asks: "Should we talk about the spells first?"

In the reading rehearsals she directed, the author herself explained the spells in her play. Now the director steps in, and the writer is silent. "They're heightened emotional moments," Esbjornson says. "Something that stops the characters in place. They go through it before moving on. It doesn't necessarily relate to the words. It's not always the same thing. It's a thought, a memory, an impression." He gives, as an example, suddenly seeing an ex-boyfriend on the street, having an unvoiced reaction, and then saying, "Oh, hello." There are murmurs of comprehension. He continues: "It has a little more dimension than a beat. Just acknowledge that they're there by just stopping today. It's hard to do in a reading. . . . 'Rests' you should treat as more potent pauses."

The read-through begins. The playwright, wearing a black skirt and black T-shirt, sits between the director and dramaturg John Dias. Her eyes focus alternately on her script and the actors exploring the rhythms and intonations of their dual roles as adults and children. She makes notes on both her pad and script. The director, wearing black pants and a black-and-gray long-sleeved shirt over a black T-shirt, makes notes rarely as he listens and watches, occasionally whispering to Parks on his left. From a distance, seated at the far end of the table, I see the playwright make proofreader's marks for cuts on her script. The actors scrupulously observe rests and spells, as directed.

When rehearsal resumes after a break, Reggie Montgomery (Reverand D.) says, after an explicit sexual episode: "Oh, my momma can't come see this show." The cast cracks up. During the astonishing first reading of the scene between Charlayne Woodard's Hester and Rob Campbell's Chilli, I see the playwright's lips form the words, "It's perfect." Parks now sings the song she composed for the play, its title, lyrics, and tune revised. ("The Wedding Song" becomes "The Looking Song.") "The tune last year was faster," Parks tells the cast. "Now it's a slower Hank Williams thing." As the reading continues, I watch everyone's lines land on the expressive face of Deirdre O'Connell (Amiga). As she reads Hester's last monologue (later cut), Woodard is quietly crying; O'Connell, head down, fingers over forehead, cries soundlessly.

The read-through ends; the company applauds. During the break, Woodard says to the playwright: "Good words." Parks replies: "You're not just reading them. You're *workin'* them." When rehearsal resumes, the director says: "It's very exciting. And you're all terrific. It's an interesting situation, hearing all of you read it for the first time. What I'd like is to have the evening to assimilate it."[38] He asks stage manager Kristen Harris to schedule a forty-five-minute session for him with each actor at the beginning of the next day's rehearsal, to be followed by a group discussion at the table.

Nine months earlier, Parks told me that she wanted "to sit in on a production [of *In the Blood*] with a director, not just to see the production but to watch the director at work," later adding as a caveat: "The production shouldn't do a number on the play. . . . Any elements that are added—like light and sound—should bring out and not cover up the play. I'm not looking for distance to be created between the play and the audience."[39]

In a new author's note on the title page of the revised script, Parks has written: "*The setting should be spare, to reflect the poverty of the world of the play.*" In consultation with set designer Narelle Sissons, the director has decided on a gray cement set,[40] placed between two raised platforms of spectators. At one end is the door to Hester's home underneath a bridge; at the other is the site of what will be Reverand D.'s "new pre-fab church" (87). "We've gone in a different direction with the set—revised it, designed it, and got it approved in three days," Esbjornson says. "It's not conventional, not proscenium. . . . The environment will be urban, harsh." Esbjornson tells the cast that he "would like to develop all the internal scenic elements *with* you . . . [and] find an organic way to create that environment in the next few weeks."

The following afternoon the director continues his presentation of design choices. He speaks of "the unforgiving relation between concrete and human beings."

> *So the concrete floor means all sorts of things, including noise. The set will have a voice. It's winter. It's cold. People will huddle differently, put cardboard down on concrete [murmurs of interest from the cast]. It's also a transitory culture. And in that world we're also trying to find an interesting specificity that is not cliché but also finding what is* true. *So it's an interesting fine line. . . . The scenic elements are related to the characters in the play.*

In certain design choices the director at first seems to create the distance Parks is "not looking for." He tells the cast:

> *We're going to try to put a barrier in between you and the audience to create a kind of formality that is sort of like a jury box. When the audience is watching things that are unsavory or difficult or Jerry Springerish, the audience can be*

watching the audience responding, watching the public judgment. We're doubling the amount of platform, making the audience section steeper, so that the audience gaze is down. . . . *We may mike some speeches softly.*

The playwright speaks for the first time during today's rehearsal: "But only for the Confessions." "Or lighting may accompany that," Esbjornson says, "or the space pulls down, or becomes more distant in relation to that audio shift." O'Connell says: "The play is obviously about how much this culture hates Hester. And if we distance ourselves too much, the audience will, too. . . . We have to make the audience feel and know, 'When I react to Hester that way, like the Doctor and the Welfare [Lady], and the Reverand, I am *wrong*.'" The playwright smiles, and nods appreciatively at the last sentence. Reggie Montgomery (Reverand D.) talks about how people in New York City walk "way out of their way" to avoid coming near people like Hester living on the street. "I think everyone should practice their audience skills," the director says. "Here I am voyeuristically watching . . . and then the actor [delivering the Confession] turns to me and addresses me directly."

In the midst of discussion of design and staging choices, the director proposes a textual revision. In scene 4, Hester visits the welfare office; Chilli, her first lover, walks by the window, seen only by Hester. Esbjornson speaks to Gail Grate [Welfare Lady] about "an adjustment in your scene so you go out and make a visit to Hester's world. . . . There may be one piece of furniture the kids bring out, for example, their best chair. . . . And you may be using Handiwipes." This is, of course, not merely "an adjustment" in one character's scene. Who visits whom, what it means for the Welfare Lady to be making a home visit, and the staging of Chilli's appearance are matters of some importance to the play as a whole. Later, the playwright says to the director: "I think you're bringing a staging idea to the scene which is actually a new interpretation of the scene. And I like it."[41]

In rehearsal Esbjornson raises a troubling question: "The issue for me at the moment is the church: does the Reverand make it himself in the middle of the night?" Parks remains silent. After the actors leave, she tells Esbjornson: "I'm afraid of the reading of the Reverand as a charlatan. He believes what he says. . . . I don't want him to seem just a homeless guy. . . . I just want it to appear that they actually gave him a Bible, the cross—something fancy."[42]

During a break, I ask the playwright why she changed the final line to "Big hand coming down on me." "It articulates the action better," she says. "It's not only the hand of fate, but [Hester] realizes that the hand of fate is her own." As she says this, she raises her hand above her head and looks at it as it curves back toward her face. Later in rehearsal, Parks, alluding to Hester's line "My life's my own fault. I know that" (54), says to Woodard, "You know that." The actress nods in agreement as the text is quoted by the author in support of a reading of the text. The director is cautious: "We have to be careful about saying, 'It's your own fault,' but I know what you're saying." Parks repeats her earlier gesture. As she gazes at her upstretched hand circling back close to her face, the playwright says: "I'm just trying this out. [Hester] keeps seeing things." The playwright's gesture deconstructs the apocalyptic image: she makes us, and Hester, see the hand of the visionary *in* the vision.

Asked by the director to talk about her play, Parks tells the company:

> *The thing that was a surprise was the Confessions. Sometimes you're* writing, *and sometimes things just come out. I didn't know what these Confessions were dramaturgically. But that's not my department. I don't have to. [Laughter] Then came these "things"—these little "knobs"—the Confessions. There's a horizontal action and there's a vertical action—the Confessions. And I'm thinking about how the Confessions* feed *the horizontal action.*

Joking that dramaturgy is not her department, she becomes, for the moment, her own best dramaturg. The director responds with appreciative interest: "I've got to think about that—the vertical action. I can do that. Gotcha. I knew I'd learn something." The playwright, in sharing what was a "surprise" and a puzzle in her play, articulates for the director its deeper structure.

Esbjornson asks: "Am I right, Suzan-Lori, that [the whispered lines] represent the general public, not the characters in the play?" "Whichever you like," the playwright says. Dramaturg John Dias says: "Some of the lines sound like individual characters." "Right," says Parks. "And some don't."

After the actors leave, Parks says to Esbjornson: "I don't want to get into rewriting in general." Then she adds: "I don't mind cutting."

On September 30, O'Connell, currently performing in Irene Fornes's *Mud*, is not present at rehearsal. The playwright is asked to read the dual roles of the missing actress. For over an hour the director rehearses the four-and-a-half-page prologue, suggesting various exercises in which both playwright and dramaturg take part. The actors whisper the "wissa's" quietly whenever they are not delivering lines; they slow down, then increase the pace; they provide whispered echoes of each other's lines. At one point Parks says: "It's difficult," and the director, responding to her as he would to a member of the cast, says: "We won't get it right at first." Esbjornson asks Parks to move to a seat nearer certain actors at the table. The seat formerly occupied by the playwright at the far end of the table remains empty; at the other end, the director sits, flanked by actors reading aloud. Suddenly Parks says: "I have to add a word." Reassuming her authorial voice, she dictates the word, "HO," added to the prologue between the lines, "BURDEN TO SOCIETY" and "HUSSY" (4). When the prologue is read again, the new line falls to Parks, who fails to deliver the word she has just added. The cast dissolves in laughter.

The dramaturg asks if the lines can be read less rapidly. The director replies: "Let's begin rather slowly and then if we're feeling confident [laughter], we can begin to go faster," adding: "Suzan-Lori, you're not allowed to make that decision." There is more laughter, but Esbjornson's joke is a serious reminder that Parks is no longer the authorial director of the voicing of her text. A few minutes later, the reading breaks off. An actor says, "We failed miserably." Others agree, including the director. "Really?" Parks asks. "It *sounded* good." The playwright is not merely "sit[ting] in on a production"; she is temporarily "inside" the reading, reliant on the director's "third ear" as she joins the actors voicing her text in rehearsal.

Giving a note on the prologue, the director says: "I don't want it to be too hip; it's already stylized. There's something nasty and haunting, mocking, about these little whispers." After the next whispered repetition of each line, Dias says: "It's interesting. It's both a haunting reverberation of the whole world and also little kids repeating what you said." The playwright's whispered response, "Right. It's both . . . ," is greeted with delighted laughter.

After the break, the actors begin reading scene 1. The director asks Parks if "part of Hester's speech to Jabber could be to the audience." In the playwright's reply, there is an almost imperceptible shift from an authorial to a directorial note: "I think she's talking to herself. She does that a lot. . . . The Confessions are not within the play. These things she says here are within the play." On the other hand, when an actress gives a line two different readings, and the director asks the playwright which she prefers, she replies: "I actually like both choices." Discussing the implications of the line with the dramaturg during the break, Parks says: "I'm listening. I like it both ways." To Grate and Woodard, she says: "It's actually more interesting to watch you *do* it. It's much better than I could ever articulate what it means."[43]

As the playwright reads aloud the lines of Beauty, Hester's seven-year-old daughter, in a lovely, soft, low voice, the other actors smile in appreciation.[44] Esbjornson is directing a beat-by-beat "reading work-through" at table. After three and a half hours, the actors have read seven pages of scene 1. They are smashing cans, cooking soup, running about panting, all without leaving the table. The director now adds unscripted sound. For example, he asks the playwright: "Do you mind if [the children] have a reaction to 'Bedtime'?" "No," Parks replies. In the next reading, the actors playing children voice their protestations.

Questions at the table are usually addressed to Esbjornson[45] who at times redirects them to the playwright. For example, Grate says, facing the director: "Question. Is this the first time we've heard this bedtime story?" "Don't you think it's the story they want to hear again?" Esbjornson asks Parks. "Right," she replies. "It's funny. The joy is even *more* intense if they've heard it before." Esbjornson adds a directorial note: "It can be *just as fresh* as if you've heard it for the first time." At other times, the playwright herself responds to questions addressed to the director. For example, Esbjornson interrupts the reading: "The 'Where are you?' is in quotes." "So go there?" Woodard asks him. "You could sing it if you like," Parks says.

Sometimes voices overlap but remain distinct. There is intense discussion of the imagery in Hester's monologue: "Bugs in my skin. Theyre gonna eat me up first. So when I go wont be nothing left" (18). Esbjornson asks Parks if "there are bugs in her skin now." Parks mentions "fleas, any kind of parasite," as Woodard says simultaneously: "When I say I have bugs in my skin, I'm referring to my bad feeling." The director says: "The strongest imagery for me is that when a person dies, maggots start to grow and eventually there's nothing left. . . . It's a flip of your own hunger. They eat you." (The monologue continues to give trouble and is cut on the last day of rehearsal.)

When the six-hour table reading ends at 5 P.M., the actors are still three pages from the end of scene 1. The playwright tells me that she needs to be unobserved for the next few weeks: "I want privacy as I explore the 'me's' around the table. All these actors are somehow embodying characters that are an aspect of me." "I don't know how to write 'me's,'" she adds, glancing at my notebook. "It's all right," I say. "I do." I have been watching her me's with not a little awe for a long time.

When I return to rehearsal a few weeks later, on October 19, the cast is performing off book for the first time. The playing area marked on the floor is on a diagonal to the director's table. Next door there is already a gray concrete floor on the stage of the Shiva Theater. The playwright, wearing black jeans, a purple sweater, and black sweatshirt, arrives with a draft of her new play, *Fucking A*. Before rehearsal begins, Esbjornson and Parks agree to cut one and a half pages of the prologue. "Cut the spell too?" the director asks. "Yes," Parks replies. "There's been no build for it."

Woodard, standing center stage, whispers "wissa" repeatedly while the other actors walk about her, delivering lines of the newly cut prologue. An actor misses his cue. Woodard asks: "Are the whispers sotto voce or full voice?" "Full voice," the director replies. "Let's try something. Everybody whisper the 'wissa's' together and then drop out after you deliver your first line." The actors are continuing to explore the voicing of the first few pages of the play.[46] It is almost as if I had never left.

Parks suggests further cuts in the prologue. The new revisions are dictated to the actors, with no explanation, as before. The director jokes, "We're just going to keep cutting until you get it right."[47] The prologue is rehearsed over and over. There is much laughter—at times, the high spirits of nervous tension—as cues are missed. The playwright, listening, suddenly says: "I don't think we need a 'HAH!' before they spit. It *crowds* it." Esbjornson says: "Okay. You want to try it?" "It's minor. We can go on," Parks replies. But no change is minor in a text this closely woven: a monosyllabic sound can be de trop. Parks suggests a further cut. This time Esbjornson demurs, saying that the actors need those lines to "build" the prologue. The writer's sense of what the text needs is in conflict with the director's sense of what the actors need.

Astonishing as it may seem, at times during rehearsal the playwright is working on the script of the unfinished parent play, *Fucking A*, as she listens to the lines of *In the Blood*. The quick pace of the reading at table has given way to a much slower playing of beats and realistic staging of physical action. There are many pauses between lines. The actors inadvertently omit, add, or rephrase lines in the script. Occasionally, Parks gives a note to the director on a missed or wrong word. Like verse, the lines in her plays yearn to be delivered precisely as written if they are to be heard as intended.[48]

At times Parks's notes walk the line between the authorial and directorial. When Woodard seems to question a particular staging of Hester's frustration, Parks suggests a different motivation: "It comes more from your inability to make the letter 'A'. . . ." Esbjornson agrees and redirects the scene. Later the playwright suggests certain unscripted props—a pill box for Amiga, for example, and a "square piece of cloth, the size of a dishrag," which Baby puts in his mouth. These props are tried out in rehearsal and retained in performance. Parks's notes to actors, like her plays, offer complicated perspectives. Moving her hand in a swirly way, she says to Woodard: "It's a little tricky. You have some tricks." The actress smiles and immediately replays the scene more knowingly.

If Parks gives notes with directorial implications, Esbjornson suggests cuts, redefines the setting of a scene, and adds stage actions that potentially alter the style and rhythm of the play. During a break the director suggests moving Hester's Confession from the end of scene 8 to the end of the final scene. Two days later he announces the anticipated change to the actors: "I'm thinking of reversing the jail scene and Hester's Confession, and Suzan-Lori is cool with this." Woodard responds: "I think [the Confession] won't make sense unless it comes right *after* what I did [she has just murdered her son]." Esbjornson says: "We'll see." The actors question the director when he is "playwriting"; rarely do they openly challenge or resist an authorial revision in the presence of the playwright.

That afternoon, Parks and Esbjornson discuss cutting scene 9 almost entirely, transferring a handful of lines to the epilogue. Hester's Confession would be closer to the end of the play but follow the killing of her child. The director says to Parks: "I'm concerned that maybe you're making a decision that you're not sure of." The playwright replies: "We could change it later." It is hard to tell whether this is a comforting thought.

Esbjornson says to the cast: "We're going to put some of scene 9 into the epilogue. Then if we're successful, we'll cut scene 9." Parks begins to dictate lines to be inserted in the epilogue. An actor suddenly interjects: "I have an idea," suggesting that one scene become an undertext for the other. The director says: "The problem is purely logistics." The author says: "The question for me is what works for the play. Several things could work for the play. This one [the revision she is dictating] works well. . . . What we do with the epilogue is *frame* the play so it's not just a story about Hester. It's much *larger*." "So we'll try it out and see," the director adds. Esbjornson now proposes cutting only the first eight lines of scene 9, and leaving the epilogue unchanged. "Want to try it? Both ways?" he asks Parks. "I can't do it now. I've done it this way. I have to leave. I'll be back in forty-five minutes," she replies and is gone.

The playwright's willingness to make revisions in rehearsal seems to elicit a sense of possible collaborative reauthoring: the writer's sole ownership of the text *itself* undergoes revision, a process temporarily interrupted when the writer leaves the room.

The cast reads the new ending as first proposed. "Neat as a pin," the director says. "I feel a little responsible," he tells the cast, "for pushing Suzan-Lori into cutting this scene. She said she's okay with it, but she's not really going to know until we start doing it. I appreciate everyone's input, but we're not going to know until it's on its feet." After a break, Esbjornson rehearses the second version of the revised ending. The playwright is still absent. The director makes a textual change, adding a repetition of a previous line and stage direction ("HAH!" *THEY spit*, 103) to the end of the epilogue. He then gives a strong note on Hester's Confession, asking the actress to "shift the blame to the audience." In the rehearsals that follow, Woodard delivers her Confession to the audience with mounting, explosive anger.[49]

When the playwright returns, an actor says: "You really had a big interview? We thought you were mad." "Honey, when I'm mad, I'm scary," Parks replies. The director says: "We added a spit and a 'Hah!'" "Add as many spits and 'Hahs!' as you want," Parks responds. The first version of the revised ending is run again. Parks says: "I like it going from Hester's Confession to the epilogue. What do you think?" The director says: "I'm concerned that you're getting ripped off on something you want to hear." "We cut scene 9 a lot already. Now we've cut it to the essentials," Parks replies. "Do we need the *whole* epilogue?" the director asks. After cutting more lines, including the spit and "Hah!" added by the director, Parks says to Esbjornson: "We're not cutting after this. Freeze it. From *now on*, it's your fault." The cast laughs. Parks dictates the new cuts to the actors who then read aloud the once again revised ending. "No more cutting," the playwright says to the actors. "I think we're pretty close to having a production script that will be intact," the director says. There has not yet been a full run-through of the play.

Rehearsing her "Bugs in my skin" monologue the following day, Woodard remarks: "I don't know what I'm saying here." "And that's a problem?" the director asks, laughing. He redirects her question: "Suzan-Lori is in the room. Let's ask her." On its feet, Hester's monologue needs to be entered again like a new country. "You're sort of telling a story but you're talking to yourself," Parks says. Standing close to the actress in the playing area, the playwright says, in between the lines: "It's irrational." Standing on the other side of the actress, the director says: "And it's pride."

The first run begins at 12:30 P.M. on the next to last day of rehearsal. The actors are wearing parts of their performance costumes: baggy jeans, an oversized flowered child's dress, thick glasses, a doctor's jacket. During the run Parks's gaze shifts from the actors to the gathering pages of notes she writes on a small white pad—a sign of what is to come.

The run-through takes well over three hours. "There's double beating, thinking between the lines, trying to remember the lines," Esbjornson says to Parks while the actors chat on the other side of the room. There is an intense private discussion of pace and possible textual revision. Afterward, while the director gives brief notes to the cast over a shared pizza, the playwright sits apart, revising the script in the presence of the dramaturg and associate producer. Later she speaks inaudibly to Esbjornson. "It sounds brutal," the director tells the cast, "but I'm going to have to say: 'You can do that faster. You can say that faster.' . . . We are going to have to pace it better so we can feel better about it." The playwright is silent. Rehearsal ends.

Exempt from the to-be-quickened pace are the Confessions, as directed, and the spells, as scripted. "With the Confessions," the director tells the actors, "it's as if the play stops and then picks up again. . . . You have to stop 'acting' and just start talking." Like soliloquies, in which an actor alone on stage voices unspoken thoughts or feelings in the presence of the audience, Parks's Confessions are literally confessional. As Esbjornson says, "In these Confessions no one is ever conning us." The Confession is that familiar paradox in the theater: a private moment conducted in public, during which an actor speaks in the rhythms of carefully scripted language but is somehow just "talking" to the audience. "It's difficult," O'Connell says to the director, "because there's still a *style* there in the language." For actor Bruce MacVittie, the Confessions are what is "most impressive about this text. . . . They live separately as poetry as well as being actable theater."

The spells are as difficult to get right as the Confessions—and as problematic as they were during the reading rehearsals. Esbjornson directs them as "freezes with eye contact." In a rehearsal directed by Robert Wilson, these would be pre-calibrated to the millisecond.[50] Here the duration and, at times, the placement of the spells are negotiated with the actors.[51] Grate says:

> *I can do a spell without movement, if that's what the director wants, but I still have my emotional change: the moment is still alive for me. . . . I always considered spells to be moments of connection between . . . actors. If it's a spell of just one character, something unspoken happens to the character emotionally, subtextually. . . . The nature and length of the spells are determined by what's going on between the actors before and after the spells.*

Rob Campbell, whose sheer bodily stillness in rehearsal at times makes Chilli's spells uncanny, remarks:

> *When I first got the script, I thought those names [without dialogue] represented places where she hadn't finished the text and lines were going to be added. Now it translates into a moment where lines aren't needed. . . . It's almost like an animal waiting to see what another animal is going to do—like a hunting animal. . . . The spell is a totally listening moment for me.*

For Campbell, "Changing spells is like requesting a rewrite." But it happens. During rehearsal an actress pauses, stares at the actor delivering the next line, and says: "I'm spelling you." "What?" the actor replies. "It's a spell," she says. "You're acting like it's normal." Later the actor asks, "Is *that* a spell?" "No," the actress responds, "I'm just looking at you." A more potent example of spell trouble occurs when two actors twice misplace their shared spell. The director gives a note: "The spell comes after the 'No.'" One actor says: "I've been adding an extra spell." The other says: "The spell felt better where we put it." Like Ruben Santiago-Hudson in *Topdog/Underdog*, the actors are "hearing another symphony." "I liked that, too," the director replies. "Spell, then 'No,' then another spell. Let's try that, let's keep trying that." After running the scene again, Esbjornson decides simply to relocate the scripted spell, and it remains in that new position in performance.

On October 24, the last day of rehearsal, Parks and Esbjornson together give notes on the first run. The three-hour session includes almost every possible variation on the interconnected roles of playwright and director in rehearsal. Parks cuts speeches and stage directions; revises and relocates part of the text; and answers actors' questions about character, subtext, and staging. Esbjornson gives detailed notes on pace, blocking, subtext, and delivery of lines; comments on political and psychological implications of particular speeches; makes adjustments in staging; and speaks for the author in her presence.

On October 21, the director had said to the cast: "At this stage in rehearsal, pace is not what we're concerned with. We'll get to pace." Now pace is what they have to get. Parks and Esbjornson in their different ways attempt to break the present pattern of performing actions between the lines rather than on them, so that acting moments do "double duty." Parks revises and cuts text, speeding up scenes by removing stage directions that have been realized in extensive detail. She combines certain actions and reverses a sequence of events in a scene of courtship so that Hester is already wearing a wedding dress when her lover sings and dances with her. Esbjornson tightens the blocking, encouraging more rapid line delivery and quickened stage action. Each has to give up something she or he has created: for the playwright, it is text; for the director, it is realistic details of staging. Each revision is negotiated with the actors who will run the play as revised that afternoon without further rehearsal as an ensemble.

Some authorial revisions are welcomed. "Here's a cut I think you'll like," Parks says to Woodard as she removes most of Hester's "Bugs in my skin" monologue. "Good," Esbjornson responds. And it is gone. An actor asks Parks a question about an entrance and exit: "Does it have to be realistic?" "It's more than a plot point and not just a costume change for Chilli," she replies. "You could just come in and it could be in [Hester's] head." The director, turning to Parks, reframes, and then defers, the problem: "The question is: how can we heighten a realistic entrance and exit? Let's wait and discuss it more later."[52]

After the other actors leave the room, Hester and Chilli rehearse their restructured courtship scene. Off book, the actors perform the revised lines and action while Parks and Esbjornson stand watching without scripts. As Chilli sings and dances with Hester, the playwright says to me: "Works better with the [wedding] dress." Her authorial revision is a directorial reenvisioning.

At 3:45 P.M., the newly revised play is run again. In attendance are George C. Wolfe, set designer Narelle Sissons, costume designer Elizabeth Clancy, assistant costume designer Michael McDonald, sound designer Don DiNicola, assistant sound designer Obadiah Eaves, artistic associate Brian Kulick, associate producer Bonnie Metzgar, dramaturg John Dias, associate production manager Narda Alcorn, and associate prop master Chris Fields. Lighting designer Jane Cox, who attended the previous run, is next door setting lights in the theater. Wolfe, wearing jeans, a white long-sleeved jersey over a white T-shirt, and white running shoes, sits in the front row with a note pad in his left hand. To his right sits the playwright, in black pants, a black long-sleeved jersey with blue sleeves and neck, and new running shoes. The director, sitting to Parks's right, dictates notes to assistant director Nora Francescani, his gaze intensely focused on the actors who speak more rapidly, pause less frequently, and deliver lines during stage action.[53] The quickened pace resuscitates the play.

Sitting on the opposite side of the playing area, for the first time I have a full view of playwright and director responding simultaneously in rehearsal. The changing emotions of the actors are replayed on the face of the director; the playwright is often impassive. Esbjornson's eyes and body follow the actors as they move; Parks's eyes often gaze downward, her body still, except for the hand holding her moving pen.

During the newly revised courtship scene, Wolfe and Parks beam with delight. There is audible laughter, but also something else—a sweet sadness—in the eyes of the audience on the other side of the playing area. Chilli, retracting his offer of marriage, ultimately disappoints, though he says *he* is disappointed that his "dear Hester" is not "triumphant . . . like Jesus and Mary" (84). But for a moment, in his song, Chilli seems a flawed, funny possible solution to a tragedy that insists on its own inevitability.

After the run-through, I wander into the semidarkened Shiva Theater where Jane Cox is directing the placement of lights. Voices in the air overlap. "6-97?" "Is this light another audience light?" "134, please." Bright blue dazzles my eyes. A huge ladder swings around over my head. "Don't worry. You're okay," a voice in the dark says to me. Sounds continue to echo in the theater, lit at intervals with blue and white spots. How different is this work from that in the rehearsal hall, and how equally essential to what is being readied for performance. I feel a familiar shiver as the stage prepares for the arrival of the actors.

In performance on November 2, 1999, the theater is brightly lit during the Confessions; members of the audience can see each other's faces reacting. I see the playwright across the stage, high up in the last row. Her gaze is focused intensely on an actor. Then her eyes lower; she makes a note. She looks again at the actor, and again makes a note. As the lights fade on the last lines of the first Confession, she is writing.

At the end of the play, downward projected light creates a large blood-red 'A' on the stage floor; it remains after the play ends. I see Suzan-Lori Parks still writing. Like her protagonist, she writes and rewrites a text that is finally illuminated "in the blood" on the stage.

5

Tony Kushner in Rehearsal

"It's an Undoing World" and *Terminating . . .*

The difference between a good playwright and a bad playwright is caring about every single word that comes out of a character's mouth.

I believe that everybody in a room together having the same experience creates something.

*T*ony Kushner has been called "one of America's most revered playwrights in the last decade of the twentieth century, the nation's voice for the turn of the millennium."[1] Best known for his Pulitzer Prize– and Tony Award–winning play *Angels in America, A Gay Fantasia on National Themes, Part One: Millennium Approaches*, and *Part Two: Perestroika*, Kushner has also written the Obie Award–winning *Slavs!: Thinking About the Long-standing Problems of Virtue and Happiness*, as well as *A Bright Room Called Day, Hydriotaphia or the Death of Doctor Browne*, and adaptations of Corneille (*The Illusion*), Goethe (*Stella*), Ansky (*A Dybbuk*), and Brecht (*The Good Person of Sezuan*). A new epic work, *Henry Box Brown or the Mirror of Slavery*, which he has described as "a play about the relationship between the textile industry in Britain and American slavery,"[2] is in progress. Kushner has studied painting and drawing, and he holds an M.F.A. in directing from New York University's Tisch School of the Arts. His plays have been produced in New York City on and off Broadway, at regional theaters, and in more than thirty countries abroad.

On December 15, 1997, I attend an author-directed reading rehearsal of *"It's an Undoing World" or Why Should It Be Easy When It Can Be Hard?*, presented that evening in the Public's Anspacher Theater as a benefit for the New Caucus, a faculty-staff labor organization at the City University of New York. Four days later I observe the playwright at a rehearsal of *Terminating . . .*, Kushner's contribution to *Love's Fire*, a program of new works by seven American playwrights, each taking as its inspiration one or more of

5.1 Tony Kushner (photograph by Susan Johann/© 2000 Susan Johann)

Shakespeare's sonnets.[3] Commissioned by The Acting Company and produced in association with the Barbican Centre in London and the Guthrie Theater in Minneapolis, *Love's Fire*, directed by Mark Lamos, premiered at the Guthrie Theater Lab on January 7, 1998. It was produced in New York at the Public's Newman Theater, June 22–July 5, 1998.

"I think that we are both created by and create history, and that we have to have an idea of what we're creating in order to have the thing that we create create us into something that we want to be. That kind of Möbius strip is important to me," Kushner has said.

> *I believe that everybody in a room together having the same experience creates something. It creates an energy. It creates a community. It creates a phenomenon that didn't exist before, and that in almost a mystical way creates good in the world, and it also empowers people and makes it more likely that they will act.*[4]

When I arrive at the Public Theater a little before 2 P.M. on December 15, 1997, production stage manager Benjamin Krevolin hands me a newly revised script of *"It's an Undoing World."* Kushner's play about a Jewish immigrant and her three cancer-stricken daughters is subtitled *Notes on My Grandma for Actors, Dancers and a Band.*[5] Kushner tells me later: "In a funny way, [*"It's an Undoing World"*] has to do with the relation of Jews to writing. It's a piece about trying to uncover history and write it down."[6] In the lower right corner of the newly revised script, "First Draft 8/7/95" is crossed out and underneath in black ink is handwritten "$1\frac{1}{2}$ Draft 12/7/97." The script is accompanied by a letter to the cast, announcing that the play is "still . . . IN PROCESS for godsake."[7] The staged reading of the work-in-progress includes music by the Klezmatics, a well-known klezmer band, and dances choreographed by Naomi Goldberg.

A lone musician plays a double bass on the Anspacher stage. Members of the tech crew check the locations and functioning of microphones. More musicians arrive and begin to play: drums, violin, keyboard, clarinet, saxophone. Suddenly Tony Kushner appears, as if materializing in response to the sounds filling the theater. He is wearing a purple and blue cardigan over a black T-shirt, dark gray pants, and black shoes. "I wanted to do it mostly with writers," he explains.[8] "They're all getting the script when they arrive today. I'll probably talk to them first in the lobby before we rehearse just to get them out of the energy in this room for a while. I don't know how exciting this is going to be." It is exciting already.

Seven members of the company are playwrights: Holly Hughes (The Middle Daughter), Larry Kramer (Benjamin Nathan Cardozo), Ellen McLaughlin (Polish Countess; Annie and Emma Lazarus), Suzan-Lori Parks (The Solemn Grandchild), Lola Pashalinski (The Voice of the Teapot), Susan Sontag (The Eldest Daughter), and Yehuda Hyman (dancing as Benjamin Cardozo). Poet and editor Katha Pollitt (The Youngest Daughter) and Kathleen Chalfant (Sarah, the grandmother), who recently performed the role of a professor of seventeenth-century poetry in Margaret Edson's *Wit*, complete the cast. "We live in—we are made of—words," Kushner has said.[9] The composition of the cast seems emblematic.

"Readings are really, really hard," Kushner comments later. "The first time through, the actors are great. The next few times they're going to be terrible because they're going through the process of figuring things out."[10]

"Tony loves actors," Chalfant tells me. "And he knows how to explain things so that you can play them, which is one of the great directorial gifts. And he's pretty good at keeping order, which is another directorial gift that can't be overestimated. And this was a fairly disorderly group."[11] The actors arrive at unpredictable intervals between 2:30 and 5 P.M. The musicians continue to rehearse on stage, joined by the dancers. Kushner conducts the musicians, humming the tune and using his hand as a baton, until he is shooed away, laughing, by choreographer-dancer Naomi Goldberg, who takes over the role of onstage director. The playwright exits with Ellen McLaughlin, who has arrived early and is studying the script.

The lights dim. The Klezmatics play. Goldberg and Hyman dance. "A little faster," Goldberg says to the musicians. Later she asks: "Can you do it slower?" In between rehearsals of the dance, the musicians discuss among themselves adjustments in tempo, phrasing, and volume. "We're going to do it for real now," Goldberg says. The playwright is still absent. Vocalist Lorin Sklamberg sings "Undoing World," one of three songs in the play, all with lyrics by Kushner. Goldberg and Hyman dance a stylized version of the story the song tells:

> . . . easily the ties that bind us break in fibrillations of the heart. . . .
> Dispossession and attrition are the permanent conditions that the wretched modern world endures. . . .
> A refugee, who's running from the wars, . . .
> Desperate in this undoing world (43).

Asked if the playwright has seen the dance I have been watching, Goldberg replies, "No. He trusts me."

It's 3 P.M. Kushner reenters and stands on stage, arms crossed over his chest, head tilted, watching and listening as Lola Pashalinski, who arrives during the dance rehearsal, sings "The Heart of the World."[12] Downstage right, Goldberg dances by herself and then lies, listening, on the stage floor. Kushner gazes intently at the actress as she sings. "Oh, that's gorgeous," he says. "I'd only like to make one small adjustment. Could you slow down just one line, 'Unto the heart is given'?" Pashalinksi sings the line again. "It's a little bit rushed," Kushner says, and sings the line himself. The actress sings it again. "Yes, just don't rush it," the playwright says. "It's just after he dies." (The song follows the line: "*In my heart as I traveled on the boat to America this was the song I sang for my dead father*" [13].)[13] Goldberg, still lying on the stage, says: "Oh, it's so beautiful." Now Pashalinski reads the lines of The Teapot (in which the grandmother's spirit lives after her death). Kushner, still standing onstage, interrupts her. His comments are inaudible. She reads the lines again. He moves closer to her. She rereads the lines. "Good," Kushner says. "Exactly. You sound terrified, like my grandmother." The "texts" that inspire this play are the undying voices of the dead.

The playwright sits in the front row center, the fingers of his left hand pressed against his lips, his right arm lying on his thigh. His left hand curls over his heart as Pashalinksi begins to sing "The Heart of the World," accompanied by the Klezmatics. Singing and music stop while a microphone is adjusted. Kushner speaks inaudibly to the actress. The musicians argue among themselves about levels of softness and loudness, giving each other notes, with no clearly designated directorial figure. Kushner oversees the repositioning of a floor mike. Holding a small teapot, he asks vocalist Lorin Sklamberg: "Do you want the teapot on your head? We could do it." "Tony, Tony, give me the teapot. I'll come on with the teapot," the actress says. Kushner begins to make further suggestions: "I think you should have the teapot behind [you]. . . ."

Kathleen Chalfant enters. "Here's a prop," Kushner says, handing her a pink hat with roses and veil. "You may not want to use it." The stage directions indicate that the grandmother *"wears a pink hat with roses and a net"* (1). The actress puts it on expertly; she will wear it throughout rehearsal and in the staged reading. "It's great," Kushner says, and hugs her. "It was clearly the right prop," Chalfant tells me later. "I believe it is the actor's job to express the writer's intention."[14]

Pashalinski sings her song once more; she receives loud, prolonged applause from everyone in the theater. Kushner, who has left briefly, reenters carrying a large green replica of the Statue of Liberty which he carefully places upstage left. Later he will tie a hoe to the statue's handless right arm and hang the little teapot from the end of hoe. (A tiny sticker, "Stop Starving CUNY," is visible on the hoe's handle.) Now Chalfant and McLaughlin rehearse their duet, a Christmas carol ("O Holy Night") in French, with keyboard accompaniment. Kushner stands next to them, listening and then singing along to indicate pace. Standing beside the actresses, one of the Klezmatics begins to direct the singing; standing on the other side, the playwright continues to "direct" by humming along. "Great, great," the musician says; the playwright smiles.

Larry Kramer arrives: "Hi, Tony. I'm here. I haven't seen the script yet." "We're going to keep developing this," Kushner says. "It will be bigger and unrecognizable." Holly Hughes arrives, receives a script, and immediately begins reading it. The playwright joins the actors sitting in the aisle and first few center rows of the auditorium. "You're our Vanessa Redgrave," Kramer says to Kushner, who then tells an anecdote about a benefit performance in which Vanessa Redgrave "wore a very long Isadora Duncan scarf" which Lynn Redgrave stood on during most of an entire act. Pashalinksi is introduced to Kramer and objects to a recent op-ed piece he wrote. Kramer defends it and hands out Xeroxed copies. The choreographer interrupts to ask: "Are you going to rehearse them now?" Kushner replies: "It's an ensemble piece. We can't. Not everyone is here."

The dancers and musicians continue to rehearse on the stage. Katha Pollitt enters and is introduced to the other members of the cast. Kushner announces that "food for eight hundred people" has arrived in the green room. At 4:30 P.M., the author-director says: "Okay. *Up!*" The staged reading will begin in three and a half hours. Kushner hands head scarves to Pollitt and Hughes, and arranges the seating order of the actors on a motley collection of wooden and aluminum chairs downstage of the Klezmatics. Scripts are placed on music stands in front of the actors. Kushner stands center stage, surveying the seated cast. Then he walks to the second row, right of center, looks again at the company on stage, and asks that several chairs be moved further downstage. Having abandoned his plan of first assembling the actors in the lobby, he addresses them now in the theater:

> *Let me just say a couple of things that might be helpful. This was a piece I wrote for a dance concert Naomi [Goldberg] gave in 1995. This is something that [director] Brian Kulick and Naomi and I are going to continue to work on. I think a certain amount of speed is important, although it is entirely unfamiliar to you, largely because of me.*
>
> *I think an important thing is line pickup. It's written in a kind of Yiddish English. It shouldn't have a strong accent. The Countess could try a Russian accent. I think you should be you.*

"*That's* a stretch," Kramer replies. "We'll see," Kushner responds. "We don't know that. We haven't heard this."

Susan Sontag arrives. "God," she says to Kushner, "don't get any thinner." "Everybody's here except Suzan-Lori," Kushner says. After the choreographer volunteers to read Parks's lines, he reconsiders the seating arrangement, makes a slight adjustment, and introduces Susan Sontag to members of the cast she doesn't know. "Okay, I'll stop you if I need to," he tells the cast. "Let's just start." There is a further delay during which stage manager Benjamin Krevolin quietly tries to hasten the beginning of the reading rehearsal. As his contribution, the playwright jokes: "Oh, I'll just leave."[15]

The read-through begins. Kushner sits on the steps of the left center aisle, the fingers of his left hand pressed against his lips, his right arm resting lightly on his right thigh. He interrupts the reading to correct the pronunciation of "Chiroszchjew," saying it himself several times. A note added to the revised script gives very detailed instructions on the pronunciation of this hard-to-locate town on the Russian-Polish border: "Chiroszchjew is pronounced Ha-RUSS-cheff; the H is a hard, back-of-the-throat phlegm-rattley H, as in Hannukah." Like Suzan-Lori Parks, Kushner gives precise, and repeated, notes on pronunciation, accent, and pace in the author-directed reading rehearsal.

Pashalinski rereads her line, pronouncing "Chiroszchjew" with great flair; the playwright laughs. He gets up and moves to a seat in the first row, then again interrupts the actors: "That's great. I want to make a little note. 'A leaf uncurled inside her head' is a pause—a five-count pause—just a little breath.

Please make a note in your text." Kushner's emphasis on breath is like that of Parks but more meticulously calibrated: "a five-count pause." Again he gives a note on pace: "This is really one long story. It can go a little faster. Give it a sense of galloping forward." Sontag responds: "I think the reason it's a little slow now is that there's a half a beat pause while we're saying, 'Is it my line now?' and it will be faster when we've read it a few times." (There will be only one complete read-through before the audience arrives.) Kushner continues to give notes: "Either . . . [the audience] will be stone-deaf when you begin or they'll laugh at the first line. So tame them down if they are laughing from the beginning."

Hughes rereads the line, "A leaf uncurled inside her head" (7). Kushner asks: "Can you 'end' that line more?" He speaks the line himself. "Yes," the actress says. The read-through continues. Kushner sits with his right hand resting on his right thigh and the fingers of his left hand pressed against a now smiling mouth. As Chalfant reads Sarah's lines, "I got three daughters, two got cancer and they died" (11), his smile disappears. Now four actors repeat the statement "My father was dead" in Yiddish, German, Russian, Polish, and French. Kushner interrupts the reading to correct certain actors' pronunciation and compliments Sontag on hers. She replies: "Well, I do know several languages."

Suzan-Lori Parks arrives with apologies for her lateness, receives a hug and a script, and takes over the role of The Solemn Grandchild. Kushner asks the actors to begin again from the beginning. He stands downstage, walking in place, smiling, as Parks reads, slowly and expressively, her first lines in the play: "This ain't ready yet this is rough. This is notes on my Grandma" (1). When she reads her next speech, Parks spontaneously quickens her pace. Kushner interrupts: "Grandma is there," he says, pointing to the actress seated to the left of Parks, who redirects the rest of her speech to Chalfant. Kushner again corrects the pronunciation of "Chiroszchjew," a word whose frequent appearances in the script are now accompanied by smiles and quiet laughter.

Kushner remains on stage, walking back and forth, downstage right, arms behind his back, hands clasped. He is without script. Interrupting the actors, he says: "Another pause after 'I did.' Another beat." McLaughlin's reading of the Countess's lines is greeted with visible delight by the other members of the cast. Kushner continues to pace onstage, arms crossed over his chest; he smiles broadly as McLaughlin reads the lines: "And so I take you on a midnight moonlight sleighride, And Why? Because I love little Jewish girls! . . . I do not keep them I only borrow them for the night!"(9). The stage manager interrupts: there is a dance. ("*The Klezmatics play the sleighride*" [10].) The choreographer announces that there *is* no sleighride dance. It is 5:10 P.M. The stage direction is provisionally canceled.

Chalfant and McLaughlin sing their duet. Kushner moves to the second row of the auditorium. In another minute he is standing center stage, again choosing a position more conducive to listening than to viewing. He begins to pace, ranging further to the left and right, then upstage and down. "I want more of a keening there," Kushner tells Parks after she reads the line, "Your father was dead" (12). She rereads the line. "That's fine," Kushner says, and then corrects an actor's pronunciation of a variant of the line in German: "Mein Vater war tot" (12). "The way I see it," Kushner says, speaking indeterminately as author/director, "is that the younger daughter believes it more. The older daughter doubts it a bit." (The identity of the father is also indeterminate: he seems to be now Sarah's father, now Sarah's husband, and now the father of her grandchild.)

"When Sarah says your name [Cardozo], start to stand," Kushner says, giving notes on blocking to Kramer, "and when Youngest Daughter says, 'Not yet, Ma,' then sit down. Okay, begin, page 8." "Even louder," he says to Pollitt (Youngest Daughter). "Just scream it. Kind of Primal Scream therapy. It'll be good for you" (laughing). He asks Hughes and Pollitt to read/scream "Not yet, Ma" in unison. As he directs, the author is revising the script: he asks two actresses to read a line with a single speech tag and when the line is repeated later by the Eldest Daughter, he asks all three daughters to deliver it. That evening the multiply voiced, and yelled, "Not yet, Ma" receives appreciative laughter from the audience.

Kushner sits in the front row, diagonally to my left. The fingers of his right hand press together against his mouth; then he laughs openly at one of Parks's lines. He interrupts rehearsal: "I'd like to go back to page 18, 'Who is Annie Lazarus Grandma?'" (giving the page number with no script in his hand). He asks McLaughlin, Pashalinski, and Chalfant to stand as they read particular speeches, adding: "You can sit after 'free.'" Asked later if this suggestion felt helpful or arbitrary, Chalfant replies: "Tony was very clear about what he wanted, and there's no point in not doing it. . . . If we had six weeks of rehearsal, you could discuss issues like that." The author's directorial note is surprisingly effective when enacted during the staged reading.

Kushner continues to correct pronunciation and give line readings. He demonstrates the pronunciation of "abubbadah bubbudah bubbudah" (20)— a line which receives a wild burst of laughter from that evening's audience— and later asks Sontag to emphasize the word "now" in her line, "Now, Ma. Tell us how you met Cardozo" (22), speaking the line aloud himself. He asks Hughes to scream her line, "BENJAMIN NATHAN CARDOZO" (22). A few minutes later he corrects Parks's pronunciation of "schoss" in the line, "So you can see how smart I am, I am a pizzle-schoss!" (23); playwright-director and playwright-actor say the word over and over. He hears a typographical error in one of McLaughlin's speeches—"Emma" should be "Annie"; its correction changes the actress's reading of the line. (The speech tag for the lines of the Lazaruses, read by McLaughlin, is always *Annie & Emma Lazarus*.)

Kushner hunkers down on the step just below the first row of seats. Parks asks him: "I'm in a bad mood?" "You don't have to be in a bad mood. *Deep down* you're happy," he replies, and they both laugh. He sits on a step in the right center aisle, then raises his seated body slightly, his hands and arms supporting his weight from behind, as he joins the cast in appreciative laughter at

Kramer's reading of Cardozo's speeches. Then he stops the read-through: "It gets a little elegiac here. . . . On page 28, Larry, could you sort of hand 'the words, the deeds . . .' to Ellen?" Kramer directs this phrase to McLaughlin who reads the next speech of Annie/Emma Lazarus. "Ellen, could you hand these lines back to Larry?" Kushner asks.

Several dancers enter the theater. The choreographer says to the director-playwright: "Go ahead. Finish." "You guys have a little dance here," Kushner tells the cast. Parks's eyes light up. Other actors ask: "Can we just keep going with the reading?" "Yes," Kushner replies, smiling. He paces downstage again, arms crossed over chest, eyes focused on the actors. He corrects the pronunciation of a sentence in Yiddish by speaking it himself.

The seated actors continue to read. The authorial director continues to move over the stage, back and forth, upstage and downstage, in a kind of full-court davening. Interrupting the read-through, he gives a familiar rehearsal note: "'She died a hundred and three, grandma.' It's not *to* grandma." "Oh. Thank you," Parks says. Playwright-to-playwright clarification of a comma functions as a directorial note on where not to direct a speech.

The first, and only, full read-through ends. Kushner gives five minutes of private notes to the actors. During the dinner break, I ask Parks what it's like, as a playwright who directs reading rehearsals, to be directed by a playwright in a reading rehearsal.

> *It feels great. It's a reading. He's great. I have more respect for actors every time I do this. How aware and attentive you have to be. You have to give and take. I have the feeling that Tony knows what he wants. It's nice to hear it from the author, from the horse's mouth. And being a horse, I enjoy that kind of thing.*
>
> *Not to say anything against directors, but I think I gotta say that. In [the next few months] I'm going to direct my own reading [of* In the Blood, *described in the preceding chapter]. I think plays are better when the readings are directed by writers. It's not about set and lighting and coordinating the talents of a multitude. It's about hearing the voices you've heard in your head for years and making sure they're coming through. A writer knows. Tony knows, because he's heard the voices in his head. He doesn't need a director to step in.*

While the actors apply themselves to an assortment of boxed dinners in the green room, Kushner, sitting in the second row of the auditorium, watches Goldberg rehearse one of her dances. "Great," he says. A small child, Alice Tolan-Mee, enters. "Alice, you remember everything, right?" Goldberg asks. A tiny voice replies, "Yeah," as she is lifted aloft in the arms of a tall male dancer, Sven Toorvald. Returned to the stage floor, she expertly performs dance steps I previously saw rehearsed by the choreographer. All of Goldberg's dancers have now arrived, and she directs them, standing in the auditorium, as they swirl and turn and fill the small space of the Anspacher stage. Alice watches intently from the first row. Goldberg is counting: "5, 4, 3, 2, 1 . . . 1, 2, 3, 4, 5, 6 . . . Good. . .good. . . Keep going. That's going to be *great*. Where are the Klezmatics?" From the second row Kushner silently watches another director-figure.

At 7:25 P.M. the dance rehearsal is over and the actors again sit in their assigned chairs in front of the Klezmatics. Their dance, deferred earlier, is now rehearsed ("*The Klezmatics play and the dancers and actors dance the glaziers' hora*" [31]). The choreographer teaches the actors to dance the hora in a seated position as Kushner watches. "And Naomi will be on stage right here," he interjects, "and will point to who stands when or it will never work." Goldberg and another female dancer sit on the floor, center stage, facing the cast, as they demonstrate and direct the dance. "It's totally great," Kushner says. "We're going to start at the top and go from cue to cue." He begins to give directions on how the actors are to enter the stage. "Let's just sit here, Tony," Pashalinski says, "until [the audience] comes in" (laughter). "You'll all just file in in this order and sit down," Kushner says. He conducts a cue-to-cue rehearsal, listening to a few lines of dialogue and then to a few minutes of music before repeating this procedure for each of the scripted songs and dances. Only during this part of rehearsal do I see Kushner carrying and consulting a copy of the script. "And don't be afraid if you want to turn around and look at [the Klezmatics]," Kushner says to the actors. "Can I mouth the words [the vocalist sings]?" Kramer asks. "Yes," Kushner responds, absently. "Really?" Kramer asks. "Yes," Kushner says. "Yes." (That evening Kramer mouths the words, adding gestures and facial expressions, to the delight of the audience.) At 7:55 P.M., the cue-to-cue rehearsal ends. "One last note," Kushner says. "Actors, remember: storytelling energy. Remember [to play to] both sides of the house. We don't really have curtain calls. So take your music stands and leave. Thank you very much."

At 8 P.M., I stand in a hallway beneath the auditorium listening to the not-so-dull roar of voices, like endless ocean waves, filling the three hundred-seat theater above my head. The "energy" the community of actors, musicians, and dancers has created is now replaced by an amassed energy waiting for them. As Kushner has said, "a phenomenon that didn't exist before" is about to occur, and it will occur only once—not merely because it will literally not be repeated but also because each encounter of audience and actors is unrepeatable. The uniqueness of the theatrical event is merely highlighted, not conferred, by its being a one-night run.

Stage manager Benjamin Krevolin motions to me; he has found an empty seat. I enter the auditorium. Moments later, Queens College Professor Barbara Bowen, the main organizer of the benefit, welcomes the audience; she talks about New Caucus, a labor-education-arts alliance, and about "Tony Kushner, who dreamed up the benefit, who invited the performers, who has been supporting the efforts of New Caucus."[16] During the applause that follows, the actors file in and take their appointed seats. Kushner appears on stage. "It's a work-in-progress," he tells the audience, "which means it's rough, it's unfinished, but you're the very first audience to hear it. So sort of squint your way through the rough parts." After introducing the performers, he says: "This is a birthday present to my aunt [Martha Deutscher, the surviving middle daughter] for her birthday in August when I was out of the country. The Klezmatics have prepared a birthday piece for her." The Klezmatics play and sing; Kushner asks his aunt to stand up; she does, with grace and poise, as the audience applauds.

Parks begins reading the opening stage directions, describing a tin Statue of Liberty, a teapot, three women with breast cancer, a solemn grandchild with a pen, and Sarah in a pink hat with roses. As Kushner anticipated, the audience laughs at Chalfant's opening lines. Subdued titters follow: the audience is "tamed down." Except for his instructions to quicken pace[17] ("a sense of galloping forward"), all of Kushner's notes—on accent, pronunciation, "breath"/pauses, line readings, screaming, and standing—are observed. The absence of the sleighride dance is announced by Pashalinski in an unscripted line: "There's no dance yet for this number." The Klezmatics play the rousing music for the missing dance and the audience spontaneously claps along. Chalfant, McLaughlin, and Parks look at the musicians as they play ("And don't be afraid . . . to turn around and look at them"). There is hearty applause. For the glaziers' hora, the two dancers enter in peasant costume, sit center stage facing the actors, and mime/direct the seated dance which the laughing cast clearly enjoys performing.

After the actors, dancers, and musicians take their bows, there are cries of "Author, author, author," from the audience.[18] He doesn't appear. There are more cries, more applause, for him. He doesn't appear. Finally, a chant emerges: "We want Tony." Bowen disappears backstage and returns with the playwright, who is holding red roses. He immediately invites everyone to a reception in the lobby.

Like Suzan-Lori Parks, Tony Kushner has directed the first public reading of a new work, not its premiere production. He tells me:

> *John Lahr talks about seeing Beckett direct his own plays and he talks about "the dead weight of the playwright's authority"—in both senses of the word. The playwright knows too much. It precludes experimentation. There's not going to be enough discovery. The nicest thing in rehearsal is always to be surprised. Suddenly there's a scene that has a completely different energy and works with a different energy.*

In a letter to Desmond Smith, who wanted to produce *Waiting for Godot*, Samuel Beckett wrote: "I am not at all sure that the author's views are without danger for the director of production. Perhaps a wrong production, wrong for me, but with the coherence of your purely personal experience of the work, is to be preferred to one in which you try to combine with your own ideas others springing from a quite different conception. Nor is the author necessarily right."[19]

Kushner's attitude toward the "dead weight of the playwright's authority" in rehearsal is clearly ambivalent, as is his attitude toward the dead author whose Sonnet 75 inspires his new one-act play, *Terminating . . .* :

> *I never really liked the sonnets. . . . The aggregate effect of them read in sequence is to portray their maker as a grossly selfish lover who . . . seems*

mostly to be in love with himself in love—seems, in fact, to be rather annoyed at his lover for failing to be a sufficiently appreciative audience. . . . The sonnets, perhaps, mark an anguished attempt to break out of the prison of narcissism. They sound to me like a brilliant patient on an analyst's couch; the beloved of the sonnets is a silent, attentive analyst, buried beneath glittering heaps of her/his prolix analysand's gorgeous, jeweled transferential fantasies.[20]

Unsurprisingly, Kushner's short play with a very long title—*Terminating, or Sonnet LXXV, or Lass Meine Schmerzen Nicht Verloren Sein, or Ambivalence*[21]—presents the final meeting of Esther, a lesbian analyst, and Hendryk, her gay patient, both intermittently appealed to by their respective lovers, Dymphna and Billygoat.

On December 19, 1997, a little before 11 A.M., I enter a fourth-floor rehearsal studio at 420 West Forty-Second Street in New York City to observe an off-book run-through of *Terminating*. . . . Erika Rolfsrud (Esther) and Stephen DeRosa (Hendryk) are rehearsing the dialogue of analyst and patient. Neither director nor author is present. An hour later, Kushner arrives, wearing a leather jacket, brown scarf, brown jeans, a gray wool sweater over a dark pink shirt, and black shoes. Soon after, the director, Mark Lamos, enters, wearing a green long-sleeved sweatshirt over a green collared T-shirt, blue jeans, and white running shoes. Lamos immediately gives the playwright a hug, saying, "Sorry I'm late."

The set consists of a red sofa, covered with a white sheet, and two chairs. Director and playwright sit, squeezed against the wall, just beyond the downstage edge of the playing area marked on the floor. The run-through begins. Kushner, seated next to me and to the right of the director, is again watching rehearsal without a script. A legal-size yellow pad rests in his lap. His left knee is crossed over his right thigh; his right hand, lying in a relaxed position over his left forearm, holds a pen. Both arms remain in his lap; the graceful fingers of his left hand curl against his lower lip and chin, then press against his lips, covering a smile. He drinks from a cup of coffee held, along with his pen, in his right hand. The playwright smiles, laughs, makes a tiny note on his yellow pad.

As the analyst, Esther, delivers her long final monologue, Lamos, his face serious, makes notes with a pencil on white sheets of paper to his left on the director's table. Kushner, his expression equally serious, makes a two-word note, another tiny note, and two further, single-word notes on the yellow pad in his lap. I notice that the playwright and director do not make notes at the same moment.

At the end of the run-through, the director reads aloud, quite beautifully, Shakespeare's Sonnet 75,[22] followed by recitations of the same sonnet by Lisa Tharps (Dymphna, Esther's lover) and Hamish Linklater (Billygoat, the lover of Hendryk). "That was wonderful," the playwright says, clapping. "That was great." Lamos asks, "You like it?" "It was great," Kushner replies. "A few notes," Lamos says to the cast. "It's a little cool at the beginning," he tells the actress playing the lesbian analyst. "Ultimately, it has to be seen that the dike doesn't hold the water" (laughter). He continues: "The playwright asks for a laugh on the line, 'You're gay,' and you're not [laughing]"; and, turning to Kushner, he inquires: "How do you feel?" "It's all right," the playwright says, surrendering the stage direction after the speech tag: "*Esther (laughs)*" (8).[23]

"Do you want to say anything?" Lamos asks Kushner in the presence of the actors. "No, I'll talk to you," the playwright replies. "I want to apologize," DeRosa (Hendryk) says to Kushner. "I was too much in my head today."[24] "I thought that, too," Kushner says, without losing a beat. "I think you need to be replaced. In fact, I'm going to replace you" (much laughter). The director says to the actor: "You need to hold [Billygoat's] head more," as he walks into the playing area to demonstrate by tousling Linklater's hair. "As simple and as uninvested with personality as possible," Lamos says to an actress. "Don't ever smile. Don't force it. . . . Also, the sonnet was too announced and *performed* today. Make it more private."[25]

"Do you want to say anything?" the director again asks the playwright. "I thought you guys were great," Kushner replies. "Physically?" the director inquires, trying in vain to elicit more detailed response. "I want to talk to you [alone]," Kushner reiterates. Voluble as he is when directing, the playwright is now notably silent with actors present.[26] Lamos persists: "I want to ask you two questions [about costumes and hair]." Kushner discusses with the actress and director the length and style of Esther's hair.[27] The director asks if Esther's lover, Dymphna, could have a slightly dowdy look; right now, Lamos points out, the look is "slightly hip." "I think both women are slightly hip," the playwright replies. "I think they should look equivalent. I don't think Dymphna should look like [Esther's] child bride."[28] "This is the only play where I'm feeling jangly about the costumes," Lamos tells Kushner. Linklater and DeRosa describe their costumes for the playwright.[29]

There is a break in rehearsal. When the actors have left the room, the playwright gives detailed notes to Lamos on pace, staging, tone, vocal emphasis, and textual revision. "Does everybody have sonnets [recited] at the end?" Kushner asks of the other six writers whose plays Lamos is directing in *Love's Fire*.[30] "Yes, everybody has one. You have several [recitations of Sonnet 75]," the director replies. "Does it bother you?"[31] "Not really," the playwright says. There is no authorial indication in the script of even a single recitation of Sonnet 75; only the first four lines appear in the play, delivered by Billygoat during a dialogue with Hendryk, who says, between the third and fourth lines: "SHUT UP! I hate the sonnets. Boring boring boring" (11).[32] (In performance on June 27, 1998, Sonnet 75 is repeated three times at the end of the play, first on videotape by Daniel Pearce, then live onstage by Lisa Tharps and again by Hamish Linklater.)

Giving notes on pace, the playwright suggests to the director that one speech is "a bit too fast" and that several long speeches "are a bit too rushed." Still without script, he quotes lines from the play as he talks to Lamos: "'You are very beautiful but you have no soul.' The first time Hendryk said that, it went by too fast. I don't know if I'm right about that, but I think it ought to be looked at and maybe you'll go back to your first choice." The notes of the author seem grounded in the experience of rehearsal's circuitous explorations, a process that sometimes at first takes one away from, rather than toward, the right choice.

The playwright comments on staging: "I wish [the two male actors] were more physical in a more dangerous way," and makes specific suggestions. Lamos walks into the playing area and sits on the couch, gesturing, while the playwright remains outside the playing area, near Lamos's chair, as if temporarily replacing the director as "third (or fourth) eye." Now Kushner suggests reblocking Esther's long monologue: "When Esther says to Dymphna, 'Inexplicably, I hate you,' I'm wondering about the choice of having her on the floor. I think it should be more aggressive, more like Hendryk. It's more to Dymphna. It's a little more like an accusation. It feels more like a wallow now." "Yes, that's great," Lamos replies. "She should be in the chair or moving." "There's a rage," Kushner continues. "It turns into a lament about Dymphna's anonymity to her patients." The author's note, as mediated by the director, is embraced by the actress. In performance, Esther delivers the line standing up. Later Rolfsrud says of the change:

> My monologue was on the ground. I was crying in the run you saw. Mark told me that Tony said that was great because of the emotional connection to the work. But at that point what Tony wanted as the next step was a manic explosion, on my feet, and a sort of manic ramble. I realized then that Esther doesn't really speak in the first part [of the play]. Her speeches are very short. The person who is on the manic roll is Hendryk. And so for me to finally get the chance to let it out makes perfect sense, especially at the crux point in the play. What the playwright said made complete sense to me. I'm very glad he said it.

In his notes after the run, Kushner makes a textual revision in Esther's monologue: "Could we add a line now to the script? Could we do it now?" He dictates the added sentence, "You know, that island with the whatchamacallit . . . the volcano," after the line, "I do live on the island of Montserrat" (22), to Lamos who writes it in his script. (The new line appears in performance and in the published text.)[33] The playwright corrects vocal emphasis in Esther's question "What about paternal ambivalence?" (25): "The operative word is 'paternal,' not 'ambivalence.'" "Oh," Lamos replies. (In performance, the actress's stress on "paternal" gives the line point.)[34]

At the end of the play Hendryk falls asleep in the analyst's office, and she leaves. In rehearsal Esther touches Hendryk before she departs. "I don't think she would touch his knee when he falls asleep because that's her escape," Kushner says. "Yes," Lamos replies. This authorial note on restaging a critical moment is not incorporated in performance.[35]

Esther's long monologue begins: "I want to die. God has closed my womb and I want to die" (21). Her lover, Dymphna, says to her at the end of the play: "Don't kill yourself. Work. Each evening come home to me" (26). "I think this agony of Esther is gone through every single day for five years," the playwright tells the director, in a final illuminating note. "It's an old, thoroughly explored, overarticulated landscape. I think what *Dymphna* says is new." "That's great," Lamos responds. Kushner has prefaced his note with the remark that most people would think the opposite: that Esther's rage and lament are new and that Dymphna's response is the familiar refrain. Instead, Esther's "old landscape" brings forth something new from her lover. "You did a great job," the playwright says to the director. "You wouldn't say that if you didn't mean it, would you?" Lamos asks. "No," Kushner says, very firmly.

"The playwright's notes are more powerful, have more weight, at the beginning of the process—at the table reading, at the initial run-throughs— because he has the most information and is the source of the play," Erika Rolfsrud says.

> His notes are still important throughout the process; it's just different in that the actors are owning the performance more and the director is pulling out, and so the notes become about finessing and giving little tweaks to what has been created among the three of us: the director, the playwright, the actor. . . .
>
> When a playwright gives a note, it sets off a wonderful chain reaction. Tony sets the first push, then Mark goes: "Oh yeah, okay." Then I go: "Okay, okay, okay."

Rolfsrud gives as an example the directorial note (understood by her as coming from the playwright)[36] that Esther's monologue "was an old monologue, her usual diatribe when she's in this bleak emotional place." Lamos, she says, told her: "And don't for a moment feel sorry for yourself or let self-pity creep in because you'll kill the monologue, especially the humor of it"—a note, Rolfsrud concludes, "which, because of his dialogue with Tony, I think Mark was inspired to give."

Like many other actors, Rolfsrud prefers that authorial notes be "filtered through" the director:

> We were scuttled out of the room, but in part that's a respectful gesture toward the director. I preferred that to having . . . [the playwright] give you direct notes because, one thing, I trusted Mark Lamos so greatly and Tony as well, but I feel that in their collaboration Tony is filtered and processed through Mark, so as a result Mark can continue to guide us as Tony wants but in the dialogue that the director and actors have created. . . . For example, should Tony say something to us as an acting note, the way he chooses to phrase it may sound contradictory to what we've been working on; it may confuse the picture the director has created, and not because he doesn't know what the director wants. His word choice may make it sound contradictory to the way we're working on the play under the guidance of the director.

In the "chain reaction" of the three-way creation of playwright-director-actor, the author's "voice" is always "filtered," even when the playwright directs his or her own work. The author is the first reader/"speaker" of the text;[37] all subsequent reading/speaking of the text mediates authorial voicing.

For Stephen DeRosa, both the "filtered" and the actual presence of the playwright are productive. On the one hand, "a playwright giving actors directorial notes is tacky. . . . And frankly, when an actor is expected to serve too many voices, the performance and production will suffer, and the morale will be catastrophically destroyed." On the other hand, "it's an actor's responsibility to serve the vision of the author."

> I think it's a tragedy for a playwright to create a character and have that character unfulfilled in production. [Kushner's] blessing for us to go forward was inspirational. Had he been unhappy, panicky, or angry, I think the morale would have suffered. I know my mental health would have suffered. And I think we would have gone further and further away from the experience . . . of the first read-through when he was present.[38]
>
> If he didn't trust the process of rehearsal and his own play as being a means of a transcendent experience just as written, it would have been a lot harder.[39]

Hamish Linklater takes a somewhat different position from that of Rolfsrud and DeRosa. The playwright's watching the run-through "was actually just a weight off my mind," he says.

> He gave so few notes. The rumor is that when he is displeased, he lets you know. . . . He was putting his smile and his blessing on what we were doing and where we were in the process, and that was gratifying.
>
> Tony didn't meddle and was probably the most "hands off" of the [seven] playwrights. We probably saw him the least during the run. . . . It was fine what we did see of him but you want to get feedback from all sources, and particularly from the playwright, and of course it would have been lovely to hear more expansively and more directly from him his ideas about my character.

"When I have a new play, I'm in rehearsal almost every day," Kushner says during a long interview after the run-through of *Terminating . . .* on December 19, 1997. "Even when I'm not in rehearsal, I'm in rehearsal. I don't go off and do something else." The role Kushner takes in rehearsal is complicated by his professional study and experience:

> Because I know the plays as well as I do and because I'm trained as a director at NYU, I think I have very valuable advice to give the actors. I usually give thirty to forty pages of notes to the director after a run-through. I am often angry, but I was really, really happy with what I've seen this week. I'm a really bad liar.
>
> I really love directing, and it's frustrating watching other people do it and not having any power. To be directed, you're surrendering so much control. Everybody has a terrifying amount of control and a terrifying lack of control in the theater. The playwright has the words.
>
> George Wolfe screamed and screamed about the epilogue in Perestroika and wanted it changed. And I didn't, in spite of the fact that I believe George's dramaturgical skill is spectacular. It's my baby. It's something I suffer terribly to produce and I care about passionately. . . . Theater is very hard, and my theater

*is very hard because it's big and untidy and not safe. Then I chicken out and get
really scared that it's not going to be a guaranteed hit. And that tension in me
produces a kind of rage.*

He describes his relationship with directors in rehearsal:

*As a playwright, I have made several directors cry and one throw up after notes.
I'm not proud of it. My worst thing was when I typed up forty pages of notes
after watching a run-through of* Millennium Approaches *at the National in
London. I flew home and I faxed the notes from New York to Declan [Donnellan,
the director] at what was 3 A.M. in London. I didn't realize the fax machine was
in his bedroom. He said it was one of the low points of his entire life, forty pages
of faxed notes from me coming into his bedroom at 3 A.M.*[40]

In *Terminating . . .*, Hendryk is openly angry at his analyst, whose own
anger and depression remain unexpressed until the end of the play. Kushner
compares the relationship between director and playwright to the relationship
between analyst and patient, much like that of Esther and Hendryk:

*I do feel it is the director's job to handle the playwright. Like a patient has to be
free to be angry at his analyst, a playwright has to be free to be angry with the
director, and it's the director's job to be able to hear what is legitimate and what
comes from unfamiliarity with the process or with a particular actor's process.
That dyad of playwright-director is at least as important as the relationship between director and actor and may be even more important, at least with a new play.*

When Kushner and Lamos watch the run-through of *Terminating . . .*, the director asks questions of the playwright, listens carefully, and evaluates the legitimacy of what he hears. The "attentive analyst" and "brilliant patient" in
Kushner's reading of Shakespeare's sonnets have become figures of the director
and the playwright in rehearsal.

Kushner characterizes his writing for the theater in relation to that of
Suzan-Lori Parks and Arthur Miller:

*On some level my work is basic, traditional, narrative realism. . . . All you have
to say to an actor is: "What's your objective?" What Suzan-Lori is doing is somewhat different. What I'm doing is like what Arthur Miller is doing, though I
don't know if I'm doing it as well. It's narrative, realistic, American drama. . . .
I was watching [Arthur Miller's]* A View from the Bridge *last night and thinking,
"Why can't I write something so tight and short?"*

*Narrative realism is a text-based theater. The difference between a good
playwright and a bad playwright is caring about every single word that comes
out of a character's mouth. The tension between that kind of fastidiousness and
the seeming spontaneousness that comes out of the actor's mouth is what theater
is about.*

As he talks, Kushner shifts easily back and forth between the subjects of writing and directing, just as in the reading rehearsal of *"It's an Undoing World"*

his voice is alternately authorial and directorial. Now he offers an interesting, untested theory about the authorial director:

> When you're directing your own play and it's new [and, he adds, directing is "a skill you can learn"] . . . if a moment isn't working, I feel as if I might possibly have a clear sense of whether the problem is in how it's being played or in the writing. I have to do more work to hear where the problem is if I'm not directing. That's a theory. I haven't really had a chance to test that out. [emphasis mine]

"There's a trade-off," the playwright adds. "If you have a good director you have a third eye, a collaborator. You get rid of them and you lose a perspective." The playwright speaks of the director as a third eye, just as an actor might, and yet in rehearsals attended by the playwright there is more than one third eye.

"Playwriting is really hard and really lonely," Tony Kushner says at the conclusion of the interview.

> Part of being a playwright is about triumphing over that loneliness. The playwright must have courage to face what all other writers face all the time: isolation, aloneness, sitting down and writing in the silence in which your only company is your horrible self and the characters you create.

With characteristic ambivalence he adds: "I worry about the seduction of that world of the rehearsal room, which is infinitely more inviting than the room where I write."

6

Arthur Miller in Rehearsal

The American Clock, The Last Yankee, and I Can't Remember Anything

What I can do is to impart to the actors the original image that the characters should spring out of.

It's an expansion of the vision of the playwright through the imagination of the actor. . . . If his imagination doesn't catch fire, you've got a dead thing. What the audience is relating to finally is the actor's imagination.

*T*here is no day when one of Arthur Miller's plays is not being produced somewhere in the world. A playwright "has a responsibility to himself first," Miller says, "to deliver up whatever vision he's got. Not bend it around to whatever fashion is going. If he can do that, he might endure."[1] "Endure" almost seems a word designed to characterize Arthur Miller who, at the turn of the twenty-first century, has been writing plays for six decades. Included among the nearly two dozen plays of "this longest-running of American theater icons"[2] are *All My Sons*, *Death of a Salesman*, *The Crucible*, *The Price*, *After the Fall*, *Incident at Vichy*, *Broken Glass*, and, most recently, his 1998 play, *Mr. Peters' Connections*, starring Peter Falk. Miller has also written several novels; a collection of short stories; essays; plays for radio and television; film scripts (*The Misfits*, *The Crucible*); three books of reportage with photographs by his wife, Inge Morath; and an autobiography, *Timebends: A Life*. He has received two Emmy Awards, three Tony Awards, an Obie Award, a John F. Kennedy Lifetime Achievement Award, a Pell Award for Excellence, and a Pulitzer Prize, along with many other honors.

Inaugurating an all-Miller season, *The American Clock*, staged by James Houghton, founding artistic director of Signature Theatre, was presented at its new home on West Forty-Second Street in New York City, October 7–November 16, 1997. It was followed by a double bill of short plays, *The Last Yankee* and *I Can't Remember Anything*, both directed by legendary Open

6.1 Arthur Miller writing in rehearsal of *The American Clock* (photograph by Susan Johann/© 2000 Susan Johann)

Theater founder and six-time Obie winner Joseph Chaikin, December 30, 1997–February 8, 1998.

Miller's *The American Clock: A Vaudeville*, with its four onstage musicians and fifteen actors playing fifty-two characters, has the largest ensemble in the history of Signature Theatre. The play is based in part, as the title page announces, on Studs Terkel's *Hard Times*, and in part on the author's memories of the Depression years in this country. "At bottom, quite simply, I wanted to try to show how it was and where we had come from," Miller has written. "I wanted to give some sense of life as we lived it when the clock was ticking every day."[3] *The American Clock* has its own history of hard times, its "seemingly endless changes" represented by two quite different published versions. The cast, somewhat expanded in the revised script, features the Baums, a family resembling Miller's own, and includes characters as diverse as an Iowa farmer, a man who was president of General Electric for one day, a female socialist comic strip writer, a seaman, a prostitute who accepts dental work as payment for her services, and a black hobo.

Miller distinguishes between the two versions of the script in this way:

> *The first emphasizes the family, whereas the second emphasizes the society. . . .*
> *The family is there to illuminate the social crisis. . . .*
>
> *It's a nonrealistic form. . . . Those characters in* The American Clock *are like signs objectified. I don't want them to have a whole inner life. I wanted a cavalcade notion, so that instead of intensity you get extension. It's the difference between a portrait and a mural.*[4]

The revised text introduces new characters, scenes, and monologues; reassigns certain speeches without regard to gender;[5] removes the narrator figures framing the play; and adds music and dance. Perhaps the most significant formal change is the stage direction indicating that all actors (and a small jazz band) remain on stage throughout the performance. These changes, in combination with the play's "cavalcade" of multiple brief scenes, seem clearly to invite what Miller calls a "style of . . . presentational declarativeness."[6]

"The vaudeville has to be done with a flair," Miller said in the mid-'90s, "the way it was done in London [in 1986]. They were able to put a whole jazz orchestra on stage. We can't afford that here . . . . [W]e have an impoverished theatre in this country."[7] Enter Signature Theatre Company.

At 10:30 A.M. on September 9, 1997, I arrive at a still-under-construction 160-seat theater at 555 West Forty-Second Street where a press conference precedes the first table reading of *The American Clock*. Muffins, bagels, grapes, coffee, tea, and orange juice are plentiful on tables in the brand new lobby. Inside the theater, seated on aluminum chairs, are Arthur Miller, director James Houghton, architect Mitchell Kurtz, and set designer E. David Cosier. On the peripheries are men measuring and sawing wood, painting walls, hammering. The workmen do not acknowledge those of us milling about nor do they make any attempt to subdue the noise of their continual labor. Nails are pounded in at a terrific rate; a buzz saw whirs just behind me. It seems the perfect setting for a playwright who is himself an amateur carpenter.

Miller is a wonderfully relaxed presence. He wears a beige safari jacket over a green short-sleeved jersey and black- gray- and red-striped suspenders, gray-brown corduroy pants, very well shined shoes, and dark socks. He looks tanned, immensely healthy. The belt of his jacket is tucked into one of its pockets, a grayish tweed cap into the other.

The first question addressed to the playwright by a reporter is: "Are you revising *The American Clock* for this production?" Miller's reply, "No, it's been revised enough," is greeted with laughter. He continues:

> *This production is the result of a lot of experimentation that has gone on over the years. . . . It's a very liquid form with a background of music. It's not a musical.*
>
> *The music of the '30s was very important to me growing up. It conveys a spirit, oddly enough, of a very optimistic kind. It's hard to find a sad song in that calamity we were going through. That's what this play is about. It's about the survival of the human spirit in what could have been, in another society, the end of democracy.*

When he is asked, "Can you comment on your strengths and weaknesses as a playwright in the past and today?" Miller provokes laughter with his counter-question—"You want that all today?"—and then goes on:

> *What we have in this country are shows, not theater. In other countries we have theater. We in America simply seize on the latest thing, run with it as far as it can go, and then forget about it. I don't want the theater to be a library; [I want it to be] . . . less of a crapshoot and more of a spiritual engagement. The last time I was in a theater that was being built was at Lincoln Center. . . . It became, in effect, a commercial theater. I hope this theater will [be one] . . . of spiritual engagement. . . . That's not answering your question.*

There is more laughter.

It is 11:45 A.M. and the actors who have been listening to the playwright's dialogue with the press are asked to go to the rehearsal room at Raw Space, next door to the theater. Reporters and photographers immediately surround the playwright. A carpenter, pausing in his work, asks me what this gathering is. I explain and point out Arthur Miller. He says: "I guess you can't tell a book by its cover. He looks just like anyone else."

At 12:15 P.M. in studio O, a windowless basement room, the playwright, director, dramaturg, and fifteen actors seated at a table begin the first read-and sing-through of *The American Clock*. Miller is brought a bag lunch—a sandwich and pickle wrapped separately—and a cup of coffee, as music director Loren Toolajian, accompanied by pianist James Besch, sings "Smilin' Through," "I'm Always Chasing Rainbows," "Yankee Doodle Boy," "Take

Me Out to the Ballgame," and "Get Happy." The director talks the cast through the preshow music and action; the reading at table begins with the pianist still playing in the background.

With no script in sight,[8] Miller listens intently as he finishes his sandwich. Laura Esterman (Rose Baum) and Jason Fisher (Rose's son, Lee Baum) make immediate eye contact and then play to each other as they read their opening lines (which will later be delivered to the audience). There are sounds of appreciative laughter from those of us (designers, choreographer, stage manager, assistant stage manager, photographer, and the director's wife, Joyce O'Conner) seated just behind the actors at table. The playwright does not laugh; he continues to listen with great concentration, looking at each actor as he or she reads. The director, seated next to the writer, looks down at the words of his script, turning pages as the cast reads.

Miller sits erect, his left hand in front of his mouth, the forefinger curled around his lips. He leans forward, right hand on cheek, then sits back in his chair. A small, appreciative smile appears; then his right hand covers the right side of his face, blocking my view of his expression. Three feet from his chair, I sense his silent laughter in the slight rocking of his body. Now he folds his arms over his chest, crosses his right leg over his left knee, then leans far forward and looks sideways as an actor seated at the corner of the table to his left begins to read. His laughter is audible for the first time when Stephen Pearlman (Lee Baum's grandpa) says: "When I went bankrupt I didn't pay *nobody*!" (31). As he listens to Lee Baum announce to his mother: "The bank has just been closed by the government! It's broke!" (32), a tender look appears in Miller's eyes.

The afternoon reading continues, uninterrupted. The playwright looks a little tired, but his attention is unflagging, intensely focused. His right hand again momentarily covers his mouth. He sits, quite erect, in his aluminum chair (the only one with a back cushion—the single deference to him in the furniture arrangements), his eyes always moving from one reading actor to the next. Beyond him, leaning against a wall, photographer Lia Chang focuses her camera lens on the playwright.

When Lee Baum talks about his father, Moe, who "always got drowsy when the news got bad" (37),[9] Miller sits further back in his chair, his lips together, unsmiling. His body is almost immobile, except for the slow rise and fall of his arms crossed over his chest, the visible rhythms of his steady breathing. Moe Baum's dryly mocking speech, "He's a farmer from Iowa. He tried to lynch a judge, so she [his wife, Rose] wanted him to live in the cellar" (40),[10] elicits laughter from the cast and a smile from the playwright. Miller leans forward, left hand and arm resting casually on the table, but is immediately erect again, arms across chest, head tilted slightly as he gazes intently at Patrick Husted four seats to his right, reading the speeches of Theodore K. Quinn. He laughs, almost inaudibly, at the end of Quinn's monologue describing his corporate rise and voluntary resignation after one day as president of General Electric.[11]

During a scene in which Rose's sister, Fanny (Mary Catherine Wright), tries to convince her songwriting son, Sidney (Chris Messina), to marry the landlady's daughter, the playwright seems to be gazing at something far off. Then he laughs appreciatively at Fanny's last line: "Write a big hit, Sidney!" (49).

"The tone is good," Miller says to the director during the first break. When I ask him what he is looking for and listening to at the table reading, Miller says, just before the actors return:

> *The main thing is to see whether they're on more or less the right line. At this stage all I can do is see if they're locating the kind of people they're impersonating. I'll be coming back as they generate more detail, and I'll try to correct where they go wrong. Jim [Houghton] is very good—so I'm just icing on the cake.*

"If they start going off in the wrong direction," Miller adds, "it gets more difficult to change later. They progress at different rates. Some of them are just reading their lines. . . . I also want to see how the music works in and whether we have the right music."[12]

The actors begin reading act 2. The playwright borrows the director's pencil and, for the first time, makes a brief note. A few minutes later, during a scene between Lee's friend, Joe (David Kener), and Isabel, a prostitute (Keira Naughton), Miller makes a second note. He laughs as Joe explains Engels's Marxism to the prostitute: "Well, it's the idea that all of our relationships are basically ruled by money" (57). He again laughs audibly during a scene between Sidney and the landlady's daughter, Doris (also played by Keira Naughton), who urges him to sing his "greatest" song, "Sittin' Around" (64). (Lyrics and music are included in the script with no mention of authorship.) After Toolajian sings "Sittin' Around" with piano accompaniment, it is identified for the company: "Words and music by Arthur." The cast applauds. Like Suzan-Lori Parks and Tony Kushner, Miller writes his song—the only one he has ever composed[13]—for a particular moment in the play. Music director Loren Toolajian says later:

> *I think it's a great song—a fun tune. . . . I can't think of any higher compliment for something written for a play than that a song sounds like it was written by the character in the play. It doesn't just sound like an Arthur Miller song that he put in the play. It sounds like a Sidney song.*

As Myra Lucretia Taylor begins to read the lines of Irene, a middle-aged black woman, the playwright's lips move silently, forming the words she speaks: "And while you're at it, you can remind Mr. Roosevelt that I done swang One Hundred and Thirty-ninth Street for him in the last election, and if he want it swung again he better get crackin'!" (67–68). I see Miller again mouth the words an actor speaks[14] when Stephen Pearlman's Kapush, an applicant at the emergency welfare office, says: "Greatest public library system in the entire world and nobody goes in but Jews" (69).

During the second act, the playwright responds with visible appreciation and audible laughter. He sits, his jacket now removed, elbows on the table, fingers of his right hand leaning against the right side of his face, his left hand near his chin. He clasps both hands in front of his mouth for a moment, then presses them against his left cheek. Miller's lips move, almost imperceptibly, as David Kener reads the lines of Stanislaus, a seaman sleeping in the Baums' cellar: "I was captain's personal steward . . ." (80).

When Laura Esterman reads Rose Baum's lines of Depression-induced hysteria near the end of the play, the author's eyes again take on a distant look, as if he is responding simultaneously to the text he is hearing in rehearsal and to some earlier current of feeling out of which it was born and which he now reenters in the presence of the actors. His left hand covers his mouth; then his right forefinger presses his lips.

The pianist begins to play. Miller makes a final note. The piano continues underneath the actors' voices. Suddenly—and for the only time in today's table reading—the director stops rehearsal, and corrects the musical "underscore." The tune changes to "Hail, Hail, the Gang's All Here" (not specified in the script). As the actors read the last scene, the playwright borrows the director's copy of the script and looks at his own writing for the first time in rehearsal. Then he puts the text down and taps rhythmically on the tabletop as the music director sings "Life Is Just a Bowl of Cherries."

The reading ends. Everyone, including the playwright, claps. During the break, Miller studies the script and confers privately with Houghton, who leaves briefly and returns. The playwright underlines several speeches on the last page of the director's spiral-bound script. "Sounds a little teachy here," Miller says, to no one in particular. He pauses, pencil poised. Houghton stands to Miller's left, looking over his shoulder; dramaturg Suzanne Bradbeer sits to his right.[15] The playwright reads a speech aloud. He studies the text, pencil in hand, then pauses. Still seated at the rehearsal table, he writes on the director's script with the director's pencil, then erases, then writes again, cutting and adding lines as Houghton watches intently.[16] Miller reads the lines he has just added aloud to Houghton. "That's right. That's good," the director says and then asks an inaudible question. "I'm not sure that's going to register very much," the playwright responds. "It's a little bit editorial, in the wrong sense." Houghton says: "That feels right."

Miller cuts or rearranges more than a dozen lines in the script he has earlier said would not undergo revision in rehearsal, and adds two lines, both delivered by Sidney: "And his brother got it in Korea"; "And his son was in Vietnam." "You can [have the whole company echo], after each of these mentions, 'Korea,' 'Vietnam,'" he tells Houghton, writing in the director's script the words "Korea" and "Vietnam." When Houghton asks for clarification of the revisions, the playwright replies: "It sort of straggled along, I thought." "That will tighten it up," the director comments.

"It's like listening to music," Sam Shepard says, explaining his rehearsal revisions of *Curse of the Starving Class*. "You hear a note that can be elaborated on or eliminated. . . . It's in response to live actors." Asked about his own revisions of the script during rehearsal, Miller tells me, "It's a bit like playing music. You write the notes, and you hear the sound. Things can some-times occur to you when you hear the sound. I don't normally make a lot of changes. Sometimes I make none. It depends on the play." Listening to actors is, for the playwright, both a return to the moment of composing and a hear-ing of new soundings of the notes.

Miller continues to study the final scene. "I'm not sure about this, either," he says, rereading a page of the script. "I'm not sure that we shouldn't lose all that [marking the director's script]. It gets a little teachy." Production stage manager Amanda W. Sloan and assistant stage manager Fran Rubenstein walk over and stand watching as the playwright makes cuts in the text. "What [song] are you playing now?" (under Rose's hysterics), Miller asks Houghton, who replies: "The Last Rose of Summer." "Seems a little flat there," the playwright says. (This song is removed from the production.) "Maybe we could get some-thing that had more comment on her." He suggests a tune, beating the rhythm on the tabletop with the fingers of his right hand, and says: "I'm not sure about that song. It's rather dull." "I'm not sure, either," the director replies. "What would you want that bit of music to say, whatever we choose?" Houghton's question, especially in its shift from "you" to "we," clearly invites an authorial-directorial exploration, as does his earlier repetition of the playwright's "I'm not sure." Miller's response, curtailed by the return of the actors, is not so much a search for a song as a rethinking of a moment in the play: "I suppose that"—very long pause—"there's an irony there. If you make the music repeat what she's done, that's defeating the point. [It becomes] sentimental."

When rehearsal resumes, Houghton says to the cast seated at the table: "We have our first cuts," and dictates the playwright's revisions.[17] The actors record cuts and additions, presented without explanation, in their scripts. Asked by the director if he would like to talk to the cast before answering questions, Miller replies: "I don't know if a general speech is of any use. Spe-cific questions and details are better."

Jason Fisher, playing Lee Baum, who—like Arthur Miller[18]—was em-ployed by the Roosevelt-created Work Projects Administration, asks Miller "exactly how the WPA worked." The playwright explains:

> Writers would go into some area and talk to the people. In the '30s there were still families whose members were continuously there for the last 150 years. And so the writers wrote the memories and histories of individual local regions. The project was canceled in the 1930s. . . . So it's very exciting for a young guy to go up there and write it. They had to be historians on the spot.

Like Sam Shepard's comments to the actors at the table rehearsal of *Curse of the Starving Class*, Miller's "details" are both sociological and autobiographi-cal. A young actor asks what a speakeasy (where an early scene in the play takes place) was like in the days of Prohibition. Miller says:

> Speakeasies were illegal. You spoke easy. Meaning you got an address, knocked on the door, a little window would open, you'd ask for Harry. That was the

nightlife. It was illegal. You weren't allowed to drink above ground. You had to do it underground. They brought in liquor from Canada in trucks. Paid off the border patrols.

Stephen Pearlman says: "I'm confused about Grandpa's politics." "A large part of the Jewish population was socialist. But some were quite conservative,"[19] Miller replies. Pearlman is playing both Grandpa and welfare applicant Kapush with foreign accents. "Why don't you try it [the role of Kapush] once without an accent?" the playwright suggests. The actor tells me later: "I felt that Kapush really is an immigrant and it's important that he have an accent. And I am using a Slavic accent for Kapush [in rehearsal and performance]. And once Miller explained that the grandfather was actually German, I could change his accent."

Myra Lucretia Taylor asks the playwright if he can talk more about Irene. "Irene is a real woman," Miller says. "I didn't know her, but I was born on 113th and Third Avenue. I went to public school in Harlem. I knew women like Irene." He compliments the actress: "You do it marvelously. Like an aria in an opera." "The play is a mixture of Studs Terkel and me—his reportage[20] and my memories," he tells the company, then adds: "You're a wonderful cast. It's terrific."

Choreographer Annie Loui inquires about the music of the era. Miller seems tired, but his response is full of energy: "The music at that time was some of the best jazz ever written. And some of the most cheerful. . . . There was no television, only radio. Everybody hung on the radio." Then he spontaneously sings part of an Irish ballad.

Asked by the director to talk about the history of the play in production, Miller says:

> *Initially, we hadn't solved the staging problems. There are a lot of seemingly unrelated people in the play. It's difficult in that sense.*
>
> *Music played little or no part in the initial production. In London a very good director [Peter Wood] filled it with the music of the time. And that was sociologically true. It was in the background of my mind. He added that. If I'm not mistaken, he made Quinn into a dancer.*

Later, director Joseph Chaikin, in rehearsal of *The Last Yankee*, will add to Miller's play a stage image that may be even further "in the background" of his mind.

"Is the clock running out on us?" an actor asks. "I have no idea," Miller replies. "I'm always ready." The cast laughs. Just before the playwright leaves, costume designer Gail Brassard passes out photographs of New York City during the Depression. The eighty-two-year-old playwright looks intently at these black-and-white images as do the actors, most of them not yet born in the thirties. It is 4 P.M. "We have to let this man go now," the director says. As he leaves the room, the playwright says, with a smile, "I'm old," not at all looking the part.

*gives a chance
actors to ask questions —
to ask q*

At noon the next day, in a third-floor studio at 412 West Forty-Second Street, Houghton begins the second rehearsal at table: "We're going to read through. Take as much time as you want. We want to take advantage of Arthur's being here." He asks the cast if there are "questions for Arthur that came to you overnight." The initial question has to do with the bending of time. Rose Baum's first monologue in the play seems to shift, without transition, from a nostalgic glance at the past to an immersion in it. Esterman asks: "Am I talking in the moment or from a different time?"[21] The playwright, dressed as before, his beige jacket and umbrella resting on a nearby chair, consults the director's rehearsal script. "You're talking from *now* about the '30s. Then you go back into . . . [the summer of 1929]. *I don't know how Jim will stage it*" (emphasis mine). Even as he "answers" the actress's question, the playwright awaits rehearsal's answers.

"Would hobos actually come to your house?" the dramaturg asks. "Yes," the playwright replies. "Rose expresses the more generous [response] to a hobo." Miller tells the cast a joke about two cars passing each other, one with a California license going east and the other with a New York license going west; as they pass, the passengers in each car yell to the other: "Go back! Go back!" The playwright describes a hobo who turned up at the University of Michigan, got a job washing windows, became interested in lectures he heard through the windows he washed, began taking classes at the university, and eventually earned a master's degree. Then he launches into a story punctuated by actors' laughter:

> There was a certain relaxation. I remember when I first went to the University of Michigan [in the '30s]. I didn't know anything about geography west of 111th Street. I got on a bus and it took twenty-six hours to get to Ann Arbor. It went wherever anyone wanted to go. I had a tour of the U.S. for $12, and I was nearly dead when I arrived there. As a matter of fact, when I got there I went to sleep and was shaken awake by a woman who said, "Are you all right? I was about to call an ambulance." I had slept thirty hours.

Rehearsal begins. The pianist plays, and the music director sings "Look for the Silver Lining." Miller sits back in his chair and stares into space, far beyond the third-floor rehearsal room on Forty-Second Street. The read-through is interrupted frequently by actors' questions: How old is Lee's boyhood friend, Joe, now? How much would $12 then be worth today? (about $60, Miller says). Suddenly the playwright himself interrupts with a "directorial" remark: "Rose [Laura Esterman], you're terrific. You're starting to do something I would encourage. Your instinct is right: 'Everything is going to be great.'" Houghton, sitting to Miller's left, smiles appreciatively at the playwright. "Oh, can I ask something else—while you're here?" Esterman says. "What's 'the real problem' [mentioned in a stage direction] on page 28?" "The real problem is how are you going to get dinner," the playwright replies. "Like everybody else, Rose and Lee figure this thing is going to be over in a month rather than ten years. . . . We do the same thing today—the school system in

New York. I read in the newspaper today that kids are being turned out of schools because they're overcrowded. I'd call that an emergency." And then without transition the playwright gives another "directorial" note: "Be faithful to the present. This is as much as you know now. Don't forecast, or you'll be played out at the end of the play."

Miller's comments at the table rehearsal continue to alternate between responses to acting choices and commentary on the psychological or social problems that form the background of the play. He presents at once his personal history and that of the country to the cast, who occasionally appear stunned by what they are hearing.

> *When the crash occurred, I was about thirteen. There was no price on shares of, say, the Chase National Bank. Well, there were a lot of suicides. People were living on borrowed money. A lot of companies had been investing more and more in the stock market. . . . I want to remind you: there is no relief, no government relief. By a month, people knew that a catastrophic event had occurred. There were two events in the history of this country that affected everybody: the Civil War and the Depression. We were just lucky that a lot of things happened the way they did, but everything could have been over. I know it's difficult to comprehend because it was difficult to comprehend at the time. It was on a* dead *level. If you went to college, you could escape it for a little. I personally think it affected the American psyche. . . . What happens? Can the whole thing just capsize?*

"Suicide was very popular," he adds, with a wry smile.

The director asks the playwright for a "time line" of the Baum family, beginning with the stock market crash. Like Shepard, Miller does not offer this kind of information. Instead, he says to Esterman's Rose: "First, you sell off jewelry, property you may have; you borrow money from friends." The actress replies: "But we still have enough food for people who come over. We eat. We have meals." Miller does not respond directly. Like Shepard, he talks about the land:

> *The agricultural life of the country was hit first. [Farmers] were actually wiped out. In the 1930s a terrific drought began. Then a terrific wind blew the farms away, blew the soil away. As late as the early '40s, I had a friend who bought a 160-acre farm for $3500 in Connecticut. That included machinery. The government was even burying crops, burying little pigs, to raise prices. That's part of the psychology of the time: that it made no sense. It was insane. That's why Marxism was so attractive: it made sense.*

An actor asks: "Were you sympathetic to Marxism?" Miller replies: "Yeah, sure. Part of any intelligence would be." The eyes of the cast are riveted on him as he speaks, just as his were riveted on them yesterday when they read the play in his presence for the first time.

> *The craziness of the thing was not lost on anybody. If you went down to Fourteenth Street, Union Square, which looks a lot different now than it did then, you*

> *would see knots of people there, arguing. The thrashing about of this great*
> *machine was ferocious.*

Then he makes some sense of the craziness:

> *The exact same thing was happening in Germany except that they were Germans.*
> *In a clutch they would reach for more authority, given their traditions. In a clutch,*
> *we reached for more democracy. So in a sense we were saved by our traditions.*[22]

Myra Lucretia Taylor asks: "What about segregation?" "It was a totally segregated society," he replies without hesitation. "Nobody denied it. The prejudices in the country were, I think, far worse than they are now." He tells "a quick story" of when he was "recording dialects, black and white," in North Carolina in 1939 and was reprimanded by the head of Health Services there because he addressed a sixty-year-old black worker as "Mister" instead of "boy." He follows this with a story of anti-Semitism in the same time and place.

After a break, the reading continues. The actors seem more energized, more in rapport with each other and with the play. During a Baum family scene, the playwright reaches past me, borrows a page from the white lined pad of actor David Kener, and makes a note: "Grandpa—imperious—"; beneath that, he writes "Lee—" Then he interrupts rehearsal with clearly directorial comments:

> *First, Grandpa. Grandpa thinks of himself as an authority in most things. So*
> *don't plead with her [Rose]. When you say, "When I went bankrupt I didn't pay*
> *nobody," and when you tell her about Germany, there's never any argument*
> *with her.*

To the actress playing Rose, Miller says: "And that will help you with him [Grandpa]. He's a big weight. He's a pain in the ass." "Oh," Esterman responds. In contrast to Tony Kushner's reticence in Mark Lamos's rehearsals of *Terminating . . .* , the playwright continues to give notes directly to the actors: "And, Lee, try to encourage your mother. Try to make nothing of these difficulties. It's very painful to see her in this distress. She's really getting tragic, and you don't want that." Far from being "the icing on the cake," the playwright in rehearsal is helping to bake it.

The time line looms again when Esterman asks how long ago Grandpa's wife died. The playwright answers: "It was quite a while ago." "Roughly, it's three years since the preceding scene," the director proposes. Esterman then asks where the Baums are living. If time bends for the playwright, space is both literal and symbolic: "They're about Avenue M, Gravesend Avenue, in Brooklyn. An appropriate name for this time."

The pianist plays and the cast sings the first verse of the beautiful Iowa Hymn, introducing a scene in which farmers threaten to lynch a judge. David Kener (here playing Brewster, a farmer) interrupts the reading: "Okay, let's talk about this scene." "It's Iowa," several actors say, laughing. "That explains it." The playwright again offers a historical perspective:

Just remember that what they did in Iowa generated a whole movement. . . .
The so-called heartland was becoming a kind of radical place. At one point there
was a barbed-wire compound. It was very, very violent. . . . The farmers would
dump milk on the highway in an attempt to force the government to raise the
price of milk. Meanwhile in the cities people are dying for lack of milk. I men-
tion this as a part of the chaos, the insanity, of the time.

As before, Miller's "details" dramatize for the actors "the psychology of the
time."

Rehearsal resumes. At the crowded table, a few inches from me, the playwright sits with his long legs stretched out, ankles crossed. Suddenly he leans
forward and makes another note: "Judge = Decent, kindly.—" He sits back in
his chair, his left hand under his chin, the pencil in his right hand poised over
the borrowed sheet of white lined paper. As David Kener reads the lines of
Brewster, the Iowa farmer who leads the attack on the judge, the playwright
makes a final note: "Brewster—scared." Miller leans forward slightly, looking
at the actors, not at the script that sits face down on the table before him.
Then he interrupts the actors, giving notes that include the words he has just
written in response to their reading of his play:

Let's make it that for the Judge this is the first time [he has levied a deficiency
judgment on a farm]. He is a very decent chap, kindly. He believes in the law and
in order. . . . [Brewster's] got to be scared. He's an amateur. The whole thing is
an improvisation. Nobody knows what his role is. Okay. [emphasis mine]

Miller's opening phrase ("Let's make it that . . .") suggests that he is directo-
rially reauthoring his text. Houghton does not ask the actors to reread the
scene the author has just commented on. Instead, he says: "Let's continue with
Banks [the black hobo whose monologue begins the next scene]."

6.2 Arthur Miller's rehearsal notes for *The American Clock*:
"Grandpa – imperious—
Lee –
Judge = Decent, kindly.—
Brewster – scared."

The playwright sits with hands crossed in front of his mouth, his pencil leaning on the cover of the script. His cheek rests for a moment on his right hand; then he sits back in his chair, arms folded over his chest. Houghton stops the reading, explaining that he has to "talk with the management for a few minutes," and leaves the room. The actors immediately begin to chat with each other. During the director's absence, the playwright talks to Isiah Whitlock, Jr. (Banks). "There's an abstract quality here," Miller tells the actor. "When people talk to themselves, there's a kind of romantic quality, a kind of music in it. You're almost there." For the playwright, "an abstract quality" and "a kind of music" seem equally important, and related.

Houghton returns; rehearsal continues. After the following exchange between Rose and her son:

> LEE: I think maybe I'll try looking for a job. But I'm not sure whether to look under "Help Wanted, Male" or "Boy Wanted."
>
> ROSE: Boy! (47)

Laura Esterman interrupts the reading: "I'm not sure what that 'Boy!' is about." "You don't want him to . . . ," Miller begins. Esterman involuntarily cuts him off: "Oh. Of course!" The actress's immediate understanding of the author's half-finished thought has the rhythm of a private conversation conducted in public.[23] After listening again to the scene in which Fanny (Mary Catherine Wright) tries to arrange the marriage of her son, Sidney (Chris Messina), the playwright comments: "I don't want to interfere with anything in that scene. It's going wonderfully."

The actors begin to read act 2. The pianist plays the music of Schumann underneath the spoken lines. The script lies face down on the table in front of the playwright; underneath is his single page of rehearsal notes, a pencil beside it. The playwright's legs are extended, crossed at the ankles. His left hand supports his chin; his right hand, slightly clenched, rests on his hip. He leans forward, glancing quickly to right and left as actors on opposite sides of the table read lines of dialogue. Just in back of him, a few feet to his left, the pianist plays songs of the 1930s. There is an unintended appropriateness in the placement of the piano: the music of the past enters the rehearsal from behind the playwright as he gazes at the actors before him reading his words.

Rehearsal pauses while director and actors discuss at some length exactly how much time has passed between two scenes. The author listens and is silent, offering no advice. Finally, he says: "This reminds me of a story." The cast laughs. "In the interval during a performance of his play, a woman came up to Ibsen and said: 'It's impossible for that woman to be the other woman's daughter because of their difference in age.' And he said: 'Mind your own business.'"[24] The company roars with laughter and stops discussing the time line.[25]

Actress Keira Naughton asks the playwright what Isabel means by "hey?" in her line to Joe: "Ain't that uncomfortable—hey? Two pairs of pants?" "Where are we in the script?" Miller asks. "Page 56, Mr. Miller," the director says, playfully. The author looks at the page and says simply: "Forget the dash." "Thanks," Naughton says, and immediately gives the line a different reading. Like Suzan-Lori Parks, Miller "directs" voicing and pace by attention to details of punctuation. His authorial-directorial comment here is a rehearsal revision of the text.

During the dialogue between Joe and the prostitute, Isabel, whose new filling is payment for her professional services, the playwright suggests to the director, in a distinctly audible whisper, that Isabel should be chewing gum constantly in the scene. "Good," Houghton replies. Gently taking hold of the arm of David Kener (Joe),[26] Miller tells the actor: "You know, [Isabel's] really a challenge to you. In a completely naive way, she's putting Marxism on the griddle. She's giving you the *human* situation which doesn't match what you came into this [apartment] building with." When the actress asks the playwright about Isabel's circumstances, he responds that, working on her own as a prostitute, "she would be living in the Brooklyn neighborhood in an apartment."

The black hobo's monologue in the next scene contains a line that becomes a haunting refrain in the play: "I still hear that train, that long low whistle, *whoo-ooo!*" (59).[27] As if the actor reading the speech in rehearsal brings back for the playwright the experience of composing it or perhaps of composing the play itself, Miller says to Isiah Whitlock, Jr.:

> *You know, while you were speaking, it reminded me of putting it all together. There are a lot of little pieces, aborted ideas, and what holds them together is a feeling. The most specific I can get is when you've been told someone is special. There's a romantic side to all these reminiscences, something beautiful. That man is really a testimony to the survival of the human spirit. If we could figure out a rhythm—a way to get it all together . . . it's songlike. Maybe I can figure out another way to say this later.*

For a moment the playwright's characteristic articulateness seems to fail him, yet this is the note the actor will remember and make use of. The "we" is prophetic: director-like, the author assists the actor in getting it "all together." Whitlock says later that Miller

> *gave me one note that all the ideas were like musical notes and I needed to be able to connect them together so it would be almost musical. It was a very helpful note. I thought about it overnight and then I came in and I started putting a lot of ideas together, trying very hard not to break that rhythmic pattern, still shifting ideas. And I'm still doing it. Those are the kinds of notes that are very helpful from a playwright.*

Then he adds, with an actor's double perspective: "Maybe I could have discovered that on my own after three or four weeks. But I got it in two or three days, so I felt the freedom to move on to something else."

Miller smiles, and laughs quietly, arms folded over his chest, as he listens to the music director sing "Sittin' Around" (which has an added resonance at the table reading). He whispers inaudibly to the director. Then in his eyes appears a faraway look, very like Suzan-Lori Parks's gaze into a middle distance no one else can enter.

The playwright's final comment during the read-through shifts from an authorial to a clearly directorial mode. He says to Melissa King, playing Edie, a socialist comic-strip artist:

> *You started to do something I found quite interesting. Her natural personality is quite* cheerful. *If you could find any way to show that. . . . She's got a* small-town *girl's cheerfulness and warmth which . . . [Lee Baum is] responding to in the wrong way. As the scene progresses, you get more* strident *and irritated.* Try it that way. *[emphasis mine]*

"Okay," the actress responds, and does. The playwright leaves at 3:30 P.M. before rehearsal ends.

A week later, Melissa King spontaneously quotes the playwright's words in rehearsal:

> *He said to me: "You started to do something right which is she's a* small-town *girl and in general she's a very* cheerful *person. And she becomes more* strident *as the scene goes on." It was great for a couple of reasons. It's the development of the scene. It's where the scene goes. Do you know what I mean? It gives the scene somewhere to go. On top of that, as actors we are called upon to discover things about the text, decipher the clues that the playwright has given, and it's a lot easier when he's in the room. It's also nice to know that I was on the right track.*

King's precise repetition of Miller's words—*cheerful, small-town, strident*— suggests how closely the actors attend to the words of the playwright in rehearsal—as closely as they do to the words of his script.

All chairs and tables are now pushed against the walls. At the center of the room are the piano and pianist. Houghton sits near me on a couch, drinking a cup of coffee and watching as music director Loren Toolajian and then choreographer Annie Loui rehearse the company in what will become daily singing and dance practice. Repeating Miller's words from yesterday's press conference, Toolajian reassures the cast: "This is not a musical. This is about you as actors." The actors sing up and down the scale on the sound "la," then together find a note, B flat, on the sound "o," before singing "Get Happy" in unison. Most of the cast stand in a clump between the piano and the six-foot-high windows open to the sounds of street traffic below. A few actors remain seated; some gesture as they sing. They rehearse the Iowa Hymn; Toolajian adjusts the key to C and they repeat it, followed by a rousing rendition of "Hail, Hail, the Gang's All Here." After a break, Annie Loui instructs the company in the foxtrot: "I've talked to Jim [Houghton] about this. Even if you think your character doesn't dance, I'd like you to learn the dance."[28] Apparently, this includes those who are just sitting around. To provide needed women for couple dancing, for the next thirty minutes I learn to foxtrot with two elegant dancing partners. Afterwards, the director, smiling, says: "You're getting more than you bargained for." But I always am.

"The dynamics today are funny," actor David Kener says after the second day at table.

That's weird—to see the playwright giving acting directions to the actors. But then it's Arthur Miller, for God's sake.

I feel that every moment of that director-writer-actor dynamic is understood and recorded simultaneously by everybody in the room. When the playwright is commenting on or complimenting the actor on what he or she has just read, that too is recorded in the actor's psychology. And I think it's the creative and talented artist that lets in what's useful, and the rest is put to the side for future grazing.

Kener gives as an example the moment during his scene with Keira Naughton's Isabel when Joe checks her fillings. "As I said, 'Open,' Arthur Miller, seated to my left, stage-whispered into Jim's ear, 'I think it would be a good idea if she was chewing gum.'"

And the actress heard it too. There is the whole dynamic we're talking about. Specific notes about physicalizations, about staging, Arthur Miller wouldn't give out loud—or even to the actors. There you see him maintaining his writer's status in the room, *because that was truly a directorial and actor choice. But I still believe the atmosphere in this rehearsal room is so open that that will not become dictum. And that atmosphere was dictated from the beginning by Jim Houghton— not specifically or contractually or verbally. It's a feeling that I have, having worked with many different kinds of actors and directors. [emphasis mine]*

"When Arthur Miller suggests that the actress chew gum, it's an impulse he throws out," Houghton tells me the next day.

It's just that—a suggestion. And that's how it's received. And I will assure the actors that that's how it should be received by them, as I'm sure Arthur will agree. *It's an idea, like many ideas, that may or may not be put into the production. That's what the creative process is about. [emphasis mine]*

There is no gum chewing in performance.

Keira Naughton's perspective is very similar to that of Kener and Houghton: "[The playwright] was trying to filter it through the director. It just happened that we all heard it."

It could be potentially very difficult and intimidating to have Arthur Miller in rehearsal, or any playwright. . . . I asked at the table how Isabel used the word "hey," and he gave me a line reading [laughs]. It's not usually helpful but in this particular . . . [pause] it's Arthur Miller . . . [pause], and I can now take it and use it or I can make my own choice and I don't think he'd be offended. But maybe he would be and he wouldn't tell me, but that's okay, too.

"You sort of forget that he's an icon at the moment you're listening to him," Laura Esterman (Rose Baum) says, "and then you remember this is the man who wrote *Death of a Salesman*. In this instance, he seems to like what I'm doing and that gives me confidence." Her response to Miller's rehearsal notes is entirely positive: "He talks like a director, not like a writer, which is great. He doesn't intellectualize. I'm sure that he's going to let Jim do what he's going to do." Stephen Pearlman's response to the playwright's presence in rehearsal is ambivalent. On the one hand, Miller's comments on the Iowa judge were "tremendously helpful." On the other hand, the actor does not want even the positive feedback valued by King and Esterman:

> *I don't like it when the playwright is there at every rehearsal. . . . Whoever it is, I don't like my work evaluated after each rehearsal. . . . I'm not talking about making a suggestion or giving a direction, which is fine. I'm talking about some-one saying, "You're on the right track" or "You got that wrong."*

For Chris Messina (Sidney), "It's like a dream. . . . I find myself staring at him."

> *It's not anything but me being green and young, but it has almost been impossible up to this point not to be aware of him and wanting to impress. During the first run-through of the first act this week, he was there and I got up to sing and I'm sitting next to the piano and I could see a reflection in the piano of him and the director. And the actor said, "Concentrate, focus, be in the moment," but all I could concentrate on was Arthur Miller in the reflection.*[29]

"I've been acting for thirteen years, and this is one of the few times when I've mentioned the playwright's name and *everyone* knows who I'm talking about," Myra Lucretia Taylor (Irene) tells me.

> *And there is a sense of awe. You know, he's very smart. He seems to really under-stand the actor's process and the actor's language. So I find myself leaning in to receive his wisdom. It's true. And he's so gorgeous. It makes you feel great about growing older.*

The actress compares the playwright in rehearsal to "a griot, the person who has the wisdom and history of an African tribe. So he's like the one who has that for us in this piece."[30] Then, without transition, she says: "We're going to have to put him aside. As much respect and love and gratitude as we have for this treasure, we're going to have to create our own reality. Because if it's not real for us, the people might just as well sit and read it."

Jason Fisher (Lee Baum) seems to agree with Taylor:

> *I feel liberated doing the part [the Arthur Miller figure in the play]. I don't feel constrained to be faithful to what I think Arthur was going through. . . . I feel that he chose me to do the role because of what I am and what he saw. So if I can just be faithful to my impulses, I feel as if that's getting closest to the heart of the matter. . . .*
>
> *The times he was here had a feeling of celebration. . . . Of course, you want to please. But the best way to do that is to take your own time with it. But he is a playwright, and I am an actor. And he's not an actor. Without me the thing couldn't get voiced, and without him there'd be nothin' to say. Any good play is dependent on the living people. And he knows that. He writes for that.*

Asked what he gets from watching actors in rehearsal, Miller tells me: "I get their personalities which are always different from production to production.

They always color what the impression will be. That's always very interesting. They can add something unexpected, and that's wonderful."

The next day (September 11), the company returns to the windowless basement studio, next door to the theater. The playwright is expected, but back pain prevents his immediate return.[31] Houghton sits, listening, as Loren Toolajian conducts the cast's daily singing with piano accompaniment: "Try to focus on your sound. The point is to develop your inner ear and your outer ear. . . . Work on picking up the tempo. . . . It's 1929. Life is good." The music director replaces the playwright as a quasi-directorial figure in rehearsal.[32]

"These actors are all my first choices before Arthur saw them," Houghton tells me during a break. "Arthur came for the callbacks and saw two or three actors audition for each role. I want the writer completely involved in that process."[33]

I think often the writer's initial impulse in creating the character is still alive in them. It's a visceral thing for the writer, and I was happy that his visceral responses to the actors in the audition were the same as mine. The writer's visceral response to the actors in audition is directly related to the initial impulse of creating the character.

Then the director adds: "There is an extension of this in rehearsal. The development of character is not restricted by that initial impulse of the writer. That initial impulse is the springboard."

Like director Garland Wright and playwright Elizabeth Egloff in rehearsal of *The Devils* or—in a different way—director Douglas Hughes and playwright David Rabe in rehearsal of *A Question of Mercy*, Houghton and Miller here seem to be speaking with the same voice. "What I can do," Miller later tells me, "is to impart to the actors the original image that the characters should spring out of."

I don't expect that a director will necessarily perceive that image from the script. He might. I look and listen for departures from the image. It doesn't mean that the actors will necessarily re-create that image. The information I can give the actor will make the image more persuasive than if he simply got it from the director or from himself alone.

My rendering of that image might be not quite what the actor portrays. That's all right. He will have a grounding in the image as I saw it. He may go on from there. In fact, I hope he does. But he will have some starting point.

"He's had enough distance from this play," Houghton says of its author, "so that it's almost as if he's hearing it for the first time. Even in the rehearsal at table the first day, he told me he didn't know what was coming next. At the end [of the read-through], he felt very comfortable with the structure and flow of the scenes. He felt as if the country was having a conversation with itself."

This sense of the whole country in conversation with itself has as its starting point the stage directions of the revised text: there are no individual entrances and exits. "We're always on the stage," actor Christopher Wynkoop says.

> And therefore we are a part of the whole ten years of the Depression, all of its facets. So, for instance, when I sit down as Frank the chauffeur, inside I have the freedom to become any other character in the play. I have to keep alive on the stage. I could be a dockworker in my mind. I think what all of us represent when we're not actually performing up there is all of America in that era—and in a way so do the characters.

Keeping alive on stage means being ready to have a conversation with any character in the world of the play. Isiah Whitlock, Jr., who, like Wynkoop, plays six roles, tells me:

> I'm not Banks [the black hobo], I'm not Clarence [a shoeshine man], I'm not Isaac [a café proprietor], but I'm not Isiah either. At that point I'm an actor who's got six characters to play and basically you're at the ready. Your mind is following along and you're preparing for the next character. . . . You need the rest of the play, what you're watching, if that makes sense, to get to the next character. They all grow; they're stacking on top of one another.

Houghton begins rehearsal at table on September 11 by charting a course for the company, one that actress Myra Lucretia Taylor has anticipated: "The great thing about having Arthur here is that we can get clarity on certain things. But ultimately what you need is to be clear about your own impulses." The actors continue to raise questions about the circumstances in the play. During the next few weeks, the playwright responds by telephone to a growing list of rehearsal queries compiled by dramaturg Suzanne Bradbeer.[34] What was the welfare office like? ("It was a five-ring circus.") What kind of card game are the women playing? ("Bridge.") Was Rose's niece, Lucille, a stripper? (She had performed "sexy dancing" in "a tight, suggestive costume" with a traveling circus in the Northeast.) Where is Lee when the Baum family is evicted? (He is a newspaper reporter living in New York.) Is Moe Baum out of work? (Moe sells women's clothing—blouses, dresses—on commission at two stores.) Who wrote: "It's a braw bricht moonlicht nicht tonicht"(80)? (There are many guesses, ranging from Chaucer to Robert Burns. Miller says: "It's something people used to say on the street." Later he confirms for the dramaturg that the line is from a Scottish song by Harry Lauder, and then he sings on the phone, imitating Lauder's voice.)[35] The playwright's responses to the actors' questions are a kind of "extratext," a resource for the creation of new subtext.

As in his rehearsals of Shepard's *Curse of the Starving Class*, Houghton characteristically raises questions in response to the actors' questions, provoking further inquiry into the "given circumstances"—which turn out to be not so much "given" as constructed by continuing rehearsal explorations. Rehearsing the play on its feet, an actor wants to energize a scene: "I feel as if we should be *doing* something." "Good," Houghton says, entering the playing area. "Let's create the givens. Let's imagine what has immediately preceded this conversation." The absent playwright is not consulted. Lewis J. Stadlen (Moe Baum) tells me: "An actor's job is to write your own subtextual play under the words."

> *That's not to say that I can't learn from Arthur Miller, but let's say I'm doing a production of* American Clock *during which Arthur Miller never appears. . . . It's still my responsibility to try to figure out what Arthur Miller intended when he wrote the play.*

But this sense of responsibility is tricky, as the author himself knows: "My rendering . . . might be not quite what the actor portrays. That's all right." Were he to attend every minute of every rehearsal, there would still be, as Miller well understands, a creative interchange between the desire to draw closer to and the need to depart from the authority of the playwright.

Two weeks later, on September 26, Houghton begins rehearsal with a series of questions: "What room are you in? Where are the front windows? What time is it now? How long have you been playing cards?" In a scene being rehearsed on its feet for the first time, Rose, her niece Lucille, her sister Fanny, and Doris, the wife of Fanny's son Sidney, play bridge with invisible cards. In the middle of the game, Rose, fortune-telling, sees in the cards the death of a young man. (In a previous scene, Lee's boyhood friend Joe throws himself under an approaching subway train.) "Does it have to be bridge?" an actress asks. "None of us plays bridge." "Arthur says it's bridge, but . . . ," another actress responds. "In real time it can't really be bridge," the director says. "I suggest hearts. No one will ever know, but we have to decide." There is an extended discussion of other possible games (whist, gin). Laura Esterman (Rose) suddenly asks: "Could I have another deck of cards for the fortune-telling?" As stage manager Amanda Sloan searches for a pack of cards, the director inquires: "Are you asking for a real deck of cards?" "No," Esterman replies. Actress Mary Catherine Wright exclaims in disbelief: "You're asking permission for an *imaginary* deck of cards?" An explosion of laughter halts rehearsal.

Like the revised text itself, the staging of *The American Clock* is precariously poised between the realistic and the nonrealistic. Miller's stage directions at times suggest, and at times specifically prohibit, a realistic rendering. For example, Rose "*[e]nters in housedress and apron, wiping her hands on a dish towel*" (37), but then "*Rose, at the piano, has her hands suspended over the keyboard as the band pianist plays*" (53). In performance on October 10, 1997, characters dressed in period costume stand, walk, and dance on an abstract set. During a scene in which imaginary cards are played on an imaginary card table, real lemons arrive in preparation for "lemonade" poured into real glasses. Lee's invisible bicycle is stolen, but the borscht his mother serves is a visibly red liquid. A sign as one enters the auditorium prepares the audience for the fairly loud sound of a gunshot during the performance, but a noose around the Iowa judge's neck is so implausibly placed that he is in no danger of being lynched. The noose is visibly as harmless as the gunshot, but the latter is staged within the conventions of realistic theater; the former is not.

On the stage floor and side walls of the set designed by E. David Cosier are red and white stripes in a kind of Jasper Johns American flag motif. A blue sky with wisps of white clouds painted on a scrim is superimposed on a blue brick wall, so that open sky and a wall constructed behind it are ironically indivisible. Like the disjunction between the upbeat lyrics and the wistful music of certain songs of the 1930s, a wall opens into a sky that turns out to be, in fact, a wall.

Near the beginning of *The American Clock*, a speakeasy owner describes Randolph Morgan's fall to his death after the stock market crash: "It was still that blue light, just before it gets dark? And I don't know why, something made me look up. And there's a man flyin' spread-eagle, falling through the air. He was right on top of me, like a giant!" (22). For Miller, who lived through the era he writes about and hears the clock ticking, the play "ends on a very positive note. The teller of the tale is still alive to tell it, and hopeful."[36] While the cast sings "Life Is Just a Bowl of Cherries" in *"a soft, long-lost tonality,"* soft-shoe dancing Theodore K. Quinn delivers the new last line in the revised edition of the play: "God, how I love that music!"(87).[37]

At the press conference inaugurating the Arthur Miller season at Signature Theatre, James Houghton had said: "Arthur was very excited by the idea of Joe Chaikin directing his plays. I hadn't expected that these two would work together, would have the same dynamic." Joseph Chaikin, well-known for his work in experimental theater, at first seems strangely paired with a figure whose plays have been labeled as traditional American realistic drama. But Miller's work at times resists as much as it invites realistic staging, and the choice of Chaikin seems appropriate for a playwright who insists: "If you look at each play separately, you see that I have written in many different dramatic forms. . . . But the critics keep repeating the same things they found in the morgue."

A stroke left Chaikin aphasic in 1984. Poststroke, what Eileen Blumenthal calls his "new, blasted language" requires that actors in rehearsal listen to the director in the same way they enter a dramatic text: by learning "to understand its particular . . . grammar rather than . . . [struggling] to translate it into approximations in standard English."[38]

Several weeks after the closing of *The American Clock*, at 11 A.M. on December 2, 1997, in a studio on the eighth floor of the Manhattan Theatre Club in New York City, the company assembles for the first table reading of Miller's one-act, two-character play *I Can't Remember Anything*, in which Leonora, a woman with seemingly impaired memory, spends a great deal of time visiting Leo, a friend and former colleague of her deceased husband. The playwright is not yet present. After brief announcements by Elliot Fox, associate director of Signature Theatre Company, and production stage manager Donald Fried, the director says simply: "Let's read the play."

Rebecca Schull (Leonora) and Joseph Wiseman (Leo) read the opening dialogue. The director looks at his script and makes notes on a small, yellow lined pad, glances back and forth at the two actors, and continues to write. At the end of the read-through, Chaikin says: "It's wonderful, it's wonderful."

Like *The American Clock*, *I Can't Remember Anything* appears in two different versions. Miller has added several pages of dialogue to the revised text, including a new final page. During the break, Joseph Wiseman looks at my copy of the earlier edition of the play and says, "Throw it away." Later he explains: "It doesn't impel me. I have to work with what's in front of me."

Chaikin gives brief notes to the actors and asks them to read the play again. Now there are more pauses, suggestive of new explorations of subtext and relationship. In the first read-through, Wiseman, who is older than the actress he is addressing, omits the phrase "twelve years" in Leo's line to Leonora: "You're twelve years older than me."[39] This time the actor stops at that line and asks the director if he should omit "twelve" or read the line as written. Chaikin turns to dramaturg Catherine Sheehy who says: "I think we should leave it. Twelve is a big number." Later, after the playwright has attended rehearsal, Wiseman tells me: "I left out 'twelve years older.' Arthur didn't say anything. I'm leaving it out for the time being." (In performance on December 30, 1997, the actor says: "I don't think you're a year older than me." The author, who sees several run-throughs before opening, does not object.)

After the second reading at table, Chaikin gives further notes: "Some ideas. You're cooking rice [to Wiseman]. And it's a failure." (Leo burns the rice.) To the actress he says, without elaboration: "Leonora, 'look out the window' [14] is a shift." He says to Wiseman: "Leo, it's not clear about Frederick [Leonora's deceased husband]. Can you tell about Frederick?" "You mean the backstory?" the dramaturg asks Chaikin, and then addresses the actor: "Tell about your relationship to Frederick." "He was my master," Wiseman says. "He was the greatest man I ever met in my life." There is a long pause. "You find something lacking there?" "No, no," the director replies. "I see, I see," the actor responds. "What he really meant to me. I'm passing over it too lightly." Chaikin's notes, often telegraphic, invite more nuanced readings, further exploration of hidden narratives. "Shift," an important word in Chaikin's rehearsal vocabulary, asks the actors to notice and play, rather than smooth over, discontinuities in the text.

Though not so pervasive as in *The American Clock*, music and dance are central to both *I Can't Remember Anything* and *The Last Yankee*. The play-long dialogue between two old friends in *I Can't Remember Anything* pivots on a samba. In his notes to the actors, Chaikin says: "Maybe you dance. Maybe celebration of [Leonora's] birthday. Maybe it's wonderful to dance in the last scene. Then a shift: 'breakfast.'" The actress asks: "Do you want us to dance together? Because the stage directions say I dance alone." Chaikin suggests that Leo join the dance by beating out the rhythm ("*He moves his shoulders to the beat*" [24]). Assistant director Kevin Kittle tells the actors: "Arthur says that the dance is very important, that the dance expresses everything you really feel toward each other but can't say. That it's a love story." The playwright's voice has entered the rehearsal, and the actress responds: "That's interesting—that it's a love story they're not admitting. I had read it as his being condescending to me." (Leonora to Leo: "Every evening I feel this same condescension from you" [21].) Kittle again brings the authorial voice to the actors: "Arthur has said that he believes Leo loves her," then adds: "But let's let him say what he thinks tomorrow." Wiseman offers his view: "We have two caring people who cannot bear the burden of caring anymore. Caring becomes a burden." The director does not speak for the playwright, whose back pain has prevented his coming to the first day at table. He simply tells the cast: "Arthur will be here tomorrow, interpreting the play."

At 1 P.M., *I Can't Remember Anything* is rehearsed on its feet. A small table and two chairs are placed in the center of the room. The actors begin and are almost immediately interrupted by Chaikin: "It's interesting, Leonora. You have nothing to do. Nothing to do. Today. The future. Nothing to do." They begin again. The tentativeness of the first read-through has returned; improvising physicalizations and blocking, the actors are again exploring new territory. Chaikin interrupts after Leo describes what it would be like to have a stroke. "You know, I had a stroke [13] years ago," the director tells the actors. "I had a heart problem when I was a child. I had a stroke, I couldn't talk at all. I can talk now. There's a different color in that. . . ." "I see," Wiseman says, and rereads the line: "Well, that's how you look when you have a stroke" (10). "Good," Chaikin says. He interrupts a little later with a note for Schull: "That's funny, very funny." She rereads Leonora's line: "I can't for the life of me figure out why I haven't died." Leo's response, "Well, maybe it'll come to you" (10), is greeted with laughter.

A new cast arrives at 2:30 P.M. for the first read-through of *The Last Yankee*. Again there are two versions of the text, but here the revisions are more radical: three female characters and a second scene, twice as long as the first, have been added to a one-scene play with two male characters. In the original version, two husbands meet in the visiting room of a state mental hospital; the new second scene introduces their wives, both suffering from depression, and a third, never identified, silent woman, also institutionalized. At 3 P.M., sitting at the table with the actors, Chaikin announces, in his elliptical style: "So can read the scenes, the play, *The Last Yankee*." After the first scene, he says: "Changing angles." Shami Chaikin, the director's sister (playing Karen Frick), changes her seat at the table so that she and Kate Myre (playing Patricia Hamilton) can face each other. After an uninterrupted reading of the second scene, Joseph Chaikin says: "Very nice."

As before, the director gives brief notes to the actors and asks them to read the play again. After the first scene, he says to Kevin Conroy (Leroy Hamilton): "You know, Arthur is a carpenter. And Jesus is a carpenter. And Leroy, you are a carpenter." The note is glossed by Shami Chaikin: "You're in good company." "Small details," the director says, at the end of the second read-through. He gives a note to Shami Chaikin: "Your husband [John Frick]. Shame." In her reply, "He's ashamed of me? Yes. I know it. And I'm ashamed of me," the actress models a way of reading, and responding to, the director's telegraphic speech.

Remarkably, at the close of the first day of rehearsal, there have been two complete read-throughs of each script; in addition, the director has begun to put the shorter play on its feet. Chaikin says to the cast of *The Last Yankee*: "Arthur will come tomorrow. We'll read again."

At 11 A.M. on December 3, nearly thirty people—the artistic and administrative staff of Signature Theatre, the director, and the casts of both Miller plays—slowly gather in the rehearsal studio for read-throughs at table of both plays in the presence of the playwright. At 11:15 A.M. Miller enters unobtrusively, wearing a black V-neck sweater over a red T-shirt, a beautiful green wool jacket, olive corduroy pants, black-laced shoes, and dark socks. He looks fit, as usual, but his posture is a little bent. Asked to introduce himself, he says: "I can't remember." General laughter. Set designer E. David Cosier displays a model of a fairly realistic set for *I Can't Remember Anything* and mentions that the director has suggested "a kind of shift" in lighting, from green to blue, during the samba.

In performance on December 30, shadows of leaves are visible on the dark green interior walls of Leo's house. The green turns a deep blue and stars begin to appear on the walls—a clearly non-naturalistic design choice—during Leonora's dance. Upstage right are a sink, dish drainer with dishes, and a small pile of wood near a wood-burning stove. The set emblematizes the same tension between a realistic and a nonrealistic presentation as did the staging of *The American Clock*.

Cosier shows the company a model of the set for *The Last Yankee*: several chairs, low tables, two beds. A single white cloud is magically suspended in space in front of the coal-black upstage walls of the mental institution. The non-naturalistic skies, calling into question the inside/outside distinction in both set designs, are neither indicated in the stage directions nor challenged by the playwright.

Now Teresa Snider-Stein presents her research on costume design directly to Miller, who expresses clear preferences. I overhear fragments of his responses: "That's too elegant" he says. "This is more like it than that. . . . Don't make her too Spanish. . . . But it shouldn't be cheap. . . . Black tights, red top: she looks like a ringmaster." (In performance of *The Last Yankee*, Karen Frick wears a black tuxedo with sparkles on the lapels, a short black skirt, and black top hat as she tap-dances while her embarrassed husband tries not to watch.) Just before rehearsal begins, Shami Chaikin discusses Karen Frick's singing of "Cheek to Cheek"[40] with Miller, who sings part of the song for the actress, saying: "You can go as far as you want to go. I only know the second verse."

At this table, in this room, each cast has read each play twice, but the situation is entirely different once the playwright takes a seat at the table. Miller sits without a script, his arms folded across his chest; he looks back and forth at Schull and Wiseman as they read the dialogue in *I Can't Remember Anything*. The director shifts his gaze from the script to the actors, his face serious, unsmiling. In contrast, the author smiles often and laughs easily.[41] Although focused on the script, the actors seem to take in every vibration of the playwright's responses. I hear Miller laugh deep in his throat when Wiseman, who bears an uncanny resemblance to the playwright, reads Leo's line: "I've been a Communist all my life and I still am, I don't care what they say" (17). Miller leans back in his chair; the fingers of his right hand curve under his chin, then his arms cross over his chest, as he watches and listens intently. At the same moment, the director, sitting immediately to the playwright's left, studies the text; the fingers of his left hand mark a particular passage, and he makes a note on his yellow pad. The playwright gazes at the actors; the director gazes at the script and writes.

During the reading of new dialogue in the revised script—Leo asks Leonora not to visit him all day every day—Miller's left forefinger presses against his mouth. I see his lips move. As the actors read the revised ending, in which Leo again futilely attempts to redefine his relationship with Leonora, the playwright's lips move soundlessly and then, for a moment, the faraway look that I saw during rehearsal of *The American Clock* appears in his eyes. His right hand, fingers slightly splayed, moves to cover his right ear, as if to block out traffic noise on West Forty-Third Street eight stories below. He gazes steadily at the actor across the table reading Leo's final monologue, laughs, and then claps as the read-through ends.

After a short break, a new cast assembles at the table to read *The Last Yankee*. Miller sits, again without a script, arms folded over his chest, eyes on the actors. His right hand moves to cover his mouth, two fingers against his lips. Then I see the words of Leroy Hamilton form silently on the playwright's lips as Kevin Conroy reads: "Well, what's it going to be, equality or what kind of country—I mean, am I supposed to be ashamed I'm a carpenter?"[42]

The actresses begin reading the new second scene. Miller leans forward, his elbows on the table, looking intently at Kate Myre and Shami Chaikin. As the actress sings "Cheek to Cheek," he grins broadly. During the first dialogue between Patricia Hamilton and her husband, Leroy, the author's left hand covers his mouth while the fingers of his right hand shield his ear from the sound of street traffic. His long legs are stretched out. He leans forward, then sits back in his seat, his face serious, intent, as his arms slowly fold over his chest. A faint smile appears. Then, almost imperceptibly, he mouths the words Leroy speaks: "I'll say it again, because it's the only thing that's kept me from going crazy—you just have to love this world" (61). The read-through ends. The company applauds.

During the break the playwright confers privately with the director and stage manager and then compliments individual actors. When he pats veteran actor[43] Joseph Wiseman on the back, the actor says: "All right, tell the writer to go home." Miller grins.

"Maybe I should leave you with these folks," the writer says to the director, who indicates that he would like him to stay longer. After a brief discussion, Miller says: "Okay," and cups Chaikin's head fondly in his right hand.

As he did at the table rehearsals of *The American Clock*, Miller talks to the company as a whole only after he has heard a reading of the entire play. Now he tells the actors:

> *I won't say that much because I'm very happy with it all and I think you're all in the right place. With the first play [I Can't Remember Anything], these are two people who have a boundless affection for each other, are bound at the hip. With him she can be quite daring, open; with others she'd be quite repressed. She comes from an old, wealthy New England family. . . . My vision of the play is that it is a kind of love story. They're very deeply attached. In the course of the play their attachment becomes sealed in a kind of crazy way. They'll never break this off. We don't know if she'll remember that he's told her she'll drive him to his grave. It doesn't matter.*

In his comments on the first play, Miller offers the actors the original image that the characters should spring out of: his "vision" of the play as "a kind of love story." In his comments on the second play, he talks about rhythm, breath, and heartbeats, first giving the director freedom to reorchestrate the play through rehearsal exploration:

> *As for* The Last Yankee, *it's all Joe's orchestration from here on out. You know, the rhythms of the play are reproducing depression and optimism. She [Patricia Hamilton] is a roller coaster. In a way, it's replicating what happens in this country, in perhaps every country. For a while everything works and then suddenly nothing works. This play was written at a time of great doubt. I can't remember the date, maybe the '80s.*
>
> *In both scenes it starts with the heart barely beating. Then the breaths start getting deeper, and the end is what it is. I hardly need tell you [to Kate Myre] your feelings are euphoric, which you're very delicately trying to preserve. In the corner there's a darkness which you're aware of.*

Like actors in *The American Clock*, Kate Myre later recalls Miller's exact words in rehearsal:

> He said something that described Patty [Hamilton] so well. *There's a darkness in the corner, and every time she's appreciating this clarity she hasn't had in so long and feels able to take a little hopeful step, then there're shadows and darkness.* And that's true for everybody, isn't it? [emphasis mine]

The character she plays, as the actress clearly understands, is illuminated by Miller's rehearsal note on the rhythms of optimism and depression.

After the playwright's commentary, Chaikin gives elliptical notes in which the word "shift" appears with increasing frequency. Like Suzan-Lori Parks's "spells," Chaikin's "shift" takes on incremental meaning only as the plays are rehearsed on their feet. Miller addresses the actors again, giving more detailed descriptions of particular characters in each play:

> *Maybe I could tell you more about the lives of these characters. Leo [in* I Can't Remember Anything] *was married for fifteen years. His wife was nutty. They*

lived in a good neighborhood in the Midwest, in Ohio. One day he went up on the roof to fix something and when he came down she said she was going to leave. She was embarrassed by this. He was relieved and left. [None of these events is mentioned in the play.]

He is very attractive to women. Women keep bringing him food in pots. He barely has to cook. He's quite alive to his life. Not like her [Leonora]. We don't know what she remembers.

As he continues to talk about the "lives" of the characters, he casually adds "directorial" notes:

[Leonora] doesn't want to be involved with her own life. She drinks and sits with him. She doesn't bother with her children, and they don't bother with her. . . . [Her deceased husband's] greatness consisted in the fact that he was a genius in his work, and he was a spirit. He emanated great energy in his house. You became his equerry. However, there were moments when you wished you could shine a little more and not just as his wife. But he treated you with respect, and you can't complain. The great tragedy, as you [Leonora] say, is that he died first.

Miller's comments on the carpenter, Leroy Hamilton, in *The Last Yankee* are also somewhat directorial:

He fell in love with wood. In a very quiet way he's a very passionate person. Nobody else in his family has that aesthetic sense he has. He's an artist, really. What we're talking about is an artist. We'd never think of him that way but he is.[44]

The playwright's last note in the reading rehearsal is directed to Kate Myre (Patricia Hamilton):

[Her] family didn't want her to marry him. So what you fell from was a very self-congratulatory family. You know the family in Fanny and Alexander; *the love and [self-]admiration in that family was enormous. . . . She ends up marrying a "swamp Yankee." You know that phrase? [Leroy describes himself to John Frick as "a . . . swamp Yankee," 24.] Someone who comes from where the water is, where no one else wants to be.*

The actress says later: "He talked about the *Fanny and Alexander* family. And my father's [Norwegian] family *is* that family." In the playwright's extra-textual notes, actors continue to find their own subtexts.

During the break James Houghton greets the playwright, who takes out a pocket calendar and asks him if he knows anything about an appointment marked for 6 P.M. that evening at a certain address with no name listed. The director, smiling, says he doesn't have a clue and suggests that Miller consult his wife, Inge Morath. Morath, whom he relies on to keep track of such things, is in Arizona for five days, the playwright says, and adds, in a joking tone: "I don't think I'll go. Why should I spend time with *those* people?"

When I ask how his back is today, Miller says: "Medium rare." While he is giving a more detailed response to my next question, we are interrupted by several actors who have received no individual comments from the playwright after the read-through. As in rehearsals of David Rabe's *A Question of Mercy*, the playwright's silence can be disconcerting.[45] Actor Peter Maloney says: "You didn't say anything about my part [John Frick] or Shami's [Karen Frick]." "Your character belongs to the Rotary,"[46] the playwright responds. "You got him right on the nose. . . . Frankly, I like to talk after you've got some form."

After the actors leave, Miller discusses his relation to rehearsals of earlier productions of *The American Clock* and the two one-act plays.

> *I wasn't present at all during the rehearsal for the British production [of* The American Clock*]. . . . They were working off a script I developed during rehearsals of the Mark Taper production. . . . Peter Wood amplified that script. . . . We discussed this at length on the phone and with letters. I told him that one problem with the original production in New York was that it wasn't vaudeville enough and he ran with that. . . . I've never written a play just like this so it just grew.*

A director reauthoring a play by Arthur Miller keeps in touch with the author's "vision" (and revision). Just as a new text of *The American Clock* sprang out of the playwright's response to rehearsals in Los Angeles, the new ending of *I Can't Remember Anything* was written "after watching rehearsals of an American production" (he can't remember which one, he says), and the "expansion" of *The Last Yankee* followed his viewing of a production in New York City. "I've done this before," the playwright says. "*A View From the Bridge* was originally a one-act play." After its New York production in 1955, "I expanded it to full length for the Peter Brook production [in London in 1956]." Six decades in the theater have not left Arthur Miller uninterested in, or uninfluenced by, the collaborative creative process in which director, actors, and author together seek the "final form" of the play.

Asked how he reconciles a writer's need for solitude with a playwright's need for some contact with rehearsal and production, and whether there is any danger of compromise when he opens his private vision of the work to a public realm, Miller says: "There are two different processes: one is the creation of the work; the other is performance." He characteristically turns to music for an analogy:

> *Consider the case of music. Mozart wrote some stuff. When it came time to play it, it's far less introverted. You're dealing with the public, not with your own memories and your own vision. You've got to make it open and available to others.*
> *It's not a compromise. It's an expansion of the vision of the playwright through the imagination of the actor. This is a vital part of the whole procedure. If his imagination doesn't catch fire, you've got a dead thing. What the audience is relating to finally is the actor's imagination.*

He is leaving for lunch and an uncertain evening appointment. Asked when he will return to these rehearsals, he transfers the fire imagery to the director:

"I want Joe to be alone with the actors for a while. He has to catch fire."
Then he adds:

> *I love Joe. His devotion is so intense and unmitigated. I love his theatrical imagi-*
> *nation. And I hope these plays will evoke it. I think he seems excited [tentative*
> *tone]. . . . I have no idea what he's going to do. I'm not sure he knows.*

He pats me on the shoulder; it's a strong, firm pat. "I'm off. Take care."
Though he will return several times to watch run-throughs, this is my last view
of Arthur Miller in rehearsal.

After the lunch break, Chaikin tells the cast of *The Last Yankee*, "We'll
find a black woman [for the role of the non-speaking woman in bed]," and he
reminds Maloney (John Frick) of his character's racial prejudice. In this casual
note about casting, Chaikin is quietly initiating what will eventually become a
powerful reimagining of the play's ending. That afternoon and in the weeks
that follow, Chaikin creates a space in which actors unselfconsciously question
the text, not by way of interrupting the open rehearsal process but as an ongoing form of it. For example, Kevin Conroy, looking at the stage direction,
"*LEROY, holding a secret*" (16), asks: "What is my secret?" "I don't know, I
don't know," Chaikin replies. "Do you know, Kate?" Both Kate Myre and
Shami Chaikin offer suggestions. The director listens; he doesn't "solve" the
problem. Rehearsal continues. Suddenly the actresses interrupt a scene in
which they do not appear: "We know what the secret is!" It is a suggestive and
a representative moment in Chaikin's rehearsals. The playwright is absent; the
actor's question is not put on an "Arthur list"; the director's silence leaves
open the possibility of further discovery.

Once the plays are on their feet, "shift" becomes a key word in directorial
notes. Even when it is not clear what the nature of the "shift" is to be, the
word jolts the actor into a new choice. Chaikin tells me: "A 'shift' is like a light
bulb going off." It is as if the director were proposing a change in lighting but
not specifying the color of the light: the actors provide the new color.[47] At
times Chaikin simply gives a note in the "shifted" tone (of excitement, remem-
brance, sudden joy).[48]

On December 16, choreographer Gail Gilbert watches the actors rehearse
the dance scene in *I Can't Remember Anything*. Chaikin suggests "a shift in
perspective," an exercise from the Open Theater. The actors sit at the director's table; the director and choreographer enter the playing area and perform
the scene. As Chaikin grows stiller and stiller, Gilbert's samba becomes more
sensual, self-delighting, seductive (as it will be in subsequent rehearsals and in
the performance I saw). There is a problem with the heavy, slightly unwieldy,
beautifully crocheted shawl worn by Leonora. "The dance changes every time
we change the scarf," the choreographer says. There is talk of finding a lighter
one. "But Arthur said he wanted a crocheted scarf," the actress says. "Arthur
will be here tomorrow," Chaikin announces. "Tell him," Wiseman says, "to
stay home." Directors watch actors; actors watch the director, even when they

don't sit at the director's table; but not every actor is pleased to be watched by the playwright in rehearsal.

"I love having the playwright around," Rebecca Schull (Leonora) says.

Hearing him talk about the characters as if they were living, breathing human beings: he knows their history, where they lived, who their family was. The sense you get from him of a whole person with a history really informs a lot. . . .

It's completely different when I'm working with a playwright who is also a director, as I did [playing Fefu] in Irene Fornes's Fefu and Her Friends. *This is different. He was here . . . and now we'll work on our own, and we may find things that haven't occurred to him. For an actor I think it's more comfortable to work with a kind of freedom to improvise. . . . But I think if Arthur said, "This isn't the way I visualized the character," I certainly do have to pay attention to that, because I think the whole play will make more sense if I play the character as he envisioned it.*

"Rehearsing a play is really very tricky," she adds. "Everybody feels inadequate a lot of the time. . . . So it's difficult if you get another perspective from someone who is an oracle. You already have a relationship with a director whose suggestions can be translated into something palpable that will *work* on the stage."

Asked what it is like having the playwright in rehearsal, Joseph Wiseman (Leo) replies, without hesitation: "Capital punishment."

It's exasperating. First of all, rehearsal for me is a place where I need to make a damn fool of myself. And I'm making a damn fool of myself in front of a man who's already got something finished, and I'm in a most unfinished state. You feel like it's a rape on the man's work. You just feel terrible.

The next day the actor says: "You know, the question you ask is a complicated question. You desperately need them [playwrights in rehearsal], but you feel you're never ready for them."

For Kevin Conroy (Leroy Hamilton), the writer's presence is "a blessing. But it's a mixed blessing."

It's an example of be careful of what you wish for: you just might get it. It's a once-in-a-lifetime opportunity, but it comes with enormous consequences and an enormous sense of responsibility. . . . When you look at a script, you tend to look at it from the actor's perspective and you might take liberties with the words. But when you're working with the playwright, you're reminded that the theater is about the words and it obligates us to respect that. And that's the burden. It's a wonderful burden but it's a burden. That in a nutshell is what I think working with the playwright is like.

Fifteen minutes later as Conroy is reading one of Leroy Hamilton's lines, the director says: "Cut the 'but.'" "Take it out of the text?" the actor asks. "Thank you. You could tell that word was hanging me up. It's incredible how much that one little word throws me off."[49]

Peter Maloney (John Frick), who, like Shami Chaikin, worked with the director in the Open Theater, says:

> *I learned from Joseph Chaikin thirty years ago how powerful the actor can be. We created those plays in the Open Theater [he mentions* The Serpent *and* Terminal*] with the author [Jean-Claude van Itallie and Susan Yankowitz, respectively]. . . . Most of the time you have to kick the playwright out for a time to give everyone the freedom to do their work. And what is their work? The work is to explore the world the playwright has imagined, not to get it right but to find out what there is to find out about all aspects of life in that world. And the things that are to be discovered are not known by* anyone *before the work of rehearsal begins—not by the playwright, not by the director, not by the actors.*

Shami Chaikin (Karen Frick) has a slightly different view. The author, she feels, "doesn't need to be here on a daily basis because we, the actors, have to discover *that which he already knows*. And when it gets in my bones more, I'd love him to come back" (emphasis mine). I ask if the playwright is important in this rehearsal process, and she replies: "I don't think he is. He gave us the jewel, and it's up to us and the director to accomplish what's written."

"I like these two Arthur Miller plays," says Joseph Chaikin during a lunch break. "Jim Houghton sent me eight plays. I found two I really like. It's fun to work with. I usually don't like naturalistic plays but I like these plays. I don't know why." Then he adds: "Some people don't like Arthur's plays because the women are below the men. But I found one idea: we cast a black woman [Betty H. Neals], very good."

In *The Last Yankee*, an unidentified, nonspeaking woman lies on a hospital bed, "*motionless with one arm over her eyes. She will not move throughout the scene*" (26). "There's no woman in that bed before me," actress Betty H. Neals says.

> *[The playwright] has put the bed there. . . . But in this case the space is there for the character not to be defined by anyone except the actor. . . .*
>
> *The other characters have been defined. So you say: "What will I use of me that fits in here?" Here I think the director is so important and wonderful because he helps you to get to your own reading. With every character he has to say, "How does that read?" With me, he has to say, "How do you read?"*

The playwright has created a "space . . . for the character not to be defined by anyone except the actor." If the imaginations of the director and actress in rehearsal catch fire, who lit the fire?

In performance, Betty H. Neals, alone on stage at the end of the play, slowly rises from her bed and walks downstage where she stands looking out at something, shifting her gaze from left to right; she keeps looking further, deeper; her eyes open wider, then close a little in concentration. As the lights dim, she is still looking out beyond the world of the stage, taking in something the audience can't see. One of the most powerful moments in the play, Chaikin's animating of a "motionless" woman may have roots in his own experience,[50] but it also reproduces, in fruitful tension with the "authority" of the text, the rhythms of depression and optimism that characterize not only *The Last Yankee* but also much of Miller's writing for the theater, including *The American Clock*, and, most famously, *Death of a Salesman*. "For a while everything works and then suddenly nothing works," Miller said to the cast at the table reading. By suddenly mobilizing a motionless woman in the final moments of the play, Chaikin takes up and reverses this pattern, but the reversal asserts the pattern. Like the wall/sky in *The American Clock* that suggests both a beyond and an enclosure, the risen woman at the end of *The Last Yankee* looks "beyond" yet is still enclosed.

When Arthur Miller cupped the director's head in his hand, he knew what he was holding. In the final stage image, a woman looks out beyond the conventional frame of the play. What seems to be a rejection of the play's "naturalism" is also a celebration of the author's openness to investigation and exploration of forms beyond naturalism. A playwright who dared to direct the Beijing rehearsals of *Death of a Salesman* in a language he did not understand deserves to be listened to when he calls in question notions of realistic and nonrealistic staging. Urging his Chinese actors to use less makeup, he argues:

> *The poetry in this play arises . . . out of the expansion of the real into many dimensions of dream, memory, and the projections . . . of . . . imagination; but without the real it won't work.*[51]

7 Maria Irene Fornes in Rehearsal
The Summer in Gossensass

[I]n the beginning all the author has is that there is something to be discovered. That is all she has. And the writing of the play is its discovery. . . . [B]y the time the author gets halfway through, she knows what the question is. Then, answering the question begins to shape the play. . . . [E]very answer creates another question. . . . When the questions begin to dwindle, that means the play is coming to an end. The last question is the one whose answer doesn't invite another question. At the start the subject haunts the writer. And at the end the writer is in a state of bliss. Do you think that's right?
—The Summer in Gossensass, scene 5

Which revised script are we revising?
—a cast member

"*I*rene is the real deal,"[1] Sam Shepard has said of famously under-recognized playwright Maria Irene Fornes, who has written some forty "elliptical, passionate, hypnotic plays"[2] over the past four decades. Alisa Solomon suggests that Fornes "has redefined American drama as profoundly as . . . Arthur Miller."[3] The playwright's own view is characteristically Fornesian: "For me, being on the margins is the only place to be. Sometimes maybe it is advisable to get even a little bit farther away."[4]

The Cuban-born playwright immigrated to New York at the age of fifteen. Originally trained as a painter, she has taken formal classes in both acting and directing; in the 1960s, she observed Lee Strasberg's sessions at the Actors Studio as well as Open Theater sessions with Joseph Chaikin, who staged her Obie Award–winning play *The Successful Life of 3* in 1965, the same year that her Obie-winning *Promenade* was produced at Judson Church in New York City. Since 1967 Fornes has directed almost every first production of her plays, including *Fefu and Her Friends*, *The Danube*, *Mud*, *The Conduct of Life*, *Abingdon Square*, and, most recently, *Letters from Cuba*. She has also staged the works of Calderón (whose plays she has translated and adapted), Ibsen, and

7.1 Maria Irene Fornes and interested onlooker in rehearsal (photograph by Sylvia Plachy)

Chekhov, among others. Awarded eight Obies for writing and directing, including one for Sustained Achievement in Theatre, she founded the INTAR Hispanic Playwrights-in-Residence Laboratory in New York City and conducts playwriting workshops across the country. She was Signature Theatre's playwright-in-residence during its 1999–2000 season and has been artist-in-residence at Women's Project and Productions, an independent producing organization founded in 1978 by Julia Miles as a response to the underrepresentation of women playwrights and directors on the American stage.

Women's Project and Productions presented a work-in-progress production of *The Summer in Gossensass*, directed by the playwright, at the Harold Clurman Theatre, February 1–2, 1997, and subsequently its author-directed world premiere, with a largely new cast, at the Judith Anderson Theatre, March 31–April 26, 1998, in New York City.

"*Hedda Gabler* was the first play I read from start to finish without stopping," Fornes has said.[5] In her 1987 staging of Ibsen's play at the Milwaukee Repertory Theatre, the seeds for a new play were sown. *The Summer in Gossensass* is about two American actresses, Elizabeth Robins and Marion Lea, and their small circle—Elizabeth's brother, Vernon; Lady Florence Bell; and David, a theater-smitten eccentric—who are involved in arranging for the British premiere of *Hedda Gabler*. (Gossensass was the summer resort in the Tyrol where Ibsen met Emilie Bardach, the young woman who inspired his creation of Hedda.)

The Summer in Gossensass is a play in which the object of desire is a play: it enfolds and unfolds, repossesses and is possessed by, *Hedda Gabler*. David is possessed by Hedda; Elizabeth is possessed by Ibsen. Actors are possessed by playwrights who are themselves possessed. The script abounds in vampires. Fornes's characters are vampirized by Ibsen's. As the author later remarks to the cast in rehearsal: "There are many Draculas in this play."

I have observed Fornes's work in rehearsal as playwright-director for more than a decade.[6] At times her scripts seem even stranger and more arresting in her choreographing mind than on the page,[7] almost as if she writes one play and directs another—but this is not true. "The sitting is part of the libretto," Fornes tells an actress. "The timing is part of the libretto, too." In rehearsal her authorial and directorial impulses are met, challenged, and occasionally rescued by each other. Directing her own plays is, for Fornes, writing in another mode.[8]

Having just learned of the work-in-progress production of *The Summer in Gossensass*, I arrive at the Harold Clurman Theatre on West Forty-Second Street at 9:50 A.M. on January 31, 1997. Three actors are rehearsing on a bare stage in the presence of stage manager Annette M. Smith and lighting designer Philip Widmer. Fornes, who only yesterday finished writing a draft of the play that will be presented tomorrow, enters wearing a gray down jacket and brown leather headgear with gray furry sideflaps. Rehearsal begins in the darkened theater, and the playwright is in full directorial mode: "More red on left" (to the lighting designer); "Take one step upstage because you're a little bit out of the light" (to an actress); "Make it a little more like you're holding the venom inside you. From your stomach the venom comes up to your shoulder. Then your head moves . . . even slower" (to actor Ron Bagden). Like Sam Shepard and Arthur Miller in rehearsal, Fornes, composing for the stage, chooses the vocabulary of music: "More vibrato. . . . More contralto voice, a little lower. . . . You are catapulting to a suicide—you have a high fever. Think of opera" (to actress Molly Powell). As the actors rehearse bows after their in-the-play performance of the final scene of *Hedda Gabler*,[9] I see Fornes gesturing in the darkness from her seat in the front row.

At the end of *The Summer in Gossensass*, Elizabeth Robins delivers a speech she has written, celebrating Ibsen's *Doll House*. The final stage directions indicate that toward the very end Elizabeth's *"voice is inaudible. She is now mouthing the words."*[10] The speech continues, but the actress's voice is silenced. The playwright has written a text she wants represented on the stage but not actually produced as sound.[11] Molly Powell, playing Elizabeth Robins both in the workshop and in the world premiere the following year, politely but clearly states that she wishes to read her final sentence aloud, sotto voce. (The final "inaudible" line is: "Those who were present [at the first performance of Ibsen's *A Doll House* in English], Marion Lea, myself and many others were to be affected by that evening's event for the rest of our lives" [sc. 10, p. 1].) The actress resists the authority of a text that refuses to be sounded. In rehearsal Fornes mediates the conflict between actress and authorial text by allowing a sotto voce reading. (In performance the following year, I hear the actress speaking the final line, although Fornes does not.) Like Suzan-Lori Parks's "spells," Fornes's silences are negotiated in rehearsal.

"To me it is a miracle when I have an impulse about the interplay of images, movements, and words, and it works for the actors," Fornes tells me during a break in rehearsal. "You cannot plan it." Working for a quarter of an hour on one minute of stage action, she suddenly, in the midst of intense directorial activity, revises the text, dictating a cut that she does not explain: "Leave out 'What part is that?'"[12] Amie Quigley (Marion) enters the revision in her script. Ron Bagden (David) asks: "Do you want me to speak more from here?" (pointing to his diaphragm). Fornes immediately resumes her directorial role: "I want the images to be your own. Then I will notice it in your voice."

When I ask about the cut she has just made, Fornes explains: "In rehearsal I hear it over and over, and make changes. Perhaps if I were typing the same scene over and over, I'd take out the same words. . . . It's like smoothing a wrinkle. The line didn't go with the sense and rhythm." In rehearsal, Fornes responds in her continuing dual roles to each new wrinkle:

> *It could be a line is not working, like a false flat. If I think the line would work, I ask the actor to make a different movement; then I correct the physical configuration. For example, a line might work if the actor is standing up, not sitting down. Sometimes it's a matter of inches. . . . A line can work if a person is a few inches further away from the table.*[13]

She continues to speak as a director, but what she says seems equally true of her work as a playwright: "It's like a photographer who takes thirty shots and then later chooses the perfect shot. He didn't know in advance or he would have taken one photo." She adds: "I may make different changes in rehearsal from those I make when I'm typing but the feeling of what it should be is the same."

Just before the matinee on February 1, 1997, the playwright tells me: "I feel good because the [actors'] work is good, but the play isn't finished yet." In a later interview, she analyzes this early version of the play:

> *With* The Summer in Gossensass *the first workshop production in 1997 helped me to understand what things are there but without full force or full clarity. . . . It's almost as if I know some things are not there yet and if you asked me to give you a list of what the things are, maybe I don't know yet. But when I have put away the play for some time and I next read it, I immediately see it. . . . In the case of* Gossensass *it's a little more than that. I want to get to that point which inspired me to write the play, which had to do with the question of interpretation and misinterpretation. Usually when I write a play, I don't want to make a point, but in this case I do.*[14]

When I enter the Women's Project offices at 55 West End Avenue at 10:20 A.M. on March 5, 1998, during the first week of rehearsal for the world-premiere production of *The Summer in Gossensass*, I am handed three different scripts, none of which is up-to-date; the first five pages were rewritten after yesterday's read-through. Actors gather, go outside to smoke, return. In the rehearsal room are two rectangular tables at right angles, surrounded by brown folding chairs. An old Pianola sits against a wall; at the other end of the room, on a small table, are a coffee pot, sugar, milk, and coffee mugs with the names of members of the company pasted on each. The playwright-director arrives, wearing brown laced short boots, a red-and-orange plaid long skirt, a gray jacket over a long-sleeved purple blouse, and her signature red-rimmed eyeglasses. Production stage manager Bryan Scott Clark hands her a thick packet of revised pages of script "typed by elves" late last night. The playwright is asked if she has brought more changes to rehearsal. "No," she replies, but she has brought "research material." Out of a fairly small leather bag she produces pile after pile of Xeroxed pages, including Elizabeth Robins's own writings, scholarly articles on Ibsen and Robins, and some notes on Ibsen's additions to the second draft of *Hedda Gabler*.[15] "He added these to make the play more dramaturgically correct," Fornes says. "I'd like to see that," actress Molly Powell murmurs quietly. "I brought it," Fornes continues, "because my interest in writing the play has to do with interpretation and misinterpretation of *Hedda Gabler* . . . which has to do with making the play accessible to a middle-class, middle-brow audience," and she adds: "There are things in that territory which are mysterious and odd, rather than good or bad." Then she reaches into a second leather briefcase and removes another huge pile of Xeroxes, saying: "Oh, and this is Ibsen's correspondence." There is immediate, loud laughter.

The actors seated at the table begin to read the opening scene. Fornes sits, leaning slightly forward, staring intently at the revised script before her. She interrupts to ask an actress to pause longer, but her eyes remain steadily focused on her writing as she listens to the voices of the actors at table. Her hands rest in her lap, the right hand over the left wrist. Then her right hand, holding a pencil, moves to her mouth, forefinger pressed against her lips. The character who does not voice the words she authors—Elizabeth Robins, silent, at the end of Fornes's play—here finds an image in the figure of the playwright in rehearsal.

Fornes interrupts the actors, dictating a new revision in the newly revised script: Elizabeth's description of Hedda—"To be so wild and to be so conventional. It's very difficult"—becomes "To be so wild and so very conventional is very difficult."[16] Throughout today's read-through at table, after each dictated revision the actors return to the beginning of the speech and immediately reread it in its new form. Sometimes the actors suggest textual changes. "Can I use a contraction?" ("That's" instead of "That is"), Powell asks. "Yes," the playwright replies. Then, after a pause: "No. Emphasize every word." The actress reads Elizabeth's lines as written: "That is right. That is right. That is more interesting." The speech would have a completely different rhythm with contractions.[17] At times, Fornes hears an actor's misreading of a line, likes it, and retains it in the revised script.

Fornes writes as she rehearses and rehearses as she writes. Like Suzan-Lori Parks at table readings of *In the Blood*, Fornes "lags behind" the actors as she listens to them read. The playwright makes new changes only after she hears the revised script. While the actresses read speeches on page 12 of scene 1, Fornes is whispering lines on page 11. She makes a note, and quickly turns to page 12. The actresses read page 13; Fornes continues to study the preceding page and then dictates a cut on page 12. The actors read page 8 of scene 3. Fornes, her lips moving soundlessly, is reading page 4. She circles a speech, then turns to the following page, writes at length on the script, erases it all, writes again, her lips continuing to move as she writes. Then she again erases what she has written, and writes again, lips moving. The actors are now reading scene 4. Fornes continues to look at scene 3, page 5. Suddenly I hear Clea Rivera read Marion's line: "I stared at the place [a rehearsal room] and I imagined the play going on" (sc. 4, p. 3). Fornes's gaze is fixed on a moment in the earlier scene and yet she is listening, in some sense, to scene 4, to the play going on.

The actors continue reading scene 4. The playwright makes revisions on page 3 of scene 3. The fingers of her right hand press against her lips. She writes again on page 3 of scene 3 and then, astonishingly, seconds later dictates an addition to Vernon's speech in the *next* scene, a revision retained in the April 25 script: "You can tell when a person doesn't like another just from reading the lines. Isn't that amazing?" (sc. 4, p. 8).[18] The playwright is looking at the revised, typed script for the first time *as* she listens to the actors at table: her first "reading" of her rewriting is a hearing of it voiced in rehearsal.[19]

Fornes moves effortlessly from authorial revision—eyes on the script, lips moving soundlessly, pencil marking pages the actors are no longer reading—to comments on the delivery of lines. Just as Fornes's continual rewriting in rehearsal transforms the script, her directorial notes transform acting style. Gazing across the table, she interrupts Joseph Goodrich (David) over and over as he reads a speech describing Hedda. "Take a breath. . . . It's like a sigh," she says. "Be a little more her. . . . You're still looking at her rather than being her. . . . When you say, 'She looks like a saint,' you're already seeing the devil in her. . . . She's coming at you again." The actor is wholly transformed as he delivers his lines:

> She's beautiful. Unusual face. Like a cat. . . . Her eyelids move slowly. She blinks. . . . She breathes again. . . . She speaks fast, you get dizzy. She puts her teeth on your neck. . . . That's what Hedda is like. . . . She's very interesting. [sc. 5, p. 18]

Goodrich's head and shoulders are twisted upward. Fornes laughs with pleasure; the actor does, too. He has been possessed by a fictional character—but whose? Ibsen's? Fornes's?

Later in the same scene, Elizabeth Robins reads aloud from Ibsen's correspondence. Fornes, who has just dictated small textual revisions, including the reassignment of half a line,[20] tells the actress playing Elizabeth: "Would you do that speech again, Molly, and do it fast, as if it's Ibsen's heartbeat?"

Now Clea Rivera reads an excerpt from the diary of Emilie Bardach. Fornes, listening, cuts six lines. The actress is asked to reread the speech, as revised, three times; Fornes crosses out words in her script as Rivera reads. She dictates further cuts; the actress reads the new version; more cuts are dictated; the actress reads the revised speech; the playwright listens and dictates another cut. Altogether, at the table, Fornes removes 145 words from a speech of 187 words, a reduction of more than 75 percent.[21] Afterward she says to the cast:

> *Yesterday after I made changes, if anybody had asked me why I made these changes, I wouldn't have been able to answer. It's like an actor's impulse. Usually, I understand why something is cut or moved. But perhaps because I'm working with Ibsen's play, I don't know why I'm reshaping it as I am. It's not as if Ibsen's spirit is moving through me. It's not he who is doing it. I think it's a little bit different from him. [She laughs.] Maybe it's Oscar Wilde.[22]*

During the lunch break I ask Fornes: "What do you hear in your mind when you write words a character says? When you write, do you hear your words in your own head with your own accent?" She responds: "What accent? I never hear my own accent. Do you hear yours?" and she adds:

> *I hear the state of mind.[23] It produces a mood, a tone, a particular reading with stresses in my mind when I write. It's not my accent. It's not anybody else's voice. I don't hear a voice.*
>
> *I hear changes in rehearsal because it's coming at me. If I see the actor misinterpret the mood, I would see if by revising it I could make it clearer what mood it is, because when I'm not directing it, the director may not see the mood I intended. I want to make things clear to the actor, not the director. Sometimes when I add or take out a word, I'm doing that rather than saying, "Change the mood or tone." I don't tell them why I make a change mostly because I think it's obvious. I want to make it clear for other productions.*

Fornes's role as playwright-director is trickier than it appears. She is not merely revising a text for a particular production, as other authors might do in rehearsal. Nor does she simply rely on her considerable directorial gifts to "change the mood or tone." She constructs and reconstructs a script not for future directors but for actors, present and future. Michael Goldman's definition of playwriting is nowhere better exemplified than by Irene Fornes in rehearsal: she practices "an art of composing in the medium of the actor—of composing in action."[24]

Now Fornes explains her earlier revision of the script:

> *The speech was directly from the diary of Emilie Bardach. It was too repetitive in a boring way. [She remarks that she herself uses repetition in her writing.] It just goes back into itself. I was too respectful of the words of a real woman speaking. I find it interesting to read anything that Emilie Bardach wrote about Ibsen.*

Then she adds: "Maybe something unconsciously was telling me that that's enough about Emilie: that the play is not about who inspired Ibsen. That's probably why I cut the speech." Rehearsing a play about actresses who learn about a text by rehearsing it, Fornes relearns her own script, moment by moment, page by page, in the presence of the company.

At the end of the read-through Fornes asks: "Shall we read the play again? But, first, are there any questions?" There are, and the kind of information supplied in other rehearsals by dramaturgs is provided by the playwright-director, and later supplemented by the actors' independent research.[25] The cast raises questions about the length of Robins's rehearsal period (two weeks), the style of acting (largely declamatory, Fornes says), and the acquiring of rights for the first British production of *Hedda Gabler*. Powell then raises a question about Elizabeth's seemingly contradictory lines describing Hedda: "She is wild with company in the parlor. She's not wild. That's why she doesn't go out much."[26] Fornes says simply: "What I meant is that Elizabeth is getting this sense of her as so powerful, so magnetic, so attractive in that world [the parlor], but not outside of it." Even as Fornes is answering her question, I hear the actress quietly repeating the line with different stresses.

A year ago, during a break in the 1997 workshop rehearsals, Fornes said that in writing *Gossensass*, she "wanted to clarify the question of what comes out of the words of the text." What she wants for Ibsen's *Hedda Gabler*, and for her own work, is "an honest reading of and an honest listening to the play." Fornes reads Hedda as suicidal (her marriage to Tesman is already the beginning of her suicide, Fornes says), not pregnant, "a little kinky for her time period," and agoraphobic. She tells me: "The play is not about the issue of interpretation directly. . . . I don't want them to discuss, for example, whether Hedda is agoraphobic or not."[27] Now the issue is "coming at [her]" in rehearsal. She tells the actress: "What it is is that [Hedda is] . . . afraid to go out. This is what *I* know. . . . What Elizabeth knows is that Hedda is a conformist as well as irreverent." Powell again questions the seeming inconsistency in Elizabeth's lines describing Hedda. "I thought—as long as it's clear to you—of not specifying," the playwright-director responds. "It's a contradiction but not 100 percent." Then she offers a revision: "Add '*only* in the parlor.' If that's too clear, we'll take it out later." (The line is later cut.)

In the afternoon read-through, Fornes continues to revise the script, rewriting lines and reassigning speeches. At one point, as the cast reads page 12 of scene 1 while the playwright, whispering audibly, lingers on page 11, one of the actresses breaks off: "I stopped because I felt you were rewriting."[28] The actors wait while the playwright continues to whisper, less audibly. Sitting next to Elizabeth Egloff while she silently made cuts during rehearsals of *The Devils*, I watched lines "audition" for the playwright, but Fornes's actors, unlike Egloff's, witness the "auditions."

At 5 P.M., Julia Miles, artistic director of Women's Project and Productions, and set designer Donald Eastman enter the rehearsal room. Fornes tells the cast that her mother, Carmen, would say, whenever Eastman was expected: "Oh, the man with the toys is coming." The designer presents a small cardboard model of the set to the company. Fornes looks at it and says: "I would prefer that the kitchen be further back. . . . Is that curtain [stage left] going to be blocking the audience view of the skylight?" (In performance, the stage left portion of the twenty-foot-high, red velour curtains that hang in a graceful swirl above the stage is folded back so as not to obscure the skylight on the set.) When Sam Shepard and David Rabe were not fully comfortable with certain design choices, they communicated privately with the director and set designer. The design presentation for *Gossensass* is conducted very much like Fornes's rehearsals: it is interrupted, interrogated, and frequently revised by the playwright-director. Now Fornes asks if there could be another door.[29] "Yes, that would be wonderful," Eastman replies. As they continue to discuss adjustments in the set, Eastman says: "We can resolve it one way or the other. The glue is literally just drying on this." After answering an actress's question, he adds: "Irene, I'm looking at it for the first time myself." "And you're not even looking at it," Fornes says, laughing, to the designer standing behind his model of the set. "Do you like it?" she asks the cast. "I want to live there," an actor replies. After the cast leaves, Eastman, in a joking voice, says: "Here's my idea. Then you can change it." Fornes makes several specific suggestions, drawing her own diagram of the set. Eastman brings forth his large blueprint and they discuss precise dimensions and spatial arrangements, including the placement of the upstage door. Their conversation is serious yet filled with laughter; the designer begins to redraw part of the set as they talk. "But wouldn't it be more interesting if we have an opening, not necessarily a door, here?" Fornes says. "I have another idea, a better idea," Eastman replies. "Better?" Fornes asks, in a joking tone. "I'm going to contradict myself," the designer replies, beginning to present his idea. As I leave the rehearsal room half an hour later, they are still studying the model of the set, agreeing on where doors and pathways are to be. It is like today's table reading: a looking together at what is to be looked at again and again, in altered forms.

The following morning, the floor of the rehearsal room is marked with brown tape to indicate the dimensions of the performance space. Four folding chairs have been placed in the playing area; a large, square wooden box is stage center and another is far left. Fornes, wearing fur-lined brown boots, a maroon patterned wool cardigan over a purple blouse, a long red-and-orange plaid skirt, and a bright blue beret, is seated at the director's table on the edge of the downstage playing area, studying the script. She looks tired. After he explains revisions in the design of the set, stage manager Bryan Scott Clark says to the cast: "I'm going to walk you through the tape." The actors follow behind him as he traverses each imaginary room. Just before rehearsal begins, the stage manager asks Fornes: "How do you want to proceed? Shall the actors move at will?" "At *will*?" she responds, in a tone of mock horror. Loud laughter erupts from the cast.

Two actresses sit on the folding chairs behind the large box. Fornes immediately says, "No, reverse." They exchange positions.

The play is rehearsed on its feet for the first time. Fornes leans forward slightly in her seat, watching the actresses. Her left hand moves across her chest, coming to rest under her right elbow; the fingers continue to move rhythmically. Her right hand presses against her lower jaw and mouth. She stares at the script, her pen in her right hand, her lips moving; the fingers of her other hand press against her lips. She raises her head and gazes, smiling, at the actresses, then interrupts Powell's reading of a thrice-repeated line ("I am about to understand Hedda," later cut),[30] with a note that is indeterminately authorial-directorial: "The repeats have to do with an exciting investigation." When the scene is replayed Fornes interrupts again, asking the actresses to move their chairs and "table" (the large box) downstage. Powell reads another thrice-repeated line describing Hedda: "But in public she is not wild."[31] Fornes interrupts: "It's more sober. It's darker." "Darker," the actress says. "Or more analytical," Fornes responds. "Uh-huh," Powell replies. The scene is rehearsed again. This time the actress stands up at a certain point during the dialogue and Fornes asks her to return to a seated position. After the speech is replayed five times, Fornes says: "Let's cut the repeats."

Throughout rehearsal the playwright-director, shifting her gaze from the script to the actors, makes continual reassessments and adjustments, textual and choreographic. Lines audition and reaudition; speeches are added, cut, rewritten, reassigned; staging is explored and reenvisioned. New text and blocking vanish like footprints in the sand.

At times in rehearsal Fornes enters the playing area to redirect physical positions or clarify the location of parts of the set not yet built. The entrance of Marion in scene 4 requires steps. Fornes decides to move the rehearsal to the foyer of the Women's Project offices where there are two steps leading to the front door.[32] Clea Rivera climbs the steps, knocks, and walks out onto the sidewalk where not only Molly Powell but also Fornes and her assistant, Dawn Williams, stand shivering in the cold. Rivera and Powell rehearse the entrance once; then the four women return to the warmth of the rehearsal room to continue work. What might seem to a passerby a realistic staging is, in fact, a reversal of "outside" and "inside": a person knocks on a door as she exits. This tiny moment in rehearsal is a playful emblem of Fornes's indefinable theater, what Ross Wetzsteon calls her "matter-of-fact surrealism."[33]

During Elizabeth's response to the announcement that Edmund Gosse will translate Ibsen's play without knowing Norwegian, Fornes interrupts: "You have to take all the emotion out." "All the emotion out?" the actress asks. "You know, when a pigeon is taking a bath and then. . . ." Fornes demonstrates what appears to be the behavior of a hyperventilating pigeon. When the laughter subsides, Powell replays the scene.

In the afternoon rehearsal Fornes watches the actors intently, right hand pressed against her mouth, left hand in her lap. Then she rises and stands behind the director's table, studying the entire playing space, not just the actors seated together at its center. She bends over her script, turns pages, straightens up, and then sits down again, looking alternately at actors and text. Suddenly it is discovered that an actress is reading from a version of scene 5 that is one revision behind the others. It is announced that further changes in the text will be dictated later. Fornes says to a cast trying to ascertain which draft of the script they are now reading: "I'm just as confused as you are."

Now Fornes redirects Marion's speech to Vernon: "Everyone is upset. Elizabeth is upset, Archer [who believes Gosse's translation has "defaced Ibsen's play"] is upset and I'm upset" (sc. 5, p. 1). There are no stage directions in the script. Fornes enters the playing area and demonstrates a kind of stylized semi-curtsy and turn, a theatricalized flirtatiousness, on Marion's line, "and I'm upset." As she repeats this demonstration over and over, the cast cracks up, but Fornes is serious. Rivera replays the line; Fornes, unseen by the actress, stands behind the director's table, repeating the choreography she has demonstrated in the playing area. It is a motion so idiosyncratic and specific that it cannot be reproduced exactly, but it transforms a "realistic" acting style into a kind of quirky, theatricalized gracefulness. Daniel Blinkoff (Vernon) jokes that he needs to take a shower. Fornes continues to direct the actress: "Stand in a kind of swooping movement when you say 'Thea Elvsted.'" Clea Rivera removes her shoes and rehearses the blocking over and over without speaking the text. Then she sits, rises, moves upstage, turns in a kind of swirl, takes a stately step backward, and says (in answer to David's question, "What part are you playing?"): "Thea Elvsted" (sc. 5, p. 5). None of these intricately arranged stage movements is indicated in the April 25 script. Fornes is "composing in the medium of the actor."

Just before rehearsal ends on March 6, Fornes directs a speech in which David describes Marion's performance in a play he has seen. "The hand goes up like this," Fornes says, demonstrating, "to the brow . . . and the chest goes up . . . and the head goes down very slowly. . . . Oh! gorgeous!" As Joseph Goodrich replays the scene upstage, facing away from her, Fornes continues to perform these gestures from her seat at the director's table. It is a director-actor dance, performed together and apart, both inside and outside the playing area. Now Fornes enters the playing area and places her hands on Goodrich's upper back and right arm, directing and supporting him as he moves. She stands facing him and they move in unison. She stops abruptly, saying that she has forgotten how he moved while she was watching earlier. "Wasn't it like this?" he asks and demonstrates.

After rehearsal, Goodrich tells me:

> With other playwrights, they bring in a block of ice and chip a little away. For practical reasons, an actor can't say a line a certain way, or the theater couldn't afford a door. But Irene is willing to melt the block of ice and it's not a question of hesitation or indecision or lack of concern for what she's written, for the vision that she brought into the theater. What it is is a willingness to surrender to the moment.

When I enter the rehearsal room on March 7, Molly Powell is discussing Elizabeth Robins's distinctive blue eyes[34] with Fornes, who today is attired in various shades of blue: marine blue culottes, a turquoise blouse under a green wool jacket, and an aqua blue beret. As they talk, Clea Rivera silently practices her swirly turn in scene 5, blocked for the first time yesterday. Rehearsal begins. The actresses read the first two pages of the script five or six times. Fornes's lips move rapidly, soundlessly, before uttering a new revision. At one point Rivera interrupts: "Oh, I thought that line was cut!" (laughter). Fornes says: "I got lost here because I started making a change where I shouldn't." After a short break, during which she rewrites a page of dialogue in scene 1, Fornes exclaims: "Ah ha! Ha! Ha!" The cast laughs. "Shall I dictate it?" As she reads aloud what she has written, she begins to revise it: "For now, let's take that line out." The playwright dictates a new mini-scene; actors and stage managers copy it down in their scripts. Powell and Rivera read the new dialogue aloud; Fornes makes further revisions as she listens; they erase, rewrite, and read again. Fornes makes new revisions. They erase, rewrite, and read again.[35]

Revising in rehearsal, Fornes hears her own textual changes in the context of what she has already seen and heard, and makes further revisions as she continues to listen and watch. The "final" version, whatever and whenever that will be,[36] is shaped by a process in which the playwright-director and actors continually exchange roles, each at some point listening, voicing, writing. Fornes listens to the actors and writes; the actors listen to her voice dictating new text and rewrite; Fornes hears new voicings of what she has newly rewritten, and rewrites, redirects. The continually rewritten script in rehearsal exists as a text-to-be-transformed (or extinguished) until it finds its life as words voiced and heard. In the revised scripts are ghosts, traces of vanished texts.

"I first did a workshop version of this play at the University of Iowa [in 1995] with student actors and one outside actor to play Elizabeth," Fornes tells me during the lunch break. One student, formerly a professional actor, "had a beautiful speaking voice. There was something about his voice, and the intensity of his voice, that made me want to write the part of David."[37]

> *When I was auditioning, the play had not been written. I had been doing research, and I had material. I had not decided what the scenes would be and what material I would be using. A writer gets inspiration from anywhere. That fellow there buying lunch [we are at Claudio Trattoria Pizzeria on West End Avenue] might end up in one of my works—something about his height or his hair.*

She mentions that there were several additional characters in the first workshop production who have since been removed.

> *It's as if I put things in my refrigerator to cook but it doesn't mean I'm going to use them when I cook. Don't you do this when you get material and then you write? You cannot have all kinds of interesting elements. You must think of the structure of the unit. . . .*
>
> *I think I learned a lot about form in theater from painting. I learned to pay attention to form, whether in words or in movement on stage. When you do an abstract painting, you understand the power of elements in proximity to each other, the power on each other, how they affect each other. You look at that column [inside the pizzeria] and see the blue-green in the center and what it does to the white on the sides and what the white does to the blue-green and the width of blue-green and how it would be if it were a little wider.*

In a later rehearsal, Fornes gives a note to Molly Powell as if she's directing her into a painting: "You know those paintings of Renaissance saints that are being tortured. . . . And a little bit sideways. Feel it in the shoulders and the head. . . . Let the eyes try to reach up as if you're trying to find God." As she speaks, Fornes demonstrates in her chair at the director's table. The actress's body, utterly transformed, takes on an amazingly tortured posture as she delivers Elizabeth's lines: "In plays unlike real life characters may not always have a past but they will always have a destiny. The destiny of this character [Hedda Gabler] is to revert into herself and to consume herself. Like an uroboros [a serpent with its tail in its mouth]" (sc. 1, p. 7).

During the afternoon rehearsal on March 7, Fornes enters the playing area, stands next to Marion, to whom David is bowing, and directs the placement of her left elbow, wrist, and hand; the tilt of her shoulders and head; the position of her right foot. She demonstrates the placement of the left arm, watches the actress approximate that position, takes away the actress's script, adjusts the arm, seems to approve, then says: "There is something wrong with the left arm," and readjusts it. Fornes and Molly Powell (who is observing from outside the playing area) simultaneously exclaim: "Oh, yes." The script is then handed back to Rivera who, as she takes it in her left hand, slightly alters the position so painstakingly found.

Marc Robinson has observed that in Fornes's play, with its incorporation of so much writing by and about Ibsen, "the two playwrights seem to jostle for space."[38] He could have been describing the rehearsal of March 12. Fornes enters with Xeroxes of some of Ibsen's first jottings for *Hedda Gabler*, and tells the cast: "He's making notes and writing scenes for an earlier draft." The stage manager then hands out revisions of an earlier draft of a scene from *Gossensass*. It is the writing process itself—both Ibsen's and Fornes's—that is being brought into rehearsal.[39]

A year earlier, after rehearsal on January 31, 1997, I had asked Fornes about the difference between writing and directing her own plays. "For the director," she said, "it's seeing the character in the person of the actor."

> As a writer you have to be inside your character and observe from the outside. That's a trick! You have to write from a character's mind and from a character's heart. You still think in the third person yet you feel it in your heartbeat—but you're watching it from outside. It's like watching someone step on a nail, and your foot goes like that [demonstrates]. . . . The difference is a matter of degree. The observation is more important for the director. For a writer the identification with one character, and then another, is more important, but then one character is observing another character. It's very difficult.
>
> The more I talk about it, the more I think there is something demented about the whole experience.

In rehearsal on March 12, Fornes, as director, "rewrites" without changing the text. Sitting at the director's table, she interrupts the actors as they begin playing scene 7: "Take a little moment, because the sentence [in the script] doesn't lead you to what I'm asking you to do." She moves into the playing area. "So you create it when you say: 'This is the night.' Think of a magician who brings forth a tiger and the woman disappears because the tiger has eaten the woman." The lines and the scene have nothing to do with magicians and tigers. Powell reads Elizabeth's next speech: "That's what we call opening night. We say *the night*" (sc. 7, p. 1; later reassigned to Vernon). Fornes interrupts: "Don't lose your magician. You're still there waiting for the next miracle."

Fornes has said that when she writes, she does not hear a voice: she hears a state of mind. In rehearsal she directs the state of mind she "hears" as a writer. For example, she says to Powell: "A little too hot. It's really peaceful, almost religious. Every word is a different landscape." Two hours later, Fornes dictates a fairly conventional stage direction: "*A pause. Dark thoughts.*"[40] Then she gives Powell an astonishing note *on* the new stage direction: "A cloud passes through you." (Later the actress tells me: "I wrote it down, too. It's wonderful!")

"No one that I've worked with works like Irene," says Molly Powell (Elizabeth).

> *I feel that she works very viscerally, like a little animal that is entirely alert. All of her senses are working. There's a kind of animal focus: she's very, very, very focused on what's right in front of her. Everything that we do in rehearsal—every tone of voice or tilt of the head or angle of the body—somehow lands on her, is perceptible to her. So she starts sorting and pulling and sifting and extending what we do. . . . When we do work on longer stretches, her attention expands to look at the whole arc. But right now each little second is passionately looked at. That's how I experience it.*[41]

When I ask Clea Rivera (Marion) if she thinks of Fornes as a director when she blocks a scene and as a playwright when she revises the text, the actress responds: "She is a director who might also change lines, and she's a playwright who likes to get involved with the way those lines are spoken and with the way the actors move. And she's just a full entity unto herself."[42]

Daniel Blinkoff (Vernon) says, "Rehearsal is 're-hears-all.' It's a process where you rehear it all." But the "full entity" of the playwright directing her own work is problematic for the actor:

> *I think that to try to combine those two roles into one person is a difficult task . . . a dangerous task. . . . You get in a situation where the purpose of rehearsal can become more concerned with the writing of the play itself than the mounting of the play. . . . I think the director and playwright have to be distinct.*[43]
>
> *I'm formulating ideas with a great concern for their clarity. As a result, our conversation is periodically sporadic. And that's the feeling you can sometimes have when the playwright is the director.*
>
> *She is an amazing writer. . . . It's obvious that Irene is passionate and seemingly on a pilgrimage towards her own work. And I love witnessing that. But does that witnessing benefit you as an actor? And the answer is: Sometimes. Does it benefit me as an artist and a person? Absolutely.*
>
> *I'm trying to be respectful of all the different levels on which that question resonates, and they're contradictory feelings.*

Scene 4 Page 21

ELIZABETH

Hedda has an interesting mind. she uses it to be destructive and to complicate her and lives

(short pause)

Thea is different. She's kind. She's studious and thoughtful. She's not imaginative. Hedda and Thea are incompatible. that's quite clear in this scene. In fact it's quite clear they're headed for disaster.

MARION

Yes.

ELIZABETH

Thea is provincial. But she is smarter than Hedda because she is sensible, generous and Hedda is neither. And that is being smarter because Hedda uses her brain senselessly. Thea is constructive. Hedda is a person who could do anything she wants to do. But doesn't. She is missing a part of herself and a part of the world. She is like a person who is color-blind, therefore is connected to everything but color. When people who are color blind first learn the words for colors, they do not know what they mean. Then they begin to think that they refer to an abstract quality of the subject. But they don't know what that quality is. They think it may describe something like a mood or a state of being. Until one day someone says, "Pass me the blue ribbon." And someone picks up a specific ribbon and hands it to the person. The colorblind person then understands that color is not an abstract quality, but a specific one. When a person is color-blind, we who can see color are well aware they can't see color. But with other abstract qualities we do not realize when a person is lacking a particular sense or a sensitivity to something. Do you know what I mean?

Rev: 2/27/98

7.2 Maria Irene Fornes's rehearsal revisions of script: "(A pause. Dark thoughts)"

In rehearsal later that day, Blinkoff raises realistic questions about the psychology of his character. After some discussion, Fornes tells him that he is "a double character: you're Vernon and Vernon's brother." As will become startlingly clear a week later, Fornes does not take a "realistic" view of identity as continuous: discontinuous identity *is* her realism.[44]

Driving downtown in her 1989 maroon Bronco II after rehearsal, Fornes tells me: "I have done more revision on this play than on any other. . . . It's been difficult to write because there are no emotional relationships. . . . [Elizabeth and Marion's] greatest joy is when they find another page of the play [*Hedda Gabler*]. It's almost as if I'm learning how to write a play in which personal relationships are secondary to the longing and desire for this play, and [the characters] share that."

The following week, on March 20, there is to be an afternoon run-through of the play for the designers and artistic director. When I arrive at 11:30 A.M., Fornes's assistant, Dawn Williams, is dictating a series of changes in scene 1.[45] An actor asks: "Which revised script are we revising?" Williams, beginning to dictate substantial changes in a dialogue between Vernon and Lady Bell, says: "Don't throw anything away. . . . Hold on to page 3, scene 6. . . . Irene is holding on to it, so let's all hold on to it. We don't have a place for it yet." Then she announces to the cast that in scene 7 the lines of Elizabeth will be reassigned to Vernon and the lines of Vernon will be reassigned to David. The actors seem a little dismayed. Fornes says: "This is necessitated by costume changes." Then she adds: "Anybody can play these lines."

The assistant to the director now begins to include in her answers to actors' questions the phrase "as far as I know at this time." She continues to dictate changes, reading first from her handwritten notations and then glancing at the playwright's own revised script. During the dictation of changes in the script, assistants xerox and hand out typed copies of the newly revised pages. At one point, Valda Setterfield (Lady Bell) says of a revised exchange in scene 6: "I understand it when you explain it, but I don't understand it" as written. When questions proliferate, Williams suggests that they may perhaps be answered when the cast begins to read aloud the revised scenes. Instead, the actors continue to discuss the reassignment of speeches in scene 7. "Let's talk about the lines, not about the character who says them," Fornes tells the cast. Blinkoff (Vernon), whose former speeches in scene 7 have all been transferred to David and who must now himself take over the speeches of Elizabeth, responds: "I feel as if I'm on unstable ground because now you've given me lines that another character was speaking." The actor's metaphor for his sense of disequilibrium recalls director Garland Wright's comment during rehearsal revisions of Elizabeth Egloff's *The Devils*: "It's quicksand."

After a short break, the actors begin reading the revised dialogue between Lady Bell and Vernon in scene 6. Setterfield interrupts with a question: "Do I look in or out?" "Let me explain that when I'm writing a scene I imagine a world," Fornes replies. "I imagine a scene, a mood. I write a lot more stage directions; then later I take them out. So take out all the stage directions to do with looks." (The stage directions, "*SHE looks at him. . . . SHE looks at him again*" [sc. 6, p. 1, of the March 20 script], do not appear in the April 25 script.) Directing her own script, Fornes eliminates, rather than adds, stage directions.

During the lunch break before the 3 P.M. run-through, Fornes talks to me about her father ("erudite, read all the time, read everything"), who died when she was fifteen, and her mother who died several years ago at the age of 104. She says that she would explain to her mother, who always commented on the clothing and hair of the actresses in her plays: "It's a *character*, not a real person" (a comment that, in more sophisticated forms, is repeated in her rehearsals).

At the afternoon run-through are Women's Project artistic director Julia Miles, lighting designer Philip Widmer, costume designer Gabriel Berry and her assistant Caitlin Ward, and literary manager Lisa McNulty. The actors, mainly off book, begin a fairly low-key reading. Fornes, wearing gray wool slacks and a gray wool jacket over a maroon blouse, sits behind the director's table, a pencil in her right hand, her gaze shifting from script to actors. The gestures and movements of the actresses, now wearing rehearsal versions of nineteenth-century costumes, seem a triumph over restraints imposed by their garments: inevitably, the more stylized movement becomes the more natural choice.

During scene 4 Fornes puts her pencil down and stares steadily at the actors. The scene is a *mise-en-abîme*. Elizabeth Robins and Marion Lea are reading over and over a few pages of script stolen from a rehearsal of *Hedda Gabler*. Like the cast of *Gossensass*, Elizabeth and Marion construct their roles and relationships, page by page, from a text that is incomplete as they rehearse.

The stage manager announces that scene 6 is "a very new scene; it has been read but not blocked" and that scene 7 (in which the speeches have been reassigned) will be "a cold reading." There is a break after the run-through/reading ends. At 5:30 P.M. the costume designer opens four boxes of clothing, and each actor presents himself or herself in costume as Fornes watches and comments ("But that cape doesn't go with that dress").

The following morning there is a full company meeting, attended by Julia Miles. During discussion of recent and ongoing revision in rehearsal, an actor says: "I wish I was the script." "You wish you were the script?" Fornes asks. "Yes," the actor replies. "I wish I was the script because it's gotten more attention than we have." Hidden in the actor's lament is an understanding of the nature of the play he is rehearsing. The object of desire in *The Summer in Gossensass*, as in Fornes's rehearsal of it, is a script, figured and reconfigured, read and reread. What is disorienting for the actor is his sense that the directorial gaze has become authorial.

"The play changed because of you," Fornes tells the actors. "Your presence inspired me. . . . Maybe inspiration is a word no one wants to hear anymore."[46] Commenting on the issue of "realistic" motivation and consistency of character, she says: "I wouldn't want to work on a play that worked conventionally." The play is "mysterious" even to its author: "You don't know because I don't know."[47]

The reassignment of every speech in scene 7 elicits clearly distinct responses in the actors most affected by it. Blinkoff feels himself to be on "unstable ground." Goodrich, on the other hand, tells me:

That kind of switch embodies the idea that character is mutable. The notion of discontinuous character . . . breaks the back of expected behavior, so characters cannot merely contradict themselves but assume a different character which to a realistic actor or dramaturg would appear to be bad or faulty playwriting. "He or she just wouldn't do that" is a typical response. . . . This kind of approach to acting and to the liquidity of script is second nature to me. It's certainly my preference as a way of writing and a means of acting. It's certainly more interesting.

The next day the actor brings me a quote from Max Jacob's *Art poétique:* "Personality is only a persistent error."[48]

In the afternoon rehearsal on March 21, Fornes reblocks five lines of dialogue. She asks that an actress move closer to another, then slightly farther back; that one cover the eyes of another with her hands and that the eyes open wide when they are uncovered; that a third actress hold her hands a little higher in the air. The actresses do not raise questions of motivation or logic; they seem fully at ease exploring differently nuanced stagings of a tiny moment in the scene. Fornes's revision of text in rehearsal is very like her revision of physicalizations: she works with words the way she works with the bodies of the actors, reexperiencing an embodied script. The actor who wishes he were the script is wishing he were the *only* script: there are many scripts in Fornes's rehearsal, and the actor is one of them.

In the late afternoon, after several actors have left, Dawn Williams and I are asked to enter the playing area during rehearsal of a new monologue in scene 5. I read the part of Lady Bell: five lines. For twenty minutes, directed by Fornes standing a few feet away, I feel the currents of energy I have only guessed at from my seat outside the playing area. Goodrich reads David's new monologue over and over, as Rivera lies curled and motionless on the floor. I sit unmoving in a chair; it is difficult work. Finally, I come to know what it means to sit quietly in a play by Irene Fornes.

On March 22 it is snowing heavily. Most sidewalks are unswept, with only a few footprints. Today New Yorkers walk in single file, with an uncharacteristic lack of haste. "Let's take out a moment to have applause for the snow," an actress says. Off book, the actresses begin scene 1. Fornes studies the script, revising speeches only after hearing them voiced. As she writes, her lips mouth the words. She interrupts the actors: "I have just clarified. Wait. Complain after you hear." She dictates several revisions, has second thoughts, and sits quietly at the director's table, writing. The stage manager announces a break and several actors leave the windowless rehearsal room to take in the snow.

After the break Fornes dictates revisions of her previous revisions. "There's a total change in mood," Fornes tells Powell. "You have to get into a dark mood, a new way of sensing her [Hedda] which is darker." As she talks to the actress, Fornes enters the playing area and redirects her movements: "The fast stuff doesn't work. [It] is quieter." "The blocking is going to change," Powell says to the stage manager, who has asked the actors to read the revised dialogue. After new blocking is found, the actors read the new lines aloud and Fornes makes a further revision.[49] The actors reread. Fornes looks again at the text, and rewrites. Her assistant dictates the fourth set of revisions to the actors. "I know that everything that is happening here is unconventional," Fornes says, "but also that there is [something] very beautiful."

A week earlier in rehearsal, Goodrich had said that it is "fascinating . . . watching Irene work her way out of corners created by rewriting on the spot." It *is* fascinating to watch the playwright-director reblocking what she has rewritten, rewriting what she has reblocked, "on the spot," again and again. For example, in rehearsal on March 22, Fornes directs David's downstage walk and reverential bow to Marion in scene 5. She fine-tunes the timing, duration, and tone of Marion's one-word response ("Oh"). Then she gives David a new line,[50] watches the scene replayed, and reblocks his bow.[51] In Fornes's rehearsals, revision of the script calls forth directorial reenvisioning. Acts of rewriting and acts of restaging continually interact.

That afternoon, for example, Goodrich ends up kneeling at the moment when Rivera says to him: "David, why do you have your head on the floor?" After discussion with the actress, Fornes changes the line to conform with this new blocking.[52] A few minutes later Fornes directs David to approach Lady Bell in a puppylike/froglike motion and to whisper, from a seated position on the floor near her chair, lines that he had been delivering rather formally in a standing position. As Goodrich replays the scene, Fornes says: "A little hunched . . . your knees bent." A matter-of-fact speech becomes peculiar, arresting. In a further directorial note devoid of reference to "realistic" psychological motivation, Fornes says: "As you come down[stage], you feel that oxygen comes into you. So you open up more." "With Irene," Goodrich tells me during a break, "movement is character. That's where character is found. . . . It's all about alternating from being hunched or low to arms up[stretched] or in motion."

The following day, birds are chirping; the blue of the Hudson River matches the blue of the sky over New Jersey. Fornes runs the opening scene several times, making further revisions in the text and its staging. The cast seems miraculously to memorize these new additions and cuts before replaying the scene. At times the actors add a word or phrase to the latest version of the script, just as, at other times, they inadvertently contribute to the reblocking of a scene.[53] During the lunch break, Fornes tells me:

> Through revisions in rehearsal, the play has changed. The logic used to rely more on storyline. Now the logic, the movement of the play, is different. The plot is the characters' understanding of the play and what playwriting is and what drama is. That is the evolution of the play, of how an author can create, based on a real person or an invented character. It's like a theory of how one creates a play. That is what is forming the movement of the play.

In *The Summer in Gossensass*, actresses (Elizabeth and Marion) read and rehearse an incomplete script to learn more about a fictional character (Hedda) who was possibly inspired by a real person (Emilie); in Fornes's rehearsal, actors read and rehearse an incomplete script inspired partly by a real person

(Robins), whom the playwright knows only through her writings, and partly by a play whose characters fascinate her own.

On March 25, the last day in the rehearsal room, Fornes asks the actors to read a newly revised scene while she decides where to locate a line without a speech tag—a line in search of a character. Standing behind the director's table, listening to a dialogue she has been revising in rehearsal, Fornes interrupts Goodrich and adds the unassigned line to a speech of his.[54] I hear Fornes's assistant reassure her that "everything has a home."[55] "You mean everything is done?" Fornes asks. "Everything is done. You can go home," Williams jokes. "Well, we'll see you opening night," remarks Goodrich, laughing. Standing with her arms outstretched against the wall of the rehearsal room, Fornes says: "Don't tell me it's all done. Can I come down off my cross?" As he leaves the room, the actor says: "I just want to reassure you that descent from the cross is optional."

That afternoon the play is run. Fornes sits at the director's table, looking alternately at the actors and at the script. Her lips shape soundless words as the pencil in her right hand hovers over a page in scene 1, darts down, circles a word. She writes carefully in spidery handwriting on a sheet of white unlined paper to the right of the script. Her page-turning keeps pace with the actors' delivery of lines, even as she circles words and makes notes. Her gaze, refocused on the actors, is steady, intense. At times the fingers of her left hand press against her mouth, then move to turn pages of her script. David begins to deliver his new monologue in scene 5.

Two weeks earlier, when I entered the rehearsal room before the actors arrived, Fornes was talking to Dawn Williams about gambling. She said that Hedda was a gambler and that for a gambler the thrill is the moment of greatest risk, where you either live or die, win or lose. I asked whether she herself had ever gambled. No, she said, except for a lottery ticket, but her mother, at the age of ninety-nine, once asked Fornes to drive her to Las Vegas to gamble at 2 A.M., and they did. The following week a new speech on gambling appeared. I listen to it now:

> More common among men, but women have a more intense, although secret, yet untapped gambling instinct. In a sense, something like a religious drive—an urge to stand on a line so fine, a tightrope that lifts upwards and upwards even further, higher and higher. In a state of balance so perilous, and yet so consuming that rather than wish for safety, one is greedy for more height, more distance from the land.

The monologue ends: "The moment of bliss.—A deal" (sc. 5, p. 21). Standing on a line so fine, in a state of balance so perilous, greedy for more distance from the land, Maria Irene Fornes is gambling all the time.

8 Jean-Claude van Itallie in Rehearsal

The Tibetan Book of the Dead

I'm merely a translator. And so are you. What will block that process will be your ego attempting to impose itself on the text.

If you get the answers from the playwright before you begin, then what is there left to discover?

"**I**t's a great thing to see a group of actors who have worked together for ten years," Tony Kushner has said. "It's great to see a director who has worked with those actors for ten years. . . . [A]ll of the theatre that is historically significant and generative of other kinds of theatre comes out of some sort of collective movement."[1] This book closes with an account of such a group, Pilgrim Theatre Research and Performance Collaborative, in rehearsals during the summers of 1997 and 1998 that culminate in a production of Jean-Claude van Itallie's play, *The Tibetan Book of the Dead, or How Not To Do It Again*, at the Boston Center for the Arts, August 13–29, 1998.

Pilgrim Theatre was founded in Poland in 1986 by two American actors, Kim Mancuso, now artistic director, and Kermit Dunkelberg. For over a decade the award-winning company, with its four core artists and a circle of more than two dozen associate artists, including musicians, composers, designers, and actors, has been performing classical and modern theater works in this country as well as in Europe and South America. During the summers of 1997 and 1998, I am invited to witness their extraordinary research and improvisatory work during intensive weekend rehearsals at a nineteenth-century farmhouse with attached barn in Ashfield, Massachusetts.

Like Sam Shepard and Maria Irene Fornes, Jean-Claude van Itallie was a seminal figure in the off-off-Broadway theater of the 1960s. One of the original playwrights at Ellen Stewart's La MaMa Experimental Theater Club and "the writer most central to [Joseph Chaikin's] Open Theater,"[2] van Itallie has written more than thirty plays and musicals, including *America Hurrah* (a trilogy of one-act plays) and *The Serpent*, created in collaboration with the Open

8.1   Jean-Claude van Itallie and director Kim Mancuso under the sycamore in rehearsal of *The Tibetan Book of the Dead* (photograph by Matt Samolis)

Theater; he has also translated several major plays of Chekhov. Having taught playwriting courses at Yale, Princeton, and Columbia, among other universities, he currently gives workshops on the healing power of theater all over the country.[3] Recently, the playwright made his debut as an actor in a three-man performance piece, *Guys Dreamin'*, directed by Kim Mancuso and Joel Gluck, presented at La MaMa E.T.C., November 6–16, 1997, in New York City. He returned to La MaMa in the spring of 1999 to perform in his one-man, song-and-dance, autobiographical theater piece, *War, Sex, and Dreams*.

"What interests me is the relationship between realities," van Itallie has said. "If you follow *The Tibetan Book of the Dead*, it's what goes on at the moments before dying, and it goes on most strongly between death and rebirth."[4] His 1983 play, based on English translations of an ancient Tibetan text, the *Bardo Thödol*, has itself undergone various reincarnations. In 1996 the script of the play became the libretto for an opera, *The Tibetan Book of the Dead, or The Great Liberation Through Hearing*. In 1998 van Itallie republished the text in an altered form—with all speech tags, stage directions, music and light cues removed—under a new title: *The Tibetan Book of the Dead for Reading Aloud*.[5] While Pilgrim Theatre rehearses his play, the playwright is revising his script as a text *not* meant to be staged—even as he prepares to enter the stage himself as an actor.

The Tibetan Book of the Dead "is navigational instructions, spoken-as-you-go, for the moments surrounding death, and the days that follow it," van Itallie has written. "It is a guide to the in-between place." If the "traveler-after-death" does not experience and merge with "the clear white light of universal mind," then three days after death "majestic manifestations of color will appear," "beneficent forms of the five [basic] energies." But if these visionary experiences are not apprehended rightly, the manifestations will reappear "in angry forms." Ultimately, *The Tibetan Book of the Dead* asks us to pay attention, stay alert, as we "choose an auspicious place of rebirth."[6]

"The success of the play depends on a long rehearsal process, including group improvisation (not verbal) to find expression for and become familiar with the primal energies and the emotional realms," the playwright says in his published production notes.[7]

> *The final staging must be precise, but it is vital that an exploratory attitude be maintained by the actors. The audience should not be patronized by an attitude of pretending to know, nor preached at, nor bored with pseudo-religiosity. The actors should think of the audience as friends. The play is as much about life and rebirth as it is about death. It is, in a profound sense, a celebration.*[8]

I arrive at the 1839 Ashfield farmhouse, nestled in the hills of Western Massachusetts, at 6 P.M. on Saturday, August 2, 1997, the first day of rehearsal. Tomorrow the playwright will meet with the company. On the wide front porch of the farmhouse she shares with co-founder and actor Kermit Dunkelberg and their daughter, Zoë, artistic director Kim Mancuso, wearing a long, sleeveless, dark print dress, greets me warmly. "Our process here can be described as finding a way to work in life: theater in domesticity," she tells me. This afternoon she asked the company to

> *go into the landscape and choose an element to work with: wood, air, water. And to remember a story or a dream that has some connection to someone who has left this life, someone whom they can celebrate—so the assignment is not simply to mourn but to mourn by celebration.*[9]

The actors will later be asked to present this "story or . . . dream" in the first-person present tense, an exercise to which van Itallie introduced Mancuso in his graduate playwriting course at Yale. "There's no point in my addressing the work in a formulaic directorial way," she says, as her beautiful four-year-old daughter passes by, "when a script or a piece has its own life. I wouldn't raise my child by a predetermined set of principles that would hold true for every child."

This evening the actors and musicians will gather around a fire in the middle of the meadow behind the farmhouse. There they will read the script together for the first time, with some vocal and musical improvisation, "just addressing the presence of the text," Mancuso says.

After that, we'll sing. I asked the actors to bring paper and pen tonight to jot down questions to ask the playwright tomorrow or to mark places in their script where they need clarification.

None of the actors comes from a Buddhist tradition. Jean-Claude and I both feel that we must approach the material from our own authentic starting points. We're not trying to be Buddhists. We're not even trying to present a sympathetic version of what we think Buddhists or Tibetans might want from this piece. . . . Tonight I'm going to listen to the text. The actors' immediate response is what's important to me at this point.

Just before we are called in to dinner, she adds: "I do not plan to make any changes in the text of the script"—a decision unique in the ten-year history of Pilgrim Theatre, a company known for its original, collaborative theater pieces.

At a long wooden table in the welcoming kitchen of the farmhouse, four-teen adults and three small children[10] share a communal meal of chicken, potatoes, green beans, peppers, and asparagus,[11] preceded by the saying of "grace," an improvised chant accompanied by the holding of hands. There are many toasts; the first expresses the director's gratitude to her company.

At 10 P.M., in the meadow visible from the kitchen windows, the actors and musicians, their faces lit by four tall torches, sit in a circle around a large fire pit. Writing about Chekhov, van Itallie has said: "In the quiet is the quality of listening. The characters listen, and the audience listens. For that . . . to happen successfully, the playwright had to listen."[12] Kermit Dunkelberg opens rehearsal with some comments on this theme:

Actual silence we never experience. Even if we could shut out all outside sound, we would still hear internal sound. The Tibetan Book of the Dead makes hearing and listening very important. I'd like us to start with ten minutes of silence. Think of the fire, listen to it. The fire is an image of a powerful transforming force.

Before the silence begins, he tells the actors: "Jean-Claude has said that the text of a performance is the bridge between the audience and the performers. So I'd like to hear the words clearly when we read the text aloud. I think it's always better to be simple than to make an effect, so if you have an impulse to make an effect, do nothing." (This last admonition is not always heeded tonight.)

I, too, listen in the "silence." For the first time in rehearsal, I do not write. I hear the crackling of the fire, the director's low breathing to my right, an ac-tress's louder breathing to my left, a small burst of crickets, cars passing in the distance, then my own breath, and, always, the steady sound of water moving over rocks somewhere in the darkness beyond our circle of lights. Dunkelberg rings a small bell, and one by one the members of the company, their eyes closed, utter sounds that seem gradually to call out to each other without losing their individuality. There are low cries, frenetic whisperings, and long, beautiful, melodic intonings, accompanied by didgeridoo (an aboriginal Australian pipe), double kalimba (an African thumb piano made of an hourglass-shaped gourd and metal spokes), and dumbek (a Middle Eastern hand drum). I begin to hear vowels, parts of words. The fire brightens.

Dunkelberg sings the opening lines of the play:

Oh you,
Who have come to this place.
Sisters and brothers, friends,
This person is dying (9).

As Susan Thompson joins him, speaking lines from the first scene, Monica Gomi repeats phrases from the lines Thompson speaks. Patricia Flynn begins to read lines aloud as Dunkelberg continues to sing them. Court Dorsey pants audibly, not yet shaping words. Four actors spontaneously repeat in unison a single phrase, "My friend" (9). As Erica Stuart begins to read the second scene, entitled "The Moment of Death," Dunkelberg stands, traveling in place. In the company's first sounding of the text, there is no clear distinction between the speaking and the singing voice.

In their rehearsal-at-fire, the actors do not alter the language in the script but the text is uttered by voices that overlap, echo each other, or return to earlier spoken or sung phrases, so that lines are not delivered sequentially but are interwoven in ever new patterns, accompanied by musical improvisation. Astonishingly, despite their experimentation with the sequence and repetition of speeches, actors and musicians bring each scene to a close at the same moment.

The director, seated next to me on top of a sleeping bag, studies the script in the dying flicker of the fire. Thompson suddenly stands up and moves halfway around the seated circle to join Dunkelberg's rhythmic swaying. The director watches intently this first sign of ensemble playing, of putting the text on its feet. Now almost all the performers play musical instruments, whose sounds gradually replace the human voice. It is nearly midnight. The director, quietly swaying in rhythm with the company, glances at her daughter sleeping soundly beside her. Suddenly Dunkelberg circles the circle of performers, removes one of the lit torches, and returns it unlit. There is silence. The actors disappear, one by one, and later return with new instruments to play and sing for several more hours.

"It is very difficult for me not to participate, to stay aloof," the director tells me, "but I have to hear them taste the words and understand the relationships as they begin to unfold."

> *We're all trying to listen to each other's energies and to meet through the text. They were bringing out certain textures of the language that I can't get by reading alone. Each word, phrase, construction of words, is like a bar or several bars of music. And they can do it in twenty different ways. That gives me some information about what Jean-Claude is doing.*

The next morning I revisit the site of the first company gathering. It seems quite ordinary now. The great fire pit appears smaller, like certain actors you meet in the green room after a performance. The large logs have become dark, rounded chunks intermingled with gray ash. Most of the company is still asleep on mattresses placed throughout the upper level of the barn. In the meadow I see three tents where several actors have spent the night. Two dogs, Nausicaa and her mother, Brzezinka, named for the village in Poland where she was found, nose by me on their way to the river where rocks have been arranged to create a pool deep enough for bathing.

Jean-Claude van Itallie arrives in a blue Mercedes-Benz at 11 A.M. He wears a brilliant bluish-green shirt over a lilac T-shirt, light blue jeans, white socks, and white running shoes; he has a full head of white hair, a warm smile, and a soft, resonant voice. The company sits with him on the grass in a large circle underneath the branches of an old sycamore tree behind the farmhouse. "I think it would be good to hear everyone's voice," the playwright says. "If you would stand and say where you were born and give a flash, an image, of something from yesterday but in the present tense." After each person in the circle has spoken, van Itallie offers his voice to the company:

> *I'm Jean-Claude. I'm born in Brussels, Belgium. I awaken this morning exhausted. The house I live in has a woman and her son scraping paint off the outside of it. . . . I look in the mirror. I wonder when I'm going to die [laughs]. I wonder if I'm going to get through the next few minutes. . . . I go downstairs. I observe my battery of vitamins. . . . I take all my vitamins. . . . I'm coming here. I think this may be the fullest, happiest day of my life.*

Then he says: "Theater is about the present moment, about now, always about now. *The Tibetan Book of the Dead* is about now. It's about this moment."

The playwright, who describes himself as a practicing Tibetan Buddhist for thirty years, instructs the company in sitting and walking meditation: "The purpose of meditation is to slow you down, to be more present in the moment. . . . You're paying attention as you walk to your breathing. . . . The reason you focus on the breath is that it's not a still point. It's always moving." He goes on:

> *In sitting meditation it's important that your back be fairly straight; your hands are comfortably on your knees, preferably hands up, eyes open to connect you with the external world, but not a striving gaze. Allow the gaze to fall wherever it falls. Concentrate on your breathing. . . . Your mind will wander. When you notice it wandering, bring it back to your breathing. Don't put yourself down or congratulate yourself on having noticed its wandering [laughter]. We're not meditating for a purpose, even though I've said that it will slow you down. We'll do this for ten minutes. When I get up, follow me.*

After the sitting meditation, we walk single file in a figure eight, led by the playwright. Nausicaa places herself in our path so that we have to step either on or over her. The director removes her dog from the meadow and then continues the walking meditation alone in a space apart from the company.[13]

We sit again on the grass in the shade of the sycamore. "The subtitle of my play is 'How Not To Do It Again,'" van Itallie tells the company. "The 'how' is what I want to focus on."

> *I would suggest that the instructions for living and dying in* The Tibetan Book of the Dead *are identical. The "how" has to do with the quality of awareness. It's as much what you observe as what you're feeling.*
>
> The Tibetan Book of the Dead *has to do with the five senses, just as life does. A good poem, a good story, a good life have to do with the full use and expression of the five senses. The process of working on this play has to do with your own process of learning to be more aware—so it's very personal.*

He asks that all of us "focus on the very full emptiness in the center of our circle" and that "demonic neurotic impulses remain outside the circle." Then the playwright speaks more particularly about his play:

> The Tibetan Book of the Dead *is a journey. Any play, of course, is a journey. My image of the shape of this journey is a funnel constructed of possibility. At any moment it is possible to break out of the funnel. The greatest moment of possibility is the moment of death. You keep getting opportunities to recognize the clear white light and merge with the majestic peaceful deities. At any moment you can be the universe. Deities is a misleading word in Western culture. A deity is universal energy outside you as well as inside you. What it wants is recognition. That's all there is.*
>
> *You spiral down. The narrowest part of the funnel is the birth canal. If you haven't managed to merge with these deities, you have to try it again [laughter]. That funnel, by the way, is my own image.*

He talks about the intricate correspondences among the images of the play. West is associated with the spring and with colors ranging from red to pink. "Red is warm, passionate, seductive. It's lust [in its negative form] or incredible compassion [in its positive form]." East is associated with the season of winter and the color blue; south with fall and orange-yellow; north with summer and green. White "contains everything, all colors, but it's nothing. . . . So that's what's flowing through us." As he speaks, everyone except the playwright is writing.

"Now is the moment for questions," van Itallie says. "What happens when you achieve enlightenment?" an actress asks. "I haven't reached it," he replies, "but you are one with the greatest, the most wonderful. . . . There's a vow among Buddhist monks that you won't step off the wheel [of time] until everyone has achieved enlightenment." The actors share titles of books they have been reading on Buddhism. Then van Itallie says, "Do this fearlessly: find the personal in your theater work with this play. If you blunder, Kim will tell you." Court Dorsey now asks about the author's role in rehearsal:

> *I have a question for you as a playwright. You've written your own conceptualization in this text. We come to this script as actors. Now, [as] the playwright in juxtaposition and collaboration with us, I'm wondering how you see your role in this process.*

"I was taught by working on this play a great deal about what a creative act is," van Itallie replies. Rather than define his role in rehearsal, the playwright draws a parallel between the author's work and that of the actors:

> *I see myself as a conduit. I think the playwright is like a seismograph. I'm record-*
> *ing with my hands the tremors I feel through my feet. I'm a vessel through which*
> *energies are moving.*
>
> *The Western view of the artist as someone imposing order on something was*
> *not useful to me. This is a holy text. I'm merely a translator. And so are you.*
> *What will block that process will be your ego attempting to impose itself on the*
> *text. To the degree that ego is out of it, you can do no wrong.*

Dorsey tries to elicit a more specific response to his question: "I understand that to mean that as a playwright you have a certain amount of benevolent detachment from our project." "Forget the playwright," van Itallie replies. "I think the creative act is always a translation. I think the idea that we create something out of nothing is paralyzing." A "translation," of course, is always also a transformation, a reimagining. Like Sam Shepard at the table reading of *Curse of the Starving Class*, van Itallie declines to answer an actor's question directly, but the reverberations of this exchange will linger all summer.

The actors now ask about particular Buddhist references in the text and their pronunciation. Occasionally, van Itallie offers to refer these questions to someone more versed in Tibetan Buddhism. At the end of the question-and-answer session, Mancuso says: "Our first encounter as a group with the text yielded in the first moments an incredible reverence. Then we gave ourselves permission to break that moment, to laugh, to be irreverent. I think you're giving us permission to do that." "Yes," the playwright replies. "The only caution I can give is: respect the banks of the river. Go deeper, go lighter. . . . Improvise. You can even do improvisations, but eventually I want you to come back to the language of the text."[14]

After a ten-minute break, Mancuso asks two actors to present for the playwright the work they have done on her "story or dream" exercise. Dorsey stands with his feet in the moving water of the river. He begins: "Jack. Giant. Over seven feet tall at the time I met you."[15] As he continues his narrative, his arms and hands move in the slowed-down rhythms of *mudras*, the symbolic gestures employed in Indian meditation and theater. Thunder and rain drive the company into the farmhouse where Thompson presents an eloquent piece on monsters. Rehearsal ends. "It's considered a great blessing to hear *The Tibetan Book of the Dead* even once or to read it," van Itallie says to the company. "So it's a great blessing to play this play and . . . experience its blessing." He asks that everyone stand and chant a prolonged *Om*. Nausicaa walks into the center of our circle at the moment of intensest sound, listens, investigates something on the floor, and departs as she entered, between a pair of legs. The playwright has not yet heard the actors read his play. He will not return to rehearsal until the following summer.

On the front porch, as the rain falls steadily, I ask van Itallie what he feels he is giving, and receiving from, the actors. "First of all," he replies, "when you say that, I think of the breath. I think it has something to do with inspiration."

> My relation to a first production of any play is different from my relation to subsequent productions. My role is more active in the first production. I feel no play is ever finished, really, completely. It's reborn with each production and each performance.

"And so you have an important role in this production," I respond. "Yes," he says, and explains what that role is.

> [I]n this situation I think of the play as a vessel. The written text is the walls of the vessel. It needs to be infused with new life. I'm familiar with those walls. I know what possibilities they might offer, so I can shine some light on those possibilities for the actors. More importantly, perhaps, if we're lucky, I can inspire them with some of the same groundswell which inspired me to begin with, inspire them to explore the territory within themselves which I explored.

Maria Irene Fornes in rehearsal of *The Summer in Gossensass* says that she is inspired by the actors. Van Itallie here reverses the trajectory of that inspiration. But what he desires is what every playwright desires *for the script itself in rehearsal*: that its vanished origins, its groundswell, be recovered, and revisited, by those who give it new life.

In the midst of our conversation a small boy, the son of one of the actresses, suddenly appears beside us on the porch and asks, indignantly: "Why are you writing?" Laughing, I say the playwright is talking about something important and I want to write it down in order to remember it. The boy nods and disappears. "In further response to your question," van Itallie continues, "and extending the metaphor of breathing, I think the play breathes, too, in many ways. Each new production requires an intake, an inspiring. Perhaps the playwright's presence may provide this."

> There is a way in which actors new to a play imbue the living playwright with semi-divine powers. It may be useful to a production for the playwright with as little ego as possible to give back this energy as an empowerment the way a therapist or a guru might hand back their center to a person. I think that's actually the dynamic that goes on between actors new to a play and the playwright.

I ask how he would distinguish the playwright's relationship with the cast from that of the director.

> In an ideal world, work on a production can be visualized as a circle of people seated around an empty space. In that space may be embodied the questions that concern the play. The playwright and the director are part of the circle, but it's necessary that they sit a little farther back in order to maintain perspective. There's no reason for the playwright and director to sit on opposite sides. [Mancuso and van Itallie sit next to each other in all circles today and next summer.] There is no need for the relationship between the playwright and the director to be polemical.

> *Ideally, they are two pairs of eyes viewing the same empty space in the middle of the circle. There's no reason why they can't be friends.*
>
> *The director is dealing with the actors and the energy of the play on a day-to-day basis. The communication is more about the specific ingredients that go into the soup. If the playwright were present at every rehearsal, the degree of his or her participation would depend on agreement and trust between the director and the playwright. I don't think there are hard-and-fast rules about that.*[16]

Like Maria Irene Fornes, van Itallie is willing to enter rehearsal in the double role of playwright-director:

> *I have taken a vow that for future productions of any play of mine over which I have any control, the director will be known to me as the talented, appropriate person for this play, or I will direct the play myself, or the play will not be done. . . . I don't believe there is any edict engraved in stone that says, "Thou shalt not direct thine own play."*

We are called to a hearty lunch of chicken, zucchini, potatoes, fresh salad from the garden, watermelon, and cantaloupe. After the playwright leaves at 5 P.M., the company spends the evening transforming a section of the upper barn into a rehearsal studio: sweeping, vacuuming, cutting sheets of plywood, scraping off a hundred years of bat guano. Late in the evening the director comments on the effect of the playwright's presence today in a way that partly echoes his own sense of his role: "It is important because he, by being here and addressing their questions, gives the work his blessing."

The following morning Mancuso discusses her own role in rehearsal, distinguishing it from that of the playwright:

> *I provide a context or a safe place within which an artist can develop his or her own voice, discover how it joins with other voices, and in that meeting discover and reveal the text. I don't tell actors what to do at first. I provide a context of controlled freedom. Later on when we discover the material, rediscover the text, explore the nuances, when we come at the material from the very personal work of each actor, then I begin to choose, to make suggestions. . . . And then, finally, my role is as a painter's, bringing the colors together on a canvas, making decisions about textures, borders between colors, what stands out in relief or retreats into the background. . . . I breathe with every word and every rhythm in rehearsal and performance. . . . I'm breathing the life into the performance. It's like keeping a plane aloft by thinking. . . .*
>
> *Jean-Claude and I sit on the same side of the circle but our roles are different. As I described the three stages of my role as director, I was thinking through what the differences are between the playwright and director. At the end I have to say: "This is mine."*

Different as they may be, both director and playwright in rehearsal lay claim to acts of inspiration; each breathes into a company at work on a play that itself "breathes, too, in many ways."

As I am about to drive back to New Haven, the director shows me a color photograph of her in 1995, standing on a cliff in Macchu Picchu. She is facing away from the camera; one cannot see her remarkable eyes or the object of their gaze. The photo, she says, is an image of her rehearsal process: she has "left the known, is heading for the unknown, possibly about to fall off a cliff, walking into a question." Walking into a question that one may eventually answer only by keeping track of where one is in relation to it is the journey Pilgrim Theatre takes in rehearsal, as well as that offered by *The Tibetan Book of the Dead*.

In a small room between the barn and the farmhouse live four Polish laying hens (though later one crows, revealing himself to be a rooster), all named Murray, and a venerable white rabbit named Rascal. When I return to Ashfield two weeks later, on August 15, Rascal has died of diarrhea and old age, and Nausicaa's mother, Brzezinka, has killed one of the Murrays. The mood in the farmhouse is somewhat subdued. Music director Katherine Down, told on her arrival what has happened, says: "Oh no! *Which* Murray?"

Rain that evening prevents the company from rehearsing outdoors. After a dinner of homemade chili, rice, bread, broccoli, and salad, and some talk at table with the children about where the dead rabbit is now and whether he is happy, the actors leave to prepare improvisations on particular scenes which they will present to the director in the upper barn. Just before midnight Mancuso and I enter the barn to observe the improvisations. Susan Thompson, wearing a white jumpsuit, red sash, wool hat, gloves, and goggles, is knocking on a glass door. On the other side of the door, Patricia Flynn, her hands pressed against the panes, says: "I'm here. Don't cry. I'm here./So. I am dead" (29). Erica Stuart, all in white, darts through a door at the top of a set of stairs, delivering lines that intersect Thompson's and Flynn's. In another room Christopher Crowley sings and chants text as he plays a steel cello curled around his body. As I move past many small enclosed spaces in near-total darkness, I hear the tormented cries of one actress, the steady insistent vocal prodding of another, maracas punctuated by the roar of the steel cello, a song sung in Spanish, the sounds of a flute, a softly rhythmic drumbeat—the strange, arresting polyphony of the entire company.[17]

"We're playing with his text," the director says.

We have to go away from the text in order to recover the text. And I think in going away from it, we would make the playwright anxious. I trust him. But there's no guarantee that each actor is as comfortable with him as I am, and my first responsibility is to the actors and their relationship to the text. If that is compromised by self-judgment, then the precious time that we have to work together is lost.

Court Dorsey offers a complicated perspective on the collaboration of actor and author in rehearsal:

I like what has happened so far. I like the fact that Jean-Claude has spent many years dealing with the subject of the play, and with the practice of Buddhism, and that he is sharing his experience with us as a resource and a subject matter. . . .

What I feel somewhat cautious about is that as a playwright his having his own individual vision fixed in the language already gives him a lot of influence as a collaborator on the final product. So the actor's role in the collaboration is to meet the written word, using a language of sound, movement, and image with relative freedom. Now to have the playwright there to further require that those elements come into line with, in this case, his vision as articulated in the language is of concern to me. And the reason I asked him the question about his role was both to sound him out and get him on record as to his intentions as a visiting playwright.

This is a dilemma for an actor working on any play: what allegiance do you owe the author? How much are you expected to re-create a writer's vision and how much are you allowed to draw the absent author into a collaboration with you? That's always the problem. Now on top of that, to have the absent writer present . . . what can you say? [We both laugh.] And especially on a work like this, where Jean-Claude himself acknowledged that we are all interpreting universal material that goes beyond any individual vision, that seems to toss the pendulum further to the side of allowing or encouraging a light hand on the author's part.

During van Itallie's visit, Dorsey had said to him: "I'd like for you to break a bottle over the bow and launch us," and the playwright had responded, in a joking tone: "It sounds like you want to get rid of me." But Dorsey meant something different:

We needed some sort of closure to this day, but he articulated the more underlying discomfort of the whole relationship. I guess the truth is I welcome his part in the process in that resource way and also as an equal, present co-collaborator but not as a representative of the authority of the written script.

And he wonders aloud: "Does the very act of choosing the written word as the form of language in the theater indicate a tendency toward overarching control of collective vision?" This question is one "whose answer doesn't invite another question."[18]

Rehearsal on August 16 begins with morning training in *silat*, a form of martial arts, conducted by Indonesian White Crane master Max Palar.[19] In the afternoon, the extreme heat of late summer sends the company, garments left behind, to the river. That evening, Patricia Flynn teaches the cast an Irish set dance, the circular movements of which translate into bodily terms a metaphor employed earlier by the playwright:

Jean-Claude spoke to us of the funnel, envisioning this journey not merely as a circle but as a circle spiraling downward. . . . It occurred to me that Irish dancing might be helpful in our finding the physical life of what at first glance appears to be an abstract text. . . . And we would all have the commonality of the [dance] language, just as the silat training we did with Max today has grounded us and given us a common starting point as a company.

On the side lawn women in flowered dresses and long skirts and men in slacks and bright shirts dance, accompanied by two flutes and thunder rumbling low in the hills as twilight falls; the dogs and children watch carefully. Earlier the remaining Murrays were carried into the farmhouse in a covered cardboard box. Every sentient being in this house is thriving tonight.

After a meal of stuffed eggplant, salad, and Irish beer, the director asks the company to return to the upper barn where they will explore their improvisations, transforming agony into celebration: "What I'm looking for is like the Irish wake, a kind of conjuring." But we are waylaid by the spectacle of a nearly full moon and a wall of mist that moves through the trees beyond the meadow as bat after bat whirls by overhead.

Just before she and I enter the barn, Mancuso says: "Each time the actors do an improvisation, they make me look at the black and white on the page differently." Tonight, the actors' presentation of every speech is altered but the text is not. For example, "I'm here. . . . I'm here" (29), from a scene entitled "Realizing I Am Dead," is now punctuated by high-pitched laughter. The tone shifts abruptly as an unseen actress in another part of the barn repeats these words. In one room Dunkelberg, bowing a mandolin, sings: "You die when you die" (a line from a song by Allen Ginsberg), over and over, to a country western tune. Eventually, the actors—speaking, chanting, and singing—gather in a single room where music director Katherine Down and musician Eve Lindi stand face to face, playing flutes. All the sounds of the company seem simultaneously to emanate from and flow back into the voice of Dunkelberg singing. The flutes now follow, now lead the human voices as the refrain, oddly, becomes more comforting: "And you die when you die, die when you die." The repeated words become softer and softer until only fragments of text are audible; the blending of human and instrumental voices is unearthly, indescribable, as if the dying voices of this non-Buddhist company have together found a way to make a good end. The director has extinguished lights as she passed through the upper barn and now there is only one small white light in a corner of the "music room" where the actors have gathered. All there is to respond to is sound, and it is a liberation of hearing. It feels like the blessing the playwright hoped his play would bring to its performers and its audience.

But it is, of course, only a moment. The voices grow louder again, seeking more life. The unearthly beauty has been lost. The repetitions become a little weary. The director gives a note: "Don't fall into mood."[20] But the falling into mood continues. Dunkelberg begins to recite lines from the play: "Don't be afraid"; "Death has happened./ It happens to everyone" (13). As he speaks, the other actors sing Ginsberg's "You die when you die." Then they begin to laugh. "Listen," the director says. The laughter persists, loud and raucous, partly covering Dunkelberg's speaking of the text. The director repeats her note: "Listen to Kermit." Dunkelberg says: "Now is the moment of [long pause; the cast laughs] death" (12). He continues to voice the text, slowly, with longer pauses and different intonations, amid quieter, sporadic laughter. There is now no light in the room. The improvisation continues for a long time. Actors leave and return. The director carries a small lamp into the room. Then everything begins again as an actor speaks the lines: "I'm here. . . . I'm here."

Suddenly I see Max Palar, like an apparition, seated in the lotus position by a doorway, listening to the wailing, chanting, singing, speaking chorus of voices. His head is bowed; his left hand forms slow, stately *mudras* as it moves downward to rest on his knee. His eyes are closed. He is utterly still, listening. He seems almost to be the figure of the absent playwright.

The director stands behind him, to his right, swaying rhythmically with the music. The *silat* master's left hand moves upward in a *mudra*; then he raises his arms, as if in response to the sounds of the chimes and the long puffing growl of the didgeridoo in the next room. His hands remain outstretched, left palm up, right palm down. His arms reach upward, then fall. The music director enters suddenly through the doorway playing her long pipe. The actors dance in after her, moving rhythmically to a celebratory beat. As I leave at 2 A.M., the director herself dances in the darkened hallway. Later she will tell me: "I felt as if the barn was haunted."

On August 17, I accompany the director on a visit to Shantigar ("Peaceful Home") in the nearby town of Rowe, where van Itallie has established a non-profit foundation dedicated to the union of artistic and spiritual practices. Inside a house and barn are spaces set aside for rehearsal and meditation; there are stone buddhas, brightly colored rugs, flowers, theatrical accoutrements. Two former temple columns have become pillars for an arch leading to a movement room; there is a stone chimney carefully laid by hand. It is an environment designed by the playwright: nothing is lavish or ostentatious nor is much left to chance.

That afternoon at the Ashfield barn, the actors formally present improvisatory pieces based on scenes in the play. The scene containing the lines, "I'm here. . . . I'm here," is rendered very differently by Flynn and Gomi. Dunkelberg sits on a blue wooden chair, head bent over an empty music stand. "Logic and the chair and the table are dissolving," he says. Picking up his mandolin, he continues to read the text aloud: "No more external sounds, no more internal sounds"(10). Walking out of the room, he delivers the remaining speeches in the scene as he bows the mandolin, then sings: "You die when you die." The company spontaneously joins him; the line is repeated over and over; there is gentle intermittent laughter. Lindi plays the flute; Down plays a giant bass drum and shakes a rattle filled with many goats' toenails.[21] At the end of the afternoon rehearsal, Mancuso tells the actors: "I've been thinking about the difficulty of the text today. So often you work with the text and also against it. So this helps me a lot."

"You can even do improvisations, but eventually I want you to come back to the language of the text," van Itallie had told the company. From the beginning of rehearsal, Dunkelberg explains, "I imposed a limitation not to put the text in my own words, not to change the order, and not to repeat." He goes on:

If there were a strong need to change the text for the performance, I think Jean-Claude would be open to that. He doesn't want us to improvise words for the performance. . . . That's basically the only condition he's mentioned. . . . He writes from a really deep understanding of this kind of actor's process where the actors are generating through improvisation a lot of what goes into the performance.

"My first reading of the script was at the first rehearsal at the fire," the actor admits. "I had tried sporadically to read it several times before, but I felt I needed to hear it rather than read it." Like other actors, he recalls the words of the playwright in rehearsal: "When he came the next day, it moved me that he began by talking about his own fear of death. That was the first thing he said. I do feel that this is why he wants us to do [*Tibetan*], because this is such a present concern." Dunkelberg mentions that both the playwright's and the director's fathers have recently died, and adds:

One of the things that Jean-Claude said to us about this play is that it's not just about dying or death but it's about every moment of life. I think that was a big key for me about how to approach this work because it's the problem of the actor—it's Hamlet's problem—you need to do something right now. . . . The word "now" comes up a lot in this script and in Shakespeare. And whenever it appears, especially at the beginning of a line, as in "Now is the winter of our discontent," it is a very important launching pad. "Now is the moment of death" launches that part of the scene [in Tibetan]. . . . I think this play is a tremendous vehicle. . . . If you can make the dead living [laughs].

I ask Dunkelberg what it is like this summer to be rehearsing both van Itallie's play and a performance piece in which the playwright has become an actor. "In *Guys Dreamin'* the idea of Jean-Claude as a playwright pretty much disappears," he replies. "I think of him as the other actor."

But for some members of the *Tibetan* cast, the idea of the playwright pretty much disappearing is problematic. "I expected Jean-Claude to be more present than he is so far," Erica Stuart says.

I appreciated when Court asked him that question about [his role] here. And when Jean-Claude responded, I basically translated that to mean: I'm finished writing; my job is done. And that upset me a little bit. . . . If he wants to not change the text at all, then I want him to be here to help us engage that text. And if he's not going to be here, then I feel like we should be able to call him[22] and say we want to change this part or change the order of these two texts. So it feels a little bit like he's said to us: This is it. Now you guys find it.

On the other hand, Stuart observes:

It feels like he's very present—his energy is more present than if the playwright's dead—because I know at some point he'll watch the play, and I am imagining that he will have expectations, whereas if you're doing a play by Shakespeare he's never going to come in and see the piece.

To work with those two energies—his presence and absence—is a very interesting place for me as an actress. One piece wants to rebel against his words in his absence and the other part of me that's the "good girl" wants to find exactly just what he imagined so when he comes to see it, it's "perfect, perfect, perfect"—that affirmation.

The actress resists van Itallie's double roles in rehearsal:

Perhaps I am overly sensitive to persons presenting themselves as spiritually awake and yet there was a piece of me that was so shocked by his taking on that role as well as the role of simply a playwright. That was a shocker for me. As an actress it fueled the rebellious Erica. And the rebellious Erica is more free to find ownership of the text. I mean ownership in an adoptive way. You find a child, you adopt it, and it becomes your own. I certainly have worked on other texts that were fixed. As an actor I think that's a big piece of training—being able to reinspirit texts.

Stuart, finally, seems to need both the absence and the presence of the playwright in rehearsal: "His distance does help in that it allows freedom for us to find the life of the text without his image superimposed on it. And the disappointment in that is that he is alive and lives down the street and [his coming to rehearsal more often] would have been a wholly new experience for me." "It was intimidating on the day he was actually here," Monica Gomi tells me. "I saw him as a large presence, and the image that came into my head was a large hand holding the production."[23] Referring to van Itallie's response to the question of what role he would play in rehearsal, the actress says:

He answered by saying what, if I had come to the situation rationally, I would have expected: that he wasn't going to be involved in the production; he had done his part in the first production and he was unlikely to change the text. But before I realized that, I was shocked by his answer.

But, Gomi adds, in the early rehearsals, "even though he wasn't literally there, we were aware of his presence and whenever there was any irreverence toward the text on our part, it was like a jolt of recognition."

Like Dunkelberg, Susan Thompson did not read the script before rehearsal began:

I opened the play, and I couldn't read it. I had no context, no approach; it was a world I didn't know. The first time I read the play was our first rehearsal at the fire. It was like fumbling first sex. Didn't give a lot of satisfaction. And I found myself fighting with the text.

And then the playwright came. . . . And [he said] how our job was to make a home for this text. . . . What I felt when he talked to us that day was permission to make it our own. He said: change whatever you want, but don't touch the words. And I became aware of his struggle with the words. Here's the man, right here, who distilled from the creative chaos the words we have on the page.

I've worked with playwrights who are still in process, who want to keep adjusting and adjusting and adjusting, who riff off of the actors and use them as part of their creative process. . . . I don't judge it as good or bad. It gives the actor the temptation to change every word in the play. And often as a company we have been very actively involved in the creation of the piece as co-writers, collaborators. It's good to set some limitation on the creative process.

Thompson has visited Shantigar and, like me, was struck by its uninsistent design: "The care that Jean-Claude gives to everything in his life he gives to these words. . . . He is a practitioner. He practices the creative process with actors; he's not just a writer." The actress welcomes van Itallie's sharing of information on the spiritual practice encoded in the play:

> *He gave us a lot of background information which I needed: north, east, west; the color symbolism; the wheel. I was frantically writing and then later when I actually read [the author's notes in the published script] and the stage directions which we had eliminated from the first reading, I saw it was already there. But I wanted him to tell me. I wanted to see the application of this sacred text to his life. . . . Why did he translate/create this sacred piece for the stage?*

Thompson prefers to hear the playwright speak about matters that could be researched and presented by a director or dramaturg: "I wanted him to tell me." Like Gretchen Cleevely in rehearsal of Sam Shepard's *Curse of the Starving Class*, this actress too would like to know why the playwright wrote the play. Shepard's response, "I don't want to get into it. . . . It's there," is abrupt but appropriate. And yet *he* is there, too. And that is the paradox of the playwright's presence in rehearsal.

That evening actors and musicians sit around the great fire in the meadow, as they had at the beginning of rehearsal. Each person chooses at random a passage from the play, suggests a musical style (e.g., blues, country western, Motown), and invites another member of the company to make a song of that passage in that style. Then the entire company joins in, changing pace and rhythm, adding gestures and accompaniment. Afterward the songs are recorded. When rain ends the outdoor rehearsal at midnight, the cast returns to the farmhouse to continue their music-making in the presence of the director. The enormous, seemingly endless energy of this company at play is focused on paying attention to every word, every syllable, in the script, sounded and tasted and listened to, over and over. Several of these songs reappear, with slight modifications, in the 1998 summer rehearsals and in performance.

The following morning Mancuso, Dunkelberg, and Dorsey rehearse *Guys Dreamin'* at Shantigar with van Itallie as co-writer and performer. At the Ashfield farmhouse, three actors—Flynn, Crowley, and Stuart—sit with books in hand, studying the script and its source text, *The Tibetan Book of the Dead: The Great Liberation through Hearing in the Bardo*, translated by Francesca Fremantle and Chögyam Trungpa (to whom van Itallie's play is dedicated). On the kitchen table are placards aligning seasons, directions, colors, emotions, and deities. "Nothing in me wants red to be spring," Flynn says, as they investigate the intricate, interconnecting images in the play. Like a Talmudic study circle, the actors have become close readers of a sacred book. As they compare texts, they raise questions about seeming contradictions, reading aloud alternately from the Fremantle and Trungpa translation, the authorial notes accompanying the play, and their own notes on the playwright's comments to the company in rehearsal. An actor says, "We should call Jean-Claude and ask him," but work continues unassisted. In a sense, the actors at the kitchen table do this morning what they did in their work at the barn yesterday afternoon and in their musical improvisations at the fire late last night: they are making texts listen to each other.

Unlike Stuart and Gomi, Patricia Flynn is neither upset nor shocked by the absence of the playwright. "I think that there's a danger in having access to the playwright," she tells me.

> *I love to ask questions and if the playwright is there, available for questioning, sometimes the answers wind up limiting your own imagination in approaching the text. Because it is his, his script, his creation, it can feel like his answers are the answers. I prefer to discover the answers from the text because if it isn't in the text, it isn't really helpful.*

The actress makes a distinction between authorial notes that accompany the script and those spoken in rehearsal:

> *I think his published notes are part of the text. But when he is present giving notes on the text, able to amplify what he meant, it's as if he's actually setting boundaries. . . . The playwright will give an answer and that's it: how can you argue? . . . I think the not knowing is what provokes the rehearsal process. If you get the answers from the playwright before you begin, then what is there left to discover?*

She leaps up to find her notes on the playwright's comments to the company:

> *"A skillful translation will be in bringing all you are. The energy comes through you. To the degree that ego is out of it, you can do no wrong." And then he stayed away. I mean he's down the road and he's not here.*
>
> *And that's how he's nurturing the work: by letting us find it. I have been thinking about the fact that he's not here. I don't think any of us would have felt as free to do what we've been doing these two weeks if he were here because we would have felt answerable to him.*

Finding nourishment in the author's absence, the actress wishes neither to receive answers *from* the playwright nor to be held answerable *to* the playwright in rehearsal.

Almost a year later, on July 24, 1998, the company prepares for the second, and final, visit of the playwright during the last weekend of rehearsal in Ashfield before the Boston production. "What I would like from him, I suppose," the director tells me before van Itallie arrives, "is a dialogue about certain choices I've made." Unlike Flynn, Mancuso wants a few more answers:

> *I'm not a Buddhist, and there were many questions that I had during the course of the process that I think he could have answered. There are issues in the play that arise from my study and my research and my talking to Buddhist teachers. And I find conflicts within the text that I would like to address together with him.*

Also there are design choices from the first production at La MaMa, clearly anno-
tated in the published script, and I'm concerned that because they don't speak to
me immediately and because I have no understanding of the decision processes
out of which these choices were made, I don't know whether to pay homage to
them or not, so I've made other choices. And he has not seen them until now.

The text has not been altered, but there has been another kind of change: *The*
Tibetan Book of the Dead has become a "musical."

It is a very American production. We have added a lot of original music and
songs created from the text. There's some dancing. . . . I'm wondering how
Jean-Claude will react to the new musicality of this play. . . . I trust that the dia-
logue among us after Jean-Claude sees the work will stimulate each of the artists,
including me.

That evening, after an extraordinary dinner of pasta, baked garlic, fresh
bread, and greens from the garden, a music rehearsal begins in the hay loft,
now converted to a rehearsal studio. An iron hay fork hangs from the fourteen-
foot-high ceiling. At one end of the loft are diverse instruments, played in
rehearsal and performance by three onstage musicians (Katherine Down, Eve
Lindi, Matt Samolis): Tibetan prayer bells, Indonesian *aungklung* rattles, Indian flutes, Australian didgeridoos, African shakers, a glass harmonica (wine
glasses filled with water), double kalimba, snare drum and slit drum, roto-
toms, steel cello, an Appalachian dulcimer, rain sticks, wind wands, long
chimes, detuned autoharps, maracas, guitar, banjo, trombone, a toy piano, Tibetan prayer bowls, a handsaw, dried leaves, and rocks. Music and voice cues
are checked and fine-tuned. Just before rehearsal ends at 2 A.M., an actor asks:
"Jean-Claude didn't say we couldn't say text simultaneously, did he?" "He
didn't say that," an actress replies. "Let's not ask him."

Morning rehearsal on July 25 begins with physical warm-ups in the
meadow followed by vocal warm-ups in the barn. A trail of moving sound
passes by my room in the farmhouse. The 11:30 A.M. work-through is attended by lighting designer Sabrina Hamilton, who was also present at last
night's rehearsal. "I'll be using some of the color images in *The Tibetan Book*
of the Dead," she tells me, "but in a very different way."

A lot of the lighting directions in this text are appropriate to a different set and a
different stage and different staging and a different scale. Kim's staging is to the
stage directions as my lighting will be to the lighting indications [in the published
script]. . . . What the music does with the text and what the actors are doing,
the lights do as well. . . . The lights are another instrument; sometimes they do
solo, sometimes they do harmony, sometimes they do counterpoint.[24]

Sounding very much like the director, she says: "It's really essential for me to
see the evolution of the movement and vocal impulses. It's almost a physical
impulse in my body that says, 'lighting cue.'"

The last rehearsal before the playwright arrives is a midnight run-through in the upper barn studio. "It's interesting because we're working against the text in terms of stage directions," Mancuso tells the company, "but I believe what we're doing is right, and true." The director lights candles and places them on the rehearsal floor. The uninterrupted run ends at 1:30 A.M. No notes are given.

The following morning the cast assembles in the meadow to discuss matters of publicity (news releases, posters, mailing labels), discount tickets, the moving of props from Ashfield to Boston. Conversations about decisions usually made by administrative or technical staff are conducted by the entire company on the very day the playwright is coming to watch a run-through. Background noises include the rhythmic squeaking of a large blue trampoline where several children are bouncing and Zoë's small questions: "What do you think I am? A soccer player? A sandwich?" Under a perfect blue sky with nearly palpable white clouds, actors and musicians sit in the shade of the sycamore, the site of their first meeting with the playwright a year before, discussing the tech rehearsal schedule in Boston and the peculiarities of the performance space (it has a glass ceiling).

At 1 P.M. in the upper barn, Mancuso gives notes on tone ("*not* tongue-in-cheek"), timing ("Someone has to count"), physical contact ("Don't touch her [the dying one]"), the actors' gaze ("The gaze is everything in this"), aligning text and staging ("It's a beautiful image but the image and the text have to come together. . . . I don't want to *illustrate* the text"), and slowing down the rhythm in a sexual scene. (This last note evokes several predictably bawdy remarks.) The director adds new blocking, saying: "Let's try it in the run-through. We don't have time to rehearse it." Then she seems to consider a tiny alteration in the script (from "his" to "a"). "No, that's changing the text," an actress says in a tone that is playful yet serious.

At 3 P.M. the playwright arrives. "What I did the first time I came," he tells me before the run-through, "was to enter into the spirit of the text, to explicate issues, but, more importantly, to validate that they explore the text with their own intuition."

> There's less I can do now. If I like what I see, then this is an opportunity to validate the work. If I don't like what I see, I'm in a difficult position. If I hate what I see, I won't pretend to like it. But if things fall into a middle area, as they usually do, I will need to be diplomatic. I will need to accentuate the positive and make a few suggestions to redirect the energies that I may feel are flowing in the wrong way. I need to be flexible. . . . If Kim is willing for me to talk to everybody, I would prefer to do that. . . . It creates a situation of secrecy and denial and anxiety if I whisper to the director and she filters what I say to the actors. It's not desirable. I need to be forthright and diplomatic.

In contrast to the preference expressed by several actors in the Miller, Kushner, and Parks productions, van Itallie does not wish his comments to be "filtered" through the director's voice. Voicing and listening are the heart of his play and also, for this playwright and this company, the heartbeat of rehearsal. As we walk to the meadow, he says: "I think frequently the director is afraid the playwright will upset the applecart. The responsibility is not to upset the applecart but help the applecart carry the apples better."

Watching the run-through are the director, assistant to the director Amie Keddy, set and costume designer Nick Ularu,[25] lighting designer Sabrina Hamilton, van Itallie, and four or five friends and colleagues of the director. Under the majestic sycamore tree, Mancuso welcomes the audience: "This is an adventure, a rehearsal, not a performance. Afterward we've agreed that Jean-Claude will talk to the company." In the run-through, as in the Boston performance, the play is preceded by a musical procession in which the performers (playing trumpet, trombone, flute, tambourine, snare drum, and triangle) walk in single file, leading the audience to the playing area. In the rehearsal studio, the playwright, wearing black jeans, a blue-green long-sleeved shirt over a turquoise T-shirt, a blue vest, gray socks, and white running shoes, sits on a red cushion to my right. The director sits on another red cushion to my left, a pencil in her right hand; she shifts her gaze between actors and text, turning pages of the script on the floor beside her, occasionally making notes. The playwright is without script, notebook, or pen; his gaze is steadily on the actors, his arms gracefully resting on his raised knees, his eyes wide open, his face impassive. He sits in a relaxed position of unmoving attentiveness.

Despite their exhaustion and apprehensiveness, the actors are fully present and focused. The playwright's left hand covers his other (writing) hand at the wrist; the fingers of the right hand are at times clenched, at other times splayed across his left calf. For a moment his eyes brighten with a faraway look: the gaze of the playwright in rehearsal looking into the middle distance. He changes position, his body semi-reclined as he leans on his left arm and elbow, his right knee raised, the fingers of both hands interlaced. Energy begins to ebb on this hot July afternoon in the upper barn. Every note given earlier today has been incorporated, but the run-through has a subdued, chastened quality that I have seen before during a playwright's visit. The director sits erect, then leans toward the actors. The playwright, by contrast, leans back on both elbows, legs stretched out, crossed at the ankles. In the scene entitled "Realizing I Am Dead," as the company sings the word *Sarvamangalam*[26] softly, over and over, to the accompaniment of flute and guitar, there is a softening in van Itallie's eyes, a quiet taking in of this quietly moving moment. The playwright sits up, crosses his arms over his knees. The fingers of his right hand twitch, move involuntarily. He lowers his eyes as Dunkelberg says: "I'm here. Don't cry. I'm here./So. I am dead" (29). In the silence between this speech and the next spoken words, the fingers of the playwright's right hand move almost imperceptibly, then seem to freeze, splayed, in midair. His face remains impassive.

During the funeral procession in the next scene, van Itallie leans forward, his left hand cradling his clenched right hand, then leans back again, arms around knees, left hand circling the wrist of the right hand, as if to constrain or subdue it. Dunkelberg and Dorsey dance by, their bodies gleaming with sweat. Scenes that evoke loud laughter from others (e.g., three actresses singing "Take

care" [33] with contemporary inflections) receive at most a nearly imperceptible smile from the playwright. Like Elizabeth Egloff's in rehearsals of *The Devils*, van Itallie's face does not give away much even to the most attentive eye—
and all the members of the company are, at one time or another, observing the
responses of this most observed of all observers.[27] The director mouths the text
sung by five actors. The playwright's lips do not move. He makes no sound. He
speaks only through changes in the intensity of his gaze, focused steadily on the
actors, and the movements of his writing hand. The run ends. The author claps
audibly along with the rest of the onlookers.

In the meadow under the sycamore, the company gathers once again in the
presence of the playwright. Mancuso invites van Itallie to talk with the actors,
adding: "I don't want to put you on the spot." "I *am* on the spot and I think I
should be as open with my thoughts as possible in order to be useful," the
playwright replies.

> *First of all, I think it's going in a beautiful direction. It's active, alive. A lot of
> work has gone into it. . . . Let me tell you my favorite moment: the "muddy
> swamp."[28] I was trying to think how I could be most helpful. Thinking back to
> what we were talking about under this tree a year ago, I still in some sense don't
> know what this is about.*
>
> *I think it's very important for the performance to maintain a questioning
> attitude. So when I think it's at its least good is when someone is pretending to
> know something and telling the audience that this is so. On the other hand, who
> is this voice of* The Tibetan Book of the Dead? *It's a compassionate voice.*

Then, like Arthur Miller in rehearsal of *The American Clock*, the playwright
gives explicitly directorial notes:

> *I think it might be important for each of you to visualize somebody in your life
> who has been a guide. How do you talk to someone who is dying or to the dead?
> Maybe the only thing they'll respond to is the love in your voice.*
>
> *Never pretend to a knowledge you don't have. When you do that, it goes to
> melodrama, and then you lose the audience.*
>
> *Simplicity, I think, is a strong direction to go in. When in doubt, do less. . . .
> I think there are a few too many moments when people are shouting at the top of
> their voices.*

He praises individual actors as well as certain musical renderings of the text. In
response to the cast's questions, van Itallie gives precise, practical responses,
indicating, for example, when a particular song "goes on too long"; when
"too much is going on [in one scene]"; when it "got too pompous"; when the
text is not fully audible.

Dunkelberg asks the playwright: "Is there any place where you think the
text is trivialized?" "No," he responds, "I don't feel that the text is trivialized.
But with Susan's song ["Tonada de Luna Llena," added, in Spanish, to one of
the last scenes], I didn't know who you were. I need clarity at every moment.
Maybe the lights will do that for me."[29] Van Itallie speaks not as a playwright

objecting to the introduction of new text but as a director desiring clarity in its presentation.

Almost by chance, the playwright mentions lines left out of the published edition. When Thompson comments that a particular scene is difficult, van Itallie responds: "Oh, yes. It's missing a part." At the actress's request, he dictates the omitted lines: "This is the northern shadow of your own brain/This is your own envy."[30] Actors sit on the grass writing new lines in their scripts, but, unlike the playwrights in earlier chapters, van Itallie is restoring, not rewriting, the text in rehearsal.

An actor now raises a question about a scene called "Love-Making" and van Itallie replies: "I think the text is unclear there but *I don't know how to change it right now*. [It will be slightly revised in the later version of *Tibetan* intended for reading aloud.] It's not saying: 'Don't make love.' It's not saying: 'Don't be sexually attracted.' It's saying: 'Don't be born'" (emphasis mine). "I wonder if that could be clarified in the staging," he comments, and suggests re-blocking: "I would turn away [he says to Dorsey] from the ones doing the love-making—I don't know how Kim feels about this—so that it doesn't sound as if you're saying, 'Don't make love.'" The director is silent. The author is suggesting how an acknowledged problem in the play might be resolved by restaging. Unlike Maria Irene Fornes, for whom rewriting the script in rehearsal *is* a restaging of it, he neither revises the text nor directs it himself.

"How was it to hear the words you've written, to hear them again?" Thompson asks. "I'm hearing them again as if for the first time," the playwright responds. "I'm thinking how will I hear them when I'm dying or dead. Did that answer it?" The actress presses further: "Were there times when you felt the text didn't come through?" During the run-through van Itallie's lips remained closed, he never uttered a sound, his fingers never covered his mouth. Now he tells the actress: "I'm not referring to a written text in my head. Sometimes I couldn't hear the words, and that bothers me. Sometimes I felt they were coming out too simply, like a preacher from a pulpit, and that bothers me. *I'm just listening as a human being*" (emphasis mine). In this last astonishing sentence, the playwright, who a year ago had told the actors: "To the degree that ego is out of it, you can do no wrong," now seems to manifest that very lack of ego.

"Were you honest?" I ask van Itallie after his meeting with the company. "Yes," he replies. "I hope I was skillfully so. One needs skillful means. One of those means is establishing a basis of trust in making the actors know that you are with them in making this the best possible production. Within that context one can be more direct." Asked if he heard or saw anything disturbing, van Itallie responds:

> I think of the text in a way as water flowing. I ask of the actors that they not obstruct the flow, so when their anxiety or anything else gets in the way of that flow I'm very aware of it. When their energy gets in the way of the flow, I'm thrown out of the play and that's disturbing. Then my task when talking to them and the director is how to help them not to do that.

It's as if the subtitle of his play, "How Not To Do It Again," is also the subtext of his comments in rehearsal.

Now I ask: how are the directorial and authorial gaze different and similar in rehearsal? "In this case," van Itallie replies, "the director and playwright are similar."

> *In the case of diagnosing why the actor is pushing too hard, or doing something discordant, that skill is the skill of a person listening sensitively. If I were here every day as the director is, our points of view would be similar.* We would see the same thing. *I think we make too much of the differences in function in the theater—performer, writer, and director.*[31] *[emphasis mine]*

But when I ask why he does not direct his own plays, he seems to open a gap between roles: "I like the dialogue I have with the director. The person seeing is a little different from the person doing." And the "person doing" that he most admires is, finally, the actor. Acting, he says, is "the most daring of the three functions and it's the one in which I feel most alive."

The director joins us on the front porch of the farmhouse. She mentions that she would have liked the playwright to be present at earlier rehearsals; she had given him "an open invitation." "Basically, I felt it was your initiative," he replies. "I would have come in response to any specific invitation." "I want to thank you for coming today," Mancuso says. "Actors have told me how much they appreciated this visit."

When I inquire if he would be willing to change the words of his script in rehearsal, van Itallie responds:

> *To change the words in the text would require my coming to rehearsal much more regularly. . . . My view is really holistic. I approach a work in terms of what stage it's in* now. *I can hear from a director or an actor that another word or words are needed and do it. . . . If an actor in rehearsal had proposed a minor script change, I would have considered it. I would consider a textual change not only for this production but also for a new published version.*

"I think it was a very successful meeting," the director tells me later. "[The playwright's] thinking about the work inspired the actors to think about their work in new ways because he saw this with fresh eyes."

> *He was very specific in some of his responses and later I heard from actors a willingness, because of what he had said, to open what they had done to further exploration. . . . Jean-Claude acknowledged that this was a different approach than had been taken with his text before, and was precise about what he felt was successful and what wasn't. I so appreciated the care he took with the actors—not judging. For me, because I think of myself as an enabler or a catalyst—and I've said this to you before—the meeting between Jean-Claude and the performers, actors and musicians alike, was successful because it directly stimulated their imaginations.*

Asked if she would characterize as directorial certain of van Itallie's comments, Mancuso responds: "Yes, I would," and adds: "I welcomed all of his input.

Because we work so collaboratively, the distinction between director and actor becomes blurred. . . . And the same thing happens between director and playwright."

> I will make the final choice because finally it's the director who is there all the time, who breathes the production. The director sees everything in every rehearsal all at once with peripheral vision open like a hunter and at the same time sees microscopically. It's two kinds of seeing. And that kind of seeing cannot happen accurately in intermittent visits to the rehearsal process. . . . The director's gaze is a double gaze.[32]

"I felt a difference in their gaze," Susan Thompson says of the director and playwright in rehearsal.

> She was the encouraging but adjusting eye, and he . . . [pause] I think there was a certain element of scrutiny—I hate to say impersonal, but I almost felt the words themselves were sitting in front of me in him. And I became suddenly aware of the exact order of the words in a way I'm usually not. That was the effect of his eye on me.

Van Itallie, watching rehearsals of his work, may not constantly be "referring to a written text in [his] head," but his own presence in rehearsal is, for this actress, the very presence of the text.

The playwright's words to the company after the run "were a license to create in freedom," says Monica Gomi, no longer intimidated by "a large hand . . . holding the production."

> He didn't say, "This is my play and it has to be a specific way." And that kind of generosity is great. I've changed my opinion of him. . . . There's something in the simple acceptance and also in his understanding of his place in the work, which is not that of the director or the actor. He's given us creative freedom, he's given us his play.

"Truthfully, I was terrified about what he was going to say and, more importantly, what he was going to feel," Katherine Down tells me.

> [In his responses to] the songs written by the actors and how we incorporated the songs in the piece, and also the choices I made in the instruments—for example, unusual instruments like the rocks—he seemed to be on a profound level understanding the process we are going through, the rawness of it, and was extremely gracious about it.
>
> He himself is asking similar questions of masters in Tibetan Buddhism to those we are asking of him. I liked the fact that he told us to keep a sense of awe and to never be presumptuous or preachy. And we needed to think about that musically as well.

"I was terrified," says Kermit Dunkelberg. "I was surprised that he didn't hate it. I was also surprised by his generosity. And the clarity, the real theater sense, of what he said."

It wasn't about: "What have you done to my play?" It was about what worked practically, what didn't work so well. His perspective on this as an author seems a little different from what one might expect. Sometimes he says: I didn't really write it, and sometimes I can't believe that, but the way he was being in that discussion was very much from that perspective. It wasn't about his ownership of that material.

"When I think over what is most successful in my work," the actor adds, "it's when I really attacked the text and did something I thought Jean-Claude would *not* want."

I had to get over wanting him to be happy. . . . He said yesterday that he liked my song: "the muddy swamp"; that song had come out in a rehearsal in which I felt that I was attacking the text, going against the grain, and yet he picked it out for compliment. It should be that way but it's scary. It's hard to not try to be faithful. It's that way with Shakespeare, too: the way to be faithful is not to be faithful.

I conduct a last late-night interview with Susan Thompson as her two young sons, Jackson and Skye, fall asleep beside us on the bed in my room at the farmhouse. "In speaking with us, [Jean-Claude van Itallie] disavows his authorship."

In many ways he's doing with the original text what we're doing with his text. He's taken liberties with the Tibetan Book of the Dead *just as we've taken liberties with his* Tibetan Book of the Dead. *He's taken the text and reflected on it and chosen those particular words for his play. We've taken his play and reflected on it and chosen this set of actions and sounds and gestures. It sounds directorial when he says: "Be genuine, be real," but that is perhaps integral to the process of his adaptation in the first place.*

With what license did this guy translate the sacred Tibetan Book of the Dead *into a play on how not to do it again? One has to guess: with a mixture of great trepidation and love of the material and chutzpah.*

I know that mixture well, for with it I began this book, my own "translation" of that mysterious process of theater-making in which an "author-ized" dramatic text, like the protagonist of *The Tibetan Book of the Dead*, seeks, over and over again, auspicious rebirth.

Notes

Introduction

1. See David Cole, *Acting as Reading: The Place of the Reading Process in the Actor's Work* (Ann Arbor: U of Michigan P, 1992), 221–253.
2. Some readers may ask: why these eight playwrights? Certainly there are others that it would also have interested me to write about. I have been partly governed in my choices by who was available—and brave enough to allow me to observe them—during the period of my research.
3. "I'm not somebody who says, 'Here's the play. See you later,'" Tom Stoppard remarks. "I like tinkering. I don't think I've been involved in a rehearsal in my life where I haven't changed *something*." Mamie Healey, "Stoppard Making Sense," *Time Out New York*, Issue 238 (April 13–20, 2000), 31.
4. Of his experience directing a script by Elaine May, Michael Blakemore says: "At one point I became irritated when she took the opportunity of responding to a question I'd asked by addressing the cast at large on how a scene should be played. I hope she's going to observe the rule of filtering her opinions through the director, and not speaking privately to the actors." "Backstage Notes: Death Defying Director," *New Yorker*, June 3, 1996, 52.
5. Quoted in "The Talk of the Town," *New Yorker*, Feb. 10, 1997, 31.

Chapter 1: Sam Shepard in Rehearsal

1. Liz Welch, "Choosing the Playwrights Who Can Go Home Again," *New York Times*, Nov. 17, 1996, Section 2, Arts & Leisure, 1.
2. "We spent five days around the table. I think it's really important that we did that, that we all start on the same page. That frees your imagination." James Houghton, interview, March 29, 1997. Unless otherwise indicated, all subsequent statements by the director and actors are from interviews conducted on March 26–29, 1997.

3. The issue of time lines also arises in rehearsal of Elizabeth Egloff's *The Devils* at New York Theatre Workshop. On April 1, 1997, director Garland Wright says to the cast: "Let's check the time line. So if this is evening [pauses], the next scene will be in the early morning, dawn." An actor says, "Are you asking in terms of what is his . . . [pauses]." The director responds, "No, I just want to know." The director needs to establish a time line for himself in the presence of the actors. Later in rehearsal I hear him ask, "What year did we decide to *think* we're in?" and an actor replies, "1871."

4. A particularly poignant sharing of subtext is actress Deborah Hedwall's March 28 rehearsal comment on Wesley's preplay childhood: "He used to be such a sweet little boy, so quiet. He would go off by himself and build campfires. Such a sweet, sweet little boy." I see Paul Dawson's eyes water—he wipes his eyes with his hand—as the actress speaks of his imaginary life as her child.

   During rehearsal of act 2 on March 22, Jude Ciccolella reveals: "I've got her [Ella] on my mind. *It's not in the play*, but that's where my energy is" (emphasis mine).

5. At the earlier (March 20) reading rehearsal, Sam Shepard made the following changes:

   Act 1:
   Ella's speech, "hotel" changed to "motel," 136
   Ella's speech, add "But I still wasn't sure" after "I could smell him right through the door," 136
   Ella's speech, add "Real money" after "We're going to have some money real soon," 143
   Act 2:
   Wesley's speech, change "Mr. and Mrs. America" to "Ozzie and Harriet," 162
   Weston's speech, add "It's only me" after "Sit down!" 164
   Weston's speech, add "That was me?" before "My laundry not done yet?" 164
   Weston's speech, omit exclamation mark and add "about the lawyer" after "You knew," 165
   Weston's speech, add "There's nobody to call" after "Don't call anybody," 165
   Weston's speech, add "Who needs a door?" before "I gotta sit down," 165
   Weston's speech, add "You're the daughter, not the mother" after "YOU'RE NOT DOING IT!" 166
   Weston's speech, add "It's always been confidential" after "they keep it a secret that means," 167
   Weston's speech, add "You're either growing up or you're lying" after "You're growing up," 167

Wesley's speech, add "I hate artichokes" after "You want an arti-
choke?" 168

Weston's speech, change "food" in "I'm the one who brings home food"
to "artichokes," 169

Ella's speech, add "I hate artichokes" after "It's a joke bringing artichokes back here when we're out of food," 171

All citations of *Curse of the Starving Class* are taken from *Sam
Shepard: Seven Plays* (New York: Bantam, 1986).

6. I notice that in rehearsal Deborah Hedwall, an emotionally meticulous
    actress, is always "within the play." For example, during the table read-
    ing of a scene in which she is not present, when Weston claims that he is
    the one who takes responsibility for the maintenance of the family,
    Hedwall shakes her head from side to side, and when he talks about the
    (worthless) land he bought in the desert, I hear her quiet scornful laugh.
    Later, during a read-through of act 2, as Wesley and Emma talk,
    Hedwall—not yet in the scene—shakes her head and makes small word-
    less responses to what her children are saying, then laughs quietly at
    Wesley's fantasy about escaping to Alaska. When Emma tells her father
    that her mother has left with a lawyer, Hedwall slaps her cheek with her
    hand. In all these instances, the actress is responding as Ella throughout
    scenes in which Ella does not appear.

7. Stephen J. Bottoms, *The Theatre of Sam Shepard: States of Crisis*
    (Cambridge, U.K.: Cambridge UP, 1998), 167. See also 172.

8. For example, the director says to Paul Dawson: "Wes, . . . think what
    you would imagine for yourself after you pay off the debt but don't have
    a home any more. But you don't have to share it with us."

9. On March 27, Jude Ciccolella, rehearsing act 3, tells the director, "I like
    what Sam said on Sunday about how you forget your people," and Jim
    Houghton responds, "I thought Sam hit the nail on the head so precisely,
    all across the board, on Sunday." The actor replies, "I would hope so. He
    wrote it."

10. Pagination is that of the rehearsal script.

11. Sam Shepard's "That's it"—no more revisions of the script—is a state-
    ment I never hear in Maria Irene Fornes's rehearsals, not even after open-
    ing night.

    The following is the complete list of textual revisions dictated by Sam
    Shepard in rehearsal on March 23, 1997.

Act 2:

Ellis's speech, add "I hate artichokes," after "Artichokes, huh?" 174

Ellis's speech, change "steak house" to "steak joint," 177

Ella's speech, add "We're going away" after "There wouldn't be anyone
here," 181

Ella's speech, add "I'm by myself" after "I'll be all right," 181

Act 3:

Weston's speech, change "a great feeling" to "a great sensation," 185

Weston's speech, change "your socks" to "your crusty socks," 186

Weston's speech, change "Chicanos" to "Mojados," 187

Ella's speech, change "I'm very grateful" to "That's big of you," 188

Ella's speech, add "How long have I been sleeping?" after "I must've slept right through it," 199

Ella's speech, add new final line, "How long have I been sleeping?" 200

12. Cf. Shepard's response to director and actor Joseph Chaikin:

I met Joe and came down to the Open Theater sessions . . . and started to see the way he was working with actors. There was this approach Joe had which was so startling in a way because it was away from all of the conventions of the approach to acting at that time. He was stepping outside the territory of cause and effect, the territory of motivation, the psychological way, and he was stepping way outside that . . . which is still the way he works. ("Stalking Himself," 1997 BBC documentary profile of Sam Shepard, directed by Oren Jacoby, shown in New York on WNET, July 8, 1998)

13. Don Shewey, *Sam Shepard* (New York: Dell, 1985), 47.

14. Suzan-Lori Parks, directing her play, *In the Blood*, at the Public Theater, also attempts to refine accents that are "too far south."

15. Shepard himself does not fly:

I've been upside down under falling horses at a full gallop. . . . I've rolled in a 1949 Plymouth Coup which is a hard car to flip over. . . . I would gladly go through all these dumb acts ten times over rather than get on an airplane of any kind. I admit to an overwhelming vertigo that I don't quite understand and I'm unwilling to psychoanalyze. The absolutely realistic sensation of falling without end, that's one I have no power over. ("Stalking Himself," documentary profile)

16. Shepard said in "Stalking Himself":

I'd avoided investigating the family for quite a while because to me there was a danger in . . . I was a little afraid of it, you know, particularly around my old man and all of that emotional territory. I didn't really want to tiptoe in there, and then I said, "Well, maybe I'd better," so [laughs] . . . I guess it started with Curse [of the Starving Class].

17. Interview with Sam Shepard, conducted by Amy Lippman. "Rhythm & Truths," *American Theatre*, vol. 1, no. 1 (April 1984), 12.

18. "He's my favorite playwright, Brecht." Interview with Sam Shepard, conducted by Kenneth Chubb and the editors of *Theatre Quarterly*, in Bonnie Marranca, *American Dreams, The Imagination of Sam Shepard* (New York: PAJ Publications, 1981), 202.

19. The writer's comments also send actors to other texts and other writers. Actor Clark Middleton later gave the director a Xerox of Joan Didion's

"Some Dreamers of the Golden Dream," accompanied by a note: "When we were talking the other day with Sam, I kept thinking about this Joan Didion story I'd read some years back. It . . . includes a sense of those crazy desert winds and environment of that part of the country that affected those families that Sam spoke of. Any use?" In this production, playwright, director, and actors together function as dramaturg.

Clark Middleton tells me: "I'm playing a small part. [What Shepard] . . . gave us is like a painting. You have to fit into the world of the play."

20. Harold Bloom, ed., *Modern Critical Views: Mark Twain* (New York: Chelsea House, 1986), 3.

21. "Stalking Himself," documentary profile.

22. Like Gayev, who addresses a monologue to an inanimate object (a bookcase) in act 1 of *The Cherry Orchard*, characters in *Curse of the Starving Class* deliver speeches to the refrigerator. Stephen J. Bottoms observes that Shepard's play "seems unashamedly derivative in its plot pretext, reading as a grotesque variation on Chekhov's *The Cherry Orchard*." *Theatre of Sam Shepard*, 158.

23. Since the opening stage directions include a working refrigerator and stove, the pointed omission of a sink may be a kind of in-joke about "kitchen-sink realism" in the American theater. And, in the following stage direction, the somewhat surreal placement of the kitchen curtains calls attention to the juxtaposition of realistic and non-realistic elements in the play: *"suspended in midair to stage right and stage left are two ruffled, red-checked curtains, slightly faded"* (135).

24. For the previous three productions of his plays at Signature Theatre, Shepard was present at the beginning of the design process. Because he is making a movie on location, he is unable to attend early design meetings or later, on-its-feet rehearsals for *Curse of the Starving Class*.

25. Shepard's stage directions indicate that Wesley urinates on the 4-H charts his sister is preparing (142).

26. Donald Fried, interview, March 26, 1997.

27. Shepard has said of the scripted onstage urination: "I wouldn't do that again if I had to do it over. I was looking for a gesture, for something without words. . . . It's a little flashy, . . . and overblown, and maybe embarrassing, but that's the way it came out." Lippman, "Rhythm & Truths," 41.

28. Moore invites poets to be "'literalists of the imagination,'" a definition that also characterizes the actor. Marianne Moore, "Poetry" (longer version), in *The Complete Poems of Marianne Moore* (New York: Penguin, 1982), 267.

29. Like Maria Irene Fornes, Sam Shepard was smitten in an early encounter with Beckett's play: "'I started reading the play . . . and it was like nothing I'd ever read before—it was *Waiting for Godot*.'" Shewey, *Sam Shepard*, 29.

30. Cf. David Cole: "If a character is a way to read, a kind of reader, then to play a character is to *agree to read* in that way." *Acting as Reading*, 113. See also 114–126.

31. "When I try to put all into a phrase I say, 'Man can embody truth but he cannot know it.'" William Butler Yeats, quoted in M. H. Abrams, ed., *The Norton Anthology of English Literature*, Vol. 2, 6th edition (New York: W.W. Norton, 2000), 2088.

32. Lippman, "Rhythm & Truths," 13.

33. In rehearsal on March 27, Deborah Hedwall says, "I can't memorize until I know what I'm doing," and Jude Ciccolella replies, "I memorize without knowing what I'm doing." There is a burst of laughter as Hedwall makes hand gestures suggesting that the actors, like the characters they play, are hopelessly out of sync.

34. The sweeping is an early rehearsal choice, not indicated in the stage directions. Eventually it is discarded.

35. During a break on March 22, Jim Houghton says to me that when a monologue is delivered out, "time stops and the character plays the speech *to* the audience."

36. The director later paraphrases the author's comment in his April 2 notes to the actors: "I don't think it's all one way or one thing."

    Earlier during rehearsal, in answer to the stage manager's question, "Should Weston snore?" as he lies "sleeping. . . . falling away. . . . (*unconscious again*)" (171), the director replies, "We could try it, but I like not knowing." (Weston does not snore in the performance I attended.)

37. Jim Houghton tells me: "We at Signature Theatre Company *try to eliminate the barriers that are likely to come up between playwrights and the members of a company producing their plays.* . . . It's imperative that the playwright is in residence. That's the crux for me: that the writer have a deep participation in each production. That participation varies with each production. Sam has been here only minimally, but he has been integrally involved in serious, lengthy discussions with me for a long time. And there is a history of his whole year's involvement with the theater" (emphasis mine).

38. Apropos Shepard's being "hard to understand," actor Frank Raiter tells me during a break in rehearsal of Elizabeth Egloff's *The Devils*: "Over thirty years ago, after I had just made a film, a Western called *The Mac-Masters*, I auditioned for a play by Sam Shepard, *Back Dog Beast Bait*. I had the script for two weeks and I didn't understand one word. I went in and Mr. Shepard was sitting in the theater with his long legs over the back of the chair in front of him, and I thanked him for asking me to audition for him. And then I told him I didn't understand one word of the play. And he said, 'Great.' And I did the part."

39. At the very end of the rehearsal period, however, Darrell Larson replaces the actor playing Taylor, and in the performance I see on April 15, 1997, Taylor exits stage right.

40. "WESLEY *enters from right carrying a small collapsible fence structure. He sets it up center stage to form a small rectangular enclosure. . . . WESLEY enters again from right carrying a small live lamb. He sets the lamb down inside the fenced area*" (153). "*Fence enclosure with the lamb inside is back, center stage*" (182).
41. The appearance of the naked actor under bright light in a small house, joked about in the rehearsal studio, is treated in a matter-of-fact way during tech rehearsal in the theater.
42. Apparently one of the hazards of kitchen-stove realism in the theater is that Ciccolella has to eat what he cooks. "It's awful," he says, "and you can quote me."
43. There may possibly be far in the background a literary antecedent in Book XII of the *Iliad* where a "bird sign" appears to the Trojans: "an eagle, flying high . . . and carrying in its talons a gigantic snake, blood-coloured." Hektor and Poulydamas argue about the interpretation of this "portent" (ll. 200–250). Richmond Lattimore, trans., *The Iliad of Homer* (Chicago: U of Chicago P, 1951), 263. When Shelley borrows this image in "Alastor," the eagle becomes female and the serpent green (ll. 227–237). In "The Revolt of Islam," the eagle and snake "wreathed in fight" in the air are both male (canto 1, stanza 8, l.4), as in the *Iliad*. In all three poems, however, the eagle continues its flight while the snake falls to earth. George Edward Woodberry, ed., *Complete Poetical Works of Percy Bysshe Shelley* (Boston: Houghton Mifflin, 1901), 36, 52–53.
44. Lippman, "Rhythm & Truths," 11.
45. This new final line, "How long have I been sleeping?" has its own history of unintentional slippage, becoming "How long was I sleeping?" in technical rehearsal and in the performance I attended on April 15, 1997.

Chapter 2: David Rabe in Rehearsal

1. Ben Brantley, "In a Season of Wild Cards, Actors Rule," *New York Times*, June 1, 1997, H4.

   Unlike David Rabe, Dr. Richard Selzer has taken a strong position "in favor of physician-assisted suicide in highly controlled circumstances." For Dr. Selzer, death "should be a choice." "I am opposed," he says, "to the prolongation of suffering" (Laura Collins-Hughes, "In Drama, Doctor Sees His Life Unfold Onstage," *New Haven Register*, Feb. 8, 1998, G5). For the playwright, certainty on the issue of physician-assisted suicide is impossible: "[The characters] can't figure it out. You can make it legal or illegal but you can't figure it out" (Laura Collins-Hughes, "Playwright David Rabe Returns with 'A Question,'" *New Haven Register*, Feb. 8, 1998, G2). Rabe has arrived at a position of caution:

   The play shows how volatile all the feelings can be and how everything can turn into quicksand. . . . My sense about making . . . [physician-assisted suicide] legal through the quote-unquote "authorities" is that anything that becomes bureaucratic ultimately is corrupt. I just see an endless area of danger with insurance companies or families who want to get rid of someone. That is my fear about legalizing it. Although if someone chose to do it, and managed to pull it off, I wouldn't think it was awful. It's so hard to know. (Frank Rizzo, "Life to Stage," Hartford Courant, *Feb. 15, 1998, G4)*

    Immediately following the performance on February 19, 1998, there was a "talkback" with Roland Clement, representing the New Haven chapter of the Hemlock Society. This was the first of a series of 19 "talkbacks" scheduled during the run of *A Question of Mercy*. The speakers included several doctors, a rabbi, a chaplain, a psychotherapist, a bereavement specialist, a lawyer, the director of pastoral care at a Connecticut hospice, and the director of education for the AIDS Project in New Haven.

2. Selzer, who retired from medical practice as a surgeon in 1986, "feel[s] [him]self to be in the continuum" of doctors who became writers, citing as examples Keats, Rabelais, Chekhov, Maimonides, Walker Percy, and William Carlos Williams. Christopher Arnott, "Is There a Doctor in the House?" *New Haven Advocate*, Feb. 19, 1998, 31.

3. Frank Rizzo, "An Experience Almost Too Painful for Words," *Hartford Courant*, Feb. 15, 1998, G4. The Long Wharf Theatre program says the Rabe play is "adapted from the essay by Richard Selzer"; the Grove Press edition of *A Question of Mercy* calls it "a play based on the essay by Richard Selzer." In an interview conducted by Christopher Arnott, Selzer says he considers himself "a diarist. . . . I never looked at [the piece] as an essay." "Is There a Doctor," 31.

4. Arnott, "Is There a Doctor," 31.

5. Douglas Hughes says of Selzer: "He was living primary source material, generous with his time, adding emotional details." Alvin Klein, "The Ultimate Moment, When Reason Fails," *New York Times*, March 1, 1998, Connecticut section, 13.

6. Klein, "Ultimate Moment," 13.

7. Long Wharf 1997–1998 season brochure.

8. Klein, "Ultimate Moment," 13.

9. Ronald Dworkin, "Assisted Suicide: What the Court Really Said," *New York Review of Books*, vol. 44, no. 14 (Sept. 25, 1997), 40. Dworkin quotes from Souter's separate opinion concurring in but not joining the majority opinion: "If we apply reasoned judgment to the assisted suicide issue, Souter argued, we can identify arguments of what he called 'increasing forcefulness for recognizing some right to a doctor's help in suicide.'"

10. *A Question of Mercy*, production script from New York Theatre Workshop, updated February 25, 1997, 74. Unless otherwise noted, all citations of the play are from this script, used in the Long Wharf rehearsals.

11. David Rabe, *A Question of Mercy, A Play Based on the Essay by Richard Selzer* (New York: Grove, 1998), 106.

12. The play was originally optioned by American Playhouse for television. When American Playhouse lost its funding, Rabe says, "they gave me all their rights to it, and I just had to get the theatrical rights from Dr. Selzer, which happened very quickly." Stephanie Coen, "When Reason Fails," *American Theatre* (July/Aug. 1997), 22.

13. Later, actor David Chandler, who plays Dr. Chapman, says: "David Rabe hasn't been . . . [in rehearsal] that much but he said something really wonderful which had to do with our efforts to make rationality into prophecy. I actually wrote it down." He leaves, returns with his notebook, and reads aloud: "'A plan is an attempt to turn reason into prophecy.' I thought that made a lot of sense." Interview, January 22, 1998. Unless otherwise indicated, all subsequent statements by the actors, director, and playwright are from interviews conducted on January 15, 22, 24, and 31, 1998.

14. In Selzer's narrative, Lionel (Thomas in Rabe's play) is a poet and ordained minister; Ramon (Anthony) is "a doctor specializing in public health—women's problems, birth control, family planning, AIDS." *Down from Troy: A Doctor Comes of Age* (Boston: Back Bay Books, 1992), 284. When I ask Rabe why he does not mention the occupations of the characters in the play, he says: "I left out the professions. I just did it. Then I later developed a rationale. I felt later that I was drawing on a tradition of medieval mystery plays where people are basically defined by their relation to the dilemma, whatever it is. The activities of a minister are there. He prays. But I felt saying that he was a minister would undermine the rawness of his position. I did it instinctively and understood it later."

15. Coen, "Reason Fails," 22.

16. Collins-Hughes, "Rabe Returns," G5.

17. Coen, "Reason Fails," 22.

18. I observe Sam Shepard, Maria Irene Fornes, Suzan-Lori Parks, and Elizabeth Egloff making textual revisions directly on the pages of their scripts during rehearsal.

19. In the rehearsals attended by Sam Shepard, Arthur Miller, Tony Kushner, and Suzan-Lori Parks, the playwright answers questions about pronunciation. In the rehearsals of Maria Irene Fornes, there is group discussion of questions of pronunciation and grammar, usually initiated by the playwright herself.

20. Coen, "Reason Fails," 22. About the ending of the play, Rabe says: "I would never have had the nerve to make that up." Collins-Hughes, "Rabe Returns," G5. Oddly, John Lahr, reviewing the New York production of *A Question of Mercy*, says of the ending: "Rabe wrings a final moral change out of *his* tale" (emphasis mine). "Death-Defying Acts," *New Yorker* (March 24, 1997), 87.

21. Douglas Hughes says of rehearsal of *A Question of Mercy* at New York Theatre Workshop: "I'd try options—add or cut things provisionally and

then if . . . [Rabe] came back and liked it, it would stay. If he didn't, it would go. Because he doesn't like to come to every rehearsal."

22. Interview, January 31, 1998. After the interview, when I couldn't read my own writing, David Rabe looked at it and decided that the last word was "theatricality." He said: "Put in that dash [after "theatricality"]. I'm still looking for what I'm trying to say."

23. Douglas Hughes, interview, February 7, 1998.

24. Hughes adds that he thinks the omission of "three" may be a typographical error.

25. This "left-over revision from the New York production," as David Rabe refers to it, seems to have begun as a change in blocking; the new dialogue only emerges in the course of the New Haven rehearsals.

26. On February 1, rehearsing Dr. Chapman's first meeting with Thomas and Anthony, Hughes says: "If it were a proscenium, it would be a cinch. . . . [This particular staging] may not be possible. [The Long Wharf mainstage] is a very deep thrust. I guess you'll have to bear with me as I struggle."

27. Hughes says of the Long Wharf Theatre: "We are here in New Haven in a food terminal with meat carcasses and sausage factories [much like the Bush Theatre]," located "above a pub . . . in a working-class neighborhood [of London]," where the production of *A Question of Mercy* is being transferred in April and May 1998. James V. Ruocco, "British Theatre to Invade Stage of Long Wharf," *Republican-American*, March 1, 1998, H6.

28. Hughes, "The Artistic Director's Diary," *The Loading Dock*, a publication for Long Wharf subscribers, February 1998.

29. Rehearsal script revisions, 45. None of these changes appears in the published edition of the play. Hughes transfers to the "new scene" Thomas's slightly earlier greeting of Anthony: "Chiquito! You're wearing your new shirt!" (rehearsal script, 42; revised rehearsal script, 45). This, Hughes tells the cast, is Richard Selzer's favorite line in the play. It is taken almost verbatim from Selzer's *Down from Troy*, 288.

30. *A Question of Mercy*, 56–57.

31. Rehearsing on January 24, Hughes suddenly says, "I always wanted [Anthony] to [help Dr. Chapman] put on the coat." In the rehearsal script, the stage directions indicate that Anthony picks up Dr. Chapman's overcoat and hands it to the doctor who later bends and hugs him. After some discussion of Dr. Chapman's ambivalence about an emotional leave-taking, Hughes says, "I'm aware of the stage direction," and then suggests that Anthony embrace the doctor after first kissing the ends of his coat sleeves. This staging appears in the performance I attend on February 19, 1998, and—with the exception of the kissing of sleeves—is indicated in the published text: "ANTHONY *picks up the coat and holds it for* DR. CHAPMAN *to slip into. . . . [ANTHONY] hugs* DR. CHAPMAN, *a strong, simple embrace that* DR. CHAPMAN *returns*" (95).

32. Hughes is the son of two actors, Barnard Hughes and Helen Stenborg. At Harvard College he did some acting but "liked [himself] better in the role of the person who directs." "There are prescribed limits to being a director that I am very comfortable with," he says. "And I found myself loving to watch rehearsals—seeing actors and scenes evolve on the stage." Cynthia Wolfe Boynton, "Where Now for the Long Wharf Theatre?" *New York Times*, Sept. 7, 1997, CN 3.

33. Kell adds: "As much as I want to clear the slate, I have some rhythms still with me from the original production."

34. On the director's "maternal gaze," see Susan Letzler Cole, *Directors in Rehearsal: A Hidden World* (New York: Routledge, 1992), 5–6.

35. Douglas Hughes tells me: "We went on a great trek to audition for Dr. Chapman, and we [Hughes and Rabe] mutually agreed on Zach Grenier. David Chandler was scheduled to audition for that role in the New York production, and he was stuck on a television set and couldn't come. So I asked him to do it at Long Wharf."

36. This passage appears almost verbatim in the published edition of the play. There are two minor stylistic changes: "caskets that" replaces "caskets which" and a comma is added after "Resurrection." *A Question of Mercy*, 92.

37. The resurrection of the body is one of the main doctrines of Christianity. "[T]he hour is coming when all who are in the tombs will hear his voice and come forth, those who have done good, to the resurrection of life, and those who have done evil, to the resurrection of judgment" (John 5:28–29). And yet questions remain.

    Exactly how the resurrection will take place, what will then happen, upon these points the Church has very little to go on. She has, however, determined that all will rise from the dead with their own bodies, those bodies which once died. . . . [A]fter the resurrection, there will be no marrying or giving in marriage, and . . . we shall be like angels in Heaven. . . . The resurrection should be the greatest consolation to man. (N.G.M. Van Doornik, S. Jelsma, and A. Van De Lisdonk, A Handbook of Catholic Faith [The Triptych of the Kingdom], *ed. John Greenwood [Garden City: Image Books, 1956], 465–466)*

    In the doctrine of the resurrection, the Catholic Church follows Aristotle, who held that anything must have both form and matter to be whole. Thomas Aquinas, following Aristotle, argued that the soul has its "natural perfection" only when it is united with the body. Thus, on the Day of Judgment, "the soul reunited with the body will be 'more perfect' than the soul is alone." Charles S. Singleton, commentary, *The Divine Comedy: Inferno*, Bollingen Series LXXX, Vol. 1 (Princeton: Princeton UP, 1970), 107.

38. Holden Caulfield says:

    What really knocks me out is a book that, when you're done reading it, you wish the author that wrote it was a terrific friend of yours and you could call

*him up on the phone whenever you felt like it. That doesn't happen much,
though. I wouldn't mind calling this Isak Dinesen up . . . but I wouldn't want
to call Somerset Maugham up. . . . I'd rather call old Thomas Hardy up." (J. D.
Salinger, The Catcher in the Rye [Boston: Little, Brown, & Co., 1951], 25)*

39. *A Question of Mercy*, 104–105. Thomas and Susanah have what Hughes calls "speeches of testimony," one after the other, in act 2. In the published edition, Susanah's speech of testimony is also delivered "out."
40. Coen, "Reason Fails," 22. The entire interview conducted by Stephanie Coen is included in the Long Wharf program but not in the thick packet of "dramaturgical materials," largely on assisted suicide, handed out to the actors by the assistant to the director, Jeanette Plourde.
41. In the reassigned line, "Thomas and Susanah will return to discover the body and call the clinic," Hughes changes "Susanah" to "I" (rehearsal script, 79). The line is not reassigned or altered in the published text. Maria Irene Fornes, directing her own play, reassigns characters' speeches, changing gender, with more drastic consequences in rehearsals of *The Summer in Gossensass*.
42. In the hospital Anthony is asked if he wants to live. Dr. Chapman says: "Now listen carefully. If you need anything repeated, I can do that. You have pneumonia. They can treat you for it. Or they can let you go. Do you understand? They can treat you, or they can let you go. Do you want to be treated for the pneumonia?" The stage direction in the rehearsal script and in the published text is unambiguous: "ANTHONY *stares, and then he nods, 'Yes.'*" Dr. Chapman rephrases the question: "Do you want to live?" and Anthony again "*nods, 'Yes.'*" Dr. Chapman asks a third time, "Do you still want to die, Anthony?" and Anthony stares again, then "*he shakes his head, 'No.'*" Rehearsal script, 96–97.
43. To my surprise, the set on the Long Wharf mainstage seems even barer than its facsimile in the rehearsal room. Downstage far right are a wooden chair, with a pair of men's pajamas neatly folded on its back, and a small table with a green phone. Far upstage, in a row, are two wooden chairs, a small wooden table with a plate of cookies, a walker, and an even smaller wooden table, two more wooden chairs, and a man's overcoat. (The rehearsal script indicates three playing areas and the set includes bookshelves, a bed, a plant, and curtains.) The backdrop is set designer Neil Patel's abstract version of Hughes's "smear of blood." Christopher Arnott, reviewing *A Question of Mercy*, writes: "Some elderly Long Wharf patrons sitting near me were critical of the set, a sparse arrangement of chairs and small tables, and indeed it's one of the most open and unornamented sets the Long Wharf mainstage has ever seen (even in the years before Hughes took over)." "Matters of Life and Death," *New Haven Advocate*, Feb. 26, 1998, 40.

44. Nearly thirty years ago, Rabe worked as a feature writer for the *New Haven Register*'s Sunday magazine.
45. This addition to the doorman's speech appears in capital letters in *A Question of Mercy*, 96.

Chapter 3: Elizabeth Egloff in Rehearsal

1. Michael Feingold, "Adaptive Mechanisms," *Village Voice*, June 3, 1997, 79.
2. Egloff has omitted and blended characters in her bold adaptation of Dostoevsky's novel.

    Dasha is a combination of Mrs. Virginsky [midwife to Marie Shatov] and Liza [Lizaveta Nikolaevna Drozdov, to whom Stavrogin was briefly engaged] and Mrs. Ulitin [a woman who takes care of Stepan Verkhovensky at the end of his life]. In a very early draft I tried to introduce the crippled girl [Marya Lebyadkin, whom Stavrogin had married on a bet]. She just wouldn't go. I think it's because in the crazy world of this play you don't need a psychotic mystic. She would be redundant. . . . A lot more of Dostoevsky's female characters were in my original draft, but I decided that the core of the story belonged in a man's world and that in that world women were outsiders and that was what united the remaining characters. (Elizabeth Egloff, interview, April 17, 1997)

    Unless otherwise indicated, all further statements by the playwright, director, and members of the company are from interviews conducted on April 1, 5–6, 8–9, 12, 15–17, 19, and 23; and May 7–8, 17, and 23, 1997.
3. Elizabeth Egloff, *The Devils*, rehearsal script, May 9, 1997, 9. Unless otherwise noted, all citations of *The Devils* are from this rehearsal script.
4. Michael Feingold, "Voice Choices: Theatre Short List," May 6, 1997, 17.
5. Postcard, NYTW publicity.
6. Michael Feingold wrote in the *Village Voice* after Wright's death:

    In an age when information can saturate the globe in an instant, an American theater career is still a mystery. . . . Within the theater community . . . [Wright] was a known quantity, a prominent director who had worked everywhere and with everybody, often achieving remarkable results. . . . Had he been a European director, his work would long since have become a subject of sustained scrutiny. As it stands, a long time will elapse, and many details vanish, before there is an overall sense of how he saw the world and what he achieved in putting it onstage. ("Theater: Garland Wright (1946–1998)," Aug. 18, 1998, 127)

7. William Grimes, "Life after 'Rent' for a Little Theater with Big Ideas," *New York Times*, May 18, 1997, H4.
8. *Ibid.*

9. The photographs, captions, and maps were provided by NYTW literary adviser Mandy Mishell Hackett.
10. Stepan's line, March 15, 1997, script, 162; later cut.
11. Also on the director's table during rehearsal are Webster's Ninth New Collegiate Dictionary, Konstantin Mochulsky's *Dostoevsky, His Life and Work*, and André Gide's *Dostoevsky*.
12. Fyodor Dostoevksy, *The Possessed*, trans. Constance Garnett (New York: Modern Library, 1936), 673–674. The final sentence in French means: "That's my profession of faith."
13. Among them, Peter Marks, who wrote: "Ms. Egloff has the least success with the novel's most enigmatic and exotic character, Nicholas Stavrogin. . . . Stavrogin is drawn here as pallid and marginal, in contrast to the more psychologically compelling rendering of Verkhovensky." "Plotters and Snoops in Old Russia," *New York Times*, May 23, 1997, C3.
14. The staging of Peter's final speech picks up this threefold repetition. Peter says: "The rich are still sucking the blood of the poor/The politicians are still sitting around/with their arms folded/talking about civilization/as our old people starve/our prophets are murdered/and our children devour each other/like wolves/. . . . And so I have given up civilization" (211–213). In performance on May 9, 1997, three drop curtains fall as Peter says, "And so I have given up civilization." He is no longer within the dark confines of the set. After the first of the five repetitions of "GIVE US JUSTICE" (212) with which his speech ends, lights brighten over the auditorium.
15. "I think I have been true to a Dostoevskian view which I happen to share—a world in which tragedy and comedy coexist, a world in which violence is more often than not the end of any action," the playwright says. "I think writers in general tend to be outsiders, so I think writers can be shameless conformists and unapologetic anarchists in the same breath."
16. When the Royal Shakespeare Company began work on Brian Friel's adaptation of *A Month in the Country*,

   the director [Michael Attenborough] banned Ivan Turgenev's . . . play from the rehearsal room. . . . Although he had read the Turgenev "a lot" before rehearsal began, he didn't want the actors having inner knowledge the audience didn't possess. He also didn't want his cast lobbying to adjust the play by adding Turgenev's material back in. "And the fact is," Attenborough said, "we were doing a Friel, not a Turgenev." (Laura Collins-Hughes, "From England, a Russian Play with an Irish Accent," New Haven Register, June 20, 1999, D1)

17. Daniel Oreskes (Blum) says of his reading of *The Possessed*:

   I throw most of it away but I keep the parts that might give me a spark to understand the emotional life of my character, that might be a clue as to how my character thinks or behaves. Or sometimes there's a clue in how another character thinks or behaves in the novel that I could steal for mine—which, parenthetically, I might also get from a Dickens novel. I love to read. I once heard someone say that great writers are great readers, and I think that should be true for all artists. For, after all, the world the actor inhabits is the world of literature and the world of imagination.

18. The stage direction in the play is: *"The park at night"* (186).

19. She adds: "I like to read serious literary books like that. I don't like the fun books. I want to read more books like this and understand them." Nathalie Paulding later played the twelve-year-old, anorexic daughter of Susan Lucci's Erica Kane in *All My Children*. When, after eighteen years, Susan Lucci won her first Emmy in 1999, she had submitted taped episodes focusing on her character's scenes with Nathalie Paulding.

20. Wright does not generally rehearse scenes in the order in which they appear in the play, except during run-throughs. Indeed, the order of the scenes in the play is revised several times during rehearsal. On April 1, he rehearses scenes from act 3 in this sequence: 6, 12, 16, 7, 8, 9, 2, 13, 14.

21. Liputin says to Shigalyov: "You can't quit unless we give you permission"; three lines later, he says: "If anyone else quits we all have to quit" (165). Both lines are retained in the May 9 script.

22. On Douglas Stein's complex constructivist set, actors often cannot move more than a few feet without coming upon a closed door. Marie Shatov and her newborn infant die outside doors that won't open. Characters meet in confined spaces where doors open onto other confined spaces. At the end of the play, three revolutionaries are led through two doors onto the upper stage to be executed. The closet where the raped child hangs herself is represented by a moving door on which is written the words, "I killed God." Characters live and labor, love and kill, in dark confined areas from which the only escape—with the exceptions of Dasha and Peter Verkhovensky—seems to be death by suicide (Matryosha, Kirilov, and Stavrogin); murder (Shatov, Mrs. Lembke); execution (Virginsky, Shigalyov, and Liputin); or neglect (Marie Shatov and her infant).

23. In rehearsal on April 9, Egloff refers to one speech she is considering revising as "the stanza."

24. "In a sense, I'm writing this to be read on a page," Egloff says.

   I know that much of the theater audience will never hear it as "poetry." They'll hear it as dialogue. The "poetry" exists on the page for the reader and for the actor. It's sort of a bastardized version of free verse. The reason that it's in this form—in terms of actors—is based on breath. It's more about breath than anything else. But I also don't care if the actors use all the line breaks. The line breaks are mainly intended as a way of giving some air, some lift. I tried twice to put this play into prose. But it never worked.

25. *"(Nicholas is taking off his right glove, wetting two of his fingers in his mouth. He puts them under Dasha's dress. There is a moment of searching.)"* (208).

26. The same kind of meticulous consideration and mutual agreement characterizes the rehearsal of Stavrogin and Dasha's scene of lovemaking (act 1, scene 18). In performance, the choices arrived at through laborious trial and error seem instinctive, fluid, right.

27. Nathalie Paulding's father, attending several technical rehearsals with her mother, said that Nathalie "understands everything" in the scenes in which she appears. Private conversation, April 23, 1997.

28. March 15 script, 213. Only the last five lines appear verbatim in the May 9 script. The first four lines quoted are cut entirely.

29. Wright is speaking for the playwright. "Dasha is as much a saint as it's possible to be in the world of this play, and that is her gift," Egloff tells me. "When she says the roses are 'fragile,' she's appreciating life for what it is rather than making a negative comment."

30. In the April 19 rehearsal (which the playwright did not attend), when Dasha says, "My darling my darling" to Stavrogin in act 3, scene 20, Wright quietly whispers: "Wrong words." In the May 9 script, Egloff has crossed through the line and speech tag (206) because, she tells me later, she "saw in a run of the play that *Dasha wouldn't say that*" (emphasis mine). Her words echo what the director had said in her absence.

31. "When I publish a piece, that's when I tear my hair out," the playwright tells me. "That's when the stakes are raised and that's when I finally give up on the play. To me there's a certain defeat that happens when a play is published because it's now set in stone, so you have to face the weaknesses of the text forever."

32. Asked if she keeps all the versions of her script, Egloff says: "No. I only keep the versions that are the most different. I almost never look back at them. I just need to keep going forward. If I don't remember a scene, I don't want to use it. Sometimes that backfires."

33. Kathleen Dimmick, private conversation, April 4, 1997.

34. Charles Means describes script changes from the stage manager's point of view:

    As revisions are happening, that is also changing all of the technical aspects. For example, in the salon scene [act 1, scene 10], Dasha used to sing. Now we've revised that to Dasha playing the violin. First, that involved cutting two pages of dialogue, which involved cutting a lot of blocking. It also involved adding a prop, getting a violin, which we didn't have. . . . Finding the intermission [later] and changing the order of the scenes was enormous just in terms of the fact that when you have an intermission you have ten minutes to set up for the act. When you move that intermission, things that you were going to set up in those ten minutes now have to be set up from the top. . . . It can be wonderful structurally that one scene follows another, but technically a nightmare. So when we do a rewrite or a revision, it generally affects the stage in some way, to varying degrees.

35. The reference to "pigs" was confirmed by Wright as an accurate transcription.

36. "As for Liz," actor Daniel Oreskes says, "I think she is at the top with regard to friendliness and humanness and approachability."

37. When I ask Egloff how she balances her roles as nursing mother and playwright in rehearsal, she says:

   A good question. I'm trying to find a system. I think the system is that I'll leave the baby at home during runs, but all the rest of the time he comes with me. . . . I don't want the baby to come with me when I am improvising writing. . . . When the baby is here, half my mind is generally with him. I only have 100 percent of my mind at moments when he's not with me. (emphasis mine)

38. "I'm functioning both as a production dramaturg and as an assistant director. This is probably fairly rare as an occurrence in theater rehearsal," Kathleen Dimmick says.

   I'm sort of a telephone line between what's going on in rehearsal and Liz at home. . . . On a new play, a production dramaturg operates as a liaison between the director and the playwright during rehearsal to help forge the best possible version of the script for the production. I participate in the discussions between the playwright and the director about things that come up in rehearsal in a way that will allow the playwright to deepen or clarify or enhance the text in the rehearsal period. The questions I ask Liz have to do with something as specific as how a scene is landing or with something as large as the reshaping of an entire act.

39. Liputin's line, "Tell him to shut up," April 1 script, 141.

40. *Ibid.*, 142-C.

41. The three lines cut from Mrs. Lembke's speech by the playwright in rehearsal do not appear in later versions of the script. The added line, with a change of pronoun, appears in the May 9 script.

42. April 1 script, 131. These lines are cut in the May 9 script.

43. Oreskes adds: "The bottom line is: actors don't get a binding vote, so any . . . [actor-initiated change in the script] relies on the goodwill of the playwright and on collegiality. So if you get it, it's great. And if you don't, you still just do your job."

44. "SHUT UP BLUM" appears in the May 9 script, 134.

45. May 9 script, 142-A.

46. This rehearsal revision appears verbatim in the May 9 script, 142-A.

47. Peter Verkhovensky's speech, beginning, "This is My strike," act 3, scene 1, 145.

48. "We were all improvising during the work-through of the ballroom scene," Egloff says.

49. Never again during her visits to rehearsal do I see this reaction. Egloff tells me she is usually emotional *while* writing, but not afterward. But since the birth of her son, she feels differently about this scene when she watches it. She was crying, she says, as a mother.

50. Seven of the thirty-five lines in Dasha's final speech, including the lines questioned by the director, are cut, and four others are altered in the

May 9 script. The "but" that troubled Kali Rocha in rehearsal on April 4 has also disappeared.

51. April 5 script, "version two," 40.

52. One and a half pages of loud speeches that had overlapped with Dasha's musical recital are crossed out in the May 9 script, 39–41.

53. The handwritten line, "Give me those papers over there," appears in the right margin of the May 9 script, 200.

54. March 15 script, 192–193. In the faxed version that arrives the following day, Dasha is standing, not sitting, as the scene opens. At the end of the scene, *"Dasha is gone"* and the candle remains (192–193). In addition, six lines of dialogue have been cut, along with two stage directions; two lines have been slightly altered. These changes are retained in the May 9 script.

55. Douglas Hughes tells me that Rabe's *A Question of Mercy* "was first a long one-act. . . . As we read through it in rehearsal at New York Theatre Workshop, . . . [the playwright] suddenly realized where he could put in an act break, and that remained the permanent act break [the intermission]."

56. In the May 9 script, seventeen lines and two stage directions are cut; twelve lines are crossed through and two are added. Several lines questioned by the director and actress in rehearsal of act 3, scene 6, are among those cut.

57. As revisions of the script proliferate, a "master script" of a scene will often include pages of earlier versions with passages crossed through. When new pages are added, consecutive page numbering is preserved by the use of such designations as "98-A" or even "98 pre-A," allowing superseded pages of the script with handwritten notes to be retained and new pages to be inserted without disrupting previous pagination.

58. Wright's revisions include reassigning one line ("I haven't had steady work in almost two years"), cut later in the May 9 script; revising Virginsky's line, "If Shigalyov gets a welding job he can't turn it down" to "If I get a carpentry job I can't turn it down"; changing Peter Verkhovensky's "We're doing it" to "Not soon"; and cutting "Well" at the beginning of one of Shigalyov's lines. "Well" is restored in the May 9 script (14). Egloff says: "It's usually impossible to tell who comes up with an idea— the director or the playwright. If the director is good, both of us will be foggy about whose idea it is."

59. Later Egloff will tell me:

When I look at the computer, I begin to visualize the text as I have seen it in rehearsal, so it's no longer in that abstract, personal, imaginary world that it was in before rehearsal. Now that I'm in rehearsal, I begin to see the actors themselves and their ability to perform and that sometimes backfires because an actor might be miscast or just not very good or at a stage where he or she is not doing good work. (emphasis mine)

60. Eventually, this scene will open the second act.

61. Egloff tells me after watching the run that she is making cuts because there may be "too many emotional arcs" and "too much information coming at the audience right now."

62. Michael Feingold, reviewing a play, says that it "has been rewritten, restaged, and recast, with results that make me want to call a rehearsal, like George S. Kaufman, 'to take out the improvements.'" "Less Easy Pieces," *Village Voice*, Nov. 17, 1998, 163.

63. In rehearsal Patrice Johnson deftly adjusts the timing of her groans in accordance with the director's author-influenced notes on her labor pains. I hear Wright say confidently: "one more contraction in two waves."

64. This change is noted in Egloff's handwriting on the March 15 script, 30. In the May 9 script the line remains, "I must and I shall" (30).

65. April 1 script, 50. This line does not appear in the May 9 script.

66. The director-initiated change in location is marked by an arrow in the May 9 script, 43.

67. The scene is not cut. Egloff tells me that she "watched the gang in rehearsal and *the actors made me realize* that the point of the scene was not expositional but character development and the actors were good so that [not cutting the scene] was all right" (emphasis mine). What seems to have changed the playwright's mind is not so much the resistance of director or dramaturg as observing the actors in rehearsal.

68. This revision appears in performance and in the May 9 script with the handwritten addition of two lines: Mrs. Stavrogin's "Dasha, get my carriage" and Dasha's "Yes, ma'am" (30).

69. "Finding an intermission is about making the audience comfortable and about reexamining what the real structure of the play is," Mandy Mishell Hackett says on the following day. "The true structural path of the play is not really solved yet." She adds: "We're really changing the whole rhythm of the play with the new act 1."

70. Hackett tells me:

    At New York Theatre Workshop we usually have three full weeks of previews in order to give us time to address any larger issues that only come up once you have a show on its feet in front of an audience. . . . You have to let go of the idea that making changes in previews is a bad thing. . . . To eliminate some of the jokes is a tonal issue, and I think you need to wait until you can feel the weight of the whole play before making that kind of change. . . . It's really important to trust the material you have. You just have to trust your instincts to decipher what is a change for the better and what not to change.

71. Wright will run the complete play only twice before the first preview performance: "I like it to remain in pieces for the actors as long as possible. . . . I don't like plays that are smooth."

72. "Before the word dramaturg became so overused in this country, it was just part of the director's job: letting and helping the playwright write the

play. . . . These days, it's a real gift to a writer to have a director-slash-dramaturg." Gordon Davidson, artistic director of the Mark Taper Forum in Los Angeles, quoted in Steven Drukman, "The Modern Dramatist's Secret Weapon," *New York Times*, May 18, 1997, 4H.

73. Here are two examples of the shared "wavelength." Rehearsing the last scene in the play on April 19, Wright says to Kali Rocha: "Try to put a double comma after the line, 'and there are no tears here,' so as to separate it more from the next line which is about 'him.'" In the same speech the director tells the actress "to leave the end of the line, 'and the sun was shining,' more unresolved" (213). In both instances, the line in question has no final punctuation and ends its stanza. The director's notes translate into acting rhythms these literary features of the text.

74. Elizabeth Egloff, private conversation, April 19, 1997. Cuts considered but not made are a speech in act 2, scene 3 (later, act 1, scene 13) and part of act 2, scene 7 (later, act 1, scene 16).

75. Actor Denis O'Hare says:

   Playwrights in the room generally make me nervous because it feels *like they have a right answer in their heads and if I'm not getting the right answer I'm disappointing them. So you're kind of always looking for the vigorous nod of the head. Which Liz doesn't do. She has a great poker face. That's good, in a way, not to get constant approval or disapproval, because finally you make it your own.*

76. Later Egloff tells me: "The suggestion to make the strike more explicit came from Jim Nicola and Mandy, and I think that was a good note."

77. This cut is not made in the production or in the text. After the play opens, Egloff says: "*Now* I know how to fix act 2. Mrs. Lembke's murder was a plot point and only a plot point. What I needed to fix was the play's attitude toward the plot point. I came to that recognition on opening night. I haven't fixed it yet on the computer because I'm working on a new play now."

78. "No matter what is explained beforehand, how many models are shown, you never really know where you are until standing on the stage, on the set." Lauren Bacall, *By Myself* (New York: Ballantine, 1985), 399.

79. Roy C. Ballard, technical director, interview, April 29, 1997.

80. *"Somewhere in the building, water is dripping"* (24).

81. Seven new speeches have been added to act 1, scene 4, 11–12.

82. The "Well" in Shigalyov's speech remains in the May 9 script, 14.

83. Kathleen Dimmick, private conversation, April 29, 1997.

84. Ray Anthony Thomas (Virginsky) tells me: "Working on a new script, I think you have a right to change stuff up to opening night. In the past I've been given a big revision half an hour before opening." Describing rehearsal of a new play by George Axelrod, Lauren Bacall says: "We'd work, pages in hand. . . . Nothing is more difficult than trying to unlearn a scene or a speech. Sometimes onstage you get half the old and half the new lines." *By Myself*, 400.

85. In an earlier stage direction, Blum carries a tray containing glasses of champagne, one of which Mrs. Lembke downs. This stage direction is cut, freeing the actors' hands. In the revised script, a champagne bottle with a note seemingly from Turgenev is found on the "back step" (131-A). In the previous version it was not clear how the poisoned champagne arrives in Mrs. Lembke's glass. "The major revisions made during previews," Hackett says, "have to do with clarity of action." In addition to the stratagem of the champagne bottle, a new scene and three new speeches are added to link Peter Verkhovensky more specifically with the poisoning of Mrs. Lembke. Egloff says: "The [adding of the] champagne bottle came from Garland. I'm not sure how I feel about it. I think it's a bit obvious. But I think I need more distance."

86. James Colby tells me that what he writes in his notebook during his monologues are "Kirilov's thoughts." He deliberately writes in a small, nearly illegible script so that no member of the company can decipher it. He says he will show me what he writes from a distance, and does. "It's like a fragrance," he says. "If it's out of the bottle, it dissipates. . . . It's a kind of throughline for myself, a driving through."

Chapter 4: Suzan-Lori Parks in Rehearsal

1. Robert Vorlicky, ed., *Tony Kushner in Conversation* (Ann Arbor: U of Michigan P, 1998), 145.

2. Suzan-Lori Parks, "Possession" and "Elements of Style," in *The America Play and Other Works* (New York: TCG, 1995), 4, 6. Marc Robinson has observed:

    Parks herself is intent on understanding all the forces that bring a character to life on stage, and takes almost nothing for granted about the apparatus of theater: speech, space, movement, presence. Watching her work, a spectator eventually comes to share this hyperawareness. (The Other American Drama *[Baltimore: Johns Hopkins UP, 1997], 191)*

3. Like Maria Irene Fornes, Parks revises the text in rehearsal as she directs her own plays, but unlike Fornes, she does not stage their professional debuts.

4. Jacques Copeau, "La mise en scène," in *Directors on Directing*, ed. Toby Cole and Helen Krich Chinoy (Indianapolis: Bobbs-Merrill, 1963), 224, 222.

5. Panel discussion, "Classic Colloquium—Conceiving Shakespeare: The Role of the Director in Contemporary Classical Theater," Public Theater, December 5, 1998.

6. Liz Diamond, interview, June 30, 1998.

7. Parks, "Elements of Style," in *The America Play and Other Works*, 11–12.

8. During a break Parks tells me that she "only added half a page" to the original eighty-five pages but enlarged the type; the revised script is now one hundred and four pages.

9. "I've never had a child. To me the experience of *this* play feels like a child—not all of my plays are like that—except that I was having the child from the center of my chest, which I hope does not happen." Suzan-Lori Parks, interview, June 30, 1998. Unless otherwise indicated, all following statements by the playwright and actors are from interviews conducted on June 29–30 and October 23–25, 1998; February 11, March 4–5, August 11, September 30, October 20–21, and November 4, 1999.

10. Parks elaborates on the birth of *In the Blood*:

    > *I was writing this very big play [Fucking A]. I had a lot of difficulty. I took a vacation from the writing. One day I was having a conversation with one of the characters, and I said: 'Oh, your name is wrong. Your name isn't Hester. It's Carolina Mary [later, renamed Canary Mary]. Now I know your name. I can write the play.' Then Hester said: 'But you have to write the play I'm in.' I said: 'I'm either going to write the little play or the big play or both'. . . . It was the slippery slope. So we'll see.*

    A year and a half later, on October 24, 1999, Parks tells me she has almost completed the big play. The original Hester has now "split into" Hester in *Fucking A* and Hester, La Negrita in *In the Blood*. The original Hester's five children "went into" the little play.

11. Suzan-Lori Parks, *In the Blood*, rehearsal script, September 1999, 5. Unless otherwise noted, all citations are from this rehearsal script.

12. In her essay, "Elements of Style," Parks distinguishes between a *rest* ("Take a little time, a pause, a breather; make a transition") and a *spell*: "An elongated and heightened (rest). . . . While no 'action' or 'stage business' is necessary, directors should fill this moment as they best see fit. . . . A spell is a place of great (unspoken) emotion. It's also a place for an emotional transition." *America Play*, 16–17.

13. When I ask where the actors *look* during the spells, Parks says: "It depends on what's happening. They could be looking at each other. Or out. Or one could be looking stage right and the other looking out, or toward him."

14. "Reverand" is an example of the intentional "misspellings" in Parks's plays.

15. The notes on her script are authorial: cuts and revisions. The notes on her pad are authorial and directorial. "I don't have space for director's notes on my script," Parks tells me, laughing. The script remains her authorial space.

16. Like Elizabeth Egloff, Suzan-Lori Parks generously shares her rehearsal notes with me. It seems appropriate to indicate the graphic features of her handwritten notes, another form of what she calls "the simple work of putting one word next to another" (Parks, *America Play*, 6). The cuts she notes on p. 31 (four lines in the Doctor's speeches) are retained in subsequent versions of the script.

17. When Parks relocates eight lines of Hester's Confession as her final speech in the play, she changes the format from verse to prose. By this shift she indicates how the actor is to experience and express the language in the text. (The speech is cut in the fall 1999 production at the Public Theater.)

18. Parks tells me: "When Wagner heard his music in his head, he heard it in his head. When he heard it played by musicians, he heard it played by all the instruments in real time—all the tones, nuances. Try as I might, I can't read the lines in the voice of Jonathan Peck. He got it—all the rhythms. I worked hard to get that in the writing. He did it exactly the way I had heard it without my telling him. *I heard the full-color version of what I had heard in my head in black and white with stick figures* [emphasis mine]. Michael's scene went the way I had heard it. But I didn't like it. So I rewrote some of the lines while he was reading the lines in rehearsal and dictated them to him during the break."

19. When I ask Parks if this is an author's explanation or a directorial strategy, she says: "Directorial strategy. That's to get the actor to *play* good and let the bad happen. . . . The actors were commenting on their characters."

20. Parks eliminates certain sexual overtones in the scene between Hester and the Doctor. For example, she cuts the Doctor's references to Hester as "Hussy" and "Hottie," and also the line, "Just looking atcha takes me back" (June 1998 script, 31–34).

21. The revision, "to escape her difficult circumstances," is retained in the September 1999 script, 57.

22. Tom Stoppard recalls that, when he was asked what was the first thing he expected from an actor in his plays, his answer ("clarity of utterance") "got a laugh, a nervous laugh in which I detected reproach. . . . [B]ut it really is the first thing I ask for, and, here and there, the last thing I get. . . . [A]uthors like myself find themselves begging individual actors to look after this consonant and that vowel." Tom Stoppard, "Pragmatic Theater," *New York Review of Books*, vol. 46, no. 14 (Sept. 23, 1999), 8.

23. "I wanted to place myself in one of the most visible places in the room that I could also make private," Parks tells me. "I'm not one of those playwrights hiding in the back or smoking outside. The actors could see me not being afraid."

24. "Women and the Future of American Theatre," keynote talk, October 23, 1998. The symposium is organized by Professor John Lemly, head of Mount Holyoke's Theatre Arts Department.

25. Spoken text literally becomes a stage direction when the first line of Reverand D.'s Confession, "Suffering is an enormous turn on" (69), reappears as a stage direction in a later scene (93).

26. Asked what it was like to have Parks directing her in this reading, McCauley says: "It makes me weepy. I know the theater is in good hands, not just because of her individually but certainly because of her."

27. Hellweg is an actor and director who teaches at Smith College.
28. "I only have one other two-character play," Parks says. "It's a lot of work—a two-character play."
29. "This character Booth is like Brazil [in *The America Play*]," Parks tells me. "And the Foundling Father is perhaps like Lincoln [in *Topdog*]." Father-son tension in *The America Play* becomes brother-brother tension in *Topdog/Underdog*.
30. "I went to Sundance [in 1996] to write a screenplay of *The America Play*," Parks says. "I was still playing around with this guy who is a Lincoln impersonator. The film is still there—underneath—waiting, writing itself, in *Topdog*. . . . It's kind of knitting itself together. It's like bacteria." With Parks, plays beget plays beget screenplays.
31. Some of the play's most arresting lines are about history: "People like historical shit in a certain way. They like it to unfold the way they folded it up" (37). Unless otherwise noted, all citations from *Topdog/Underdog* are from the April 16, 1999 script.
32. The multiple parentheses are really a musical notation. "The difference between three and five parens is a difference in volume," Parks says. "The more parens, the softer the voice. A single paren brings it down. . . . But you have to be audible, so it's a 'cheat.'" (In acting, "to cheat" means to modify one's position or cross slightly to make the blocking work better.)
33. March 4, 1999 script, 58.
34. Charlayne Woodard, who later received an Obie for her performance as Hester in the world premiere of *In the Blood*, says of the playwright: "She hasn't written out the subtext. Sometimes you *really* need to know."
35. The actor does not consistently observe the scripted rests in *Topdog*, nor do all the actors observe all the spells in rehearsal and performance of *In the Blood* at the Public Theater the following fall. In addition, the "musical score" of the text is at times overridden by the audience's laughter, spontaneous and contagious.
36. As a result of knee surgery a week before rehearsals were to begin, Marcus Stern has been prevented from continuing as director.
37. During a break, Parks tells me that George C. Wolfe had raised a question about Hester's final scream several months ago. Incremental repetition of the image of a big hand coming down on Hester occurs in scenes 6, 7, 8, and, now, at the very end of the play. In performance on November 2, 1999, the last line is repeated eight times, as if fading out.
38. Esbjornson was not present at auditions except for the last role cast (Amiga).
39. Parks says:

   I call it "doing a number" on my play when a director wants to leave his or her mark in a way that intentionally obscures the play and does not in any viable way develop an interpretation that would be supported by the rest of the play or by their other directorial choices. If the director really has a desire to do a number on a new play, the director should write his or her own play. . . . As a playwright, I don't do a number on the play. . . . I stand aside and let the play come through. . . . My plays are perplexing enough: just do the play.

40. During a break, Parks tells me that when asked by Wolfe what she wanted for the set, she said, "Cement." Later Esbjornson also proposed a cement set.

41. In performance on November 2, 1999, Welfare Lady places white handkerchiefs on the seat and back of a dilapidated chair. She gives Hester a Handi-wipe, asking her to clean her hands. In rehearsal, Chilli's "walking by the window"(50) becomes a surreal moment in which he walks right through the scene, invisible to Welfare. In performance, he stands far to the side, behind Welfare's back, seen only by Hester as if in a vision.

42. Later in rehearsal Parks adds lines in which Reverand D. refers to "Backers [who] are building me a church" (67-A). In performance he appears with a newly engraved cornerstone and a large illuminated cross.

43. In rehearsal of *Topdog/Underdog*, Parks says to Ruben Santiago-Hudson: "A writer can come this close to the character. [She walks toward the actor, comes very near him, and stops.] But I'm learning things from you."

44. After rehearsal, Charlayne Woodard (Hester) says: "When she read [the role of] Beauty, she was my little girl. I didn't ever deal with . . . [her being the playwright] at all. . . . She has a real lovely innocence: she's got a very good Beauty thing going easily."

45. "There are rules that I've always lived by in rehearsal," Woodard tells me. "All questions that have to do with set design, costume, the script, the character and her relation to other characters are addressed to the director."

46. In the first preview performance on November 2, 1999, prerecorded "wissa's," whispered in unison by the actors but inaudible to the audience, accompany the recorded voices of individual actors delivering the lines of the prologue. The only character visible on the semidarkened stage is Hester. On November 3, 1999, the lines in the prologue are delivered live, with no miking.

47. During a break, Parks tells me that the prologue was too long. "David [Esbjornson] thought it was too long, and I did, too."

48. Reggie Montgomery says of Parks's script: "Nothing else needs to be added to it. Sometimes actors add an 'and' or a 'but' or a 'for.' An addition like that totally changes the meaning."

49. In performance on November 2, 1999, the tone shifts somewhat to that of defiant desperation. The director's note seems to be in tension with the playwright's comment to Woodard at the table: "[Hester] knows that her

life's her own fault. You know that." The lines Parks alludes to appear in scenes 4 and 8. They are cut in the latter scene on the second night of previews (reported by production assistant Elizabeth Moreau).

50. For an example of such "pre-calibration" by Robert Wilson, see Susan Letzler Cole, *Directors in Rehearsal*, 150, 154, 165–167.

51. In the rehearsals I observe, and in the performance I attend, spells are sometimes lost, either missing altogether or simply not discernible.

52. In performance on November 2, 1999, music plays softly as the Doctor announces the scheduling of Hester's hysterectomy. His gestures are slightly stylized and he has entered from the side of the stage where only Hester and her children enter and exit. The staging is thus halfway between that of a realistic moment and a vision.

53. In performance on November 2, 1999, the running time of the show has been reduced to two hours, four minutes. Further heavy cuts were made that morning, the spells have been "tightened," and in one scene the quickened pace now allows actors' lines to overlap (reported by production assistant Elizabeth Moreau).

Chapter 5: Tony Kushner in Rehearsal

1. Robert Vorlicky, ed. *Tony Kushner in Conversation* (Ann Arbor: U of Michigan P, 1998), 1.

2. *Ibid.*, 123.

3. The other six playwrights are: Eric Bogosian, William Finn, John Guare, Marsha Norman, Ntozake Shange, and Wendy Wasserstein.

4. Vorlicky, *Tony Kushner in Conversation*, 214, 208.

5. An earlier version was published in *Conjunctions* 25 (fall 1995), with the note: "This is an early attempt at what will someday be a play on this subject" (14). Three new characters—a Polish Countess, Annie Lazarus, and Emma Lazarus, all performed by Ellen McLaughlin—appear in the revised script. All citations of *"It's an Undoing World"* are from the December 1997 rehearsal script.

6. Interview, December 19, 1997. Unless otherwise noted, all statements by Kushner are from this interview.

7. Letter, December 14, 1997. Mark Lamos writes:

   Tony Kushner, who responds to deadlines in a Perils of Pauline sort of way, called from a plane somewhere over my head, on his way between speaking engagements. He was halfway through the process of creation, he said, . . . he couldn't imagine when he'd finish it, could I substitute another writer. . . . But then "Terminating . . ." arrived, just past deadline, and when we read it with the actors, it was a completely modern version of Shakespeare's amalgamation of love and need and torment. (Love's Fire *[New York: Morrow, 1998], xiii*)

8. As David Cole remarks, "[O]ne might point to certain performance-like situations that seem designed to dissolve, or at least to perplex, the

distinction between authors and actors: Simone Benmussa's production of Virginia Woolf's *Freshwater*, 'played by writers only: E. Ionesco, N. Sarraute, A. Robbe-Grillet, etc.'" *Acting as Reading* (Ann Arbor: U of Michigan P, 1992), 225.

9. Vorlicky, *Tony Kushner in Conversation*, 214.

10. "When we first did *Slavs!* as a benefit in 1994 or 1995 with an all-female cast," Kushner adds, "we almost did it cold and it was thrilling." The all-female cast consisted of Madeline Kahn, Tracey Ullman, Kathleen Chalfant, Laurie Metcalf, and Barbara Eda-Young.

11. Interview, September 11, 1998. Unless otherwise noted, all statements by Chalfant are from this interview.

12. Kushner had originally written the lyrics of "The Heart of the World" for *A Dybbuk: Between Two Worlds*, but, he tells me, it was cut because the play was too long. For all three songs in *"Undoing World,"* the playwright had a tape of the melodies and wrote the lyrics.

13. All lines spoken by The Voice of the Teapot are in italics.

14. "I suppose there are limits to how far I would go," Chalfant adds, "but as you see you are speaking to a bald person and furthermore a woman who at the age of 53 appears naked in a very small room full of people for the very first time." At the end of *Wit*, for which she has shaved her head, the actress removes the white hospital gown she has been wearing throughout the performance and stands naked, facing the audience, as the lights dim. It is what Peter Marks calls "one of the great treatments of nudity on a contemporary stage." "New Lead in 'Wit' Transcends a TV Past," *New York Times*, Sept. 10, 1999, E5.

15. In a more serious vein, Chalfant comments on the presence of the playwright in rehearsal:

   It's good for them to come away and come back. From the actor's point of view, the playwright's presence sometimes has a dampening effect because you have to try out a number of ways, most of which are wrong and most of which you fiercely defend while you're trying them out, in order to find the right way, and the look of anguish and/or rage on the face of the playwright is, as I said, dampening to the creative impulse. It's sometimes better for them to go away.

16. "It's so exciting," Kushner says, "when political activism and theater can actually connect. The issues that we all grapple with are so related. It's a dream of what culture in the largest sense really ought to be: that kind of dialogue. And we raised $12,000 in a three hundred-seat house."

17. "What really paid off with those guys," Kushner tells me, "was that though the pacing wasn't bang-bang-bang, because they were mainly writers they had a wonderful attention to words."

18. Significantly, Kushner did not sit in the auditorium during the staged reading. He tells me that he "heard," but did not see, the play. Like Parks, his "first thing" is listening.

19. "Who Is Godot?" *The New Yorker*, June 24 and July 1, 1996, 137.
20. Andrea Stevens, "Aspects of Love: Seven Playwrights on the Sonnets," *New York Times*, May 31, 1998, AR 4, 16.
21. "Sonnet LXXV" is later dropped from the title, perhaps another indication of ambivalence. "I don't want to get 'Bloomy' (as in Harold Bloom) about it," Kushner has said,

    > but there is something to the idea that, when one is a writer, one is profoundly influenced by a very great writer the way I was profoundly influenced by Brecht. [Brecht and Shakespeare are "the two playwrights whose work I admired the most."] That one does have to engage in a struggle . . . , a struggle of someone who is fighting to find his or her own voice and persona as a writer, and to wrest an independent persona from a progenitor. (Vorlicky, Tony Kushner in Conversation, 107, 112)

22. "Mark Lamos is so fantastically literate. You heard how he read the Shakespeare sonnet in rehearsal today," Kushner says. "He knows text."
23. Rehearsal script, October 12, 1997. Unless otherwise noted, all citations of *Terminating . . .* are from this script.
24. In performance at the Public's Newman Theater, on June 27, 1998, Stephen DeRosa, who was to receive several rave reviews, is crazier, funnier, looser, more playful. Asked what it was like to have the playwright present in rehearsal, DeRosa says:

    > It was absolutely terrifying. . . . The night before he came to the rehearsal run, I couldn't sleep. Insomnia had become my new neurosis, thanks to Love's Fire. . . . When it was all over, I felt horrible. I felt everyone else had done a terrific job. . . . I would just like to add that what I went through is probably what all the other actors felt when they did their first run-through for the playwright.

    Unless otherwise indicated, this and all subsequent statements by the actors are from individual interviews on July 31, 1998.
25. Lamos's comment recalls Esbjornson's directorial notes on the Confessions in Parks's *In the Blood*, as if the sonnets were a sequence of Confessions, delivered by a single character.
26. "I remember doing a play with Tony Kushner, *A Bright Room Called Day*, at the Public, directed by Michael Greif. We never even *saw* Tony Kushner," actor Frank Raiter tells me. "He was there, but we didn't see him. One day I asked him a question when I did see him there finally and he said, 'No, those are questions that the director has to answer.'" Interview, April 8, 1997.
27. Hendryk says to Esther: "you have short hair" (9). In performance, the actress's red hair is not cut but pinned up stylishly.
28. Stage directions regarding costume are minimal: *"Esther is nicely turned out, Hendryk is a godforsaken mess"* (1). In performance on June 27, 1998, Esther wears black slacks, a black jacket, a dark brown top, a

stylish black shawl, and black high-heel shoes; Dymphna wears a beautiful long, black-and-white patterned skirt, a blue cardigan over a purple
top, and black medium heels.

29. "I had just had a costume fitting that day," Hamish Linklater (Billygoat)
tells me,

> *but I was wearing a T-shirt and jeans in rehearsal. I showed the Polaroids from
> the costume fitting to Mark—tight, tight purple velvet pants, purple vinyl Diesel
> jacket. And Tony said to Mark: "That's all wrong. Billygoat should wear a
> T-shirt and jeans, just like Hamish is wearing". . . . It brought me . . . back
> down into myself—after all, I had put those clothes on today. . . . Ultimately,
> [Lamos] completely ignored Tony's objections to the costume design and de-
> cided that this was what he wanted to see Billygoat in because, after all, he was
> the director.*

30. Anne Cattaneo, the dramaturg at Lincoln Center Theater, "first suggested
that The Acting Company . . . focus on the sonnets as the inspiration for
an evening in the theater;" she "selected the sonnets she thought most
compatible with the individual styles of the playwrights; . . . no playwright knew what the others were doing." Lamos, *Love's Fire*, xii.

31. At least one reviewer is bothered. Katherine Duncan-Jones, writing on
the London production of *Love's Fire*, says: "It was not a good idea to
have Sonnet 75 read three times." "Woody and a Choice of Bagels,"
TLS, June 5, 1998, 20.

32. The first four lines of Sonnet 75 are: "So are you to my thoughts as food
to life,/Or as sweet-season'd showers are to the ground;/And for the
peace of you I hold such strife/As 'twixt a miser and his wealth is found."

33. Kushner makes only one other textual revision in *Terminating* . . . during rehearsal: the addition of Dymphna's line, "It isn't Schmendrik,"
after her question, "What's his real name?" (*Love's Fire*, 59). Usually,
Kushner says, he does "a lot of rewriting in rehearsals for a new play. I
don't write scenes but I add and change lines in the rehearsal room."
When I ask for an example, he says:

> *The scene between Sister Ella Chapter and Hannah Pitt. It's act 2, scene 10, of*
> Millennium Approaches. *We were doing it in Los Angeles. The last line of the
> scene, which I like a lot, I came up with on the spot in the rehearsal room. I
> don't remember the original line. Hannah says: "Fifty thousand dollars for the
> house, Sister Ella Chapter; don't undersell. It's an impressive view." It's an
> incredibly important scene for me. It's a wide open breathing space. They're
> looking at the view. It's a good line: it's an impressive line, and it's true. It is
> impressive, but it's full of doubt. The cast applauded when I did it.* This came
> from me listening to actors. But it was a collaboration. *(emphasis mine)*

34. The actress tells me that associate producing director James Bundy gave
her a note to stress "paternal": "I assumed it was from James directly,"
she says.

35. Asked if she continues to touch Hendryk's knee at this moment in perfor-
    mance, Rolfsrud says: "Yes, every night. I give him a gentle little shake.
    Perhaps you didn't see it because my body blocked your view."

36. Rolfsrud explains: "I thought that note was generated either by a dia-
    logue between Mark and Tony or by a note from Tony because of the
    specificity of the details of who Esther was and what she did."

37. On "the author as first reader" of his or her own text, see David Cole,
    Acting as Reading, 221–253.

38. In that early read-through, which was also DeRosa's audition, the actor
    "felt that rare experience of the play taking me. . . . After the first read-
    ing I only saw Tony [in rehearsal] once, the time you came [December 19,
    1997]. After that I only saw him a few days after we had opened in New
    York and after the reviews had come out." DeRosa says that there were
    "only two full run-throughs before we went to Minneapolis [for the pre-
    miere on January 7, 1998]."

39. Erika Rolfsrud tells me: "I have to say I cannot even begin to under-
    stand the feeling of having written a piece that generates from the
    self . . . and then to give it to someone and trust them to capture just a
    fraction of what you had in your heart and head. I can only assume it
    must bring even to the experienced playwright a degree of anxiety and
    vulnerability."

40. "[W]e almost killed each other," Declan Donnellan says. "But it was
    wonderful in the end, and we are very good friends now." He adds:
    "Sometimes watching trains collide can be very fruitful for the audience,
    if not necessarily pleasant for the passengers." Maria M. Delgado and
    Paul Heritage, eds., *In Contact with the Gods?* (New York: St. Martin's,
    1996), 89.

Chapter 6: Arthur Miller in Rehearsal

1. "The idea is that I've been out of fashion," Miller says. "Well, the
   number of productions of my plays around the world has steadily in-
   creased over the last 20 years. It's never ceased for one year to go
   [higher] than the year before. I can tell you that there isn't a day in the
   year when they're not going on somewhere." Michael Sommers, "A
   View From the Stage," *The (Newark) Star Ledger*, Nov. 2, 1997,
   Section 4, 1, 2.

2. Vincent Canby, "This Time, Peter Falk Is Part of the Mystery," *New York
   Times*, May 24, 1998, AR 4.

3. Arthur Miller, introduction to *The American Clock* (New York: Dramatists Play Service, 1992), 4–5. Unless otherwise noted, all citations of *The
   American Clock* are from this edition.

4. Arthur Miller, in an interview conducted by Jan Balakian, in *Speaking on
   Stage*, ed. Philip C. Kolin and Colby H. Kullman (Tuscaloosa: U of
   Alabama P, 1996), 45–46.

5. Cf. my chapter 7 account of Maria Irene Fornes's disregard of gender in her reassignment of speeches during rehearsal of *The Summer in Gossensass*.
6. Introduction, *The American Clock*, 9.
7. Kolin and Kullman, *Speaking on Stage*, 47–48.
8. Cf. my account of Tony Kushner in rehearsals of *"It's an Undoing World"* and *Terminating . . .* (chapter 5). Directing *Death of a Salesman* in Beijing, Miller is able to respond to the actors in rehearsal without looking at, or being able to read, the script in its Chinese translation:

   [W]hile I don't understand the language and never will, I can still surprise [the actors] time and again by picking up a line if they are misinterpreting it or even altering its proper color. I suppose I am hearing Chinese like music, *for which I have a good ear; one does not have to be a composer or musician to know when a familiar passage is being played too fast, too slow, or too dispiritedly. [emphasis mine] (Arthur Miller, "Salesman" in Beijing [New York: Viking, 1983], 155)*

9. Speaking of his relationship with his own father, Miller says: "It was like two searchlights on different islands." Studs Terkel, *The Spectator: Talk about Movies and Plays with the People Who Make Them* (New York: The New Press, 1999), 80.
10. "We had people sleeping in our basement all the time, some old, some not. Some guy would show up at the back door and ask for a hand-out and then my mother would swear she would never do it again and she'd say, 'Where are you living?' Well, he was living in his shoes." Arthur Miller, in *Arthur Miller and Company: Arthur Miller Talks About his Work in the Company of Actors, Designers, Directors, Reviewers, and Writers*, ed. Christopher Bigsby (London: Methuen, 1990), 197.
11. The real Ted Quinn, a neighbor of Miller's, had actually resigned after a single day as president of GE.
12. In the script the playwright suggests song titles, e.g., *"Sidney begins to sing a song like 'Once in a While'"* (49). Loren Toolajian, resident composer for Signature Theatre, and director James Houghton chose the songs together. Toolajian says:

    We went to the Performing Arts Library at Lincoln Center and we did research. We looked up the music for hundreds and hundreds of songs from the period. Based on the lyrics and the musical content, we honed that list down . . . to about forty or forty-five songs. This has been going on for the last several months. . . . [We] literally put the sheet music for all the songs on the floor and then compared the notes that each of us had made on the text of the play to decide what music would be right at those places in the text where Arthur specified music. . . . I had a keyboard, and I would sing and play the songs. And we'd make a decision: Does it work? Does it belong? That's how the music took shape.

    Toolajian describes the effect of the playwright's presence in rehearsal: "Really what I've gotten from him is his spirit, and [pause] his spirit has directly helped my musical choices. . . . It's hard to capture in words. You're trying to be open to the coming together of the spirit of the man and the spirit of the music. That's really what it is." Interview, September 26, 1997. Unless otherwise noted, all subsequent statements by the playwright and members of the Miller companies are from interviews conducted on September 9–11, 18–19, and 26, 1997; October 13 and 18, 1997; December 5 and 16–17, 1997; and February 3, 1998.

13. Asked if he has written other songs, Miller says: "That's the only one." When I inquire why he didn't give himself credit in the published script as the composer of "Sittin' Around," he laughs: "Good question. I hadn't thought about it."

14. On September 19, when the play is on its feet, the director mouths the words of "You Made Me Love You" as the actor is singing it, and then begins a half dance step. Choreographer Annie Loui, standing next to him, exuberantly dances the dance steps of the actor she is watching.

15. "I see my role as primarily research and giving the cast as much of a sense of the era as I can," dramaturg Suzanne Bradbeer says.

> *I'll be bringing in lists of popular books, films, athletes, songs, plays. . . . Each situation is very different dramaturgically. This one will be more making the time alive for the cast and working with Jim [Houghton] a lot rather than being a sounding board for the playwright.*

The dramaturg is using many different resources, and the playwright is one. "He says things so beautifully off the cuff," Bradbeer adds.

16. The following lines, on pages 85–86, are those Miller considers "a little teachy," and cuts in rehearsal:

SIDNEY: But I look back at it all now, and I don't know about you, but it seems it was friendlier. Am I right?
LEE: I'm not sure it was friendlier. Maybe people just cared more.
SIDNEY: (*With Irene singing a song like "I Want To Be Happy" under his speech.*) Like the songs, I mean—you listen to a thirties song, and most of them are so happy, and still—you could cry.

17. In addition to those already noted, Houghton dictates the following revisions: "Sidney, cut: 'Lou Charney.' Replace with: 'Georgie Rosen.' Lee, cut: 'Charney?' Replace with: 'Sold me his racing bike that got stolen.' Sidney, omit: 'Hundred yard dash—you and him used to trot to school together.' Lee, omit: 'Oh, Lou, sure!' Sidney, cut: 'And you knew Georgie Rosen got killed, didn't you?' Lee, cut: 'Georgie Rosen.' Sidney, cut: 'Little Georgie. Sold you his racing bike. That got stolen.' Lee, cut: 'Yes, yes! God—Georgie too.'" Also cut is a stage direction indicating that an actor sing the first verse of "*a song like 'The Times They Are A-Changing'*" (85).

18. Miller had a $23-a-week job with the WPA Theatre Project for six months in 1939. The scene in which Moe accompanies his son, Lee, on a visit to the welfare office (a prerequisite for an application to the WPA) is

based on the playwright's own experience. See Arthur Miller, *Timebends: A Life* (New York: Penguin, 1987), 231, 246, 396.

19. The playwright's grandfather is the source of some of Grandpa's lines, including the comment: "If [Roosevelt] was king he wouldn't have to waste his time making these ridiculous election speeches, and maybe he could start to improve things!" (77). See Kolin and Kullman, *Speaking on Stage*, 47.

20. Irene is based on Mrs. Willye Jeffries in Studs Terkel's *Hard Times: An Oral History of the Great Depression* (New York: Pantheon, 1970; reissued, 1986), 397–402.

21. Cf. my discussion of similar "time-bending" questions addressed to the director, not the playwright, in rehearsals of Shepard's *Curse of the Starving Class* and Egloff's *The Devils*, by actresses Deborah Hedwall and Nathalie Paulding, in chapters 1 and 3, respectively.

22. More than a week later actor Christopher Wynkoop recalls Miller's "interesting philosophical comment comparing us to Germany during the Depression" and in particular his use of "clutch" as a metaphor. "Absolutely correct," he says.

23. This kind of communication occurred at times between actress Charlayne Woodard and Suzan-Lori Parks in rehearsals of *In the Blood*.

24. When I ask him later which Ibsen play this was, Miller replies: "I don't know. It's an anecdote I heard a long time ago."

25. Interest in it, however, persists. Dramaturg Suzanne Bradbeer hands out a time line tracking events in the play from the summer of 1929, when Lee Baum is fourteen, to the early 1970s, when he is past fifty.

26. "Arthur Miller held me in the crook of my arm," the actor says, demonstrating on my arm, "and don't think I'll ever forget it. And, by the way, did you see what beautiful hands he has—delicate and learned."

27. Miller's black hobo is based on Louis Banks in Terkel's *Hard Times*, 40–43. Several of his phrases, including the refrain, are taken directly from Terkel's transcript.

28. "Annie Loui's effective stylized group movements"—especially a full-company, slow, rhythmic shuffle in place, at the relief office—receive consistent praise in reviews of the play. John Simon, "Agitpop," *New York*, Nov. 3, 1997, 54.

29. Messina is twenty-three years old. The career spans of the actors in the company range from a few years in the theater to more than forty.

30. Later, in the author's absence, members of the cast take over his role as griot, relating their own families' memories of the Depression.

31. "Arthur Miller had an operation on his back last November," Houghton tells the cast. "He just called to say he had a shot this morning to relieve his pain and is a little more drugged up than he thought he'd be, so he doesn't know if he can come to rehearsal today."

32. Later Houghton himself will fine-tune the timing, volume, and "punch" of the songs, especially the music that becomes an undertext for spoken lines. He also fine-tunes some of the dance sequences.

33. Miller tells me: "If I didn't want them, they're not here. . . . In general, Jim and I agreed about who's right and wrong. We had no argument about it." (Miller was also present at auditions for the one-acts.)
34. Cf. the so-called "Liz list" compiled by the production dramaturg during rehearsals of Elizabeth Egloff's *The Devils*.
35. The responses documented here were communicated to the company by Bradbeer during rehearsal.
36. Arthur Miller, in Terkel, *The Spectator*, 81.
37. After the preview performance on October 10, 1997, Miller holds a notes session in which he suggests that the cast's singing of "Life Is Just a Bowl of Cherries" underneath the lines at the end of the play be "kept down." When the actors sing loudly, he says, they sound like fifteen individuals singing; when they sing more softly, they sound like a multitude singing, which is what he prefers. This note is incorporated in subsequent performances (reported by production stage manager Amanda W. Sloan).
38. "Understanding Chaikin," *Village Voice*, Dec. 19, 1995, 94.
39. *I Can't Remember Anything*, rehearsal script, 19. All further citations are from this script.
40. A song by Irving Berlin from the Fred Astaire and Ginger Rogers film *Top Hat*.
41. Actress Kate Myre says: "What is completely delightful about him is he laughs at his own jokes. . . . To see him delight in his own work is a good lesson. He can appreciate the theater, the action, without constantly thinking he's the author of it all, and yet he is."
42. *The Last Yankee*, rehearsal script, 23. All further citations are from this script. The punctuation has undergone slight revision (a question mark after "country" has been replaced by a dash; a comma has been added after "I mean."). In his revisions, Miller, functioning as a director-within-the-text of pace and intonation, pays minute attention to punctuation.
43. Wiseman has been acting for more than half a century.
44. Leo and Leonora's deceased husband were civil engineers, designers of bridges. During the break, Miller says to Wiseman: "Think of Verrazano Bridge. It's a work of art. These are thrusts of the imagination that are just as valid as any other art. They are very daring people."
45. "When he didn't give me any verbal response, I felt deprived. Getting no notes is not the best circumstance," Peter Maloney tells me later.
46. In rehearsal that afternoon, the actor tells the director: "Now Arthur said to me, privately, out there [points to lobby] that Frick was a Rotarian. . . . Did you notice that Arthur didn't say anything to me or Shami?" "Maybe he didn't like us," Shami Chaikin says, laughing.
47. "'Shift' excites me no end," Shami Chaikin says. "It means 'quotation marks'; it means 'new idea,' like a lightbulb. Ah! [She gestures with her hands in the air.] That's what a shift is. If we're talking about the sun, and

the moon, and the stars, and then all of a sudden I say, 'Do you want a drink?' that's a shift."

48. For example, he emits a wordless sound—an "o" on a rising beat or an excited intake of breath—as an actor reads a line. Without breaking the rhythm of the scene, the actor immediately gives the line a different rendering.

49. The line is: "I don't know what you [John Frick] are but I'm only a dumb swamp Yankee, but . . . *Suddenly breaks off with a shameful laugh*" (24).

50. Chaikin tells me:

   I was very depressed at first after the stroke. I couldn't talk and I had awful pain on the right side from the foot to the head. I had to use [a walker]. Now I am so glad. I'm living more and working. It's surprising. My personality is a pessimist, generally. I'm often no pessimist now. I like the lighter things.

   In a review of *The Last Yankee*, Clive Barnes writes: "There is perhaps more of a touch of hope in Chaikin's staging than is to be found in Miller's last stage direction, but presumably Miller does not resent the luminous glint of a silver lining." "Memorable Times 2," *New York Post*, Jan. 12, 1998, 42.

51. *"Salesman" in Beijing*, 207.

Chapter 7: Maria Irene Fornes in Rehearsal

1. Letter to James Houghton, April 30, 1999. Like Shepard, Fornes was part of the off-off-Broadway theater of the 1960s. In the summer of 1978, at the Bay Area Playwrights Festival, Shepard and Fornes collaborated on "a four-page sketch called *Red Woman*, about a man named Dan talking to a statue of St. Teresa" (Don Shewey, *Sam Shepard* [New York: Dell, 1985], 129).

2. Michael Feingold, "'Mud' and 'Drowning,'" *Village Voice*, Sept. 28, 1999, 75.

3. "Mud and Desire," *Village Voice*, Sept. 21, 1999, 51.

4. "A Conversation with Maria Irene Fornes," an interview conducted by Randy Gener, *The Dramatist*, vol. 2, no. 3 (Jan./Feb. 2000), 18.

5. "Maria Irene Fornes Discusses Forty Years in Theatre with Maria M. Delgado," in Maria M. Delgado and Caridad Svich, eds., *Conducting a Life: Reflections on the Theatre of Maria Irene Fornes* (Lyme, N.H.: Smith and Kraus, 1999), 248.

6. For accounts of Fornes's 1987 rehearsals of Chekhov's *Uncle Vanya* and her own play, *Abingdon Square*, see Susan Letzler Cole, *Directors in Rehearsal*, 35–54.

7. "While her plays are rooted in both the absurdist and realist traditions—and, in fact, fuse the two in many instances—her directing of the work places the plays firmly in nonrealistic territory. The disjunction

of text and staging is what often gives her work in production a feeling of being constantly on edge." Caridad Svich, "Conducting a Life: A Tribute to Maria Irene Fornes," in Delgado and Svich, *Conducting a Life*, xxiii.

8. Asked by Maria M. Delgado, "Is directing part of the writing process?" Fornes replies: "It is with a new play." *Ibid.*, 261. Fornes tells me on March 25, 1998: "I've written entire plays in rehearsal. *Mud* was written in fourteen days in rehearsal [in July, 1983]. . . . I wrote a scene a day. The voice of one of my actresses [Mary Jo Pearson] possessed me. I had her voice in my ear when I wrote the play. I would write a scene the night before; then I would wake up at dawn and do a little reworking. Then first thing in rehearsal I would dictate the scene, so each actor's script was in his or her own handwriting. And when I made changes in the script, I would go look at the actors' own handwriting." Not only does the actress's voice "possess" the playwright, but the actors literally inscribe the first rehearsal script of the play.

   Unless otherwise indicated, all subsequent statements by Fornes are from interviews conducted on January 31, 1997; February 1, 1997; March 5–7, 12, 24, and 25, 1998; April 8, 1998.

9. In the March 1998 rehearsals of *The Summer in Gossensass*, Molly Powell tells the director and the cast that Elizabeth Robins did not take bows after her performance as Hedda Gabler because Hedda was dead. "There I think Elizabeth Robins was wrong," Fornes replies. (However, for other reasons, these bows are cut in performance.)

10. Maria Irene Fornes, *The Summer in Gossensass*, April 25, 1998 rehearsal script, scene 10, p. 1. Unless otherwise noted, all following citations are from this rehearsal script.

11. Cf. the stage direction describing twelve of the heroine's speeches at the end of Elizabeth Robins's own play, *Alan's Wife: "Jean's sentences are given as a stage direction of what she is silently to convey." Alan's Wife* (London: Henry and Co., 1893), 41. (In a further self-silencing, Elizabeth Robins and Florence Bell did not admit their co-authorship of *Alan's Wife* until thirty years after the play was performed.) Analyzing the disjunction between a reader's and a spectator's experience at the end of Robins's play, Catherine Wiley says: "The theatre spectator is left with the void in language . . . a void filled by the actress's body, not the character's." "Staging Infanticide: The Refusal of Representation in Elizabeth Robins's *Alan's Wife*," *Theatre Journal*, vol. 42, no. 4 (Dec. 1990), 445.

12. This line appears in the April 25 script (sc. 5, p. 18).

13. Actress Irma St. Paule, playing Lady Bell in the workshop production, describes Fornes after rehearsal on January 31, 1997: "Her sense of timing, gesture, speech, and body is to the microsecond and to the micrometer. She has a perfect sense of what's going to work, for example, 'Tilt your chin; move your feet two inches to the right.' She reminds

me of Meyerhold." Unless otherwise indicated, all subsequent statements by actors are from interviews conducted on March 6, 12, 13, 14, 21, and 24, 1998.

14. Interview conducted by Maria M. Delgado in Delgado and Svich, *Conducting a Life*, 251. In an admiring and yet largely unfavorable review of the 1998 production, Michael Feingold says of *Gossensass*: "Centered on the theater and the act of interpreting a great play, the script is like Fornes's *ars poetica*, tossing off enough apothegms about playwriting, acting, and the sources of artistic inspiration to rank as an act of literary criticism more than a play." "Show Business," *Village Voice*, April 14, 1998, 129.

15. Throughout rehearsal Fornes moves easily among roles often performed by three people in other productions: playwright, director, dramaturg. Fornes's antipathy to production dramaturgs is well known. In these rehearsals the main use she makes of dramaturg Lisa McNulty is to appropriate her office, which adjoins the playing area, as a part of the imagined set: an offstage kitchen.

16. Elizabeth's speech undergoes subsequent changes in rehearsal. In the following versions, it is divided between Marion and Elizabeth: "She's wild, isn't she?" Marion asks, and Elizabeth replies: "Yes, and yet she's very conventional" (March 10 script); "She's very wild," Marion says, and Elizabeth responds: "Very wild, and yet very conventional" (April 25 script), sc. 1, p. 5.

17. March 4 script, sc. 1, p. 7. However, in the April 25 script, the line becomes: "That's interesting" (sc. 1, p. 10). The revision of the preceding line has also made use of a contraction. ("She is always the cat" becomes "She's always the cat.")

18. These lines repeat the previous two lines in the speech, with the addition of the word *reading*. Molly Powell says that Fornes "hears the way an actor will say a word or a phrase and something about the way the actor says it interests her, and she'll have the character repeat the same word or the same phrase. Have you noticed that? It may not be that what we're doing is so interesting. *It may be that she hears it afresh, and her mind begins to spin another way*" (emphasis mine).

19. Cf. actress Valda Setterfield's remark to the stage manager just before rehearsal begins on March 22: "When you get a [typed script revision], it looks different on the page. It's an interesting process."

20. The last three words of Marion's line in the March 4 script, "And return to life as someone else," are reassigned to Lady Bell (sc. 5, p. 20).

21. The abbreviated version, with several words added and one word altered, appears in the April 25 script, sc. 5, p. 22. In rehearsal on March 13, dialogue on one page greatly expands and then contracts, changing from sixty-one to ninety-nine to thirty-six words (sc. 1, p. 4). So far as I know, there is no transcription of this sequence of revisions except my own, itself not complete.

22. Fornes tells me on March 25, 1998: "I was in a state of creativity with this play that is completely different from any other state of creativity I've been in."
23. Fornes's striking directorial note to Molly Powell later in rehearsal might also serve as a comment on her own writing process: "It's almost as if it's a vision you see but a voice that comes through you."
24. Michael Goldman, *The Actor's Freedom: Toward a Theory of Drama* (New York: Viking, 1975), 101.
25. During a break, Powell and Rivera discuss their own research on the backgrounds of Elizabeth Robins and Marion Lea. Later Powell remarks in rehearsal that Robins and Lea memorized their lines before they rehearsed with other actors.
26. March 4 script, sc. 1, p. 5. The lines do not appear in this form in subsequent drafts.
27. In the revised script, Hedda is described as "an agoraphobic uroboros" (sc. 1, p. 9).
28. A run-through on March 24 is temporarily interrupted when an actress says: "I can see Irene making notes." A member of the cast tells me during a break:

    I've been thinking about why it's sometimes difficult to have Irene as a writer in the room running the room. And there are some little procedural, concrete differences. One is that as she's watching a scene, her mind may go into rewrite land. . . . It's exciting, and it's also irritating, because you can see a thought bubble and you think: "Oh! Maybe this will be a delicious little something." But your actor self will say: "Maybe she didn't see the last minute or half-minute of work." You don't experience that when you're working with only a director.

29. When Ross Wetzsteon noted a profusion of doors in Fornes's sets and asked: "What's going on?" she replied:

    When I was directing Eyes on the Harem *[in 1979], I had the set designer put in entrances and exits all over the place so I wouldn't have to worry about how to move the characters on and off stage. By now it's become an almost unconscious technique. I guess what it means is that if I ever get into a situation where I don't know what I'm going to do next, there'll always be an exit to help me get out. ("Irene Fornes: The Elements of Style,"* Village Voice, *April 29, 1986, 45)*

    At the end of *Letters From Cuba*, Fornes's first new play in the twenty-first century, directed by the author at Signature Theatre, two characters make a breathtaking entrance in Donald Eastman's stunning set, "through a door that hasn't previously existed." Michael Feingold, "Island Escapes," *Village Voice*, Feb. 29, 2000, 63.
30. March 4 script, revised in rehearsal on March 5 (sc. 1, p. 6).
31. *Ibid.* The line does not appear in the April 25 script.
32. Contrast Garland Wright's rehearsals of Egloff's *The Devils*, in which the multiple sets of stairs remained imaginary until the actors were on stage.

33. Wetzsteon, "Irene Fornes," 42.
34. Marion says to Lady Bell: "Don't you think Elizabeth should play Hedda Gabler? She has the eyes" (sc. 1, p. 13).
35. All that remains of the rehearsal revision is Marion's line: "Lady Bell, do you think Hedda Gabler resembles a woman Ibsen loves?" (sc. 1, p. 14), and even this is an altered version of a line assigned to Elizabeth: "Lady Bell, do you know if Mr. Ibsen is in love with a woman who resembles Hedda Gabler?" (dictated in rehearsal, March 7, 1998). One dictated line undergoes the following three revisions in rehearsal and then vanishes altogether. In the first dictated version, Elizabeth asks: "So how does he [Ibsen] know so much about a woman as complex and enigmatic as Hedda?" First revision: "So how does he know so much about a woman as complex, mysterious, and perhaps as perverse as Hedda?" Second revision: "So how does he know so much about a woman as complex, mysterious, enigmatic, and perhaps as perverse as Hedda?" Third revision: "So how does he know so much about a woman as complex, mysterious, enigmatic, and perhaps as perverse as *this* Hedda?"
36. During a colloquium entitled "Focus on Fornes," at Hunter College on April 8, 1998, Fornes says: "I do rewrites during rehearsal and during subsequent productions and even after the plays have been published. The perspective you have when you've just completed something is different from your perspective later on. . . . Twenty years after [*Fefu and Her Friends*], I was finally able to revise it the way I had always intended." More than twenty years after *Waiting for Godot* was first staged, Samuel Beckett wrote: "Finding out things about *Godot* I'm glad I never knew. Making a good few cuts in 1st act." Quoted by Dan Gunn, "The Beam of Sam's Light," *TLS*, Jan. 15, 1999, 3.

    There is another striking parallel with Beckett: "After 1967 . . . Beckett took charge of the first productions of his new plays, signaling, in the process, that the actual realization of a work on stage, and not just the writing of the play, was the essential act of authorship." Fintan O'Toole, "Game without End," *New York Review of Books*, vol. 47, no. 1 (Jan. 20, 2000), 43.

    Fornes's vocation as playwright seems to have taken fire when she saw the Roger Blin production of Beckett's *Waiting for Godot* in Paris: "When I left the theater, it was like I was in a different world," she tells me. "I didn't understand a single word because it was in French but I understood it all, the way a dog understands, without understanding words. I began writing plays two or three years later."
37. In the 1997 script David is listed as "an actor." In the 1998 script he is not, yet he wishes to take part in the performance of *Hedda Gabler*. (Another "ghost.") In rehearsal on March 25, 1998, Fornes says: "David is not an actor." Daniel Blinkoff (Vernon) asks: "David is not an actor?" "He's a theater-worm," Fornes replies. "But he's not an actor. That's just a feeling I have about him."

38. *The Theater of Maria Irene Fornes*, ed. Marc Robinson (Baltimore: Johns Hopkins UP, 1999), Introduction, 17. See also Robinson's fine discussion of reading in this play in *"The Summer in Gossensass:* Fornes and Criticism," 109–129.

39. Near the end of *Gossensass*, the actors perform the final scene of *Hedda Gabler* in which George Tesman and Thea Elvsted sit on the floor sorting out pages of notes for a manuscript destroyed by Hedda. Fornes, directing the scene, says to the actors: "If you want to see an example of this, I'll show you my notes for this play."

40. Retained in the April 25 script, sc. 4, p. 21.

41. Powell describes Fornes's gaze ("a kind of animal focus") in the same way that her character, Elizabeth Robins, describes Ibsen: "Observant. Like a wild animal" (sc. 1, p. 4).

42. Asked "When you say 'Irene,' are you thinking of her as a playwright or as a director?" Molly Powell replies: "She's it. She's Irene. That's it."

43. Later, during a break, a member of the cast tells me: "[In other kinds of rehearsals] actors can say to a director: 'This is not working. Please ask the playwright to cut or trim this.' Here there's no emissary."

44. Cf. Elinor Fuchs writing on postmodern theater: "The interior space known as 'the subject' was no longer an essence, an in-dwelling human endowment, but flattened into . . . the unoccupied occupant of the subject position." *The Death of Character: Perspectives on Theater after Modernism* (Bloomington: Indiana UP, 1996), 3.

45. A note on the process of script revision: Textual changes made in, or brought to, rehearsal are dictated to the cast by Fornes or her assistant. The actors write these revisions in their scripts. Periodically, numbered pages on which changes occur are retyped and handed out to the actors who replace previous pages of the script with the most recent version. Often a newly typed, revised page will be altered immediately after its first reading aloud by the actors in rehearsal. Midway through rehearsal, when asked by Fornes if I think she has made many revisions, I complain that the script is now too heavy for me to carry to rehearsal. She replies: "You should go to the gym."

46. In scene 1, Lady Bell considers the possibility that "a character created by the author . . . [might be] inspired by the existence of a real person," though a few minutes later she wonders "if Ibsen's talent didn't simply create Hedda without that external inspiration" (15, 16).

47. A transcript of the comments quoted here was provided by Joseph Goodrich, March 21, 1998. During a break in the 1997 workshop rehearsal, Fornes tells me: "If you write the mystery of a character under whose spell you are, you can actually get in touch with the essence of a person by a detailed attention to voice, pace of speech, face." Such "detailed attention to voice, pace of speech, face" also characterizes Fornes's work as a director.

48. Quoted in Roger Shattuck, *The Banquet Years* (New York: Vintage, 1955), 39. On March 26, during a break in the first rehearsal on stage, Fornes remarks to me and her assistant, Dawn Williams: "In my other plays, the characters serve the play. . . . In this play they're eccentric for their own purposes. They don't care about the play."

49. A few of these changes: Marion is given a new line describing Hedda: "Oh, she's an agoraphobic uroboros." This line is then repeated by Lady Bell and, later, Vernon. Other lines are reassigned. Elizabeth's "Oh that makes so much sense" becomes Lady Bell's "That makes so much sense." Pronouns lose gender or become plural: Vernon's "She's agoraphobic" becomes "That's an agoraphobic"; Marion's "She's found the key to Hedda Gabler's character" becomes "We've found the key to Hedda Gabler's character" (sc. 1, p. 9).

50. "No, it isn't" (David's response to Marion's observation that his praise of her acting is kindness). "Miss Lea" is added to that line in the April 25 script (sc. 5, p. 8).

51. Neither the previous nor the new blocking is indicated in the text. In fact, stage directions in the March 20 script, e.g., *"(Shyly)"* and *"(They both laugh gaily),"* (sc. 5, p. 9) disappear in the April 25 script.

52. The earlier version appeared in the March 19 script (sc. 5, p. 14). The new line, as revised in rehearsal and reassigned to Lady Bell, appears in the April 25 script: "Thank you, David. Why are you on your knees?" (sc. 5, p. 14).

53. The following italicized words are examples of actor-added text: Elizabeth's description of Ibsen, "He *delves* into unimaginable depths" (sc. 1, p. 4), suggested by Molly Powell as Fornes is revising the line during a break; Lady Bell's question about critics reviewing *Hedda Gabler*: "Is it that they don't like the play? If they don't *like the play* why don't they just say so?" (sc. 1, p. 14), added in rehearsal by Valda Setterfield, who then asked Fornes if she would approve this "indiscretion." Rehearsing scene 5, Daniel Blinkoff suggests a new sequence for Elizabeth's greetings of persons in the room she enters: Marion, Vernon, and Lady Bell. (She had addressed Lady Bell first. The revised sequence is retained in the April 25 script, sc. 5, p. 16.) Fornes incorporates the actor's instinctive physicalization in her reblocking of David's quirky downstage cross to Lady Bell. "You did a little skip when you turned. Do you remember?" Fornes asks the actor. When Goodrich cannot recall it, Fornes demonstrates the "little skip" over and over in the playing area. "*It wasn't in character* [emphasis mine]," she says. "You did it to make your turn. Do that and come to the chair." Earlier in rehearsal the actor accidentally fell off his chair and Fornes added the fall to the scene.

54. The line appears, slightly altered, in the April 25 script: "However, there are things that are not part of our existence but are outside ourselves, like imitation, which could also be of great value to creation" (sc. 7, p. 2).

55. A little later Fornes spies a two-inch slip of paper with lines from the February 27, 1998 script: "David is right. Hedda is suicidal" (sc. 6, p. 2), and says to her assistant: "What about this?" Dawn Williams replies: "You said this was left over for a rainy day, Irene. Today is a sunshiny day. I'm giving it to Susan," and hands it to me. The line does not appear in the April 25 script.

Chapter 8: Jean-Claude van Itallie in Rehearsal

1. Robert Vorlicky, ed. *Tony Kushner in Conversation* (Ann Arbor: U of Michigan P, 1998), 235.
2. Eileen Blumenthal, *Joseph Chaikin: Exploring at the Boundaries of Theater* (Cambridge: Cambridge UP, 1984), 17.
3. "I feel that if art or theatre doesn't have some sort of sacred intent, it's not of interest to me. It's meant to heal in some way." Jean-Claude van Itallie, in an interview conducted by Alexis Greene, in *Speaking on Stage*, ed. Philip C. Kolin and Colby H. Kullman (Tuscaloosa: U of Alabama P, 1996), 159.
4. *Ibid.*, 157.
5. "I wrote it because I felt a need to make the *Tibetan Book of the Dead* as readily available as a book of poems." Jean-Claude van Itallie, *The Tibetan Book of the Dead for Reading Aloud* (Berkeley: North Atlantic, 1998), Introduction, x.
6. Jean-Claude van Itallie, "Notes (to be placed in [theater] program)," *The Tibetan Book of the Dead, or How Not To Do It Again* (New York: Dramatists Play Service, 1983), 5–6. All citations of the play are from this edition.
7. *Ibid.*, 44. Each of these "primal energies" has its own color (e.g., blue, yellow, red, green), psychological aspect (e.g., intellectual, generous, charming, compassionate), and direction (east, south, west, north), as well as its negative manifestation (e.g., hatred, pride, lust, envy).
8. *Ibid.*
9. Unless otherwise indicated, all further statements by members of the company are from interviews conducted on August 2–4 and 15–18, 1997; July 24–27, 1998; and August 15, 1998.
10. The ages of those in the farmhouse this summer range from four to forty-four.
11. Chores at the farmhouse, including food preparation, are shared by the company.
12. *The Playwright's Workbook* (New York: Applause, 1997), 116.
13. Late that evening, sitting with the other actors in the kitchen of the farmhouse, Erica Stuart says: "Jean-Claude was talking today about meditation. That's a great solo way—meditation—to keep working on the play. And it's related to what the play is about." Music director

Katherine Down connects the practice of meditation with the company's creation of music for the play: "I've set up a room [in the upper barn] with musical instruments. Spend some time there," she tells the actors. "There are dry and wet sounds in music. Just experiment. . . . All our bodies have their own vibration. . . . Instruments and sounds evoke all sorts of colors and resonance. I'd like to guide that later, but you can begin to find it for yourselves. And that will work with meditation."

14. In an "angry letter" he wrote to the director of a production of *The Serpent*, van Itallie says:

   Actors are not poets, at least not while they're on their feet in front of an audience. Their concentration had better not be on the invention of words while they are performing. . . . The word "improvisation" is an overused one and means a lot of different things to different people. What it does not mean for a play like The Serpent *is verbal improvisation in performance.* ("A Letter," America Hurrah and Other Plays [New York: Grove, 1978], 11)

15. During the summer of 1997, Kim Mancuso and Joel Gluck are co-directing Court Dorsey, Kermit Dunkelberg, and the playwright in rehearsal of *Guys Dreamin'* in preparation for its New York debut. Dorsey's "Jack" piece, somewhat altered in content and delivery, is performed by the actor in *Guys Dreamin'* at La MaMa E.T.C. in November 1997.

16. In *The Playwright's Workbook*, 135, van Itallie writes:

   Keep in mind that the playwright's presence carries great weight and authority at rehearsals. Actors may strive to please the playwright, so at some rehearsals your absence might ease the director's task of encouraging actors to experiment. Often it works well for the playwright to attend beginning rehearsals (to hear the play read, to answer questions, and to make script changes), and then to attend later rehearsals (to see the production with fresh eyes).

17. "Somehow the deeper meaning of a text which is unfamiliar to us manifests musically or textually in an improvisation," music director Katherine Down tells me.

   It's as if somewhere unconsciously you do know what is going on in the text. We're finding it by listening. . . . Last night in the improv in my room, I could hear what every single actor was doing. . . . Gradually, the flute became an extension [of the spoken text]. . . . I listened to the actors. The flute became a voice. The flute became an actor talking.

18. Maria Irene Fornes, *The Summer in Gossensass*, sc. 5, p. 10 (April 25, 1998 rehearsal script).

19. "Pilgrim Theatre's work has always been founded in training the body and voice," the director says. "Max had a training that might open certain doors of understanding in regard to this text." Max Palar describes

one movement as we watch the actors practice it for three-quarters of an hour:

This movement is based on the idea of ever-flowing, like a river. The world—the body—moves but the face keeps looking in the same direction. . . . The feet never stop. The left foot and left arm move forward and backward together, and the right foot and the right arm move forward and backward together. As they move forward, the palm faces upward; as they move backward, the palm faces down.

Later van Itallie tells me, "I think of the text, in a way, as water flowing."

20. The next day during lunch at nearby Shelburne Falls, Mancuso tells me: "The biggest problem with the text is that it lends itself nicely to actors making atmosphere rather than specifically finding the meaning of the work."

21. In the published script, van Itallie says: "The music, crucial to the production, is primarily Tibetan in feeling—sometimes fierce and sour—with emphasis on percussion of all sorts, and unusual handmade instruments" (7). Down tells me: "We're not going to be biblically bound. We have the handmade instruments specified."

22. Cf. director Douglas Hughes, describing his relationship with playwright David Rabe: "David is someone I can call up."

23. Recall Signature Theatre Company's logo: the author's hand holding a pen.

24. In her review of the production, Anne Marie Donahue says that it is "illumined by lighting that's a show in itself." *Boston Phoenix*, Aug. 21, 1998, 9. Lighting designer Sabrina Hamilton is the founding director of KO Theatre Works and teaches at Williams College.

25. "I want to integrate people dying and costumes dying and objects dying in the visual universe of the performance," Romanian set and costume designer Nick Ularu tells me after the run.

At the beginning, in discussion with Kim, it was my idea to use a huge mandala surrounded by the four elements and the four colors in the text. Seeing the evolution of the rehearsal and seeing that the vision is not only Tibetan but universal and the music and parts of text are from different languages, I started to think more generally about the phenomena of dying and am trying to involve the visual aspects in the style of the performance.

After the August 14, 1998 performance at the Boston Center for the Arts, van Itallie says: "I liked the *embrace* of the set. It's in a circle in a big round space. It emphasizes the circularity. It's like arms reaching out to include the audience. I missed color. I wanted more color. Curiously, from the original production, what I missed most visually was the painted mandala on the floor because all the action takes place in this colorful universal mandala." While van Itallie liked Jun

Maeda's massive constructed skull in the La MaMa production, this production

had the height and they had the actors climbing vertically. They used the set as if there were some aspects of the skull. But the [La MaMa] skull was off-white and therefore reflected the color of the lights better. The blackness of this set absorbed the color more than what I would have wished. . . . I am relieved that Nick did not put dead objects on the set which he told me he planned to do. I talked about not being too grim. In 1983, Ellen Stewart said to me: "If a play is called The Tibetan Book of the Dead, *it better be a celebration of life." And I feel she was absolutely right. And I told this to Nick and he said, "I understand what you mean." I'm gratified that he modified his concept somewhat. And I think Kim agrees with me.*

26. Untranslated in the text, 28. The director translates it as "enter into the place of auspicious origins."
27. "I was watching him in rehearsal while I was playing," music director Katherine Down tells me, "and I saw on his face looks of amusement, bewilderment, and intense concentration." "When we were doing the run-through," Kermit Dunkelberg says, "I thought he was hating it. The few times I looked at his face he wasn't smiling. It wasn't a very giving expression. I'm a little bit cowardly, so I didn't look at him that much." Assistant to the director Amie Keddy says:

    I watched his face as much as I could during the run. . . . and I saw a lack of expression most of the time. I kept waiting for him to at least smile in places where everyone else was audibly laughing. And he didn't. I did see him "smile" once—his lips were closed and it was small, just pleased a bit—during Kermit's "muddy swamp" song.

28. After the performance on August 14, 1998, van Itallie says that this moment when Dunkelberg "comes out at the apex of a V-formation [of slowly advancing actors] singing, 'I've wandered so long/In this muddy swamp' remains for me the apex of this production."
29. The actress first heard "Luna" sung to her brother-in-law as he was dying. "It's a traditional Venezuelan song about the passion of life," Thompson says.

    In rehearsal Kim had us do an improv and this song came out. It was my meeting point with the text and it wasn't even in the text! . . . Jean-Claude was saying something directorial. He wasn't saying as author: "Don't put any new words in my play." . . . He was saying you can't communicate to the audience by pushing your point of view. . . . So these become my possibilities. First, he needs the moment clarified. That's emotional work I have to do as an actress. But the second possibility, more dire, is that I have not connected with the text, that I'm still battling with it. . . . He was very gently questioning a moment that happened to be very personal to me and in doing so brought me back to the work that I have yet to do on the rest of the text.

After the performance on August 14, van Itallie says of this song: "It doesn't bother me as much and there seems to be less of it. [Mancuso tells me that the song is "exactly the same length."] But I still don't understand what it's doing there." Asked why it doesn't bother him that additional text is introduced into the play, he says: "One reason is that it is in Spanish. [He doesn't know most of the Spanish words in the song.] There were a few words that could conceivably have been a translation of the text, for example, 'moon.' I would prefer that it was not there. It's a very spare text. I wouldn't mind translations of it into other languages, but extraneous text—no. In this case, I mind it less because it's a song and it's not in English and it's short."

30. Added at the end of "The Angry Energies." (This section of the text is almost completely rewritten in the later version of *The Tibetan Book of the Dead*, intended for reading aloud.) Mancuso only learns of the lacuna when van Itallie mentions it today. "I had assumed that what was logically missing was the playwright's choice, not a typographical error," she tells me later. "I and the cast had worked for hours in rehearsal trying to justify this omission."

31. Cf. van Itallie's earlier comments on the playwright and director in rehearsal on pp. 192–193.

32. For more on the directorial gaze, see Susan Letzler Cole, *Directors in Rehearsal*, especially 5–6.

Index

Note: **Boldface** indicates principal discussions of playwrights, directors, or texts.

257

Coventry University